Accounting, Finance, Sustainability, Governance & Fraud: Theory and Application

Series Editor

Kıymet Tunca Çalıyurt, Centre for Forensic Accounting Research and Enterprise, School of Finance and Management, SOAS University of London, London, UK

This Scopus indexed series acts as a forum for book publications on current research arising from debates about key topics that have emerged from global economic crises during the past several years. The importance of governance and the will to deal with corruption, fraud, and bad practice, are themes featured in volumes published in the series. These topics are not only of concern to businesses and their investors, but also to governments and supranational organizations, such as the United Nations and the European Union. Accounting, Finance, Sustainability, Governance & Fraud: Theory and Application takes on a distinctive perspective to explore crucial issues that currently have little or no coverage. Thus the series integrates both theoretical developments and practical experiences to feature themes that are topical, or are deemed to become topical within a short time. The series welcomes interdisciplinary research covering the topics of accounting, auditing, governance, and fraud.

Halis Kıral
Editor

Rethinking Enterprise Risk Management

Springer

Editor
Halis Kıral
Social Sciences University of Ankara
Ankara, Türkiye

ISSN 2509-7873 ISSN 2509-7881 (electronic)
Accounting, Finance, Sustainability, Governance & Fraud: Theory and Application
ISBN 978-981-97-5982-8 ISBN 978-981-97-5983-5 (eBook)
https://doi.org/10.1007/978-981-97-5983-5

This Springer imprint is published by the registered company Springer Nature Singapore Pte Ltd.
The registered company address is: 152 Beach Road, #21-01/04 Gateway East, Singapore 189721, Singapore

Acknowledgements

I am deeply grateful to Prof. Dr. Kıymet Tunca Çalıyurt, our Series Editor, for her unwavering support and insightful guidance throughout the development of this book. Her expertise and thoughtful feedback were essential to the final product.

The chapter authors, who are students in the Ph.D. Program in Audit and Risk Management at Social Sciences University of Ankara, also deserve my sincere thanks. The success of this publication depended on their dedication and hard work.

Contents

About the Editor

Halis Kıral is an associate professor at the Social Sciences University of Ankara in Turkey. He is also Head of the Audit and Risk Management Department and Director of the Center for Audit and Risk Management (ASBÜDRM) at the ASBU. He was a visiting scholar at the Duke Center for International Development (DCID) for the 2017–2018 academic year. He has also worked in the Ministry of Finance of Turkey as a state budget expert, public finance expert, head of the Department of Central Harmonization for Internal Audit, and head of the Budget Policy Department. He wrote several articles, books, and chapters on public finance, public financial management and control, specifically internal audit and risk management, public budgeting, and applied economics.

List of Figures

List of Tables

Part I
Introduction

Chapter 1
Introduction: Why Enterprise Risk Management Needs a Rethink

Halis Kıral

Abstract Unfortunately, enterprise risk management (ERM) activities are not high on the priority agenda of senior management in both public and private sectors. Over the years, risk management experts or internal auditors have continued to raise awareness about ERM among senior management. The purpose of this chapter is to examine the role of international standards and frameworks in the failure of ERM. Conceptual ambiguity and methodological gaps in current standards and frameworks make it difficult to implement ERM effectively. Enterprise risk management is now far from being coordinated with core management and audit functions such as strategic management, internal control, and internal audit as well as with core business functions such as procurement, production, marketing, and financing. Therefore, ERM, which aims to eliminate the unit-based silo approach of traditional risk management, adopted a function-based silo approach. In this case, focusing on managing fewer and more significant risks associated with high-level objectives, rather than all business processes of the organization, and making higher contributions to the strategy formulation phase of other corporate functions can increase the success of ERM implementation.

Keywords Strategic risk management · Risk appetite · Risk culture · Standard · Frameworks

1.1 Introduction

Since the early 2000s, there has been a growing interest in enterprise risk management (ERM) driven by the requirements and guidance of public institutions, regulatory bodies, professional organizations, and rating companies. Despite being named

H. Kıral (✉)
Social Sciences University of Ankara, Ankara, Türkiye
e-mail: halis.kiral@asbu.edu.tr

H. Kıral (ed.), *Rethinking Enterprise Risk Management*, Accounting, Finance, Sustainability, Governance & Fraud: Theory and Application,
https://doi.org/10.1007/978-981-97-5983-5_1

by Harvard Business Review as "One of the Breakthrough Ideas for 2004" (Buchanan, 2004), the interest in ERM has fluctuated considerably over time. With the impact of the published frameworks and standards, more organizations have adopted and intended to implement the ERM approach. In practice, however, criticisms have often been raised that the ERM approach is far from achieving the expected effects (e.g., Power, 2007; Mikes, 2009; Kıral, 2018).

Despite these criticisms, there remain claims and expectations that ERM has not yet reached its full potential and that its importance will gradually increase. We can divide academics or professionals who have these claims and expectations into two groups. Those in the first group argue that the importance of ERM will increase in the business world, which has become more complex with the rapid introduction of new technologies into our lives through digitalization, with new risks being added every day. The second group mostly appear in the aftermath of disasters. The academic studies or social media posts by professionals made after any economic crisis or natural disaster with devastating impacts often claim that the impact would not have been so severe if the company's risk management processes had been effective.

While we do not doubt the sincerity of either group, we see that their expectations have not been met. Excluding sectors such as banking, insurance, and energy, where regulatory pressure is intense, managers and employees in many other sectors, whether public or private, have serious doubts about the need for and effectiveness of ERM activities. Despite the accelerating pace of digitalization and the occurrence of various corporate or national crises, ERM has not achieved the expected success yet.

In fact, claims that the importance of ERM will increase with digitalization or after crises do not take into account a very simple and primitive aspect of human beings. When faced with a complex situation and the feeling that we cannot manage this complexity is overwhelming, we quickly return to our habits and routines, preferring an artificial sense of control. Similarly, the habits and routines that organizations have built up over time are the most common and fastest strategies they resort to in a complex business world or a crisis. Therefore, organizations often prefer to turn to traditional methods that have been tried before and are easier to repeat, instead of ERM which claims a new and holistic approach. In this respect, the target set by ERM is quite ambitious. It is the complete abandonment of the familiar and frequently used traditional approach in favor of an entirely new one. There is no doubt that in this battle between the old and the new, the old has a distinct advantage. The only way for the new (ERM) to prevail in this struggle is for organizations to believe that they will gain enough to enable them to leave their comfort zone. Can we say that the ERM approach, as currently structured, promises such a clear gain?

Empirical studies have attempted to answer this question by determining whether an organization that adopts ERM manages its risks more effectively and efficiently than other organizations. In this context, after the 2007–2008 global financial crisis, many studies have been conducted to examine the impact of enterprise-wide risk management practices on firm value (e.g., Beasley et al., 2008; Pagach & Warr,

2010; Hoyt & Liebenberg, 2011; Ellul & Yerramilli. 2013; Baxter et al., 2013; Bohnert et al., 2017; Lechner & Gatzert, 2018; Silva et al., 2019; Phan et al., 2020; Faisal et al., 2021; Septyanto & Nugraha, 2021). These studies have reached significantly different conclusions about the existence of any relationship between ERM practices and firm value and the direction of that relationship, if any. The main reason for such divergent results is that these studies mostly focus on determining whether a general risk management framework or standards such as COSO ERM or ISO 31000 has been adopted or whether there is a risk management officer in the relevant firm. However, studies often ignore the level of internalization and implementation of the framework or standard by an organization's senior management and employees. It should be noted that the effectiveness of risk management depends on all employees and managers setting up, coordinating, and contributing to risk management processes, rather than on guiding frameworks and standards or a risk management officer (Mikes & Kaplan, 2015).

In this respect, the success of the implementation of ERM is influenced by many factors. These include top management support (Ivancevich et al., 1998; Walker et al., 2002; Beasley et al., 2005), the industry in which the organization operates (Whitfield, 2004; Tillinghast, 2004; Golshan & Rasid 2012; Lechner & Gatzert, 2017), regulatory pressure (Plambeck & Weber, 2010), size of the organization (Colquitt et al., 1999, Beasley et al., 2005; Nocco & Stulz, 2006), and the presence of a risk expert or manager (Beasley et al., 2005; Hoyt & Liebenberg, 2011).

On the other hand, there are also studies in the literature suggesting that the shortcomings in the effective implementation of ERM stem from ERM approaches. According to these studies, factors such as conceptual uncertainties related to ERM (Hillson & Murray-Webster, 2005; Guerrón-Quintana, 2012; Kıral, 2018), risk management processes (Power, 2004, 2009; Arena et al., 2010; Mikes, 2011), risk management tools (Borghesi & Gaudenzi, 2013; Vinnari & Skærbæk, 2014), and risk analysis methods (Hubbard, 2020) are argued to be barriers to effective implementation.

Unlike the studies mentioned above, the main purpose of this book is to evaluate ERM approaches comprehensively and holistically. We aim to critically examine the existing approaches to ERM in different areas, starting with the concepts of ERM, its stages, academic studies, as well as standards and frameworks. However, we do not limit ourselves to criticisms and offer solutions for each of them. This way, we aim to contribute to the implementation of an ERM approach that is applicable and systematic and creates value for organizations.

In its current form, ERM is an approach that is applied only in certain sectors, such as banking, insurance, and energy, and only under regulatory pressure (Whitfield, 2004; Tillinghast, 2004; Golshan & Rasid, 2012, Lechner & Gatzert, 2017). As the number of similar studies increases and the tangible and measurable contributions of ERM become more apparent, many organizations will embrace the idea of implementing ERM without regulatory pressure.

1.2 Is Enterprise Risk Management Flawed?

The WorldCom and Enron scandals in the early 2000s marked a turning point in terms of ERM. Witnessing one of the most important accounting scandals in world history with the bankruptcy of Enron Company in 2001, the USA passed the Public Company Accounting Reform and Investor Protection Act, also known as the Sarbanes-Oxley Act, in 2002 to prevent similar risks from occurring again. Sections 302 and 404 thereof regulate the effectiveness of internal control and risk management processes related to the financial records of public companies and management responsibility for these processes.

The methods and approaches by which the responsibilities brought about by the Act will be implemented will be clarified by COSO (the Committee of Sponsoring Organizations of the Treadway Commission) (Kıral, 2018). Following the Internal Control Framework published in 1992 for this purpose, COSO published the ERM Framework in 2004. The first global test of the COSO Framework was the global financial crisis in 2007–2008. Enterprise risk management failed to identify the impending global economic crisis in time and did not add any value to the organizations in taking necessary measures. What could be more logical than the following question (EY, 2020): What is the real value of ERM efforts that fail to recognize that a major crisis is coming?

Following the COSO ERM Framework, the ISO 31000 Standard, the other most widely used approach, was first published in 2009. While discussions about the effectiveness of ERM efforts continued, the COSO Framework was revised and reissued in September 2017 and the ISO standard in February 2018. Would the revised approaches be successful this time? The second global test of ERM was the COVID-19 pandemic. The fact that most organizations were caught unprepared for this pandemic, which had lasting and profound global impacts, led to a reexamination of the added value of ERM. Despite the revision of the framework and standards for ERM, the result did not change and ERM did not achieve the expected success in the second global test (EY, 2020).

The existence of numerous published standards, frameworks, and guidelines as well as academic studies on ERM suggests that ERM is a mature discipline with clear proven concepts, methods, and tools (Mikes & Kaplan, 2015). Unfortunately, this is not the case. Many theoretical and practical issues need to be addressed in ERM approaches. These problems can be grouped under two headings: conceptual ambiguities and methodological gaps. If these issues are not resolved in the near future, then ERM will be at serious risk.

1.2.1 Conceptual Ambiguities: What Should We Understand?

According to Aristotle, human beings think by means of concepts and thus manage to reach conceptual knowledge of principles through abstraction (Ketenci & Topuz, 2013). Being "frames that carry what exists to the level of knowing and communicating," concepts are the basic condition that makes human beings humans (Çotuksöken, 1998: 13). We can understand any subject through concepts and use this knowledge in practice by understanding the relationship between concepts.

One of the biggest risks in understanding and implementing ERM is the lack of conceptual clarity. Conceptual ambiguity starts with the concept of risk. Some definitions associate risk with uncertainty (Knight, 1921), loss (Jaaferi, 2001), threat (Beck, 1992), and opportunity (Hillson & Murray-Webster, 2005). The definition of risk varies across disciplines, from mathematics to philosophy, to sociology, to economics, etc.

Confusion about what we should understand by risk also affects the identification of the risks that exist in the organization. The first and perhaps the most important stage of ERM is risk identification. The effectiveness of the subsequent stages of assessing, prioritizing, responding to and monitoring the risks identified depends on getting this first stage right. As Giordano Bruno said, "[i]f the first button of the shirt is not buttoned correctly, the others will also go wrong."

Conceptual ambiguity in ERM is not limited to the concept of risk. Differences in the definition of concepts such as risk capacity, risk appetite, risk tolerance, risk culture, and risk threshold, which are extremely important in the implementation of risk management, are striking. These differences can be found in the academic literature as well as in the standards and frameworks that regulate ERM.

Let us discuss just two of these concepts: risk appetite and risk culture. Risk appetite is a critical concept in ERM. This is because ERM is a process undertaken to identify potential risks that may affect the achievement of an organization's objectives and manage them within the scope of the organization's risk appetite (Rittenberg & Martens, 2012). We decide whether or not to respond to risks by taking into account our level of risk appetite. Despite being so important, there is no agreed definition of risk appetite in frameworks and standards or academic literature (Power, 2009; Kıral, 2018). In addition to the definition, it is also unclear as to how and at what stage of risk management should risk appetite be considered. As a result, the questions of whether there is a consistent risk appetite across the organization and whether the risk management process achieved its intended impact across the organization remain largely unanswered (Mikes & Kaplan, 2015).

Apart from risk appetite, another concept that remains uncertain is risk culture (Bromiley et al., 2015). The standards and frameworks published on ERM mention that organizations should adopt a risk-aware culture. However, going beyond these general statements, there is no explanation of the behavioral elements that the organizations desiring to have a risk-aware culture should possess and the processes encouraging these elements (Brooks, 2010). This shortcoming is also supported by the survey study conducted by Fraser and Simkins (2016). The risk managers surveyed think that most of the risk management literature does not provide sufficient guidance on how to overcome various organization-specific cultural and historical challenges (Fraser & Simkins, 2016).

The existence of conceptual deficiencies or differences in existing standards and frameworks as well as academic studies on ERM also makes it difficult to measure these concepts clearly and accurately. It is obvious that it is difficult for organizations to implement risk management strategies on the axis of a set of concepts whose definition and measurement are unclear (Kıral, 2018).

1.2.2 Methodological Gaps: How Should We Do It?

The ambiguity of concepts in ERM has seriously undermined the applicability of it, along with significant deficiencies in its standards and frameworks with respect to risk management processes. Let us start with the concept of risk, as we did with conceptual ambiguity. The first stage of the risk management process is the identification of risks. Without a clear concept of risk, we cannot talk about effectiveness and a common approach to risk identification. The COSO Framework or the ISO standard for risk management does not clearly define how risks should be written. This has led to different ways of expressing risks, often using problems, issues, or uncertainties interchangeably with risks. For example, it is observed that the current problems, such as staff shortages or seasonal difficulties, are written by organizations as risks.

Identifying problems, issues, or uncertainties as risks, rather than risks that have an impact on achieving corporate objectives, may result in the identification of hundreds or even thousands of risks, even for a medium-sized organization. In an organization where thousands of risks are identified, it becomes difficult to talk about the effectiveness and sustainability of ERM.

Let us move on to risk appetite, the first example mentioned in the section on conceptual uncertainties. Despite its critical importance to ERM, risk appetite is difficult to measure when it is not conceptually clear. Moreover, most of the existing risk appetite definitions ignore its dynamic nature. In this respect, the idea that risk appetite, which varies over time or for different types of risk, is invariant and can be characterized by a single financial indicator is misleading (Crickette et al., 2012; Hillson and Murray-Webster, 2012; Aven, 2013; Ullah et al., 2021).

The senior management responsible for determining risk appetite faces considerable uncertainty regarding the tools and techniques it can use for this purpose. At what stage and by which method will the senior management determine the organization's risk appetite? Moreover, the deficiencies in risk identification raise the question of how to determine risk appetite for hundreds or even thousands of risks. Even if we ignore its dynamic structure that changes over time and according to the type of risk, it is obvious it will long take to determine thousands of risk appetites. Managers who do not have the time to determine thousands of risk appetites with uncertain tools and methods will continue to rely on their individual judgment and experience rather than on ERM (Mikes, 2009).

Apart from determining risks and risk appetite, ERM standards and frameworks also contain serious gaps in the processes of assessing, responding to, monitoring, and reviewing risks (Power, 2004, 2009; Arena et al., 2010; Mikes, 2011; Borghesi & Gaudenzi, 2013; Vinnari & Skærbæk, 2014; Fraser & Simkins, 2016; Hubbard, 2020). In fact, we can say that these gaps in the standards, frameworks, and guidelines on ERM stem from the legal gaps left by the regulatory authorities. For this, let us go back to the years when the understanding of ERM was rapidly growing.

We have mentioned that COSO intended to fill the gap regarding the methods and approaches to be used in the implementation of corporate responsibilities with regard to the internal control and risk management processes regulated by the Sarbanes-Oxley Act, passed in the wake of the corporate scandals in the USA in the early 2000s. The extent to which the COSO ERM framework published for this purpose fills this gap is questionable. In addition to the conceptual and methodological uncertainties in the COSO ERM Framework, the framework's preference to include all processes of an organization in risk management, regardless of whether they are small or large, important or unimportant, has led to the emergence of a "process-obsessed risk management of everything" approach in practice (Power, 2004). As a result, ERM has become a one-off burden that requires time-consuming and detailed documentation, rather than an ongoing practice. Enduring these obligations and sometimes fulfilling mandatory administrative requirements can lead to an illusion or an artificial sense of assurance that risks are effectively managed in the organization (Arena et al., 2010; Kıral, 2018). This artificial assurance caused by improper implementation of ERM can lead to dangerous consequences. This is because the understanding of "risk management of everything" and the vague conceptual framework and superficial process design may result in "the risk management of nothing," which may be costly for organizations (Mikes, 2011).

Reputation risks have a great impact on the risk management of everything, leading to risk management of nothing. Since the late 1990s, major corporate scandals have led to the emergence of a new type of risk: reputational risk. According to Power (2004), reputation risk is a symptom of late modern insecurity. Unlike traditional primary risks such as health, safety, insurance, and project management, reputation risk, which is a "man-made" secondary risk, has become the most popular type in recent years (Kıral, 2018). The efforts of the ERM approach to combine all primary and secondary risks to form a single model have further promoted the understanding of "risk management of everything" (Vinnari & Skærbæk, 2014). The Committee of Sponsoring Organizations of the Treadway Commission's "process-oriented, risk management of everything" approach, combined with the association of every risk with reputation risk, has resulted in "enterprise risk inflation," with hundreds or even thousands of risks being identified even for medium-sized organizations. Needless to say, it is not possible to talk about effectiveness where there is inflation.

1.3 What Will Happen if This Continues?

We can clearly state that today, neither in the public nor in the private sector, ERM activities are not among the priority agenda items of the senior management. Although years have passed, risk management experts or internal auditors continue to create "awareness" in senior management about ERM (Kıral, 2018). In fact, it is not realistic to think that any manager is not aware of risk management or takes it lightly. It should not be forgotten that senior executives have risen to their positions in business life sometimes by taking risks and sometimes (mostly in the public sector) by avoiding risks, in other words, by managing their risks effectively. They continue to manage their risks with their individual risk perceptions, attitudes, and behaviors shaped by their own experiences over the years. The risk perceptions and attitudes of the top managers are decisive in identifying and evaluating the risks of the organization and taking necessary measures (Manab & Kasim, 2012; Faisal, 2020). The senior manager of an organization is the most influential person in the effective implementation of ERM. However, ERM has not yet led to a paradigm shift that changes the individual risk perceptions, attitudes, and behaviors of senior managers.

Apart from changing the senior managers' perceptions, Henriksen (2018) observed that none of the companies in his study implemented ERM to create value, but rather to meet external regulatory pressures or market expectations. External demands being decisive rather than the needs of the top manager has bureaucratized ERM to produce the necessary documentation in line with these demands, turning it into a "paper tiger" (Henriksen, 2018).

If this continues, the current crisis in internal control will soon arise in ERM. Before being sufficiently clarified, the concepts and processes related to internal control have become overused and difficult to understand and implement. As a result, internal control activities have started to be seen as a "workload" that has to be carried out in certain periods, which is not directly related to organizational objectives and activities and does not contribute to them either (Kıral, 2018).

If the uncertainties in ERM are not resolved, it would not be surprising to see more technical issues with clearer boundaries, such as information security or business continuity, come to the fore. We can say that digital risk management, business continuity, and crisis management are queuing up to fill the space that ERM cannot fill. Of these, digital risk management is more technical, while business continuity and crisis management have a natural advantage over ERM as their boundaries are more defined.

1.4 Conclusion and Evaluation

Enterprise risk management is effective to the extent that it identifies and manages critical internal and external risks that may affect the achievement of organizational objectives. However, current approaches to ERM are not sufficiently successful in identifying critical risks that may affect the achievement of organizational objectives. One of the main reasons for this failure is that ERM approaches tend to include all processes of the organization in risk management. Conceptual ambiguities and methodological gaps in standards and frameworks lead to the identification of hundreds or even thousands of risks, even for a medium-sized organization. These standards and frameworks do not suggest a clear and practical approach to ensure that thousands of risks can be reduced to a few dozen critical risks that are important to senior management and need to be managed carefully. When a manager reviews risk analyses that track thousands of risks in detail, he or she is likely to conclude that such a study is not meaningful from his or her perspective. It can only be considered as data waiting to be turned into meaningful information.

The second reason for the failure of ERM approaches to manage critical risks is the silo approach. The studies comparing the traditional risk management approach with the ERM approach often state that each unit manages its risks within the framework of its own understanding rather than an understanding that encompasses the whole organization as a result of the silo approach of the traditional risk management approach (Liebenberg and Hoyt, 2003; Lundqvist, 2014; Kerstin et al., 2014; McShane, 2018, etc.).

We do not yet have solid scientific evidence on the extent to which ERM eliminates the unit-based silo mentality. However, it is safe to say that ERM is not fully harmonized and coordinated with core management and audit functions such as strategic management, internal control, and internal audit, as well as with the core business functions such as procurement, production, marketing, and financing. Furthermore, ERM, which aims to eliminate the unit-based silo approach, appears to have resulted in a function-based silo approach. The main reason for this is that current ERM approaches focus on the execution (implementation) phase of strategies rather than the strategy formulation (planning) phase of other organizational functions.

Although the same (enterprise) risk management approach is applied throughout the organization during the implementation phase of the strategies determined for core management, audit, or core business functions of the organization, ERM cannot influence the strategy formulation (planning) phase, resulting in a function-based silo approach. In other words, ERM approaches that focus on strategy implementation instead of strategy formulation processes have failed to establish an integrated link with strategic processes (Henriksen, 2018). Strategic planning is critical in establishing this link. For ERM to be useful as a strategic management tool, it must be fully integrated with the strategic planning process. The integration of strategy formulation and risk management processes will increase the effectiveness of strategic planning as well as the added value of ERM (Andersen & Sax, 2019).

Let us take the example of internal audit to illustrate the importance of integrating ERM and other functions in the strategy formulation (planning) phase of strategic planning. As a requirement of risk-based auditing, internal audit plans and performs audits based on the organization's risk log, prioritizing the highest risk areas. If the organization does not have a risk log prepared by the unit responsible for coordinating risk management processes, or if internal audit does not take that log into account, internal auditors determine the audit universe based on the risk universe they have prepared. This separates the ERM and internal audit functions and reduces the effectiveness of both. On the other hand, internal audit is expected to decide on the areas to be audited based on the risk log prepared by the unit responsible for risk management, and this unit is expected to update the risk log based on internal audit reports. This integration of ERM and internal audit in the strategy formulation (planning) phase will increase the effectiveness of both functions.

The third reason for the failure of ERM approaches to manage critical risks is that the published standards and frameworks are generally based on private sector companies. However, public organizations have a unique structure, for instance, the duties and organizational structure of public institutions are determined by legal regulations. Let us illustrate with an example that this feature alone is sufficient to differentiate public sector risk management from the private sector.

Suppose that the duties of a country's ministry of culture and the organizational structure created to carry out those duties are regulated by law. Under this law, one of the units of the ministry is the directorate of libraries and this directorate has 20 different tasks related to the activities of the national library. If we take, as a starting point for ERM studies, the 20 tasks assigned to the directorate of libraries by law and the hundreds of processes related to these tasks, it is easy as pie to write hundreds or even thousands of risks related to these processes. Yet, do thousands of risks really make sense considering that the directorate is already carrying out the tasks assigned to it by law? Moreover, if we consider that we also need to carry out these studies in other units of the ministry, we will end up with a pile of data and documents that will be difficult to manage and to draw meaningful conclusions from.

On the other hand, if we consider that ERM is the management of risks that may affect the achievement of the organizations' objectives, risk management studies based on processes in public institutions will not be effective, as is the case for the example above. This is because these processes are not related to the objectives but to the tasks assigned to the organization by law. For public institutions, objectives are determined by top policy documents such as development plans or medium-term programs and strategic plans.

Continuing with the example of the ministry of culture, let's say that the development plans, which are top policy documents, set a target to increase the number of mobile libraries. In this case, the strategic plan of the ministry of culture, which is prepared by taking into account this top policy document, will identify the targeted number of mobile libraries by years, responsible units, and the risks that may be faced in achieving this target. This is the point where risk management for public organizations should start. Some of the tasks assigned and carried out by law have now turned into a target. Managing the risks affecting the achievement of this goal is ERM.

To the extent that development and strategic plans are realistically prepared and meticulously followed, the importance and value of ERM activities will increase. Where development or strategic plans are not effective, we cannot expect ERM activities to be effective. To the extent that the objectives are institutionalized, ERM will also achieve its objectives. It is not possible to talk about ERM where there is no institutionalization.

The starting point for addressing the issues arising from the abovementioned methodology of ERM should be the elimination of conceptual and methodological ambiguities and gaps in the frameworks and standards. Internationally published frameworks and standards set out a general framework and basic principles in the field of ERM. These guidelines are independent of country or sector in terms of identifying overarching rules, principles, and approaches to risk management. However, it should not be overlooked that these general rules and principles should be transformed into a tailor-made model, taking into account the specific structure of the country or sector. On the contrary, harmonizing these frameworks with national or sectoral realities will increase their applicability (Kıral, 2018). For this to happen, first and foremost, the regulatory authorities of the countries have a lot of work to do.

1.5 Structure and Contents of the Book

The main objective of this book is to encourage business leaders, strategy practitioners, corporate decision makers, as well as academics and students to rethink ERM approaches in a comprehensive and holistic manner. Starting from the concepts of ERM to its stages, from academic studies to standards and frameworks, we aim to examine existing ERM approaches in a holistic and critical manner. In addition, we do not limit ourselves to criticism but also offer solutions for each criticism. In this way, we aim to contribute to the realization of a viable, systematic approach to ERM that creates value for organizations.

The book consists of 13 chapters. In Chap. 2, *Aynur Zaku* argues that without a clear distinction between uncertainty and risk, risks cannot be managed effectively. One of the concepts mostly confused with risk is uncertainty. From the simplest decisions in daily life to the most strategic decisions of organizations and even governments, we make all our decisions under uncertainty and risk. Given that our brains behave differently in situations of uncertainty and risk, the distinction between these two concepts becomes even more important. While the decision-making process in the face of risk is handled by deductive and inductive methods, the decision-making process in the face of uncertainty is more intuitive (heuristic). Analyzing the theories used by different disciplines to understand decision-making under uncertainty and risk, the author first examines the developmental stages of the concepts of uncertainty and risk from the sixteenth and seventeenth centuries to the present day.

The first concept we need to consider when making decisions under uncertainty and risk is risk attitude. Risk attitude is the extent to which individuals are willing to take risks. Why do some people avoid risk while others take them? Which factors influence our attitude to risk? In terms of ERM, individual risk attitudes have an important impact like a keystone. In this regard, in Chap. 3, *Yağmur Özyurt and Ali Göksel* analyzed the factors affecting individual risk attitudes and senior management's risk attitudes specifically for ERM and the impact of these factors on ERM. They also sought an answer to the question of what extent risk attitude is taken into account in standards and frameworks. The authors concluded that the published standards and frameworks on ERM either completely ignore individual risk attitudes or do not address them in the necessary depth. Özyurt and Göksel emphasized the importance of considering individual risk attitudes for an effective ERM system, and they summarized their recommendations as "CAPSTONE."

Over the centuries, the meaning of the word risk has changed, its use has become widespread, and it has been applied in different fields. In Chap. 4, *Mecbure Aslan* draws attention to the different definitions of risk in different disciplines, from mathematics to philosophy. She argues that the different definitions of risk by different scientists, even within the same discipline, lead to ambiguity in the definition of risk in general. An effective way of removing the ambiguity in the definition of risk is to clarify what risk is not. According to Aslan, recognizing that risk is not a problem, uncertainty, danger, threat, or mere negativity would reduce the ambiguity in the definition of risk. Given that correct definition of risk is the first and most important stage of ERM, the effectiveness of ERM will increase as the ambiguity in risk definition decreases.

ERM process is a process that begins with the identification of risks that are likely to affect the achievement of the organization's objectives and continues with the assessment of risks. Risk assessment involves rating and prioritizing risks to identify the significant risks facing the organization, project, or strategy. Risk assessment is carried out using a variety of methods and tools, ranging from qualitative methods such as surveys, interviews, or risk matrices to quantitative methods such as Monte Carlo simulation, sensitivity analysis, Markov analysis, or artificial neural networks. In Chap. 5, *Ali Erdem Saatçi* analyzes the effectiveness of the methods and tools used in the risk assessment process. We can never be sure of the effectiveness of the risk management process unless we are sure of the effectiveness of the methods and tools. The effectiveness of the methods and tools ensures the accuracy and reliability of the information obtained through these methods and tools. Accurate and reliable information enables the organizations to assess their risks more accurately and make more effective decisions. The author underlines that one of the greatest risks of the risk assessment process is that no performance measurement is applied to measure the effectiveness of risk assessment methods and tools, even in organizations with the most advanced ERM maturity levels.

Once the risks are identified and assessed for impact and likelihood, it is time to respond to the risks that could affect the existence and continuity of the organization. Risk response strategies express how the organization will respond to manage the identified and assessed risks. At this stage, alternative actions are identified to mitigate threats and make use of opportunities. Management's risk appetite determines which risks will be responded to and how. In Chap. 6, *Baha Karaçolak* states that, contrary to popular belief, risk responses do not only involve eliminating the threats posed by risks, but also taking advantage of the potential opportunities that these risks present. Indeed, there are risk response strategies for threats, such as mitigation, avoidance, or transfer, as well as strategies for making use of opportunities, such as enhancing exploiting or sharing. However, Karaçolak points out that the awareness and practical use of opportunity strategies is more limited than that of threat strategies. The author also notes that there are significant differences between the risk responses included in the standards and frameworks for risk management, both in terms of terminology and the meaning, action or process.

After identifying, assessing, and responding to risks, the process of monitoring risks begins. In order to monitor risks effectively, risks must first be recorded. In Chap. 7, *Esra Güneş and Caner Erşan* analyzed the activities of recording, monitoring, and reviewing risks. Literature review is followed by examination of the methods included in the risk management standards and frameworks most commonly used in organizations. The authors also included the approaches to recording, monitoring, and reviewing risks applied in project management standards in order to reveal different understandings in risk management. They found that the differences and shortcomings in recording, monitoring, and reviewing risks in the analyzed standards and frameworks are remarkable. Güneş and Erşan emphasized the need for a common language and new regulations regarding the implementation of risk recording, monitoring, and reviewing processes in organizations, and they offered opinions and suggestions to increase the effectiveness of these processes.

The transformation of ERM into an integral part of the corporate culture depends on the existence of effective communication between all internal and external stakeholders. In this respect, dealing with risks requires not only the efforts of experts or managers, but also the cooperation of all stakeholders who are affected by risks within an organizational structure. In Chap. 8, *Murat Soner* discusses risk communication. According to the author, although the need for risk communication is emphasized in many studies, there is no common view on the definition of risk communication. For example, although the COSO framework emphasizes the need for risk communication, it does not include a definition of risk communication. Soner analyzes the approaches and models put forward to explain risk communication over time and argues that a new risk communication model is necessary to adapt to the changing nature of today's risks. The author also explains the barriers to effective risk communication and concludes that the most important organizational communication barrier is organizational awareness while the most important individual communication barrier is lack of trust.

One of the main objectives of risk communication is to manage reputation risks to the organization. Perceived risk is as effective as real risk and risk perception is more emotional than rational. When people believe something, they hold it to be true even if facts or science contradict it. Given the existence and impact of perceptions, reputation risks become more difficult to manage. In Chap. 9, *Yasemin Gök* argues that failure to manage reputation risks effectively could have devastating consequences for key elements of reputation such as financial performance, strategic plans, leadership, and sustainability. As the relationship between perceived risk and reputation is understood, reputation risks will be managed more effectively, thus protecting or enhancing the value of corporate reputation. In this case, the reputation of risk management, which enables management of reputation risks that are difficult to manage, will also be protected or enhanced.

Organizations face a variety of risks that are constantly changing. Organizations that fail to manage some of these risks effectively may face a crisis at any time. Crises are often experienced as a result of the occurrence of risks and an unpredictable increase in their impact. In this respect, we can say that risks are mostly signals of crisis. However, ERM alone cannot prevent a crisis from occurring, nor can it guarantee effective crisis management. In Chap. 10, *Turgay Çağlayan* addresses the similarities and differences between risk and crisis, as well as between crisis management and risk management. In this chapter, the author reveals the relationship between risk management and crisis management with examples ranging from United Airlines to the Tylenol crisis; from the global chip supply crisis during COVID 19 pandemic to the Wimbledon Tennis Tournament.

Internal control is an important tool for the effective management of risks throughout the organization and for the early detection of crises. In Chap. 11, *Serpil Ceylan* analyzed the relationship between risk management and internal control considering the relevant literature and published frameworks and standards. According to the author, published frameworks on risk management and internal control offer different approaches. For example, in the internal control frameworks published by the COSO in 1992 and 2013, risk management is a part of internal control. However, in the ERM frameworks published by COSO in 2004 and 2017, internal control is a component of risk management. Ceylan refers to the situation as the "COSO Confusion." Despite this confusion in the COSO frameworks, the relationship between internal control and risk management is clear in academic studies. Academic studies generally agree that internal control and risk management should be integrated and that both contribute to the achievement of organizational goals and objectives. The disagreement is about how this integration will be achieved.

In Chap. 12, *Cem Dursun* discusses risk management in the digital age. The author begins with the historical development of digital transformation. Industrial revolution, with the invention of steam machines, resulted in Industry 1.0; transition to mass production resulted in Industry 2.0; invention of the computer and the integration of electronic and information technologies resulted in Industry 3.0, and the autonomous systems developed with the spread of the internet resulted in Industry 4.0. After the second half of the 2010s, the emergence of artificial intelligence, blockchain, cloud computing, 3D printers, data analytics, predictive analytics, robotic process automation, driverless cars, Internet of Things, and drones led to digital transformation. Digital transformation has led to serious changes in management and operational processes. After digital transformation, brand new opportunities and threats arising from processes, systems and infrastructure, culture and business models have emerged. According to Dursun, it does not seem possible to manage the risks that have arisen or will arise after digital transformation using traditional methods. In this respect, digitalization will have a lasting and significant impact not only on the management and operational processes of enterprises, but also on risk management processes. In digital risk management processes, it is crucial to benefit from the innovations brought about by information systems, data analytics, and automation. In this way, significant risks can be prevented, for example, through early detection of errors and irregularities. Finally, the author addresses seven components of digital risks and risk management approaches observed in businesses following digital transformation.

Chapter 13 of the book contains, to the best of our knowledge, the first bibliometric analysis in the field of enterprise risk management. In this chapter, *Deniz Erdem,*

Ertan Güvendi, Mecbure Aslan, Ramazan Acar, and Serkan Ülger analyzed publications on ERM between 1996 and 2022. The bibliometric analysis, based on nearly six hundred publications, provides a map of keywords, authors, countries, and institutions, and an important framework for tracking the development of the ERM literature over the twenty-five-year period. Analyzing the number of articles and citations by year is analyzed, it is noteworthy that studies in the field of ERM increased between 2006 and 2020, but the number of publications decreased after 2021 and the number of citations slowed down relatively. In the field of ERM, which is an interdisciplinary field of study that attracts the attention of both the business and academic world, they have identified a decrease in the number of publications, despite the emergence of new and different studies in recent years. According to the authors, the limited effectiveness of the current methods and methodologies of ERM and the lack of expected benefits may have an impact on the decline in academic interest in ERM. It is, therefore, predicted that there will be an increase in the number of studies that offer suggestions to address the shortcomings of current approaches to ERM and to increase its added value.

References

Andersen, T. J., & Sax, J. (2019). *Strategic risk management: A research overview* (1st ed.). Routledge.

Arena, M., Arnaboldi, M., & Azzone, G. (2010). The organizational dynamics of enterprise risk management. *Accounting, Organizations and Society, 35*, 659–675.

Aven, T. (2013). On the meaning and use of the risk appetite concept. *Risk Anal., 33*, 462–468.

Baxter, R., Bedard, J. C., Hoitash, R., & Yezegel, A. (2013). Enterprise risk management program quality: Determinants, value relevance, and the financial crisis. *Contemporary Accounting Research, 30*, 1264–1295.

Beasley, M., Pagach, D., & Warr, R. (2008). Information conveyed in hiring announcements of senior executives overseeing enterprise-wide risk management processes. *Journal of Accounting, Auditing & Finance, 23*(3), 311–332.

Beasley, M. S., Clune, R., & Hermanson, D. R. (2005). Enterprise risk management: An empirical analysis of factors associated with the extent of implementation. *Journal of Accounting and Public Policy, 24*(6), 521–531.

Beck, U. (1992). *Risk society: towards a new modernity*. Sage.

Bohnert, A., Gatzert, N., Hoyt, R. E., & Lechner, P. (2017). The relationship between enterprise risk management, value and firm characteristics based on the literature. *ZVersWiss, 106*, 311–324.

Borghesi, A., & Gaudenzi, B. (2013). *Risk management: How to assess, transfer, and communicate critical risks*. Springer.

Bromiley, P., McShane, M., Nair, A., & Rustambekov, E. (2015). Enterprise risk management: Review, critique, and research directions. *Long Range Planning, 48*(4), 265–276.

Brooks, D. W. (2010). Creating a risk-aware culture. In J. Fraser & B. Simkins (Eds.), *Enterprise risk management: Today's leading research and best practices for tomorrow's executives* (The Robert W. Kolb series in Finance) (pp. 87–95). Wiley.

Buchanan, L. (2004). Breakthrough ideas for 2004. *Harvard Business Review, 2*, 13–16.

Colquitt, L. L., Hoyt, R. E., & Lee, R. B. (1999). Integrated risk management and the role of the risk manager. *Risk Management and Insurance Review, 2*(3), 43–61.

Çotuksöken, B. (1998). *Kavramlara felsefe ile bakmak*. İnsancıl Yayınları.

Crickette, G., Demian, R., Fox, C., Hach, J., Makomaski, J., Mazumdar, R., & McGuire, R. (2012). *Exploring risk appetite and tolerance*. RIMS Exec Rep 2012. Retrieved May 23, 2023, from https://ermgovernance.com/Resources/RIMS_Exploring_Risk_Appetite_Risk_Tolerance_0412.pdf

Ellul, A., & Yerramilli, V. (2013). Stronger risk controls, lower risk: Evidence from U.S. bank holding companies. *Journal of Finance, 68*, 1757–1803.

EY. (2020). *How to transform ERM into a value-added decision-making capability*. Retrieved May 15, 2023, from https://www.ey.com/en_us/consulting/how-to-transform-erm-into-a-value-added-decision-making-capability

Faisal, F., Abidin, Z., & Haryanto, H. (2021). Enterprise risk management (ERM) and firm value: The mediating role of investment decisions. *Cogent Economics & Finance, 9*.

Faisal, M. (2020). Karakteristrik CEO dan enterprise risk management. *Jurnal Riset Akuntansi dan Keuangan, 8*(1).

Fraser, J. R., & Simkins, B. J. (2016). The challenges of and solutions for implementing enterprise risk management. *Business Horizons, 59*(6), 689–698.

Golshan, N., & Rasid, S. (2012). Determinants of enterprise risk management adoption: An empirical analysis of Malaysian public listed firms. *International Journal of Social and Human Sciences, 6*, 119–126.

Guerrón-Quintana, P. A. (2012). Risk and uncertainty. *Business Review*, 9–18.

Henriksen, P. (2018). *Enterprise risk management – Rationaler og paradokser i en moderne ledelsesteknologi*. Doctoral School of Business and Management, Copenhagen Business School

Hillson, D. A., & Murray-Webster, R. (2005). *Understanding and managing risk attitude*. Gower.

Hillson, D., & Murray-Webster, R. (2012). *A short guide to risk appetite* (1st ed., pp. 1–7). Routledge.

Hoyt, R. E., & Liebenberg, A. P. (2011). The value of enterprise risk management. *Journal of Risk and Insurance, 78*(4), 795–822.

Hubbard, D. W. (2020). *The failure of risk management: Why it's broken and how to fix it*. Wiley.

Ivancevich, D. M., Hermanson, D. R., & Smith, L. M. (1998). The association of perceived disaster recovery plan strength with organizational characteristics. *Journal of Information Systems, 12*(Spring), 31–40.

Jaaferi, A. (2001). Management of risks, uncertainties and opportunities on projects: Time for a fundamental shift. *International Journal of Project Management, 19*, 89–101.

Kerstin, D., Simone, O., Nicole, Z., & Lehner, O. M. (2014). Challenges in implementing enterprise risk management. *ACRN Journal of Finance and Risk Perspectives, 3*(3), 1–14.

Ketenci, T., & Topuz, M. (2013). Aristoteles ve Augustinus'un İnsan Anlayışları Üzerine. Kaygı. *Bursa Uludağ Üniversitesi Fen-Edebiyat Fakültesi Felsefe Dergisi, 20*, 1–18.

Kıral, H. (2018). Kurumsal Risk Yönetiminin Riskleri (Risks of enterprise risk management). *Denetişim Dergisi, 18*, 5–14.

Knight, F. (1921). *Risk, uncertainty and profit*. Riverside Press.

Lechner, P., & Gatzert, N. (2017). Determinants and value of enterprise risk management: Empirical evidence from Germany. *The European Journal of Finance*.

Lechner, P., & Gatzert, N. (2018). Determinants and value of enterprise risk management: Empirical evidence from Germany. *The European Journal of Finance, 24*(10), 867–887.

Liebenberg, A. P., & Hoyt, R. E. (2003). The determinants of enterprise risk management: Evidence from the appointment of chief risk officers. *Risk Management and Insurance Review, 6*, 37–52.

Lundqvist, S. (2014). *Abandoning silos for integration: implementing enterprise risk management and risk governance*. [Doctoral thesis (compilation), Department of Business Administration]. Lund University School of Economics and Management, Department of Business Administration

Manab, N. A., & Kasim, I. (2012). A moderating affect of leadership on a success of enterprise-wide risk management practices. In *3rd International Conference On Business And Economic Research (3RD Icber 2012) Proceeding*.

McShane, M. (2018). Enterprise risk management: History and a design science proposal. *The Journal of Risk Finance, 19*(2), 137–153.

Mikes, A., & Kaplan, R. S. (2015). When one size doesn't fit all: Evolving directions in the research and practice of enterprise risk management. *Journal of Applied Corporate Finance, 27*, 37–40.
Mikes, A. (2009). Risk management and calculative cultures. *Management Accounting Research, 20*(1), 18–40.
Mikes, A. (2011). From counting risk to making risk count: Boundary-work in risk management. *Accounting, Organizations and Society, 36*(4/5), 226–245.
Nocco, B. W., & Stulz, R. M. (2006). Enterprise risk management: Theory and practice. *Journal of Applied Corporate Finance, 18*(4), 8–20.
Pagach, D., & Warr, R. (2010). *The effects of enterprise risk management on firm performance*. Available at: http://papers.ssrn.com/sol3/papers.cfm?abstract_id=1155218
Phan, T., Dang, T., Nguyen, T., Ngo, T., & Hoang, T. (2020). The effect of enterprise risk management on firm value: Evidence from Vietnam industry listed enterprises. *Accounting, 6*(4), 473–480.
Plambeck, N., & Weber, K. (2010). When the glass is half full and half empty: CEOs' ambivalent interpretations of strategic issues. *Strategic Management Journal, 31*(7), 689–710.
Power, M. (2004). *The risk management of everything: Rethinking the politics of uncertainty*. Demos.
Power, M. (2007). *Organized uncertainty: Designing a world of risk management*. Oxford University Press.
Power, M. (2009). The risk management of nothing. *Accounting, Organizations and Society, 34*(6/7), 849–855.
Rittenberg, D. L., & Martens, F. (2012). Understanding and communicating risk appetite', the Committee of Sponsoring Organizations of the Treadway Commission. Martens.–2012. Retrieved from https://www.coso.org/Documents/ERM-Understanding-and-Communicating-Risk-Appetite.pdf
Septyanto, D., & Nugraha, I. M. (2021). The influence of enterprise risk management, leverage, firm size and profitability on firm value in property and real estate companies listed on the Indonesian stock exchange in 2016-2018. *KnE Social Sciences, 5*(5), 663–680.
Silva, J. R., da Silva, A. F., & Chan, B. L. (2019). Enterprise risk management and firm value: Evidence from Brazil. *Emerging Markets Finance and Trade, 55*(3), 687–703.
Tillinghast, P. T. (2004). *Adding value through risk and capital management*. Tillinghast-Towers Perrin.
Ullah, S., Mufti, N. A., Qaiser Saleem, M., Hussain, A., Lodhi, R. N., & Asad, R. (2021). Identification of factors affecting risk appetite of organizations in selection of mega construction projects. *Buildings, 12*(1), 2. MDPI AG
Vinnari, E., & Skærbæk, P. (2014). The uncertainties of risk management: A field study on risk management internal audit practices in a Finnish municipality. *Accounting, Auditing & Accountability Journal, 27*(3), 489–526.
Walker, P. L., Shenkir, W. G., & Barton, T. L. (2002). *Enterprise risk management: putting it all together*. Institute of Internal Auditors Research Foundation.
Whitfield, R. (2004). Creating a risk-conscious climate. *NACUBO Business Officers (March)*, 27–32.

Halis Kıral is an associate professor at the Social Sciences University of Ankara in Turkey. He is also Head of the Audit and Risk Management Department and Director of the Center for Audit and Risk Management (ASBÜDRM) at the ASBU. He was a visiting scholar at Duke Center for International Development (DCID) for the 2017–2018 academic year. He has also worked in the Ministry of Finance of Turkey as a state budget expert, public finance expert, head of the Department of Central Harmonization for Internal Audit, and head of the Budget Policy Department. He wrote several articles, books, and chapters on public finance, public financial management and control, specifically internal audit and risk management, public budgeting, and applied economics.

Part II
The Zero Point of ERM: Risk, Uncertainty, and Risk Attitude

Chapter 2
Conceptualising Risk and Uncertainty in Decision-Making: A Historical Analysis

Aynur Zaku

Abstract Although decisions have been made under risk and uncertainty for thousands of years, theories on decision-making processes started to be formulated once risk and uncertainty were defined. Just as diagnosis is necessary to treat a patient, definition is necessary to theorise and manage a concept. It is not quite possible to manage risks without making a precise distinction between the concepts of uncertainty and risk. The change in the concepts of uncertainty and risk in the last three centuries has also steered the development of decision-making theories. The decision-making process is influenced by emotions, intuitions, personality and experiences. Examining this process under risk and uncertainty also makes it difficult to predict behaviour. This study aims to examine decision-making processes under uncertainty and risk from the perspective of expected utility theory, prospect theory and heuristic approach as well as the effects of cognitive perception and misperceptions on decision-making mechanisms.

Keywords Uncertainty · Risk · Decision-making · Expected utility theory · Prospect theory · Heuristic approach

2.1 Introduction

Hundreds of thousands of years ago, human beings lived in small groups, spending most of their awake hours foraging for food. They were looking for something to eat or drink, looking for safe places to live, choosing partners and protecting their children. The success of humans in fulfilling their 'duties of survival and perpetuation of their species' is not attributed to their active senses or strong physical abilities per se. Humans dominate the world today because of their distinctive ability to make

A. Zaku (✉)
Social Sciences University of Ankara, Ankara, Türkiye
e-mail: aynur.zaku@student.asbu.edu.tr

H. Kıral (ed.), *Rethinking Enterprise Risk Management*, Accounting, Finance, Sustainability, Governance & Fraud: Theory and Application,
https://doi.org/10.1007/978-981-97-5983-5_2

good decisions (Hastie & Dawes, 2010). The same skill has not led to only good and right decisions throughout history, since quite bad decisions have also been made, such as the use of weapons of mass destruction.

We do not think much about how often we make decisions in our daily lives unless there are decisions that deeply affect our lives. While making a decision is sometimes of vital importance, it appears, from time to time, as an insignificant part of human life. Our decision-making processes start from the moment we wake up; what and how much to eat, when to leave the house, which way to take to work or on what schedule we will do our work are part of the hustle and bustle of everyday life. It is also an involuntary and reflexive decision to suddenly startle by the sound of a horn we hear while crossing the street and run away from danger. It is harder to make decisions that we think will affect our lives such as choosing a school or career or getting married, which makes us analyse the gains, losses and probabilities.

Studies on decision-making processes combine knowledge in the fields of psychology, medicine, physiology, behavioural sciences, pathology, economics, philosophy or law (Simon, 1959; Asselt, 2000; Abdellaoui & Hey, 2008; Potemkowski, 2017). The fact that decision-making is of interest to that many disciplines has resulted in the emergence of quite different approaches to the decision-making mechanism. However, the focus is on revealing how the choice is made, not what the choice is. What needs to be done first is to answer the question of how a decision is made, which, then, will be followed by the question of how to make the right strategic decision. Regardless of the fact that it is a decision that is not very important in our daily life or a strategic decision to be taken on behalf of an institution, our decision-making mechanism works the same and is affected by similar misperceptions.

First of all, it is necessary to distinguish between the decision itself and the concepts of decision-making. A decision is simply defined as a non-random selection of two or more options. Decision-making has an executive function that bridges cognition and action together with mental functions such as thinking and reasoning (Hastie & Dawes, 2010).

Making rational decisions is a learned skill that can be developed with experience, as is the case for other skills (Tyburski, 2017). However, our choices are not always optimal, because our decision-making mechanism is constrained by psychological barriers (Tversky & Kahneman, 1981). Decision-making has a process with several stages determined from cognitive, affective and motivational aspects (Potemkowski, 2017). In the pre-decision stage, a problem is identified and information is gathered about the available options. In the next stage, the favoured choices are identified which is followed by making a decision. In the last stage, the result is evaluated (Svenson, 2003).

When the decision-making theories are examined from a historical perspective, expected value theory stands out as the first theory in this regard. The foundations of the expected value and probability theory were laid as a result of the correspondence between Pascal and Fermat, when C. Méré, who was a French noble in the seventeenth century and was fond of games of chance, asked Pascal, one of the famous mathematicians of the time, in a letter two problems that he experienced in gambling and could not solve mathematically (Kaivanto, 2008; Szpiro, 2020). The history of the concepts of risk and uncertainty in the field of economics dates back three centuries ago. Sakai (2019) examines the said development in six stages. While Sakai uses the term 'First Age' to describe the period before 1700, the second process that started with Bernoulli in 1713 combined the concepts of uncertainty, risk and probability with the field of economics. Over the years, these concepts have become indispensable concepts not only in the field of economics, but also in fields such as mathematics, statistics, medicine and biology. Knight's (1921) distinction between uncertainty and risk is a turning point for studies in this field (Borch & Mossin, 1968; Eichberger et al., 2008; Sakai, 2019; Szpiro, 2020). Differences between uncertainty and risk also affect the decision-making mechanism (Kahneman et al., 1982; Damasio, 1994; Lipshitz & Strauss, 1997; Sharps & Martin, 2002; Mousavi & Gigerenzer, 2014; Sproten et al., 2018).

Starting from the historical development of the concepts of uncertainty and risk in the last three centuries, this study addresses the most commonly accepted approaches to decision-making processes under uncertainty and risk, and it aims to reveal the effect of psychological barriers and pitfalls on decision-making mechanisms.

This study consists of five chapters including the introduction. The introductory part discussing the concepts of decision and decision-making in terms of different disciplines is followed by the second part where the concepts of uncertainty and risk are defined and the evolution of these concepts is examined from a historical perspective. The third part discusses the approaches to decision-making processes, while the fourth part focuses on psychological barriers and pitfalls encountered while making decisions as well as the ways of coping with uncertainty. The last part is composed of the conclusion.

2.2 Can Risks Be Managed in the Absence of Distinction Between Uncertainty and Risk?

Although uncertainty and risk are different concepts, they are often used interchangeably in daily life. The concepts of uncertainty and risk have been addressed in various disciplines such as mathematics, philosophy, statistics, physics, medicine and economics, yet there is no consensus on their definitions.

Uncertainty is a fact of life. However, it cannot be said that much effort has been spent to obtain information about uncertainty until recently. In an age where humans can go to space and map genomes, one can think that understanding and managing uncertainty should not be too complicated, but in reality the situation is somewhat different. The concept of uncertainty, which has been neglected for centuries, has started to find the place it deserves in many disciplines and practices, especially in the last 70 years (Bammer & Smithson, 2008).

The literal meaning of uncertainty is expressed as the state of being ambiguous, imprecision and vagueness. The Methodology Glossary defines uncertainty as vagueness, the state of a concept, expression and measurement being ambiguous or polysemous, whereas the Dictionary of Economic Terms defines it as the situation where the probability of occurrence of events is not known (TDK, 2021).

Uncertainty is the inability to make predictions about the current situation or future due to information inconsistency or lack of information (Yoe, 2019). According to a different definition, uncertainty is the situation where the decision-maker cannot accurately predict the consequences of an event (Nikolaidis et al., 2011).

Risk has different definitions according to the discipline in which it is addressed. Its general meaning is the probability of loss or opportunity to occur. The literal meaning of risk is hazard, danger of loss. While the Dictionary of Economic Terms defines risk as 'the situation where the probability of occurrence of the events is known', according to ISO 31000/2018 Risk Management Standards, it is defined as 'the effect of uncertainty on targets' (ISO, 31000/2018).

2.2.1 From Risk Society to the Age of Uncertainty

Wars, economic crises, technological developments, disasters and space studies in the last three centuries have deeply affected the social and individual needs and expectations. These effects are also reflected in risk and uncertainty, and decision-making processes are reshaped within the framework of these definitions. In this section, we will examine the historical development of the concepts of uncertainty and risk in order to better understand the theories on decision-making processes.

Sakai (2019) examines the development of the concepts of risk and uncertainty in the field of economics in six stages. The first stage, called the First Age, is used to refer to a long period before 1700. Here, a close connection is established between statistics and mathematics by B. Pascal, yet the economic theory itself has not been mentioned much. As can be seen in Table 2.1, while other ages are named with the names of their representatives, the last age we live in is called the Uncertain Age. Table 2.1 presents the ages, their representatives and important events that took place in that period.

First Age (Before 1700): The dominant language in which uncertainty is explained is the language of probability. The concept of probability was developed by Pascal and Fermat in the sixteenth and seventeenth centuries to be applied in the evaluation of games of chance, and then it was applied to insurance and interpretation of actuarial tables (fire, life) (Machina & Viscusi, 2014).

Second Age (1701–1880): Bernoulli, one of the most famous mathematicians, loved to devote time to games of chance, which helped him formulate the basic principle of decision-making under risk. Adam Smith's great success in the field of economy with his book *The Wealth of Nations* is also apparent in the field of risk

Table 2.1 Six developmental stages of risk and uncertainty concepts in economics

Age	Risk and uncertainty	Historical events
I. First Age	Statistics created by Pascal and Fermat	World tour by Magellan (1519–1522)
		London Royal Exchange (1566)
	Economic theory is not well developed yet	British East India Company (1600)
		Great Fire of Tokyo (1657), Great Fire of London (1666)
1700		
II. 'B–A' Age	Daniel Bernoulli (1738)	American Independence (1776), French Revolution (1789)
	Adam Smith (1759, 76)	Meiji Revolution (1868)
	Laplace (1812)	Tokyo Marine Insurance (1879)
1880		
III. 'K–K' Age	Marshall (1890)	World War I (1914–1918), Russian Revolution (1917)
	Keynes (1921, 36), Knight (1921)	Great Kanto earthquake (1923), Great Depression (1929)
	De Finetti (1937), Shackle (1938, 1949)	World War II (1939–1945)
1940		
IV. 'N–M' Age	Von Neumann/Morgenstern (1944)	Hiroshima atomic bomb (1945)
	Nash (1951), Selten (1970)	People's Republic of China (1949), Cuban Missile Crisis (1962)
	Friedman/Savage (1948), Allais (1979)	Sputnik in space (1964)
	Simon (1957), Tobin (1958)	Moon landing (1969)
	Stigler (1961), Pratt (1964)	Violent student movement (1968–1969)
1970		
V. 'A–S' Age	Ok (1970), Akerlof (1970)	Second crisis of economic theory by Robinson (1971)
	Spence (1974), Stiglitz (1975)	Oil crisis (1973, 1978–1979)
	Hurwicz (1973), Sandmo (1970)	Chernobyl nuclear disaster (1986)
	Tversky and Kahneman (1974)	Collapse of the Soviet Union (1989)
	Black/Sholes (1973)	Great Kobe earthquake (1995)
2000		
VI. Uncertain Age	Piketty (2013)	Bankruptcy of Lehman Brothers (2008)
	Old doctrines on the rocks	Fukushima nuclear disaster (2011)
	New approaches are expected	Unpredictable events (Covid-19)

Source: Sakai (2019)

and uncertainty (Sakai, 2019). Adding the concept of probability to the concept of uncertainty, Laplace (1825) attributes the main ways of reaching the truth in mathematical sciences to the vertical transfer of knowledge, induction, analogy and probabilities. Accordingly, Laplace proceeds in the light of current events, principles that have an obvious connection with previous ones, and argues that something cannot begin without a cause that produced it (the principle of sufficient reason). Therefore, he says that the current state of the universe should be treated as the effect of its previous state. He argues that if a creature with intelligence that can analyse all the forces of nature and the entities that compose it, from the largest to the smallest, could exist, all uncertainties would disappear and both past events and the future could be seen very clearly (Laplace, 1825).

Third Age (1881–1940): Keynes and Knight's definitions of uncertainty marked this period. Knight was the first to associate uncertainty with risk. Knight defined risk, in 1921, as 'the objective relation of subjective uncertainty'. He accepted the risk in uncertainty. He argued that uncertainty is immeasurable when risk is calculated (Knight, 1921).

The diagram reflecting Keynes' views on uncertainty and probability is provided in Fig. 2.1. In the diagram, the innermost is composed of the cases that are digitised, while outside this circle there are cases that are not digitised but can be sorted, and these two cases are associated with probability. In the part where the probability ends, the events in which no comparison can be made begin, which point at uncertainty. The last circle describes the area where instincts are the sole dominant factor.

Fourth Age (1941–1970): This stage was marked by the drastic development of game theory. Game theory emerged as a result of the co-operation of Von Neumann and Morgenstern (1944), two famous scientists from different fields. Scientists in this field work on quantifiable risk instead of unquantifiable uncertainty.

Fifth Age (1970–2000): As game theories kept on rising, a group of economists adopted a different perspective on human interactions. In the early part of this stage, the rise of uncertainty and incomplete information economy can be regarded as an important step towards bridging the gap between doctrine and

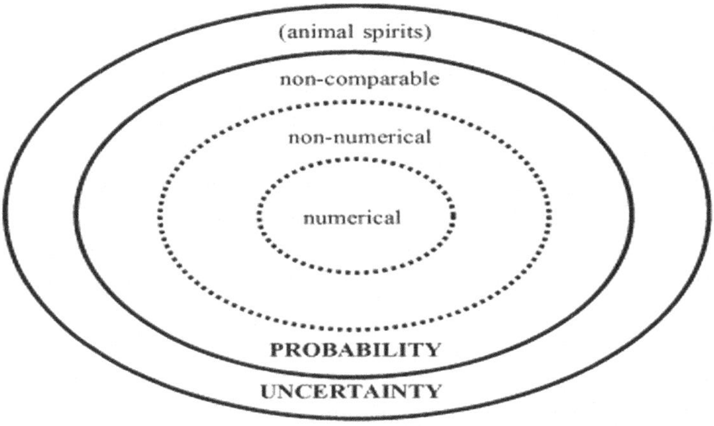

Fig. 2.1 Keynes' uncertainty and probability diagram. Source: Sakai (2019)

what actually happened. Through their work on classifying people's intuitive illusions in decision-making, Tversky and Kahneman led to the emergence of different approaches not only in psychology but also in various fields such as economics, marketing and advertising. The mathematical option problem is among the noteworthy ideas put forward in this period (Sakai, 2019).

Sixth Age (2001–): The current period: Uncertain Age. Sakai (2019) says that the term 'Risk Society' (Beck, 1986) can also be used for this period. The Uncertain Age actually refers to two meanings. The first one is the uncertainty of what the age brings, and the second one is the uncertainty of the theories developed in this age. The increase in the Black Swan phenomenon points out that the era deserves its name (Taleb, 2007). Many Black Swans are likely to be felt more deeply due to their unexpected nature. The 2008 loan crisis and the Covid-19 pandemic that started at the end of 2019 (Brown, 2020) are also examples of Black Swans. Taleb (2007) draws attention to three characteristics of the Black Swan. First, it must occur outside normal expectations. Second, it must have the potential for enormous impact (Great Depression or pandemic). Third, it should allow us to look back after the event has occurred and sort out some explanations and even excuses (Sakai, 2019).

Uncertainty is examined in three parts according to the sources causing uncertainty (Fig. 2.2), which are as follows:

- *Probability*: Future results being random
- *Ambiguity:* Lack of reliability of the information, lack of adequate and complete information
- *Complexity:* Information features that limit understanding

A different classification of sources of uncertainty is objective uncertainty (variability or diversity) and subjective uncertainty (lack of information) (Asselt, 2000; Kühberger & Schulte-Mecklenbeck, 2017). Open sources that cause the perception of uncertainty are defined as novelty, complexity and insoluble stimuli, whereas indirect sources are defined as inconsistency (Budner, 1962; Herman et al., 2010), diversity (Hancock et al., 2005), unpredictability (Greco & Roger, 2001; Norton, 1975), insolubility (Hancock et al., 2005; MacDonald, 1970), polysemy and incomprehensibility (Lauriola et al., 2015; Norton, 1975; McLain, 1993), obscurity, impermanence (Schneider et al., 2010; Geller et al., 1993; MacDonald, 1970; Norton, 1975), complexity, unfamiliarity (MacDonald, 1970), information disorder,

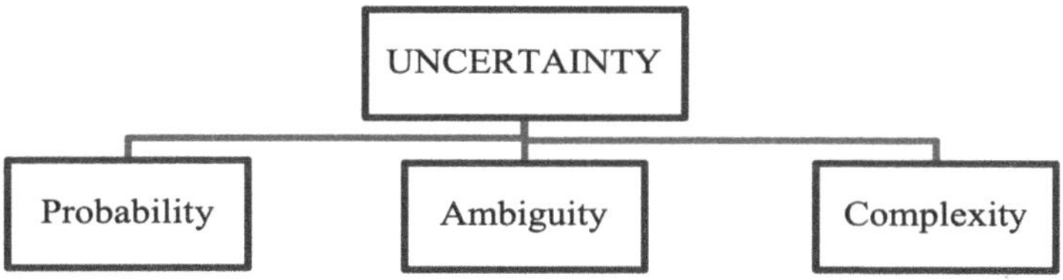

Fig. 2.2 Classification of uncertainty considering their sources. Source: Sakai (2019)

lack of information, lack of transparency (Budner, 1962; Hancock et al., 2005) and discontinuity.

Decision-making, by its nature, stands out the most in uncertain and risky environments. In strategic management, uncertainty has often been neglected and has not been given as much credit as risk. Starting from the motto, 'You cannot manage what you cannot define', each and every sector takes effort to make its own risk definitions and manage the risk. However, the scenario drastically changes when uncertainty is considered. People have sometimes confused uncertainty with risk; uncertainty has sometimes been left undefined and often ignored. The primary goal of risk management is to be prepared to make the right decisions at the right time. No matter how many risk methods and models are developed, it is not possible to manage a process where definitions are confusing and there is no unity of meaning in place. The importance of making decisions under risk and uncertainty arises not only from the difference between concepts, but also from different behaviours of our brain in cases of risk and uncertainty.

2.3 Decision-Making Under Uncertainty and Risk

In the traditional risk management literature, decision-making is typically categorised into three groups: certainty, risk and uncertainty. In the case of certainty, it is clear that every action leads to a definite result. In risk, all possible outcomes and the probabilities associated with each outcome are known. However, in the context of uncertainty, the outcomes are known, but the probabilities are not. Mousavi and Gigerenzer (2014) summarised decision-making under uncertainty and risk as shown in Table 2.2.

Table 2.2 Decision-making under uncertainty and risk

Nature of the unknown	Knightian probability	Decision-making process	Method	Information generated
Risk	A priori (design, tendency)	Deduction	Uses probability theory to model the fundamental structure, optimisation	Deterministic information (as is the case for lotteries)
Risk	Statistics (long-term frequency)	Induction (statistical inference)	Uses statistical inference, optimisation	Stochastic information, that is, correlation estimates
Uncertainty	Taking steps considering predictions, opinions	Intuitive	Picks up the most rational one from among the past experiences	Satisfactory solutions in the absence of optimisation Intuition (as is the case for entrepreneurship)

Source: Mousavi and Gigerenzer (2014)

In Table 2.2, the decision-making process in the face of risk is discussed with a deductive and inductive approach according to probability. This process is intuitive (heuristic method) in case of uncertainty. Probability theory and statistical inference are used in case of risks, and comparisons with experiences come to the fore in uncertainty.

Researchers in the fields of economics, biology and psychology have mostly agreed on the outcome variance in the definition of risk and made the definition as follows: the options with equal expected values, the one with a greater outcome variance is considered riskier. (Bernoulli, 1738). For instance, though an option with a 100% chance of winning 40 TL and an option with a 40% chance of winning 100 TL have the same expected values (40 TL), the first option has only one outcome while the second option has two outcome variances with certain probabilities (winning 40 TL; winning 0 or 100 TL). The second option, which has two outcome variances, is therefore defined as riskier. Since individuals exhibit systematic preferences for risk within various environmental and social contexts, elucidating decision-making under uncertainty and risk entails explaining the rationale behind decision-makers' preference for high-variance options over low-variance ones, and vice versa (Mishra, 2014).

Different disciplines have preferred normative and/or descriptive approaches to understand decision-making in situations involving uncertainty and risk. In this part, we will examine decision-making processes in terms of expected utility theory (economics), prospect theory (economics/psychology) and heuristic approaches (psychology).

2.3.1 Expected Utility Theory

The expected utility theory was formulated by Bernoulli as a response to the St. Petersburg Paradox.[1] According to Bernoulli's theory, the individual does not consider risk only on the basis of possible losses or gains, but focuses on the benefit derived from the risky action itself (Sakai, 2019). According to Bernoulli, money has declining marginal utility. Decision-makers may assign additional subjective value or benefits other than the absolute value of a decision outcome. The calculation of expected utility involves multiplying the utility of a given decision outcome by its corresponding probability. This hypothesis anticipates that decision-makers aim to maximise their utility. Utility is typically defined as a gauge of happiness and contentment stemming from an action (Friedman & Savage, 1948; Mishra, 2014).

As seen in Fig. 2.3, there is a difference between the expected utility under certainty and the expected benefit under risk. While the expected utility is higher under

[1] St. Petersburg Paradox: In a fair heads or tails game, the game continues until a coin flip results in heads. The player earns $2^n every time they get a tail. How much should one be willing to pay to play this game? Why are the players unwilling to pay too high even though the expected value is ∞? (Stanford, 2019)

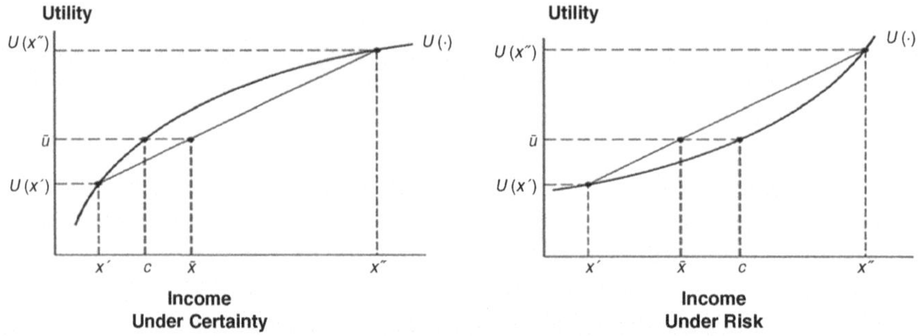

Fig. 2.3 Expected utility. Source: Friedman and Savage (1948)

certainty, it is lower under risk. According to this theory, it proposes three types of utility functions that describe the relationship between the expected value of a decision and the utility: risk neutrality, risk aversion and risk seeking.

The expected utility model is a theory of what should be done and what should be preferred in general. However, it falls short of explaining individual decisions. But the most significant criticism of expected utility theory is its inability to describe real-world decision-making models under conditions of risk. Expected utility only deals with decision-making under risk. It does not provide a model for how to make decisions in the event of uncertainty. Mishra (2014) stated that although it is very unlikely for individuals to win big prizes, they may ignore the possibility of losing rather than thinking economically and thus motivate themselves emotionally. In fact, this explains why the lottery is so popular universally.

In 1952, Allais revealed, in his study, that decision-makers decided against the expected utility theory. While decision-makers decide, considering that there is a very large subjective difference between 99% and 100% (certainty) probability of winning the award, they did not have the same sensitivity between 10% and 11% probability of winning the award. In his study, Ellsberg (1961) revealed that decision-makers behave differently in the face of risk and uncertainty. It has been observed that decision-makers prefer the one with a certain probability (even if the risk is high) over the one with an uncertain probability (uncertain). Alternative theories such as prospect theory have emerged against the criticisms of expected utility theory.

2.3.2 Prospect Theory

Prospect theory was formulated by Kahneman and Tversky in the late 1970s in response to increasing criticism that expected utility theory could not accurately estimate real-world decision-making in many cases. In cases of uncertainty where the probability is unknown, decision-makers predict the probability subjectively. Subjective probability, in fact, forms the basis of risk perception. With their work classifying people's misperception in decision-making, Tversky and Kahneman led to the emergence of different approaches in 1974, not only in psychology but also in different fields such as economics, marketing and advertising.

Kahneman and Tversky conducted a study on the framing effect in 1981. In this research, they examined how individuals perceive and interpret probabilities in decision-making problems and how they assess outcomes. In the study, the participants were asked two questions with two options and requested to make a choice. They were informed that an infectious disease, expected to result in the deaths of 600 people, had entered the country from Asia and that two treatment options were available. In alternative A, 200 patients would be cured, and in alternative B, the probability of recovery of 600 patients would be 1/3 and the probability of not recovering at all would be 2/3. When asked which option they would prefer in such a case, 72% of the participants preferred alternative A. It was said that in option C, 400 patients would die and in alternative D, the probability that no one would die was 1/3, and the probability of 600 patients dying is 2/3. In this question, 78% of the participants chose alternative D. In the first case with alternatives A and B, people were risk-averse because the word 'recovery' was perceived as a gain, even though the probabilities were the same. However, in the second case, since the possibility of losing is brought to the fore, people tend to take risks instead of losing. Kahneman and Tversky explained this as follows: 'Choices involving gains are mostly risk-averse, and choices involving losses often take risks', and they defined this problem as the trap in framing (Tversky & Kahneman, 1981).

As seen in Fig. 2.4, the value function of Kahneman and Tversky reveals risk perception against gains and losses. Individuals do not want to take risks when it comes to gains, whereas they are more willing to take risks when it comes to losses. Tversky & Kahneman, 1981) argued that people encode gains and losses according to a reference point. This coding is based on evaluating results above the reference point as gains, while results below the reference point are considered losses. These references may vary depending on the expectations or prejudices of the individual. The law of diminishing returns prevails in theory. Accordingly, the difference between 5 TL and 10 TL and the difference between 100 TL and 105 TL are not considered the same; as the share in the amount decreases, so does the expectation (Mishra, 2014).

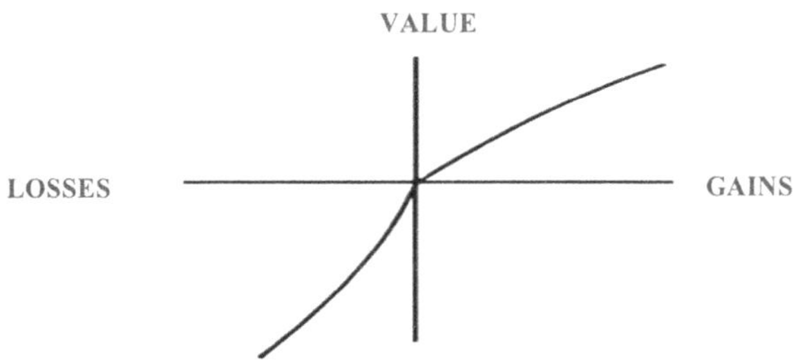

Fig. 2.4 Prospect theory function. Source: Kahneman and Tversky (2000)

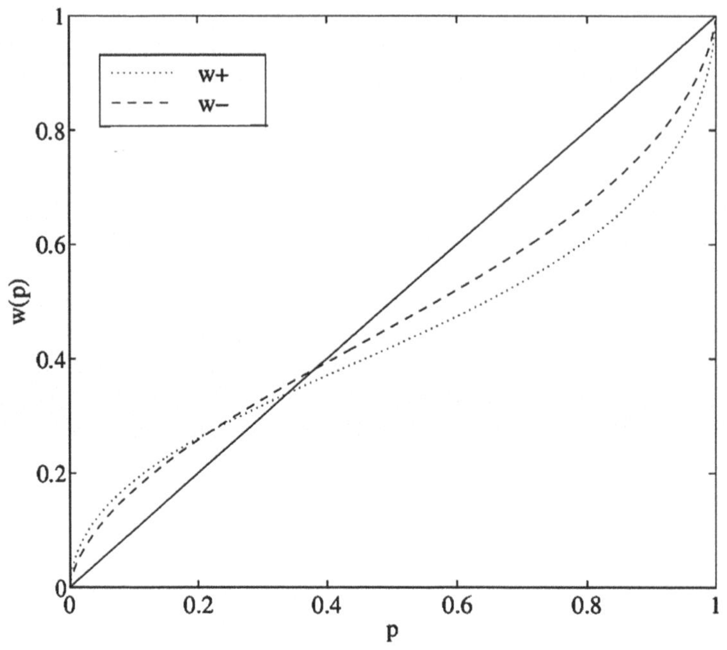

Fig. 2.5 Weight function for gains and losses. Source: Tversky and Kahneman (1992)

In 1992, Kahneman and Tversky revised their theory. In this new approach which they call the cumulative prospect theory, the weight function for gains and losses is added to the value function. The authors proposed a four-stage model of risk attitude as a result of this study: risk aversion for gains, risk seeking for high probability losses, gain seeking for low probability losses and risk aversion. The value function for gain and loss according to the cumulative prospect theory is provided in Fig. 2.5. In the new model which also includes the weight function, gain is again associated with risk aversion, whereas it is seen that the risk perception varies according to the probability level of losses.

2.3.3 Intuitive (Heuristic) Approaches

Thinking systems come to the fore in the heuristic approach. For some decisions such as choosing a profession or school, changing jobs, getting married or getting divorced, we go through an analysis process where we consider the pros and cons for days. However, it does not always take such long hours to make decisions; we unconsciously make thousands of decisions each and every day and apply them automatically in order to continue our daily activities. The fact that we make more than 200 decisions about food alone in a day is a relevant example (Wansink & Sobal, 2007).

Our mind uses some references and creates shortcuts when making decisions. This way, in the face of every new situation, the mind uses these shortcuts instead of wasting time by repeating the same actions over and over. This method is both very practical and economical and can be life-saving in the face of sudden dangers, which mostly allows us to continue our daily life in a routine manner. For example, our mind transforms the pictures of two-dimensional objects into three-dimensional objects thanks to our eyes and light, and compares and matches this object with the objects in our warehouse (brain) consisting of what we have previously perceived and experienced with our senses. Our mind has created another shortcut to determine and follow the motion direction of the matched object and its position in space: shadows of objects. Our mind follows the shadows of the objects together with the object and decides the direction of the movement. Although the direction of motion of the object does not change in the animation we watch, just making little changes in its shadow will completely change our perception of the direction it moves towards. Likewise, another shortcut created by our minds is estimating the sharpness and size of objects and the distance they are located. When we see an object clearly and large, we think that it is close to us, and otherwise, we think that it is far away. While this is generally true, it can have a misleading effect for two-dimensional images and when viewing distance is reduced.

Decision-making and reasoning are tasks that our brain undertakes systematically, and they are different concepts, albeit closely interconnected. Making a decision is a cycle that includes evaluation; evaluation includes reasoning and reasoning includes making a decision about what reasoning is necessary (Damasio, 1994). Neuroscientist Damasio observed that one of his patients had difficulty in making decisions due to the damage to his prefrontal cortex, though he was able to display many conscious behaviours; this made Damasio research similar events. As a result of his studies, he brought an alternative approach to Descartes' approach that completely separates the mind and the body. According to this view which Damasio calls the 'Somatic Determining Hypothesis', if one of the possible outcomes considered during reasoning is dangerous or bad, an unpleasant sensation will occur in the body (Damasio, 1994). This feeling will warn the person against a dangerous or bad outcome, acting as an alarm.

Options identified with automatic somatic response (feeling) and thought to cause undesirable consequences are unconsciously removed from the options list. Only then is a conscious benefit/harm analysis made among the remaining options. Not only feelings, but also emotions can play an active role in decision-making. Similar experiences or experiences unconsciously likened as well as resulting emotions related to the situation or event to be decided on can also stand out and affect decision-making mechanisms. In order to explain these thinking systems, the brain is addressed as a lower layer and an upper layer. The lower brain is the part responsible for the functions and motives necessary for the continuity of life. Right above this area is the part responsible for emotions and long-term memory, also called the limbic system. The upper layer, called the neocortex, refers to the part where the conscious decisions are made. Fast and slow thinking are not completely independent of each other and are in balance. These two ways of thinking are also called intuitive and reflective thinking. In intuitive thinking, impressions, associations, emotions and actions occur spontaneously, without requiring any effort. We do not consciously focus on how to do these things, we just do them (like walking, crossing over obstacles and tying laces). In reflective (rational) thinking, thinking and action are slow, diligent and deliberate. This type of thinking prevails at the front when we first learn how to drive, when we solve questions and when we work. Both ways of thinking are actually constantly active. However, reflective thinking is generally in the monitoring phase and waits for appropriate conditions (such as high risk or error detection) to take action (Lovallo & Sibony, 2011). Organisms with less developed brain structures use the intuitive decision-making system—which is economical and fast—much more successfully than humans. The decision-making process is also affected by our experiences and emotions. For this reason, the basis of the heuristic approach is considered as 'direct comparison' (note that the focus is on 'value' expected utility theory and prospect theory).

Our brain uses shortcuts such as likening and matching with the old ones, continuing and completing the pattern in every situation that it describes as new. Although the main reason for this is to be able to make a quick decision in case of danger, this affects every moment of our lives; while providing advantages in many areas, it also brings some disadvantages. In situations where effort is required, such as evaluating and predicting probabilities, individuals reduce the event to simpler judgement processes (Tversky & Kahneman, 1974). While doing this, they use the three most basic cognitive shortcuts (heuristics):

1. *The Representational Cognitive Method*: In the event of uncertainty, in cases where people are asked the probability of event X stemming from process Y and the probability of object X belonging to class Y, they rely on their representational intuition, in which X is judged by the degree by which it represents Y, and they think they are giving a logical answer this way. People usually guess by choosing the outcome that best represents the input (Kahneman et al., 1982). *Example*: Selma is a quiet, introverted and neat person. When people ask which is more likely about Selma's profession (librarian or teacher), most people choose librarian. The reason for this is the misperception of representing the librarian's identity with the personality traits listed. In the absence of any information about Selma's profession, our minds prefer the librarian identity rather than teaching which is more likely.
2. *Availability*: It argues that people will evaluate the frequency of a class or the probability of an event according to which instance or occurrence the decision-maker encounters more frequently (Tversky & Kahneman, 1974). The past experiences that leave deep marks, the most recent experiences or the objectives of the individual may be the first options that appear in his/her mind. *Example*: A surgeon who lost a relative in his family to cancer may tend to make more radical decisions, rather than conservative, in the treatment approach of his patients.
3. *Anchoring*: People make predictions by beginning with an initial value adjusted to give the ultimate answer, which is called anchoring (Kahneman et al., 1982). *Example*: Writing the initial price and the last price on the labels, which is very

often used in marketing. The first price will act as an anchor, and the person's mind will see how attractive the current price of the product is and be convinced that it should be bought.

These heuristics (intuitive methods, shortcuts) are both cost-effective and often efficient. Nevertheless, they have the potential to result in consistent and foreseeable mistakes. Gaining a deeper comprehension of these heuristics and the biases they generate can enhance decision-making when faced with uncertainty (Tversky & Kahneman, 1974).

The dual decision-making model, in which rational thinking and the heuristics are effective, has come to the fore in recent years (Tyburski, 2017). However, cognitive errors also play a role in rational decision-making. Accordingly, decisions consist of two stages under uncertainty: editing and evaluation. During the editing stage, simplification of the decision-making process occurs through the application of specific heuristics. During the evaluation stage, alternatives are assessed, and the option with the greatest subjective value is chosen. Kahneman (2003) states that gains and losses are relative and evaluated according to a certain reference point. Multiple responses defined indirectly (Hillen et al., 2017) and prevailing mood (Kiziukiewicz & Jaworska, 2017) when making decisions are also important.

Indirectly defined responses under uncertainty are shown in Table 2.3. Accordingly, the answers given under uncertainty are examined under three subtitles, namely cognitive, emotional and behavioural responses. In cognitive responses, approval and curiosity are among the positive responses, while distrust and denial are among the negative responses. Emotional positive responses include excitement and pleasure, while negative responses include stress, anger and fear responses. From the behavioural perspective, adaptation is among the positive responses, whereas avoidance is among the negative ones.

Moods of individuals remarkably affect the risk perception and decision-making mechanism, as well. Kiziukiewicz and Jaworska (2017) conducted research on the effects of negative emotions on risk perception and decision-making. Anger and rage accelerate decision-making, while sadness slows it down. While fear and anxiety cause individuals to avoid risk, anger increases risk tolerance. Sadness decreases decision certainty, whereas anger enhances it. Fear and anxiety lead to defensive behaviour, whereas anger can result in destructive behaviour.

2.3.4 Strategic Decision-Making and Psychological Traps

It is a difficult and risky process for the manager to make decisions regarding the institution he manages. Taking the right decision can take the manager and the institution to the top while a bad call can cause irreversible damages. Hammond et al. (1998) identified six psychological traps that influence the occurrence of wrong decisions in the human mind:

Table 2.3 Multiple responses defined indirectly against uncertainty

Positive	Negative
Cognitive	
Approval, acceptance	Denial
Entertainment	Disgust
	Distrust
Curiosity	Self-devaluation (self-doubt)
	Brain fog
	Suspicion
Emotional	
Comfort (health, relaxation)	Discomfort (restlessness, emotional sadness, feeling overwhelmed)
Pleasure	
Excitement (passion, encouragement)	Stress
	Worry/anxiety (frustration, fragility or the feel of threat)
	Fear
	Depression (sadness)
	Anger (disappointment, resentment)
Behavioural	
Approach (confrontation, following, seeking)	Avoidance (source of uncertainty)
Adaptation	
Deliberation	
	Decision avoidance, hesitation, postponing or prudence
Explanation (tendency to explain)	Non-disclosure (reluctance to admit)
	Withdrawal (lack of persistence)
	Control orientation (reducing outcome or source, problem-solving)

Source: Hillen et al. (2017)

1. *Anchoring Trap*: Used in various situations where an unknown value needs to be estimated. It starts with anchoring an existing salient point to generate the necessary estimate (Ritov, 1996).
2. *Status Quo Trap:* Decision-makers have a strong bias towards status-maintaining alternatives. The status quo approach includes not taking action to avoid harm and risk (Hammond et al., 1998).
3. *Sunk Cost Trap*: The sunk cost effect is insisting on continuing the effort after investing in money, effort or time, even though it is clear that you are making a loss (Arkes & Ayton, 1999).
4. *Confirming Evidence Trap*: Drawing conclusions based on confirmatory evidence can cause incorrect conclusions because various hypotheses may be consistent with identical data. Such inferences are evident in the choices made to justify prejudices (Wason, 1960).

5. *Framing Trap*: Psychological principles that determine how decision problems are perceived and how probabilities and outcomes are evaluated lead to expected changes in preferences when the same problem is presented in different frameworks (Tversky & Kahneman, 1981).
6. *Prediction and Estimation Pitfalls:* Our minds are quite good at estimating distance, time and weight. This largely stems from the fact that we constantly test and measure whether our estimates are correct. However, when it comes to uncertainty, it is not easy to test whether our predictions are correct. The three most common types of estimation and estimation traps, which can have a particularly disruptive effect in uncertain situations as they cloud our ability to evaluate probabilities, are listed as follows (Hammond et al., 1998):

    (a) *Overconfidence Trap*: It is an error in evaluating the accuracy of individuals' answers to questions about intellectual or perceptual problems. People feel confident more frequently about sensory and perceptual tasks (Pallier et al., 2002).
    (b) *Overcautiousness Trap*: It is the type of trap that appears when the person takes into account the precautions more than necessary in order to stay in the safe zone under many conditions. The risk appetite of the decision-maker is very low in such situations and s/he takes extra precautions to avoid risks.
    (c) *Recallability Trap:* It refers to the situation in which the experiences, negativities and traumas are always evident in the decisions of the person. Even if the probability of the event resulting in the trauma is very low, the person may make wrong decisions because s/he perceives this probability as much higher.

The pitfalls in strategic decision-making are grouped differently by different researchers. According to Russo and Schoemaker's (1991) study, the ten most common barriers to decision-making are: plunging in, frame blindness, uncontrollable decision-making, overconfidence, current and recent data creating an anchoring trap, making decisions without thinking about the outcome, group failure, inadequate use of feedback, inability to follow through on past decisions and lack of framework control.

Benson (2016) has gathered over 180 cognitive biases under four main headings:

1. Prejudices that occur when there is too much information
2. Prejudices that occur when meaning is missing
3. Prejudices that occur in situations where quick action is required
4. Prejudices that occur in situations where remembering is important

How mixed messages are internalised in our minds and how they turn into attitudes and behaviours while making decisions are also affected by factors such as age, gender and personal characteristics, apart from feelings, emotions, intuitions and prejudices. Sproten et al. (2018) conducted two experiments where they investigated how decision-making under uncertainty is affected by age. Their first experiment conducted with young adults and older adults found no difference in decision-making under risk between the two groups. It has been observed that young adults take more risks than older adults when it comes to making decisions under uncertainty, and older adults avoid risk in the face of uncertainty (Sproten et al., 2018).

Ronay and Kim (2006) investigated whether gender differences play a role in risk decisions. The study found no difference between the individual and unconscious decision-making responses of men and women. However, it has been observed that men had a tendency to take more risks than women when they come together in groups.

Busenitz and Barney (1997) examined the differences in the decision-making processes of managers and entrepreneurs considering their prejudices and intuitions. Entrepreneurial groups in large enterprises are more willing, compared to managers, to reveal their prejudices and intuitions when making decisions. Entrepreneurs rely much more on their intuition in situations of uncertainty.

2.4 Ways of Coping with Uncertainty

The decision-maker has to deal with uncertainty. As problems become more complicated, different aspects of uncertainty become more visible. Uncertainty is temporary. The extent of uncertainty changes as you learn about the unknown. In other words, uncertainty is not fixed but dynamic and constantly changing. The uncertainty about a specific subject is usually tried to be eliminated with the subjective perception of probability and the quick-thinking system comes to the fore. Although the quick-thinking system has many advantages, it also brings some misperceptions. First of all, the type of uncertainty should be analysed to minimise such misperceptions that the mind encounters in decision-making processes in the face of uncertainty. The types of uncertainty are provided in Table 2.4. Accordingly, uncertainty arises from a partial or complete lack of information or insufficient understanding. While there is uncertainty in outcomes, situations and roles in the case of lack of information, there is often uncertainty in situations and roles in poor understanding.

Table 2.4 Types of uncertainty

Type	Outcome-output	Situation	Role
Information			
–Completely lacking	√	√	√
–Partly lacking	√	√	√
–Unreliable	√	√	√
Inadequate understanding			
–Equivocality		√	√
–Instability		√	
–Novelty		√	√
–Conflict	√		√

Source: Lipshitz and Strauss (1997)

People apply tactics of reducing, acknowledging and suppressing uncertainty in order to cope with uncertainty. Some of these tactics involve rational decision-making, while others involve avoiding uncertainty and suppression. The tactics for coping with uncertainty are indicated in Table 2.5. Accordingly, tactics such as collecting additional information, asking for advice and following standards are adopted in tactics of reduction. In acknowledgement tactics, uncertainty is accepted but measures are taken to minimise its impact. In suppression tactics, on the other hand, uncertainty is usually ignored.

According to the results of Lipshitz and Strauss's research on decision-making processes in natural uncertainty using the models in Tables 2.4 and 2.5, the most preferred method for coping with uncertainty is reducing uncertainty, corresponding to 47%, which is followed by accepting uncertainty (42%) and then by acknowledging uncertainty (11%). People used different tactics in different uncertain situations. While the first strategy used in the case of inadequate understanding was reduction, the first strategy used in conflict was evaluating the pros and cons. It was observed that the prevention tactic is in the background of all strategies (Lipshitz & Strauss, 1997).

Many decision-makers, today, realise how prejudices can impair judgement in a business environment. However, it is possible to raise awareness of the effects of prejudices and take steps to confront them. As for more than 1000 large commercial

Table 2.5 Tactics for coping with uncertainty

Tactic	Definition
	Tactics of reduction
1. Collect additional information	Conduct an active search for factual information
2. Delay action	Postpone decision-making or action taking until additional information clarifies the decision problem
3. Solicit advice	Solicit advice/opinion of experts, superiors, friends or colleagues
4. Follow SOPs, norms, etc.	Act according to formal and informal rules of conduct
5. Assumption-based reasoning	Construct a mental model of the situation based on beliefs
	Tactics of acknowledgement
1. Pre-empting	Generate specific responses to possible negative outcomes
2. Improve readiness	Develop a general capability to respond to unanticipated negative developments (e.g., leave some resources unused)
3. Avoid irreversible action	Prefer or develop reversible course of action, prepare contingencies
4. Weighing pros and cons	Choose among alternatives in terms of potential
	Tactics of suppression
1. Ignore uncertainty	Act as if under certainty
2. Rely on intuition	Use hunches, informed guesses, etc., without sufficient justification
3. Take a gamble	Take a chance, throw a coin, etc.

Source: Lipshitz and Strauss (1997)

investments, McKinsey's 2010 study found that organisations achieved 7% higher returns when they tried to reduce the impact of prejudices in their decision-making processes (Lovallo & Sibony, 2011).

2.5 Conclusion

We have to make thousands of decisions each and every day in order to continue our lives. These decisions are sometimes of vital importance to us while they are sometimes just a part of our daily life and appear unconsciously. Affected by many factors, decision-making processes are complicated processes studied in many fields such as economics, psychology and biology.

We make most of our decisions under uncertainty and risk, yet we do not think much about what that means. The adventure of the concepts of uncertainty and risk, which started with the analysis of a gambling game about three centuries ago, continues to progress by incorporating different disciplines into the game. The concepts of uncertainty and risk gain a different dimension with each new period, and we have to play the game by the rules. So, can we really play the game by the rules? Can we keep up with these changes? For many years, we ignored uncertainty and watched the inevitable rise of risk and risk management. The age of uncertainty that started in the 2000s proved that risk management models actually do not manage risks very well. So what was it that was missing?

Whatever risk assessment method developed, it is the 'human' who defines the risk and makes the decision despite all the assisting methods. Revealing how the decision is made, rather than what kind of decision should be made, is closely related to the concepts of risk and uncertainty. For the efficient implementation of corporate risk management, it is of utmost importance to clarify the distinction between the concepts of uncertainty and risk, which must be followed to understand how people make decisions under uncertainty and risk, by making use of studies in the fields of psychology, neuroscience and behavioural science.

Our fast and slow thinking systems are in balance when making decisions. If we were to go through slow, strategic decision-making processes for all of the thousands of decisions we make in order to continue our lives, our lives would be far from sustainable. In fact, we might not have a life to lead because we could not react to dangers in a timely manner. Although we have cognitive biases in the face of uncertainty and risk, the practicality, affordability and benefits of intuitive thinking are indispensable. If we were only thinking rationally, as in many clinical examples, our decision-making mechanism would be incomplete and the balance would be disrupted. However, if we were only making decisions with intuitive thinking and the prejudices it brings, we might face irreversible situations. We are used to dealing with a certain degree of uncertainty in our daily lives. In cases where uncertainty is very high, our decision-making processes may be interrupted or even collapsed, and we may act based on prejudice, emotion and intuition instead of logic and facts. In general, rational thinking is at the forefront when making decisions under risk, but intuitive thinking supersedes rational thinking when making decisions under uncertainty. In the age of uncertainty, unless the concept of uncertainty is given the credit it deserves, one dimension of risk management will always remain incomplete. It will be possible to manage risks better, if the concepts of risk and uncertainty are clearly distinguished and included in the management processes and if the level of awareness of the misperceptions encountered in the decision-making process is increased.

References

Abdellaoui, M. D., & Hey, J. (Eds.). (2008). *Advances in decision making under risk and uncertainty*. Springer.

Allais, M. (1979). The foundations of a positive theory of choice involving risk and a criticism of the postulates and axioms of the American School (1952). In M. Allais & O. Hagen (Eds.), *Expected utility hypotheses and the Allais paradox, theory and decision library* (An International Series in the Philosophy and Methodology of the Social and Behavioral Sciences). Springer.

Arkes, H. R., & Ayton, P. (1999). The sunk cost and concorde effects: are humans less rational than lower animals? *Psychological Bulletin, 125*(5), 591–600.

Asselt, M. B. A. (2000). *Perspectives on uncertainty and risk; the PRIMA approach to decision support*. Springer Science+Business Media.

Bammer, G., & Smithson, M. (Eds.). (2008). *Uncertainty and risk multidisciplinary perspectives*. Earthscan.

Beck, U. (1986). *Risikogesellschaft: Auf dem Weg in eine Andere Moderne* (in German). Surbkamp Verlag, Frankfurt am Main. English translation by Ritter, M. (1992) Risk society: towards a new modernity. Sage.

Benson, B. (2016). Retrieved May 21, 2021, from https://www.teachthought.com/critical-thinking/the-cognitive-bias-codex-a-visual-of-180-cognitive-biases/#:~:text=The%20Cognitive%20Bias%20Codex%3A%20A%20Visual%20Of%20180%2B%20Cognitive%20Biases&text=A%20cognitive%20bias%20is%20an,%E2%80%93and%20often%20irrational%E2%80%93conclusions.&text=Not%20all%20'broken%20thinking%2C',thought%20are%20labeled%2C%20of%20course

Bernoulli, D. (1738). Exposition of a new theory on the measurement of risk. *Econometrica (1954), 22*, 23–36.

Black, F., & Scholes, M. (1973). The pricing of options and corporate liabilities. *The Journal of Political Economy, 81*, 637–654.

Borch, K., & Mossin, J. (Eds.). (1968). *Risk and uncertainty, proceedings of a conference held by the International Economic Association*. Macmillan.

Brown, J. (2020). *Affective decision making under uncertainty, risk, ambiguity and black swans*. Springer.

Budner, S. (1962). Intolerance of ambiguity as a personality variable. *Journal of Personality, 30*, 29–59.

Busenitz, L. W., & Barney, J. B. (1997). Differences between entrepreneurs and managers in large organisations: Biases and heuristics in strategic decision-making. *Journal of Business Venturing, 12*(1), 9–30.

Damasio, A. (1994). *Descartes' error: Emotion, reason and the human brain*. Avon Books.

Eichberger, J., Kelsey, D., & Schipper, B. C. (2008). Advances in decision making under risk and uncertainty. In M. Abdellaoui & J. Hey (Eds.), *Granny versus game theorist: ambiguity in experimental games*. Springer.

Ellsberg, D. (1961). Risk, ambiguity, and the savage axioms. *The Quarterly Journal of Economics, 75*(4), 643–669.
Friedman, M., & Savage, L. J. (1948). The utility analysis of choice involving risk. *Journal of Political Economy, 56*, 279–304.
Geller, G., Tambor, E., Chase, G. A., & Holtzman, N. A. (1993). Measuring physicians' tolerance for ambiguity and its relationship to their reported practices regarding genetic testing. *Medical Care, 31*(11), 989–1001.
Greco, V., & Roger, D. (2001). Coping with uncertainty: The construction and validation of a new measure. *Personality and Individual Differences, 31*(4), 519–534.
Hammond, J. S., Keeney, R. L., & Raiffa, H. (1998). The hidden traps in decision making. *Harvard Business Review, 76*(5), 47.
Hancock, J., Roberts, M., & Monrouxe, L. (2005). Medical student and junior doctors' tolerance of ambiguity: Development of a new scale. *Advances in Health Science Education, 20*, 113–130.
Hastie, R., & Dawes, R. M. (2010). *Rational choice in an uncertain world: The psychology of judgment and decision making*. Sage.
Herman, J. L., Stevens, M. J., Bird, A., Mendenhall, M., & Oddou, G. (2010). The tolerance for ambiguity scale: Towards a more refined measure for international management research. *International Journal of Intercultural Relations, 34*(1), 58–65.
Hillen, M. A., Gutheil, C. M., Strout, T. D., Smets, E. M. A., & Han, P. K. J. (2017). Tolerance of uncertainty: Conceptual analysis, integrative model, and implications for healthcare. *Social Science & Medicine, 180*, 62–75.
ISO 31000/2018, International Organization for Standardization. Retrieved May 8, 2021, from https://www.iso.org/obp/ui#iso:std:iso:31000:ed-2:v1:en
Kahneman, D. (2003). A perspective on judgment and choice: mapping bounded rationality. *American Psychologist, 58*(9), 697–720.
Kahneman, D., Slovic, P., & Tversky, A. (1982). *Judgment under uncertainty: heuristics and biases*. Cambridge University Press.
Kahneman, D., & Tversky, A. (Eds.). (2000). Choices, values, and frames, Cambridge University Press.
Kaivanto, K. (2008). Advances in decision making under risk and uncertainty. In M. D. Abdellaoui & J. Hey (Eds.), *Alternation bias and the parameterization of cumulative prospect theory*. Springer.
Kiziukiewicz, T., & Jaworska, E. (2017). Neuroeconomic and behavioral aspects of decision making. In K. Nermend & M. Łatuszyn'ska (Eds.), *The impact of behavioral factors on the decisive usefulness of accounting information*. Springer.
Knight, F. (1921). *Risk, uncertainty and profit*. Riverside Press.
Kühberger, A., & Schulte-Mecklenbeck, M. (2017). Economic psychology. In R. Raynard (Ed.), *Theories of economic decision-making: value, risk and affect*. Wiley.
Laplace, P. (1825). *Essai philosophique sur les probabilités* (Digitally Printed Version-2009), Cambrıdge Unıversıty Press, s.1–4.
Lauriola, M., Foschi, R., Mosca, O., & Weller, J. (2015). Attitude toward ambiguity: empirically robust factors in self-report personality scales. *Assessment, 23*(3), 353–373.
Lipshitz, R., & Strauss, O. (1997). Coping with uncertainty: A naturalistic decision-making analysis. *Organizational Behavior and Human Decision Processes, 69*(2), 149–163.
Lovallo, D., & Sibony, O. (2011). Before you make that big decision. *Harvard Business Review, 89*, 50–60, 137.
MacDonald, A. P. (1970). Revised scale for ambiguity tolerance: reliability and validity. *Psychological Reports, 26*(3), 791–798.
Machina, M. J., & Viscusi, W. K. (Eds.). (2014). *Handbook of the economics of risk and uncertainty*. Elsevier.
Mclain, D. L. (1993). The Mstat-I: A new measure of an individual's tolerance for ambiguity. *Educational and Psychological Measurement, 53*(1), 183–189.

Mishra, S. (2014). Decision-making under risk: integrating perspectives from biology, economics, and psychology. *Personality and Social Psychology Review*, 1–28.

Mousavi, S., & Gigerenzer, G. (2014). Risk, uncertainty and heuristics. *Journal of Business Research, 67*, 671–1678.

Nikolaidis, E., Mourelatos, Z., & Pandey, V. (2011). *Design decisions under uncertainty with limited information*. CRC Press.

Norton, R. (1975). Measurement of ambiguity tolerance. *Journal of Personality Assessment, 39*(6), 607–619.

Pallier, G., Wilkinson, R., Danthiir, V., Kleitman, S., Knezevic, G., Stankov, L., & Roberts, R. D. (2002). The role of individual differences in the accuracy of confidence judgments. *The Journal of General Psychology, 129*(3), 257–299.

Potemkowski, A. (2017). Neuroeconomic and behavioral aspects of decision making. In K. Nermend & M. Łatuszyn'ska (Eds.), *Neurobiology of decision making: methodology in decision-making research. Neuroanatomical and neurobiochemical fundamentals*. Springer.

Ritov, I. (1996). Anchoring in simulated competitive market negotiation. *Organizational Behavior and Human Decision Processes, 67*(1), 16–25.

Ronay, R., & Kim, D. Y. (2006). Gender differences in explicit and implicit risk attitudes: A socially facilitated phenomenon. *The British Journal of Social Psychology, 45(Pt 2)*:397–419.

Russo, J. E., & Shoemaker, P. (1991). Decision traps: Ten barriers to brilliant decision-making and how to overcome them. *Journal of Behavioral Decision Making, 4*, 75–78.

Sakai, Y. (2019). *J.M. Keynes Versus F.H. Knight risk, probability, and uncertainty*. Springer.

Schneider, A., Löwe, B., Barie, S., Joos, S., Engeser, P., & Szecsenyi, J. (2010). How do primary care doctors deal with uncertainty in making diagnostic decisions? *Journal of Evaluation in Clinical Practice, 16*, 431–437.

Sharps, M. J., & Martin, S. S. (2002). Mindless decision making as a failure of contextual reasoning. *J Psychol, 136*(3), 272–282.

Simon, H. (1959). Theories of decision-making in economics and behavioral science. *The American Economic Review, 49*(3), 253–283.

Sproten, A. N., Diener, C., Fiebach, C. J., & Schwieren, C. (2018). Decision making and age: factors influencing decision making under uncertainty. *Journal of Behavioral and Experimental Economics, 76*(C), 43–54.

Stanford. (2019). *The Stanford Encyclopedia of Philosophy*. Retrieved June 17, 2021, from https://plato.stanford.edu/entries/paradox-stpetersburg/

Svenson, O. (2003). Values, affect, and processes in human decision making: a differentiation and consolidation theory perspective. In S. L. Schneider & J. Shanteau (Eds.), *Cambridge series on judgment and decision making: emerging perspectives on judgment and decision research* (pp. 287–326). Cambridge University Press.

Szpiro, G. (2020). *Risk, choice, and uncertainty: Three centuries of economic decision-making*. Columbia University Press.

Taleb, N. N. (2007). *The black swan: The impact of the highly improbable*. Random House.

TDK. (2021). Retrieved May 8, 2021, from https://sozluk.gov.tr/

Tversky, A., & Kahneman, D. (1974). Judgment under uncertainty: Heuristics and biases. *Science, 185*(4157), 1124–1131.

Tversky, A., & Kahneman, D. (1981). The framing of decisions and the psychology of choice. *Science, New Series, 211*, 453–458.

Tversky, A., & Kahneman, D. (1992). Advances in prospect theory: cumulative representation of uncertainty. *Journal of Risk and Uncertainty, 5*(4), 297–323.

Tyburski, E. (2017). Neuroeconomic and behavioral aspects of decision making. In K. Nermend & M. Łatuszyn'ska (Eds.), *Psychological determinants of decision making*. Springer.

Von Neumann, J., & Morgenstern, O. (1944). *Game theory and economic behavior*. Princeton University Press.

Wansink, B., & Sobal, J. (2007). Mindless eating: the 200 daily food decisions we overlook. *Environment and Behavior, 39*, 106–123.

Wason, P. C. (1960). On the failure to eliminate hypotheses in a conceptual task. *Quarterly Journal of Experimental Psychology, 12*(3), 129–140.
Yoe, C. (2019). *Principles of risk analysis decision making under uncertainty*. Taylor and Francis, CRC Press.

Aynur Zaku is an internal auditor at the Presidency for Turks Abroad and Related Communities. She is a PhD candidate at the Social Sciences University of Ankara Audit and Risk Management Program. In 2002, she graduated from Gazi University Faculty of Dentistry. She worked for 11 years as a dentist in various clinics. She has worked in health workforce planning, strategic planning, the burden of disease, risk assessment methods in occupational health and safety, health professions, and education in the Ministry of Health, and she has contributed to the Ministry's publications on these issues. In 2020, she completed the Ankara University Internal Audit and Internal Control Master's Program. In 2021, she was appointed as an internal auditor. She presented a paper at an international conference on project risk management and has an ISO/IEC 27001 Lead Auditor certificate.

Chapter 3
Risk Attitude: The CAPSTONE of Enterprise Risk Management

Yağmur Özyurt and Ali Göksel

Abstract Individuals' attitudes towards risk-taking or risk avoidance when faced with risks vary depending on many factors and determine the outcome of the decisions we make. Individual risk attitudes have a keystone effect on Enterprise Risk Management (ERM). Ignoring the impact of risk attitude, which holds the ERM structure together, can cause the entire structure to collapse. Therefore, risk attitudes need to be understood and properly managed. This study aims to produce recommendations taking into account the subjective aspect of individual risk attitudes that affect ERM. Accordingly, the factors affecting individual risk attitudes and senior management's ERM-specific risk attitudes are analyzed together with the impact of these factors on ERM. In addition, the extent to which risk attitudes are taken into account in standards and frameworks has been the subject of the research. We have concluded that the standards and frameworks used in ERM either ignore individual risk attitudes completely or do not address them in the necessary depth. Emphasizing the importance of taking into account individual risk attitudes in the design or implementation of the ERM system, recommendations defined as CAPSTONE are presented.

Keywords Risk perception · Risk attitude · Enterprise risk management · ERM

Y. Özyurt (✉) · A. Göksel
Social Sciences University of Ankara, Ankara, Türkiye
e-mail: yagmur.ozyurt2@student.asbu.edu.tr; ali.goksel@student.asbu.edu.tr

H. Kıral (ed.), *Rethinking Enterprise Risk Management*, Accounting, Finance, Sustainability, Governance & Fraud: Theory and Application,
https://doi.org/10.1007/978-981-97-5983-5_3

3.1 Introduction

Each individual has different past experiences, cultural background, social capital, and personality traits. In this respect, each individual is unique. This is reflected in our actions and behaviors which are driven by our instincts. It is our attitudes that determine our actions and behaviors.

Our attitudes best reflect the uniqueness of individuals when considered in the context of risk. For example, some individuals may be overly willing to take risks, while others may exhibit risk-averse behavior. Those willing to take risks may end up earning more, while risk-averse individuals may not earn sufficient returns. The opposite is also possible. From this perspective, our attitudes towards risk make a significant difference between success and failure. The role of individual risk attitudes is also important for Enterprise Risk Management (ERM) practices. Because an organization's risk-taking attitude determines how it develops its business strategies and sets its financial targets. Therefore, risk attitude affects risk strategies and becomes a critical success factor for organizations.

To what extent does ERM take into account risk attitude, which has a significant impact on organizational decisions and outcomes? Based on this question, this study examines the role of individual attitudes in ERM. This is because individual attitudes are the root cause of failure stories in ERM initiatives (Fadun, 2013). Since individuals' risk perception and risk attitudes directly affect ERM, there is a need to both understand risk perception and attitudes well and to seek solutions to reduce the negative effects of these factors.

In this context, the second part of the study examines risk attitude in terms of different fields and discusses the variables affecting risk attitude. The third section discusses the impact of individual risk attitudes on ERM, more specifically, the impact of CEO characteristics on risk attitude and ERM. Considering the impact of individual risk attitudes on risk management, the fourth section explores the approaches of risk management frameworks to risk perception and risk attitudes. Recognizing the inadequacy of existing frameworks and standards in addressing individual risk attitudes, the final section proposes new approaches and strategies to overcome this inadequacy and take into account the effects of individual risk attitudes on ERM.

3.2 Risk Attitude

Risk is defined in many different ways, and the word is used to mean many different things. As a result, the definition of risk has become almost meaningless (French & Liang, 1993; as cited in Riabacke, 2006). The three common points in these definitions of risk are event, outcome, and probability. However, risk definitions based on probability may lead to neglect of important uncertainties. Thus, uncertainties beyond probabilities need to be considered (Aven, 2010). In this respect, risk is an uncertain situation for a decision-maker in which the outcomes are unknown in advance and one cannot be sure what outcomes may occur (Riabacke, 2006). According to another definition, risk is uncertainty that, if occurs, could have a positive or negative impact on one or more objectives (Hillson & Murray-Webster, 2004). These perspectives show that the concept of risk is seen as a positive or negative situation and involves both taking risks and risking losses (Aven, 2012).

Risk attitude is people's intention to evaluate risk positively or negatively and act accordingly. Risk attitude indicates the extent to which individuals are willing to take risks and is expressed in a wide range from risk-seeking to risk aversion (Dohmen et al., 2011). For example, some individuals (risk-averse) may prefer to stay in the right lane on their morning commute, while others (risk-loving) may prefer to cut through the traffic. Our actions, which require us to decide between these two opposite poles, are influenced by a variety of factors (Figner & Weber, 2011). So, what are the main factors that lead individuals to take or avoid risk?

Recent research has shown that risk attitudes are not always the same for all individuals (Rohrmann, 2008). Risk attitudes are domain (context) specific, so they can vary from one case to another (Blais & Weber, 2006; Macías & Andrea, 2015). Some people are more willing to take financial risks, yet more reluctant to take risks in medical decisions, such as vaccinating their children. Some people are risk-averse about ethical risks, such as filing an incomplete tax return, while others are more willing to take entertainment risks, such as skydiving (Zimerman et al., 2014). These results show that people do not have the same level of risk-taking tendency in all areas (Hanoch et al., 2006).

Studies examining domain-specific risk-taking attitudes assess two important motivations underlying risk attitudes: perceived risks and benefits[1] (Weber et al., 2002). Risk attitude is shaped by the degree to which an activity is safe or dangerous (risk perception) and the benefits that can be derived from engaging in the activity (expected benefits). If an activity seems too risky, then the likelihood of engaging in that activity is lower. On the other hand, if an activity seems more beneficial, then the likelihood of engaging in that activity is higher (Wilke et al., 2014). For example, high-risk sports (such as parachuting, mountaineering, or paragliding) offer benefits such as excitement, adrenaline, physical skill development, and increased self-confidence, but they also carry risks of injury or death. Some may participate in high-risk sports believing that the benefits are worth the risks, while others may avoid such sports believing that the risks outweigh the benefits. Accordingly, risk attitude can be seen as the result of the trade-off between the expected benefit of an activity and its perceived risk (Figner & Weber, 2011).

When risk attitude is analyzed from the perspective of investors' financial decisions, it is seen that the trade-off between risk and return shapes risk attitude. Greed and fear indexes are two important indicators that provide information about the risk perception and risk-aversion behavior of investors in financial markets (Figner & Weber, 2011). Risk-seeking (greedy) investors tend to take more risk in order to

[1] Preference $(X) = a \times$ Expected Benefit $(X) + b \times$ Perceived Risk $(X) + c$.

obtain high returns, while risk-averse investors tend to take less risk (fear) by settling for smaller returns (Weber et al., 2013; Chuang & Chang, 2013; Özer & Mutlu, 2021).

On the other hand, individuals' risk attitudes vary depending on the size of the gain or loss and whether the outcomes are perceived as gains or losses (Oliver, 2018). According to Markowitz (1952), the founder of the "modern portfolio theory," individuals generally prefer to take risks in options involving small amounts, while as the amount increases, they tend to choose the guaranteed option.[2] Similarly, "prospect theory" predicts that individuals will be more risk-averse, preferring to avoid losses than to realize gains (Kahneman & Tversky, 1979). According to the theory, "losses hurt more than gains please." Therefore, people are more interested in not losing than winning (Levy, 1996; Öztürk, 2021). Individuals primarily consider the risk of loss and prefer less risky options to secure gains.

In addition to approaches focusing on the behavioral dimension of risk attitude, approaches focusing on the sociological and anthropological dimension are also common in the literature. Research in these fields show that risk attitude varies with age (Rolison et al., 2013) and gender (Hanoch et al., 2006; Figner & Weber, 2011; Lozano et al., 2017). The common view is that men are more likely to engage in risky behaviors than women (Gustafson, 1998; Johnson et al., 2004). Contrary to many studies, Macías and Andrea (2015) found that women tend to perceive greater risk than men in all domains and that risk perception increases with age. In another study on age-related risk attitudes, it was found that men's tendency to take risks in the financial domain decreases rapidly at older ages compared to women. Women's tendency to take risks in the social domain is less than men's at older ages, and the tendency to take risks for entertainment purposes decreases sharply from young to middle age (Rolison et al., 2013). These results indicate that risk attitude will vary according to personal factors.

Another issue in sociological research is the effect of social capital on risk attitude (Hasan et al., 2020). The basic structure of social capital consists of the norms of social networks and mutual trust, and these social networks affect the attitudes and behaviors of individuals and determine their decisions (Ceylan & Kıral, 2021). According to Ferris et al. (2017), social capital allows the individual to share risks with the social network and thus the individual tends to make riskier choices. According to Powell (2007), individuals try to join groups to meet their social needs, and after joining the group, they engage in risky behaviors to gain the appreciation of group members. In this case, as the closeness of group members increases so does the individual's propensity to take risks. The literature shows that the effect of social capital on risk attitude differs according to the parameters of the social environment.

---

[2] In the study conducted by Markowitz (1952), it was found that when individuals were offered the guarantee of earning 10 cents or the chance of earning 1 dollar with a probability of 1/10, they took the risk to earn 1 dollar, whereas when individuals were offered the guarantee of earning $1 million or the chance of earning $10 million with a probability of 1/10, they preferred 1 million dollars and avoided the risk.

The factors affecting risk attitude are quite diverse and cannot be limited to the factors exemplified above. The literature on risk attitude ranges from *genetics* (Roe et al., 2009), *cultural differences* (Breuer et al., 2017; Kolnhofer-Derecskei, 2018; Czerwonka, 2019; Díez-Esteban et al., 2019; Gaganis et al., 2019), *religion* (Noussair et al., 2013; Kanagaretnam et al., 2015; Gao et al., 2017; Berry-Stölzle & Irlbeck, 2021), *personality traits* (Pavlíček et al., 2021), *educational background* (Rosen et al., 2003; McWilliams et al., 2022), *marital status* (Yao & Hanna, 2005) and *emotions* (Mikulic et al., 2011, 2012) to *prejudices* (Küçüksille & Usul, 2012). It is difficult to cover such a wide range of issues within the scope of this study. However, a common conclusion can be drawn from the studies in the literature: Our risk attitudes are shaped by the combination of many factors, the source of which we do not know, and these factors have a significant impact on our individual decisions and behaviors.

In this respect, individuals' understanding of their own risk attitudes enables them to manage these attitudes more accurately and make better decisions. Understanding individual risk attitudes is also important for ERM. Considering that ERM practices are influenced by individuals, increasing the awareness of employees and managers about risk attitudes can help them make the right decisions and successfully implement ERM. Taking these issues into account, the next section examines impact on risk management of the risk attitudes of individuals, and in the case of ERM, of chief executive officers (CEOs).

3.3 The Impact of the Top Executive's (CEO) Personal Traits and Risk Attitude on Enterprise Risk Management

In order to keep pace with rapidly changing and developing technology, globalization, and an increasingly complex economy and communication order, companies must accurately identify and assess their risks and opportunities. For this purpose, an ERM system should be adopted and implemented effectively. The effectiveness and success of this system are influenced by many factors such as company size, risk communication and personnel competence, as well as individuals' attitudes towards risk. Individuals' attitudes towards risk have a significant impact on the successful implementation of risk management (Van-Winsen et al., 2016; Khanal et al., 2022; Henschel & Lantzsch, 2022). Individuals are the risk takers within organizations, and investigating the risks faced by these individuals and their attitudes towards risk can help organizations to be more successful in risk management (Helliar et al., 2001).

The literature on ERM emphasizes that the CEO is the most influential individual in the effective implementation of ERM (Beasley et al., 2005; Desender, 2011;

Manab & Kasim, 2012; Faisal, 2020). In addition, the COSO ERM Framework[3] states that the CEO is ultimately responsible for the implementation of ERM (DeLoach, 2014; Faisal, 2020). Especially during the risk assessment phase, management's approach to risk and risk attitude is decisive (Vasvári, 2015). Therefore, the CEO's approach is vital for the success of ERM (Faisal, 2020).

The personality traits that lead CEOs to make different decisions naturally affect their individual risk attitudes. CEO's individual risk attitude is of great importance for ERM (Cen & Doukas, 2017; Mat Ludin et al., 2017). The number of empirical studies examining the relationship between CEO personality traits and ERM is almost nonexistent (Faisal, 2020). Research to date has mostly focused on the impact of CEO personality traits on enterprise risk-taking (Cain & McKeon, 2016; Farag & Mallin, 2018). As corporate risk taking is seen as an integral part of the ERM process, the results of these studies are included in our research.

In the literature, age and gender differences are considered among the characteristics that may affect CEOs' approaches to risk management. Investigating the impact of CEO gender on enterprise risk-taking, Faccio et al. (2016) found that firms led by female CEOs tend to make less risky financing and investment choices than similar firms led by male CEOs. In the long run, this may protect the company's corporate reputation and increase its success. On the other hand, male CEOs who tend to take risks may increase the company's growth potential by gaining a competitive advantage over their competitors. In this case, it can be said that both approaches have different advantages and disadvantages. There are also studies in the literature that find that the risk-taking attitudes of male and female CEOs do not differ compared to each other (Farag & Mallin, 2018). The different results in the literature leave unanswered the question of whether female CEOs or male CEOs take more risks in companies. More research is needed in this area.

Studies on the effect of age on enterprise risk-taking show that younger CEOs are more willing to take risks than older CEOs (Barker III & Mueller, 2002; Ting et al., 2015; Tang et al., 2016). Vroom and Pahl (1971) argued that as managers age, changes occur in their lives, for example, they get married and have children, and due to their responsibilities towards their children or grandchildren, they can no longer take the risks they took when they were younger; therefore, they avoid taking risks compared to younger managers. According to Orens and Reheul (2013), older CEOs tend to hold higher levels of cash as a hedge against adverse events. In addition, risk-averse CEOs tend to prefer safer internal financing over riskier external financing. This may become an important advantage in terms of ensuring business continuity, especially in times of financial crisis.

Another characteristic of the CEO that may affect ERM is the length of his/her tenure in the company. The longer the tenure of CEOs, the more risk-averse they tend to be (Farag & Mallin, 2018). CEOs who stay in office longer are familiar with events that can harm organizations. This leads them to be more cautious and

[3] COSO ERM Framework is the risk management framework published by the Committee of Sponsoring Organizations of the Treadway Commission (COSO).

risk-averse in the face of potentially damaging problems (Dickson, 1982). CEOs who have been in office for a long time tend to protect the company's position by avoiding risk in order not to lose their position. This may have an impact on financial profitability. Because less risk means less return. On the other hand, more experienced CEOs are more familiar with the operations and functioning of the company. Thus, they can promote better risk management practices and better manage organizational risks. Newly appointed CEOs, on the other hand, tend to take higher risks as they strategically focus on the external market and are more open to new business ideas (Orens & Reheul, 2013).

In addition to tenure, education level is also an important factor affecting CEOs' risk management approaches and ERM. Barker III and Mueller (2002) argue that CEOs with higher levels of education are less risk-averse and more likely to invest in R&D. The findings of Farag and Mallin (2018) are similar. They find that CEOs with degrees such as master's or doctoral degrees are less risk-averse, are likely to be more open to innovative business ideas, and are therefore more knowledgeable about their external environment. CEOs with higher levels of education may decide to launch a new product and expand the market segment, which may bring higher profits to the company and provide an opportunity for innovation and growth.

Finally, power and social capital influence the CEO's risk attitude and its impact on ERM. According to Ferris et al. (2017), social capital increases a manager's sense of power, leading to higher managerial risk tolerance and ultimately greater corporate risk-taking. Although Haider's (2018) study claims otherwise, other studies in the literature also show that CEO power is positively related to excessive risk-taking (Lewellyn & Muller-Kahle, 2013). For a CEO, the most important reason for low risk-taking is possible job loss. Thanks to his/her social capital, a CEO can take high risks by relying on a safety net that increases the likelihood of getting a new job even if he/she loses his/her job (Ferris et al., 2017). The CEO's social capital is related to his/her social networks of connections, reputation, and relationships. Therefore, social capital can be useful in providing the resources needed for ERM, obtaining the necessary knowledge and experience in identifying risks, gaining information about investors' and stakeholders' attitudes towards risk, and managing relationships that play an important role in risk management.

The abovementioned studies reveal that individual characteristics and risk attitude have a significant impact on enterprise risk-taking and ERM. Therefore, assessing risk management processes without considering risk attitudes means ignoring an important factor. Given the critical importance of risk attitude, the question arises as to how much importance is given to it and to what extent it is taken into account in risk management frameworks. The next section addresses this issue.

3.4 Risk Attitude in Enterprise Risk Management Framework and Standards

Of the five components of the COSO (2017) ERM Framework, the "Strategy and Objective Setting" component states that an organization should determine its risk appetite in relation to its strategy. The framework addresses an aspect of risk attitude through the principle of "Defines risk appetite" under the "Strategy and Objective Setting" component. While this part of the framework recognizes the variability of organizations in determining risk appetite, it does not produce any specific recommendations on how to manage or control the factors that influence the process.

In addition to risk appetite, another concept associated with risk attitude in COSO (2017) is "organizational bias."[4] According to COSO (2017), organizational bias as a factor affecting risk attitude is caused by dominant personalities, overreliance on numbers, disregarding contrary information, or disproportionate weighting of recent events. However, COSO (2017) does not include any recommendations on how such bias should be taken into account in terms of the effectiveness of the risk-taking process.

ISO 31000 (2018)[5] recommends that the dynamic and changing nature of human behavior and culture be taken into account at every stage of risk management. The standard does not provide an explanation or a road map for the impact of human factors on risk behavior.

The "Governance and Leadership" section of The Orange Book,[6] under the heading "Supporting Principles," states that human behavior and culture have a significant impact on all aspects of risk management at all levels and stages. This emphasis in the framework points to risk communication and highlights the responsibility of management to communicate expected values and behaviors and to ensure buy-in at all levels. In this context, it appears that the framework proposes a *soft control*[7] focusing on organizational culture to offset the impact of the human element on risk management. The same section states that effective risk management should support informed decision-making consistent with risk appetite, build credibility in risk responses, and provide clarity about the significant risks faced and how they are addressed (HM Government, 2020).

According to the Management of Risk (M_o_R®, 2010)[8] framework, risk-taking is inevitable for organizations to survive and achieve their goals. Organizations that

[4] COSO ERM 2017 addresses organizational bias as an important factor that the board of directors needs to understand and challenge management to overcome potential biases that affect decision-making in organizations and need to be managed.

[5] ISO 31000 is a risk management standard.

[6] The Orange Book is a risk management framework published by HM Government.

[7] Soft control includes elements in the control environment and is defined as virtues transmitted to employees during the orientation process through policy directives and invisible standards derived from company culture (Lartey et al., 2023).

[8] M_o_R® is a risk management guide published by AXELOS.

take risks to a certain extent gain a competitive advantage by managing not only hazards but also opportunities. In this context, ERM should create a culture that supports risk-taking. Because it is neither possible nor desirable to take no risks. There should be a balance between the controls taken against risk and the benefit to be obtained as a result of the risk. The cultural environment can provide this balance by considering risk-taking attitudes. Thus, individuals or groups that are persistently risk-averse or risk-seeking can be effectively guided. On the other hand, the framework argues that risk attitude contributes to the operational risk profile of the organization. Besides, the framework emphasizes the importance of stakeholders' (employees, managers, external customers, etc.) engagement and states that stakeholders' perceptions of and attitudes towards risk should be taken into account to increase the effectiveness of risk management. This requires adopting an appropriate level and style of communication. If perceptions are identified, the causes, impact, probabilities, and consequences of risks will be better explored. The framework underlines that it is possible to adopt a practical approach to risk management despite differences in individual risk perception. According to M_o_R® (2010), *facilitation* and *challenge*[9] techniques can be applied in group work to reduce the bias and subjectivity of risk management caused by risk perceptions varying from person to person and group to group.

As can be seen from Table 3.1, COSO ERM (2017), ISO 31000 (2018), M_o_R® (2010), and The Orange Book emphasize the impact of individual risk attitude on ERM from various aspects such as risk appetite, risk culture, risk communication, and transparency.

The COSO ERM (2017), ISO 31000 (2018), M_o_R® (2010), and The Orange Book all agree that human behavior and risk culture play an important role in risk management processes. Differently, COSO ERM (2017) highlights the elements of bias in ERM, while ISO 31000 (2018) highlights the fluid nature of human behavior and risk culture at all stages of risk management. M_o_R® (2010) emphasizes the importance of stakeholders' risk perceptions and attitudes, and points to the need for risk management to create a culture that supports taking risks. The Orange Book draws attention to human behavior and risk culture, which affect all aspects of risk management at all levels and stages, and highlights the elements of transparency and trust that risk communication and effective risk management should provide. There was no mention of the CEO's attitude to risk and its impact on ERM in the standards and frameworks reviewed.

[9] Facilitation refers to helping group meetings run more effectively and efficiently, while challenge is often used to refer to the questioning of a situation or idea by the group and coming up with new and creative ideas.

Table 3.1 Issues related to risk attitude addressed in standards and frameworks

Standards	Title	Issues related to risk attitude
COSO ERM (2017)	Principle 1: Exercises Board Risk Oversight (Organizational Bias)	The impact on ERM of bias elements such as dominant personalities, overreliance on numbers, disregard for contrary information, disproportionate weighting of recent events, and risk aversion
	Principle 7: Defines Risk Appetite (Applying Risk Appetite)	The need for an organization to determine its risk appetite in relation to its strategy
ISO 31000 (2018)	6.1: General	The recommendation that the dynamic and changing nature of human behavior and risk culture should be taken into account at every stage of risk management
M_o_R® (2010)	2.4: Engages Stakeholders	Stakeholders' perceptions of and attitudes towards risk should be taken into account to improve the effectiveness of risk management
	2.8: Creates a Supportive Culture	The need for organizational risk management to create a culture that supports risk-taking
	6.5.2: Fits the context	Risk attitude contributes to the operational risk profile of the organization
The Orange Book	Section A: Governance and Leadership (Supporting Principle A1)	Human behavior and risk culture significantly influence all aspects of risk management at all levels and stages It is the responsibility to communicate expected values and behaviors through risk communication and ensure their acceptance at all levels
	Section A: Governance and Leadership (Supporting Principle A3)	Effective risk management should support informed decision-making in line with risk appetite, provide confidence in responding to risks, and provide transparency on the main risks faced and how they are managed

3.5 Suggestions for Considering the Impact of Individual Risk Attitudes on Enterprise Risk Management

Various mechanisms should be used to prevent subjective risk perceptions of individuals or managers (CEOs) involved in the ERM system and to guide their risk attitudes. The specific mechanisms suggested below will complement and enhance the functionality of the issues specified in the standards and frameworks. For this reason, we summarize our suggestions as "CAPSTONE":

- Culture: Risk culture guides risk decisions through variables such as organizational and national cultures, personality, experience, intuition and mental processes, and risk perception (Kelly, 2009). Organizations should create a culture that emphasizes values such as ethics, honesty, respect, and responsibility to ensure that employees make the right decisions in risk management. To achieve this, policies and strategies on risk management should be established within the organization. A right culture helps employees adopt right risk attitudes and increases the success of ERM.

- **A**wareness: The CEO and employees should be made aware of the impact and consequences of their individual risk attitudes. This helps all staff understand the concept of risk more accurately and makes risk perceptions objective. In this way, attitudes towards risk become more informed. Different risk attitudes lead organizations to take different decisions and actions. According to Braumann (2018), in the presence of risk awareness, the organization environment and reporting processes make risk management effective. To ensure that employees are diligent in their risk management decisions and actions, roles and responsibilities in ERM should be clearly defined and employees should accept and implement these responsibilities. In addition, accountability mechanisms should be established to fulfill these responsibilities. In this way, employees have the opportunity to review the decisions and actions they take as a result of their risk attitudes. According to Cormican (2014), promoting risk awareness should be a starting point for any risk management process.
- **P**erformance: The organization should periodically evaluate its risk management process and regularly seek feedback on opportunities for improvement. Evaluating the performance of ERM may include an assessment of economic value added (Shad & Lai, 2015), measurement through integration into an existing performance management system (Rasid et al., 2017), or an analysis of critical success factors (Zhu et al., 2023). In this way, the impact of individual risk attitudes on ERM can be observed and, where necessary, risk-taking or risk-averse approaches can be better managed.
- **S**elf-Control: According to Jia et al. (2015), individuals' ability to self-control has a significant impact on risk perceptions and risk assessment processes in risk management. In order for the ERM system to be established objectively, it is important for managers and employees to recognize their subjective risk perceptions and regularly evaluate these perceptions. In this way, misleading risk perceptions can be identified and these perceptions can be corrected and a healthy risk attitude can be adopted.
- **T**ransparency: Transparency is an important factor in addressing the impact of human factors on ERM. Transparency is clearly stating stating the sources of data, methods of analysis, and how the results are interpreted; the purpose, advantages, and disadvantages of the methods used; and when, how, and why decisions are made. In this way, other units and managers can understand the accuracy and correct interpretation of the data, methods, and rationale for the decisions taken in the process of determining risk attitude.
- **O**pen Communication: Communication is an important control mechanism for the human element in ERM. Kimbrough and Componation (2009) state that ERM should ensure open communication and cooperation between departments within the organization. An open communication channel should be opened up between employees and cooperation should be encouraged. This will create awareness in terms of risk perception and risk attitude and help employees to make more accurate risk management decisions. In this context, people with different views and perspectives within the organization should be brought together

to discuss risk management strategies. In this way, a healthier risk attitude can be created by combining ideas from different perspectives.

- Neutrality: Neutrality is vital for ERM to be successful, since it helps to strengthen the organization's ability to make accurate risk assessments and manage risks effectively. Neutrality reduces the influence of bias and self-interest in risk assessment and management processes. This leads to more neutral and accurate risk analyses. It also encourages the participation of different business units and managers in risk management processes, leading to more comprehensive and accurate risk assessments and management strategies. If risk attitudes are only influenced by individuals from certain business units, this may lead to biases and inadequacies in the organization's risk management strategy and objectives. It is therefore important to seek views of different units and managers when determining risk-taking attitude.
- Education: Raising awareness about risk attitudes should begin during the educational life, many years before the professional life. After entering professional life, it would be beneficial to follow programs such as certification courses. The acquisition of a risk-based perspective should begin during education, much earlier than professional life. Incorporating risk-related topics into the curriculum enables individuals to internalize a perspective on risk. Establishing an understanding of the continuity of training in organizations leads to a better understanding and implementation of standards and frameworks and CAPSTONE recommendations. Training helps the organization achieve its risk management goals by ensuring that managers and employees have adequate knowledge and skills. It is therefore essential that organizations allocate sufficient resources to training and place a high priority on the continuing professional development of their staff.

3.6 Conclusion

Enterprise risk management standards and frameworks define the basic principles, methods, and practices that organizations should follow in their risk management processes. These standards and frameworks help organizations plan their risk management processes more systematically and implement these processes more consistently across the organization.

This study has found that standards and frameworks related to ERM do not address risk perception and risk attitude in sufficient depth. Standards and frameworks set out general and principled approaches that are applied in different countries, cultures, and sectors. As such, it is difficult for them to provide an overarching approach to risk perception and attitude, which vary from country to country, organization to organization, and even individual to individual. However, it is also a fact that any approach that does not adequately address risk perception and attitude is unlikely to be effective in ERM.

Successful implementation of an ERM system depends on the accurate assessment of risk perceptions of the employees, especially managers, and the adoption of realistic risk attitudes. Risk perceptions and risk attitudes, influenced by factors such as age, gender, experience, religion, education level, and social capital, have a critical importance that can affect the entire ERM system. It is therefore important to propose new strategies to improve ERM practices and increase success through a greater focus on individual risk attitudes.

This study presents recommendations, called CAPSTONE, to ensure that individual risk attitudes are taken into account in ERM practices. The CAPSTONE recommendations are grouped under eight main headings: culture, awareness, performance, self-control, transparency, open communication, neutrality, and education. Implementation of these recommendations will enable a clearer identification of the impact of individual risk attitudes on ERM and will serve as a keystone for the success of risk management.

In conclusion, ERM standards and frameworks provide an important basis for standardizing and making more effective ERM processes. However, there is need to consider the impact of individual risk attitudes on these processes and develop more effective management strategies. Future research focusing on risk attitudes and the human factor in ERM will help organizations achieve success in their risk management practices.

References

Aven, T. (2010). On how to define, understand and describe risk. *Reliability Engineering & System Safety, 95*(6), 623–631.

Aven, T. (2012). The risk concept—historical and recent development trends. *Reliability Engineering & System Safety, 99*, 33–44.

Barker, V., III, & Mueller, G. (2002). *CEO characteristics and firm R&D spending* (Vol. 48, p. 782).

Beasley, M. S., Clune, R., & Hermanson, D. R. (2005). Enterprise risk management: An empirical analysis of factors associated with the extent of implementation. *Journal of Accounting and Public Policy, 24*(6), 521–531.

Berry-Stölzle, T. R., & Irlbeck, S. (2021). Religiosity and risk taking: Is there a demand-side effect? *Journal of Corporate Finance, 71*, 102117.

Blais, A.-R., & Weber, E. U. (2006). A domain-specific risk-taking (DOSPERT) scale for adult populations. *Judgment and Decision Making, 1*(1), 33–47.

Braumann, E. C. (2018). Analyzing the role of risk awareness in enterprise risk management. *Journal of Management Accounting Research, 30*(2), 241–268.

Breuer, W., Kollath, J. A., Salzmann, A. J., & Nitzsch, R. V. (2017). The assessment of risk behavior: A cross-cultural analysis using the DOSPERT scale. *Behavioral Finance: Where Do Invertors' Biases Come From?*, 159–180.

Cain, M. D., & McKeon, S. B. (2016). CEO personal risk-taking and corporate policies. *Journal of Financial and Quantitative Analysis, 51*(1), 139–164.

Cen, W., & Doukas, J. A. (2017). CEO personal investment decisions and firm risk. *European Financial Management, 23*(5), 920–950.

Ceylan, S., & Kıral, H. (2021). Sosyal Sermayenin Risk Algısı ve Risk Alma Davranışına Etkisi. In H. Karabacak (Ed.), *Uzmanların Kaleminden Farklı Boyutlarıyla Risk ve Risk Yönetimi* (1st ed., pp. 313–329). Gazi Kitabevi Tic. Ltd. Şti.

Chuang, S.-S., & Chang, M.-C. (2013). Prospect theory and the investor's attitudes toward risk. *Risk and Decision Analysis, 4*(4), 303–308.

Cormican, K. (2014). Integrated enterprise risk management: From process to best practice. *Modern Economy, 05*, 401–413.

COSO. (2017). *Enterprise risk management: Integrating with strategy and performance.*

Czerwonka, M. (2019). Cultural, cognitive and personality traits in risk-taking behaviour: Evidence from Poland and The United States of America. *Economic research-Ekonomska istraživanja, 32*(1), 894–908.

DeLoach, J. (2014). *The role of executive management in ERM*. Retrieved 04.09.2023, from https://www.corporatecomplianceinsights.com/the-role-of-executive-management-in-erm/

Desender, K. (2011). On the determinants of enterprise risk management implementation. *Enterprise IT Governance, Business Value and Performance Measurement*, 87–100.

Dickson, G. C. (1982). A comparison of attitudes towards risk among business managers. *Journal of Occupational Psychology, 54*(3), 157–164.

Díez-Esteban, M., Farinha, J. B., & García-Gómez, C. D. (2019). Are religion and culture relevant for corporate risk-taking? International evidence. *BRQ Business Research Quarterly, 22*(1), 36–55.

Dohmen, T., Falk, A. H., Sunde, U., Schupp, J., & Wagner, G. G. (2011). Individual risk attitudes: Measurement, determinants, and behavioral consequences. *Journal of the European Economic Association, 9*(3), 522–550.

Faccio, M., Marchica, M.-T., & Mura, R. (2016). CEO gender, corporate risk-taking, and the efficiency of capital allocation. *Journal of Corporate Finance, 39*, 193–209.

Fadun, O. S. (2013). Risk management and risk management failure: Lessons for business enterprises. *International Journal of Academic Research in Business and Social Sciences, 3*(2), 225–239.

Faisal, M. (2020). Karakteristrik CEO dan enterprise risk management. *Jurnal Riset Akuntansi dan Keuangan, 8*(1).

Farag, H., & Mallin, C. (2018). The influence of CEO demographic characteristics on corporate risk-taking: Evidence from Chinese IPOs. *The European Journal of Finance, 24*(16), 1528–1551.

Ferris, S. P., Javakhadze, D., & Rajkovic, T. (2017). CEO social capital, risk-taking and corporate policies. *Journal of Corporate Finance, 47*, 46–71.

Figner, B., & Weber, E. U. (2011). Who takes risks when and why? Determinants of risk taking. *Current Directions in Psychological Science, 20*(04), 211–216.

French, S., & Liang, Y. (1993). Decision support systems: A decision analytic perspective. *Developments in Operational Research*, 21–40.

Gaganis, C., Hasan, I., Papadimitri, P., & Tasiou, M. (2019). National culture and risk-taking: Evidence from the insurance industry. *Journal of Business Research, 27*, 104–116.

Gao, L., Wang, Y., & Zhao, J. (2017). Does local religiosity affect organizational risk-taking? Evidence from the hedge fund industry. *Journal of Corporate Finance, 47*, 1–22.

Gustafson, P. E. (1998). Gender differences in risk perception: Theoretical and methodological perspectives. *Risk Analysis, 18*(6), 805–811.

Haider, J., & Fang, H.-X. (2018). CEO power, corporate risk taking and role of large shareholders. *Journal of Financial Economic Policy, 10*(1), 55–72. https://doi.org/10.1108/JFEP-04-2017-0033

Hanoch, Y., Johnson, J. G., & Wilke, A. (2006). Domain specificity in experimental measures and participant recruitment: An application to risk-taking behavior. *Psychological Science, 17*(4), 200–203.

Hasan, I., He, Q., & Lu, H. (2020). The impact of social capital on economic attitudes and outcomes. *Journal of International Money and Finance, 108*, 102162.

Helliar, C., Lonie, A., Power, D., & Sinclair, D. (2001). Attitudes of UK managers to risk and uncertainty. *Balance Sheet, 9*(4), 7–10.

Henschel, T., & Lantzsch, A. D. (2022). The relationship between ERM and performance revisited: Empirical evidence from SMEs. *Risk Management: Insights from Different Settings*, 95–113.

Hillson, D., & Murray-Webster, R. (2004). *Understanding and managing risk attitude*. Accessed 06.12.2022, from https://www.kent.ac.uk/scarr/events/finalpapers/Hillson%20+%20Murray-Webster.pdf

HM Government. (2020). *The Orange book management of risk – Principles and concepts.*

ISO 31000. (2018). Risk Yönetimi.

Jia, J. S., Khan, U., & Litt, A. (2015). The effect of self-control on the construction of risk perceptions. *Management Science, 61*(9), 2259–2280.

Johnson, J., Wilke, A., & Weber, E. U. (2004). Beyond a trait view of risk taking: A domain-specific scale measuring risk perceptions, expected benefits, and perceived-risk attitudes in German-speaking populations. *Polish Psychological Bulletin, 35*(3), 153–163.

Kahneman, D., & Tversky, A. (1979). Prospect theory: An analysis of decision under risk. *Econometrica, 47*(2), 263–291.

Kanagaretnam, K., Lobo, G. J., Wang, C., & Whalen, D. J. (2015). Religiosity and risk-taking in international banking. *Journal of Behavioral and Experimental Finance, 7*, 42–59.

Kelly, P. (2009). Conceptualising business risk culture: A study of risk thinking and practice in contemporary dynamic organisations. *International Journal of Business Continuity and Risk Management, 1*(1), 19–37.

Khanal, A. R., Mishra, A. K., & Lien, G. (2022). Effects of risk attitude and risk perceptions on risk management decisions: Evidence from farmers in an emerging economy. *Journal of Agricultural & Resource Economics, 47*(3).

Kimbrough, R. L., & Componation, P. J. (2009). The relationship between organizational culture and enterprise risk management. *Engineering Management Journal, 21*(12), 18–26.

Kolnhofer-Derecskei, A. (2018). Relations between risk attitudes, culture and the endowment effect. *Engineering Management in Production and Services, 10*(04), 7.

Küçüksille, E., & Usul, H. (2012). Bilişsel önyargılar ve yatırımcı kararlarına etkileri. *Yalova Sosyal Bilimler Dergisi, 2*(4).

Lartey, P., Akolgo, I. G., Jaladi, S. R., Ayeduvor, S., & Afriyie, S. O. (2023). Recent advances in internal control: Soft control overcoming the limits of hard control. *Frontiers in Management and Business, 4*(1), 289–302. https://doi.org/10.25082/FMB.2023.01.004

Levy, J. S. (1996). Loss aversion, framing, and bargaining: The implications of prospect theory for international conflict. *International Political Science Review, 17*(2), 179–195.

Lewellyn, K. B., & Muller-Kahle, M. I. (2013). CEO power and risk taking: Evidence from the subprime lending industry. *Corporate Governance: An International Review, 20*(03), 289–307.

Lozano, L. M., Megías, A., Catena, A., Perales, J. C., Baltruschat, S., & Cándido, A. (2017). Spanish validation of the domain-specific risk-taking (DOSPERT-30) scale. *Psicothema, 29*(1), 111–118.

M_o_R®. (2010). *Management of risk: Guidance for practitioners.*

Macías, A., & Andrea, P. (2015). *Validación de la domain-specific risk-taking (dospert) scale en la población colombiana*. Bachelor's thesis, Uniandes.

Manab, N. A., & Kasim, I. (2012). A moderating affect of leadership on a success of enterprise–Wide risk management practices. *3rd International Conference On Business And Economic Research (3RD Icber 2012) Proceeding.*

Markowitz, H. (1952). The utility of wealth. *The Journal of Political Economy, LX*(2), 150–158.

Mat Ludin, K. R., Mohamed, Z. M., & Mohd-Saleh, N. (2017). The association between CEO characteristics, internal audit quality and risk-management implementation in the public sector. *Risk Management, 19*, 281–300. https://doi.org/10.1057/s41283-017-0022-z

McWilliams, D., Lennon, C., & Lowery, J. (2022). Impact of experience and education on risk attitude and risk perception of supply chain management professionals. *Operations and Supply Chain Management: An International Journal, 15*(1), 56.

Mikulic, I. M., Cassullo, G., Torcassi, V., Fernández, G. L., Paolo, A. M., Caballero, R. Y., & Aruanno, Y. (2011). *Aportes de la evaluación psicológica a la psicología ambiental. Estudio de la percepción de riesgo en distintos grupos sociales*. In Memoria.

Mikulic, I. M., Cassullo, L., Melina, C., Crespi, P., Caruso, A., Mariana, E., & Roberto, M. (2012). Evaluación de la percepción de riesgo en diferentes grupos sociales: propuesta de un. *Anuario de Investigaciones, XIX*, 37–44.

Noussair, C., Trautmann, S., Kuilen, G., & Vellekoop, N. (2013). Risk aversion and religion. *Journal of Risk and Uncertainty, 47*, 165–183.

Oliver, A. (2018). Your money and your life: Risk attitudes over gains and losses. *Journal of Risk and Uncertainty, 57*, 29–50.

Orens, R., & Reheul, A.-M. (2013). Do CEO demographics explain cash holdings in SMEs? *European Management Journal, 31*(6), 549–563.

Özer, G., & Mutlu, Ü. (2021). Duygusal Zeka ile Risk Alma Tutumu İlişkisi. *Uluslararası Yönetim İktisat ve İşletme Dergisi, 17*, 146–164.

Öztürk, S. (2021). Beklenti Teorisinin Dış Politikadaki Uygulamaları Üzerine Bir Değerlendirme. *Eskişehir Osmangazi Üniversitesi Sosyal Bilimler Dergisi, 22*(2), 601–617.

Pavlíček, A., Hintošová, A. B., & Sudzina, F. (2021). Impact of personality traits and demographic factors on risk attitude. *Sage, 11*, 1–11.

Powell, C. (2007). The perception of risk and risk taking behavior: Implications for incident prevention strategies. *Wilderness & Environmental Medicine, 18*(1), 10–15.

Rasid, S. Z., Golshan, N., M, M., & Tan, G. G.-Z. (2017). Enterprise risk management, performance measurement systems and organizational performance in Malaysian public listed firms. *International Journal of Business and Society, 18*(2), 311–328.

Riabacke, A. (2006). Managerial decision making under risk and uncertainty. *IAENG International Journal of Computer Science, 32*(4).

Roe, B. E., Tilley, M. R., Gu, H. H., Beversdorf, D. Q., Sadee, W., Haab, T. C., & Papp, A. C. (2009). *Financial and psychological risk attitudes associated with two single nucleotide polymorphisms in the nicotine receptor (CHRNA4) gene* (Vol. 4, p. e6704). Plos One.

Rohrmann, B. (2008). Risk perception, risk attitude, risk communication, risk management: A conceptual appraisal. *5th International Emergency Management Society (TIEMS) Annual Conference*.

Rolison, J. J., Hanoch, Y., Wood, S., Wood, S., & Liu, P.-J. (2013). Risk-taking differences across the adult life span: A question of age and domain. *Journals of Gerontology Series B: Psychological Sciences and Social Sciences, 69*(6), 870–880.

Rosen, A. B., Tsai, J. S., & Downs, S. M. (2003). Variations in risk attitude across race, gender, and education. *Medical Decision Making, 23*(6), 511–517.

Shad, M. K., & Lai, F. W. (2015). A conceptual framework for enterprise risk management performance measure through economic value added. *Global Business and Management Research: An International Journal, 7*(2).

Tang, Y., Li, J., & Liu, Y. (2016). Does founder CEO status affect firm risk taking? *Journal of Leadership & Organizational Studies, 23*(3), 322–334.

Ting, I. W., Azizan, N. A., & Kweh, Q. L. (2015). Upper echelon theory revisited: The relationship between CEO personal characteristics and financial leverage decision. *Procedia-Social and Behavioral Sciences, 195*, 686–694.

Van-Winsen, F., de Mey, Y., Lauwers, L., Van Passel, S., Vancauteren, M., & Wauters, E. (2016). Determinants of risk behaviour: Effects of perceived risks and risk attitude on farmer's adoption of risk management strategies. *Journal of Risk Research, 19*(01), 56–78. https://doi.org/10.1080/13669877.2014.940597

Vasvári, T. (2015). Risk, risk perception, risk management–a review of the literature. *Public Finance Quarterly, 60*(1), 29–48.

Vroom, V. H., & Pahl, B. (1971). Relationship between age and risk taking among managers. *Journal of Applied Psychology, 55*(5), 399.

Weber, E. U., Blais, A.-R., & Betz, N. E. (2002). A domain-specific risk-attitude scale: Measuring risk perceptions and risk behaviors. *Journal of Behavioral Decision Making, 15*(4), 263–290.
Weber, M., Weber, E. U., & Nosić, A. (2013). Who takes risks when and why: Determinants of changes in investor risk taking. *Review of Finance, 17*(3), 847–883.
Wilke, A., Sherman, A., Curdt, B., Mondal, S., Fitzgerald, C., & Kruger, D. J. (2014). An evolutionary domain-specific risk scale. *Evolutionary Behavioral Science, 8*(3), 123–141. https://doi.org/10.1037/ebs0000011
Yao, R., & Hanna, S. D. (2005). *The effect of gender and marital status on financial risk tolerance.*
Zhu, D., Li, Z., & Mishra, A. R. (2023). Evaluation of the critical success factors of dynamic enterprise risk management in manufacturing SMEs using an integrated fuzzy decision-making model. *Technological Forecasting and Social Change, 186.*
Zimerman, L., Shalvi, S., & Bereby-Meyer, Y. (2014). Self-reported ethical risk taking tendencies predict actual dishonesty. *Judgment & Decision Making, 9*(1), 58–64.

Yağmur Özyurt graduated from Gazi University, Department of Architecture, in 2006 and from Anadolu University, Department of Public Administration, in 2019. In 2021, she completed the Social Sciences University of Ankara Audit and Risk Management Master's Program with her thesis titled "Managing the Internal Audit Function: Problems Encountered in the Public Sector and Solution Proposals." She is currently continuing her doctoral studies in the same department. Between 2007 and 2015, she worked as an architect at the Ministry of Culture and Tourism. In 2015, she was appointed as Internal Auditor to the Internal Audit Unit of the same Ministry. She has conducted many audits and consultancy activities to review and improve the institution's internal control, risk management, and business processes. Currently working as an internal auditor at the Ministry of Culture and Tourism, she holds A-3 level Public Internal Auditor and Certified Internal Audit (CIA) certificates.

Ali Göksel graduated from the Department of Mechanical Engineering at Karadeniz Technical University in 1999 and completed his master's in the same department in 2003. He worked as Mechanical Engineer at Eti Maden from 2000 to 2016 and has been serving as the Head of the Internal Audit Department since 2016. He is an active doctoral student in the Audit and Risk Management Program at the Social Sciences University of Ankara, continuing his academic studies.

Part III
Rethinking the Components of ERM

Chapter 4
Uncertainty in Risk Definition and Its Impact on Enterprise Risk Management

Mecbure Aslan

Abstract Defining risk correctly is crucial for an effective Enterprise Risk Management (ERM). In the existing literature, disciplines and researchers have different perspectives on risk. It has been observed that other perspectives are reflected in risk definitions, leading to uncertainty. This ambiguity becomes a significant risk to the effectiveness of ERM. Uncertainty in the definition reduces the effectiveness of ERM by making the stages of assessing risks and taking measures against risks uncertain. This study concludes that, for an ERM to be effective, it is necessary to take proper measures against risks and assess them correctly, which is possible with a good definition of risk. Therefore, the importance of risk definition for an effective ERM is emphasized.

Keywords Risk · Uncertainty · Danger · Threat · Opportunity · Enterprise risk management

4.1 Introduction

Risk includes threats and opportunities that organizations try to manage to survive. Organizations face threats and opportunities throughout their lives. In addition to being able to cope with threats, it is essential for the organization not to miss opportunities to survive. Therefore, as important as it is for organizations to identify, assess, and manage the risks they face, it is equally essential to identify, assess, and manage opportunities. From this perspective, the inclusion of opportunities in the concept of risk over time has added a different dimension to the idea of risk. This achievement makes the importance of the concept of risk in risk management much more meaningful and critical.

M. Aslan (✉)
Social Sciences University of Ankara, Ankara, Türkiye
e-mail: mecbure.aslan@student.asbu.edu.tr

H. Kıral (ed.), *Rethinking Enterprise Risk Management*, Accounting, Finance, Sustainability, Governance & Fraud: Theory and Application,
https://doi.org/10.1007/978-981-97-5983-5_4

As a result of the literature review, it is clear that risk is studied by scientists from different disciplines. The perspectives of scientists from different disciplines on risk have led to different definitions of risk. While some definitions are based on uncertainty (Knight, 1921; Jaaferi, 2001; Cabinet Office, 2002; Ni et al., 2010), expected loss (Byrd III & Cothern, 2005; Willis, 2007), and expected damage (Campbell, 2005), some researchers associate risk with indecision (Beck, 2006).

As is the case with the definition of risk, scientists do not agree on the origin of risk. Giddens (1999) and Beck (1999) state that the concept of risk began to exist with modern society. According to them, the idea of risk began to emerge with the idea of controlling the future. Denney (2005), on the other hand, argues that the concept of risk has existed since the premodern times.

The main reason for including the multiplicity and diversity of definitions of risk in this study is to highlight the ambiguity in the definition of risk and to draw attention to its implications for Enterprise Risk Management (ERM) which is defined as managing risk with a holistic approach (Verbrugge et al., 2003; Banham, 2004; Bromiley et al., 2015).

An accurate definition of risk is critical for effective ERM. Researchers such as Willis (2007), Aven (2009, 2010, 2011, 2022), and Hopkin and Thompson (2022) and organizations such as the Institute of Internal Auditors (2004) emphasize the importance of an accurate risk definition for effective risk management.

The study seeks to demonstrate the importance of risk definition for risk management. To this end, we aim to contribute to the correct definition of risk by showing what risk is not and cannot be limited to for effective risk management. For this purpose, the perspectives of disciplines and scientists on risk and risk definitions will be presented first, followed by an explanation of what risk is not. Defining risk by starting from what risk is not or what it cannot be limited to will reduce the ambiguity in its definition. The following sections will discuss why risk definition is essential for ERM and how best to define risk for effective risk management. The last section will provide evaluations and recommendations on the subject.

4.2 What Is Risk?

In addition to different definitions of risk in the literature, other disciplines have different perspectives. Moreover, there are debates about when the concept of risk first emerged and the reasons for its emergence. In fact, these debates are reflected in the disciplines' perspectives on risk and in the scientists' definitions of risk. The perspectives of different disciplines and scientists on risk are presented below.

4.2.1 Risk According to Different Disciplines

According to the Oxford English Dictionary, the word "risk" has been in use since the seventeenth century. It comes from the Italian words *risco, riscare*, or *rischiare* (Althaus, 2005). However, Luhmann (1991) claims that the word "risk" appears in German references in the mid-sixteenth century and that the Latin term *riscum* was used much earlier. Giddens (1991), on the other hand, argues that risk is a concept developed in the sixteenth and seventeenth centuries and invented by Western explorers. The origin of the word "risk" is therefore controversial.

A study on the epistemology of risk (Althaus, 2005) examined risk from an interdisciplinary perspective. Table 4.1 provides a summary of the study:

Each discipline has a different understanding of risk, as shown in Table 4.1. While religion views risk from the perspective of fate, philosophy views the same as a problem that must be faced and cannot be solved (Althaus, 2005). For philosophy, risk is a difficult issue to understand and needs to be seen through metaphysical, epistemological, and moral eyes (Althaus, 2005). According to logic and mathematics, risk is a quantifiable and calculable phenomenon, while art branches such as music, theater, and literature place it in an emotional framework. In social

Table 4.1 The disciplines, risk, and knowledge forms applied to the unknown that determine disciplinary epistemological definitions of risk

Discipline	How it views risk	Knowledge applied to the unknown
Logic and mathematics	Risk as a calculable phenomenon	Calculations
Science and medicine	Risk as an objective reality	Principles, postulates, and calculations
Social sciences		
Anthropology	Risk as a cultural phenomenon	Culture
Sociology	Risk as a societal phenomenon	Social constructs or frameworks
Economics	Risk as a decisional phenomenon, a means of securing wealth or avoiding loss	Decision-making principles and postulates
Law	Risk as a fault of conduct and a judicable phenomenon	Rules
Psychology	Risk as a behavioral and cognitive phenomenon	Cognition
Linguistics	Risk as a concept	Terminology and meaning
History and the humanities		
History	Risk as a story	Narrative
The Arts (literature, music, poetry, theater, art, etc.)	Risk as an emotional phenomenon	Emotion
Religion	Risk as an act of faith	Revelation
Philosophy	Risk as a problematic phenomenon	Wisdom

Source: Althaus (2005)

sciences, risk has a social and cultural basis, while in science and medicine it is seen as an objective reality.

Knowing how the abovementioned disciplines view risk makes it easier, for researchers, to understand various definitions of risk. As can be seen, the disciplines have different perspectives on risk. This difference has an impact on the definitions of risk. It can be said that the disciplinary fields of the researchers who define risk, the time period they live in, and the society they were born into have led to the formation of different risk definitions.

4.2.2 *Risk According to Different Scientists*

It is not as easy to define tangible and visible concrete objects and entities such as glasses, hats, or birds as it is to define abstract situations and events such as mind, thought, or reality. It is much easier to agree on what a glass means than on a mind and thought. The agreed definition of a glass is the same today as it was a century ago. It would be correct to consider the word "risk" as an abstract concept like mind or thought. Interest and curiosity about the abstract leads to different perspectives. Like mind or thought, the word "risk" has been of interest to many researchers and has been defined in different ways as knowledge has increased.

While Knight (1921) defines risk as uncertainty, Beck (2006) argues that risk is indecision and that being at risk is an inevitable consequence of living in the modern world. Knight's (1921) and Beck's (2006) perspectives on risk are not very independent from each other. Knight's (1921) attribution of risk to uncertainty is important in that uncertainty about the occurrence and outcomes of events is the main cause of indecision.

Risk is the probability of exposure to a loss or gain, or the probability of a loss or gain, multiplied by the impact. The probability of an event occurring ranges from 0% to 100%. There are a large number of uncertain values, within this range (Jaaferi, 2001). Uncertainty is therefore a key element of the definition. Ni et al.'s (2010) definition of risk supports Jaaferi's (2001). According to them, risk is an objective entity and an unexpected phenomenon. When risk occurs, people have to endure some things, big or small, important or unimportant. Risk is uncertain and one cannot know when it will occur (Ni et al., 2010).

Risk is conceptualized by Aven and Renn (2009) and Rosa (2010) as the uncertainty of the outcomes of an event related to something people value. According to Aven (2011), the scope of risk is generally defined as the consequences of an event related to something that people value and the uncertainty about the consequences. In essence, then, there is an event, the consequences of the event, and uncertainties about the consequences. Therefore, risk is formulated in the most general terms by Aven (2011) as "risk = (A, C, U)" as a combination of an event (A), the consequences of the event (C), and the associated uncertainties (U). It is noteworthy that the "most general definition" of risk (Aven, 2011) is associated with and limited to something that is valued by people.

According to Kalkan and Deniz (2013), considering the concept of risk only as a "risk score" is mathematization of risk. The attitude of the decision-maker towards the hazard is more important than the quantitative value of the risk. Risk is not a technical concept to be quantified, but a social concept with human elements. Therefore, the concept of risk should be considered together with "things that people value." The assessment made by Kalkan and Deniz (2013) supports the risk definitions made by Aven and Renn (2009) and Rosa (2010).

According to Byrd III and Cothern (2005), the definition of risk should have a scope that clearly expresses the unintended consequence or expected loss. In this case, the definition should include an estimate of an event as well as an estimate of the consequences of that event.

Willis (2007) considers risk as the intersection of threat, vulnerability, and consequences.

The circles in Fig. 4.1 represent probability sets showing threat, vulnerability, and consequences, and risk is the area where these three intersect. Willis (2007) also argues that risk is generally equal to the expected loss. This perspective is in line with the definition of risk by Byrd III and Cothern (2005).

Beck (1992) defines risk as a systematic way of dealing with the hazards and insecurities of modernization. According to Beck (1999), risk is "the modern approach to anticipating and controlling the future consequences of human action." Here risk is beyond time and space. Ewald (1991) agrees with Beck (1999), arguing that "calculating a risk means commanding time and disciplining the future." According to Beck's (1999) definition, risk is a modern approach. In this case, Beck (1999) has the same point of view with Giddens (1999) who argues that there is no concept of risk in traditional societies.

Considering the definitions above, the concept of risk stands out as a word with multiple and different meanings. It can be said that risk is mostly viewed from a negative perspective in the definitions. However, it is also apparent that the view of risk changes over time from a negative view such as hazard, harm, threat, and expected loss to a positive view (Jardine & Hrudey, 1997; Richard, 2003). Richard (2003) underlines that risk definitions are made by drawing attention to opportunities.

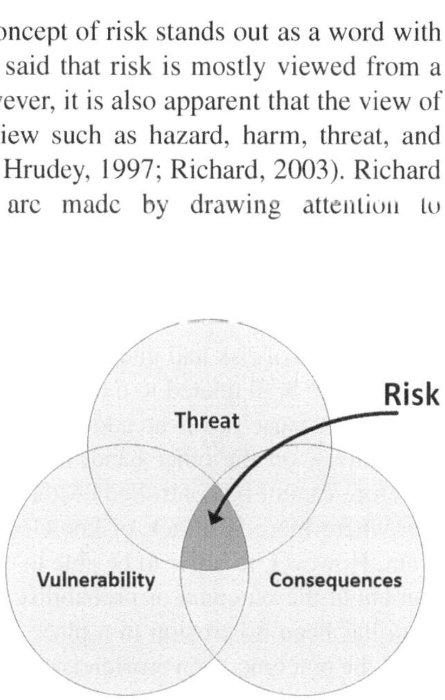

Fig. 4.1 Risk is the intersection of threat, vulnerability, and consequences. Source: Willis (2007)

4.3 What Is Not a Risk?

Looking at the definitions above, risk is generally seen as uncertainty (Knight, 1921; Jaaferi, 2001; Ni et al., 2010), indecision (Beck, 2006), undesirable outcome, or expected loss (Byrd III & Cothern, 2005; Willis, 2007) and threat (Beck, 1992; Willis, 2007). On the other hand, researchers such as Douglas and Wildavsky (1983), Bonß (1991), Furedi (2001), Althaus (2005), Williams (2008), and Hopkin and Thompson (2022) emphasize that risk needs a definition beyond these. The main reason for this idea is that the definition of risk is considered important for risk management. The most accurate definition of risk needs to be found for effective risk management. However, agreeing on a risk definition seems to be more difficult than defining what risk is not. It would be, therefore, more useful to determine what risk is not or what it cannot be limited to. This reduces the multiplicity and ambiguity in the definition of risk. Assessments on what risk is not are given below.

4.3.1 Risk Is Not a "Problem"

A problem is defined as "a situation, issue, problem, troublesome situation or trouble that needs to be researched and learnt, thought, solved and closed" (TDK, 2021). As can be understood from the definition, a problem is a situation that has already occurred. On the other hand, a risk involves the possibility of an undesirable situation that has not yet occurred. Therefore, the main difference between a risk and a problem is that the problem has already occurred. Therefore, it can be said that a risk can turn into a problem only when it has occurred (Kotb & Ghattas, 2017). For example, air pollution is a problem, but long-term exposure to polluted air has health risks such as lung disease. Lung disease caused by air pollution now turns into a problem that needs to be treated.

4.3.2 Risk Is Not "Uncertainty"

The concepts of risk and uncertainty are related to the unknown. However, the fact that they are both related to the unknown does not mean that they refer to the same concept. Because risk is an attempt to "control" the unknown through information. Uncertainty, on the other hand, represents the completely random unknown and therefore cannot be controlled (Althaus, 2005). In this case, uncertainty is a situation where there is a lack of knowledge about the outcome or probability of an event. However, in order to be able to call it a risk, it is necessary to have information about the outcome or probability of an event (Power, 2014). For example, if there has been no erosion in a place before and therefore there is no information about the outcome, then erosion is an uncertain situation for that place. However, if erosion has occurred in the past and there is information about the outcome and the probability of occurrence, then erosion has become a risk for that place.

Kıral (2023), like Wassenius and Crona (2022), states that risk and uncertainty are not the same concepts, but emphasizes that the two concepts are not independent from each other. While uncertainty encompasses all important and unimportant outcomes, risk is uncertainty whose outcome is important (Kıral, 2023). This statement by Kıral is noteworthy in terms of showing the difference between risk and uncertainty, as well as the point where the relationship between the two overlaps.

Perry and Hayes (1985) make a distinction between the two concepts by saying that "risk is a measurable uncertainty, while uncertainty is an unmeasurable risk." In this case, the main difference between the two is that risk is measurable while uncertainty cannot be measured. Therefore, it can be said that an uncertainty can only become a risk if it can be measured.

4.3.3 Risk Is Not a "Hazard"

Bonß (1991) distinguishes between risk and hazard, arguing that risks, as opposed to hazards, emerged with modern society. Luhmann (1991) also makes a distinction between the concepts of risk and hazard, and according to him, hazard is damage that has an external source, whereas risks are decisions taken about possible future damages. Luhmann (1991) sees the act of decision-making as the main difference between the two.

According to Denney (2005), the concept of hazard includes negativity and it is clear what constitutes a hazard. For example, war, drought, disease, global pandemic, or radiation are examples of hazards. Risk is different from hazard. It includes both positive and negative situations. Risk is a globalized concept and, unlike hazard, it is difficult to reach a consensus on what constitutes a risk (Denney, 2005).

Risk, unlike hazard, is related to the possibility of being exposed to any harm. For instance, as for aviation activity, hazard is inherent in the nature of the technology-based activity. Risk, on the other hand, lies in the remote possibility that the aircraft may crash due to human error, unfavorable weather conditions, etc., causing loss of life (Denney, 2005). Wassenius and Crona (2022) have a parallel view with Denney (2005). According to Wassenius and Crona (2022), defining risk only as a hazard, that is, an event or action that causes harm, limits risk. This is because risk is not only about the hazard but also about the degree to which a person is exposed to the hazard and how vulnerable he/she is in relation to that exposure (Wassenius & Crona, 2022).

4.3.4 Risk Is Not a "Threat"

Threats are limited, and risk should not be seen only as a threat. This is because the danger is associated with capabilities such as military power or military capability. The level of control or capability allows the threat to be assessed. For example, it is possible to determine the threat posed by the Soviet Union by looking at the number of tank and infantry divisions during the Cold War. The risks, on the other hand, are infinite because they are not limited to a particular power or capability but also include possible scenarios (Williams, 2008).

Williams (2008) compares risk and threat in terms of time and space. Risks cease to be risks and turn into threats once they occur, such as an act of terrorism (Van Loon, 2002). Therefore, threats exist in the present time, whereas risks exist beyond the present time and space (Williams, 2008). Williams (2008) bases the threat, unlike risk, on something that is possessed, such as military power or military capability, and limits it to a specific time and space.

4.3.5 Risk Is Not a "Negativity"

Zey (1998), Giddens (1999), and Denny (2005) emphasize the aspect of risk that enables development. Zey (1998) argues that the scientific endeavors observed in the eighteenth and nineteenth centuries are a result of the tendency to take risks. Giddens (1999) also argues that risk-taking is a fundamental element in the formation of an innovative society. Denney (2005) argues that risk-taking is the driving force behind the development of capitalism.

Furedi (2001) points out that today's efforts to negate risk have a negative impact on risk-taking. He states that one of the barriers to risk-taking is the culture of fear. According to him, the culture of fear in today's society is an important reason for risk avoidance. Because this culture turns a new problem or difficulty into a matter of life and death, which creates an atmosphere of suspicion that discourages taking action and taking risks. Thus, society is afraid of taking risks and tends to avoid them. However, risk should often be considered as a creative and constructive endeavor (Furedi, 2001).

ISO Guide 73:2009 (2009) and the Institute of Internal Auditors (2010) define risk as "the effect of uncertainty on objectives." The Guide (2009) explains that the effect can be positive or negative or deviate from what is expected. Accordingly, risk goes beyond negativity to include a positive and constructive impact.

The Institute of Risk Management (2010, 2018) provides a clearer definition of risk that includes positive outcomes. According to the Institute, risk is the combination of the probability and the outcome of an event, and the outcomes can be positive as well as negative.

4.3.6 Risk also Encompasses "Opportunities"

ISO Guide 73:2009 (2009) defines risk as "the effect of uncertainty on objectives" and explains that this effect can be positive, negative, or a deviation from the expected. This indicates that risks include opportunities, threats, or uncertainties (Hopkin & Thompson, 2022). Therefore, risk has a broader scope that includes not only negativities but also opportunities.

According to Douglas and Wildavsky (1983), uncertainty should not prevent risk-taking. On the contrary, it should be seen as a good reason to take risks. Because this point of view allows us to learn how to do better. Therefore, risk is also an opportunity (Douglas & Wildavsky, 1983). It is only by taking certain risks that a company can go beyond national borders and become a strong international organization.

In light of the above information, risk cannot be defined solely as a problem, hazard, or threat, nor can it be reduced to a definition based solely on probability or uncertainty. Instead, these concepts provide an understanding of the nature of risk. The concepts of problem, hazard, threat, or uncertainty do not correspond to what risk is. They provide information about what risk is not. This contributes to efforts to make an accurate risk definition (Kaplan & Garrick, 1981; Slovic, 1999) by reducing the ambiguity in the definition of risk.

4.4 Why Is Risk Definition Important for Enterprise Risk?

Risk management initially focused on hazard (pure) risks[1] such as fire, storm, and property damage. Over time, the focus has changed and new risks have emerged, which are categorized as speculative risks[2] such as reputational, market, credit, operational, and financial risks (ICAEW, 1999; Banham, 2004; Power, 2004). Risks have been quantified and a more comprehensive terminology for risk management has been developed. The efforts to manage new risks led to the emergence of ERM (D'Arcy & Brogan, 2001).

Enterprise risk management is the effort to manage all risks of an organization in a way that helps it to increase the value of its assets (Verbrugge et al., 2003). Banham (2004) defines ERM as the identification, assessment, measurement, and comparison of all risks arising from an organization's operational, financial, and strategic activities. According to Bromiley et al. (2015), ERM is managing all risks the organization faces with a holistic approach.

The Institute of Risk Management (IRM) outlines the risk management steps as shown in Fig. 4.2.

---

[1] These are the risks that may lead to negative results such as fire or theft.

[2] These are the risks that have both favorable and unfavorable outcomes, such as equity or commodity securities. They involve both losses and gains.

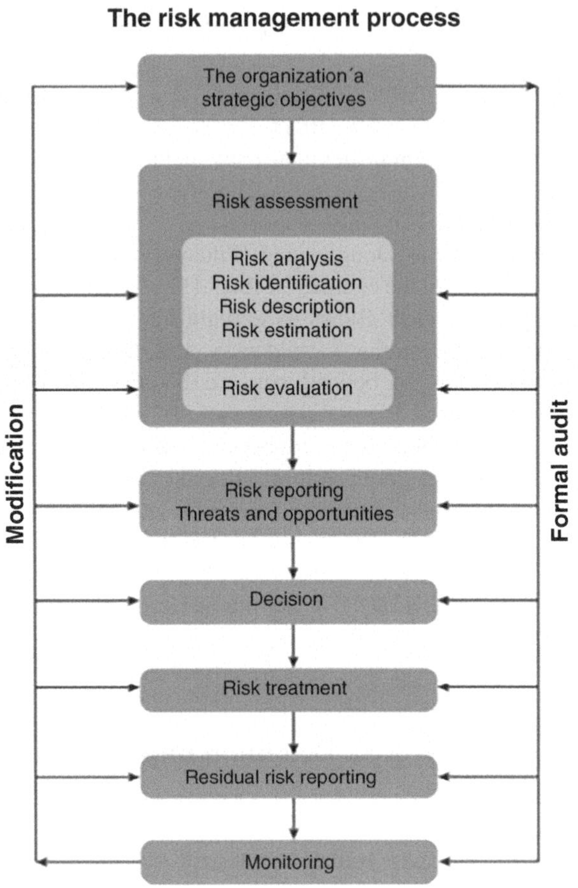

Fig. 4.2 Risk management process. Source: IRM (2010)

As Fig. 4.2 shows, achieving an organization's strategic objectives depends on managing its risks. Once the organization has set its strategic objectives, the first step is to analyze, identify, and assess the risks.

There is no doubt that risk management is an important and growing area in a world of uncertainty (Olson & Wu, 2010). Organizations adopt a risk management approach for various reasons. They may use risk management because of legal obligations and customer requirements, or they may prefer to use it to increase the effectiveness and efficiency of activities and business processes within the organization. In addition, risk management is also important because it supports organizational decision-making. In order for risk management to deliver these expected benefits, it must be applicable and effective (Hopkin & Thompson, 2022). For effective risk management, the risks faced should be well assessed and appropriate risk responses should be determined. To achieve this, accurate risk identification is critical (Willis, 2007; Aven & Renn, 2009; Aven, 2010; Hopkin & Thompson, 2022). However, more than identifying risks correctly, it is necessary to determine what risks mean for everyone. The second section emphasizes that risk is uncertainty for some (Knight, 1921), loss for others (Jaaferi, 2001), threat for others (Willis, 2007), and opportunity for others (Richard, 2003). It is obvious that these approaches have differences that may affect the risk management process from the beginning to the end. Therefore, it should be clarified what the definition of risk means for everyone. Because risk definition is the basis of the ERM approach and should be considered as the beginning of the ERM process. It would be appropriate to illustrate this with an example. In a study conducted by Røyksund and Flage in 2019, the relationship between risk definition and risk assessment was discussed. The study intended to reveal how the new risk definition adopted by the Petroleum Safety Authority-Norway (PSA-N)[3] is reflected in the risk assessment carried out by companies in the sector. The data used in the study were obtained from 178 sector audit reports made by the Authority. In 2015, the Authority updated the petroleum legislation and adopted a new definition of risk. Risk, previously defined as a combination of probability and consequence, was redefined as "the negative consequences of an uncertain event" (Framework Regulations Guidelines, 2015). The probability component of the risk concept was replaced by uncertainty. Companies in the sector used the new risk definition set by the Authority in their risk assessments. However, the new definition was not sufficiently understood by the companies operating in the sector, which had a negative impact on the risk assessment process and led to the emergence of different risk management approaches among the companies. Given the results of the study, it was observed that the difference in risk definition reduced the effectiveness of risk management and negatively affected the communication between the Authority and the companies.

As can be seen from the example, the use of different risk concepts leads to different risk management approaches and may cause some problems. It is, therefore, necessary to use a common language to make ERM consistent and applicable and to understand the risks within the organization (Abrams et al., 2007). For example, financial managers dealing with exchange rate risk in an organization may use different risk concepts from those dealing with regulatory compliance. The first group of managers focuses more on the definition of risk which is quantified and includes positive or negative consequences, while the second group focuses on the definition of risk which is often unmeasurable and includes largely negative consequences. This causes uncertainty among departments, making the risk management process uncertain and negatively affecting internal communication (Bromiley et al., 2015). Studies by Bromiley et al. (2015) and Røyksund and Flage (2019) show the importance of an agreed definition of risk for effective risk management.

Ultimately, in order for ERM to deliver the expected benefits, organizations must first clarify how they will define risk. Because unless the definition of risk is clear, the whole ERM process will be negatively affected by the domino effect. In this case, ERM will not deliver the expected benefit for the organization. It is clear that

---

[3] It is a supervisory body under the Norwegian Ministry of Labour and Social Inclusion. It has the authority to regulate the activities of the petroleum industry in Norway.

there is a relationship between risk definition and the benefits of ERM. The details of this relationship are given below:

- With ERM, management can identify challenges associated with existing opportunities and new opportunities by considering the positive and negative aspects of risk (COSO, 2017). For this purpose, risk should be defined in such a way that it covers not only negative but also positive consequences.
- Enterprise risk management helps the organization maintain and improve its current performance (Hopkin & Thompson, 2022; COSO, 2017; Florio & Leoni, 2017; Bohnert et al., 2019; Malik et al., 2019; Hanggraeni et al., 2019; Jurdi & AlGhnaimat, 2021; Pan et al., 2023). Therefore, it is important to understand risk in the same way within and between organizations and to define it in a way that does not negatively affect communication (Abrams et al., 2007; Bromiley et al., 2015).
- Enterprise risk management enables organizations to improve their ability to respond appropriately to risk. This capability helps organizations to reduce surprises and associated potential losses (COSO, 2017). Thus, it is necessary to include the cause element in the risk definition. According to Hopkin and Thompson (2022) and Kıral (2023), including the cause element in the definition increases the effectiveness of risk management by enabling measures to be taken against the risk.
- Enterprise risk management helps organizations to achieve their objectives. This requires effective risk assessment and management, and risk assessment is only useful and effective if an appropriate risk definition is used (Hopkin & Thompson, 2022).
- Enterprise risk management helps management to make the right organizational decisions by providing accurate and sufficient information (Hopkin & Thompson, 2022). To that end, it is important to use an accurate risk definition that is agreed upon within the organization (Abrams et al., 2007).

As can be seen, risk definition is critical to the ERM approach and practices. Moreover, it also assumes an important role in ensuring that ERM delivers the expected benefits. Because if you start with a correct definition of risk, risks will be correctly identified and assessed, and appropriate responses to risks will be given. On the contrary, if you do not start with an accurate risk definition, the right strategies cannot be determined to mitigate risks (Uzulans, 2018), which will lead to inadequate management of the risks faced by the organization, resulting in reducing the effectiveness of risk management. Ineffective risk management should not be expected to contribute sufficiently to achieving the organization's objectives.

4.5 How to Define Risk for an Effective Risk Management?

There is no formula for defining risk. However, risk needs to be defined as accurately as possible in order to manage it effectively.

According to Power (2014) and Kıral (2023), for effective risk management, the cause and impact of the risk should be included in the definition. This is because including the cause in the risk definition will enable clarification of the measures to be developed for the risk (Kıral, 2023). For example, let's define risk for a company producing refrigerators as "financial loss as a result of not meeting the demand due to inaccurate calculation of the capacity of the machine used in production." In the example, the reason is that the capacity of the machine used in production is not calculated accurately. In this case, the risk occurs due to inaccurate calculation of the capacity of the machine used in production. The correct calculation of the machine capacity reduces the probability of the risk occurring and allows it to be managed effectively. As can be seen, a risk definition that includes the cause facilitates the risk management process by ensuring an appropriate response to the risk.

The second element that should be included in the definition of risk is impact. Impact is the result that a risk will have on an objective if it occurs.

Let's explain this through the same example and define risk as follows:

> Financial loss as a result of not meeting the demand due to inaccurate calculation of the capacity of the machine used in production (1)

In the example above, the cause resulting in the risk to arise is that the capacity of the machine used in production is not calculated accurately. The impact is the financial loss if this risk occurs. Therefore, there must be a cause for the risk to occur and an event for the impact to occur. Knowing this relationship between cause, event, and impact will facilitate the assessment and prioritization of risks (Kıral, 2023). This will obviously increase the effectiveness of the risk management process.

Let us now take our example one step further and see the magnitude of the impact and how it is reflected in the risk management process.

Let us now define risk, on the basis of the same example, as follows:

> Financial loss and loss of reputation as a result of not meeting the demand due to inaccurate calculation of the capacity of the machine used in production (2)

In the first example, the impact is financial loss, while in the second example it is "financial loss + loss of reputation." In this case, we can write it as follows:

> Impact in example (2) > Impact in example (1)

Therefore, as Kıral (2023) states, including more than one impact in the definition of risk will determine the magnitude of the impact. This will affect the prioritization of risks and risk responses. The organization may prefer different risk responses for both examples. In the first example, it may accept the risk, while in the second, it may transfer the risk with a greater impact or avoid the risk. As the example shows, including impact in the definition of risk enables organizations to make more informed decisions and ensures effective management of risks.

4.6 Conclusion and Evaluation

In the literature, both disciplines and scientists have different perspectives on risk. These different perspectives are reflected in the definitions of risk and lead to risk being defined differently, making the concept ambiguous. However, although the meaning is ambiguous, it is clear what risk is not.

Risk is not a problem. A problem has happened and needs to be fixed, whereas a risk involves the possibility of an undesirable situation that has not yet happened.

Risk is not a hazard. While hazard is a negative concept, risk also includes the positive. What constitutes a hazard, such as an epidemic or a drought, is also clear. Agreeing on what risk is, however, is a challenge.

Risk is not a threat. Risk is twofold: Threat and opportunity. Risk has both a negative and a positive outcome. A threat represents only the negative aspect of the risk.

Risk is not uncertainty. Both concepts are about the future. Uncertainty includes significant and insignificant outcomes, whereas risk is uncertainty with a substantial outcome.

Identifying what risk is not reduces uncertainty in the definition and enables better risk management. Because risk definition is the starting point of ERM, it is critical to the ERM process. Unless the ERM process starts with a correct risk definition, making an accurate risk assessment and responding to risks is impossible. This leads to inadequate management of the organization's risks and thus reduces the effectiveness of risk management.

So, how should a correct risk definition be made for effective ERM? The cause must be known in order to respond duly to risk, and the impact must be understood in order to assess and prioritize the risk. Understanding this "cause—event—impact" relationship enables risks to be managed more effectively. Therefore, starting with a risk definition that identifies the cause and impact will facilitate the ERM process and increase its effectiveness.

References

Abrams, C., Kaenel, J. V., Muller, S., & Pfitzmann, B. (2007). Optimized enterprise risk management. *IBM Systems Journal, 46*(2), 219–234.

Althaus, C. E. (2005). Disciplinary perspective on the epistemological status of risk. *Risk Analysis, 25*(3), 567–588.

Aven, T. (2009). Safety is the antonym of risk for some perspectives of risk. *Safety Science, 47*, 925–930.

Aven, T. (2010). On how to define, understand and describe risk. *Reliability Engineering and System Safety, 95*, 623–631.

Aven, T. (2011). A risk concept applicable for both probabilistic and non-probabilistic perspectives. *Safety Science, 49*, 1080–1086.

Aven, T. (2022). On some foundational issues concerning the relationship between risk and resilience. *Risk Analysis, 42*(9), 2062–2074.

Aven, T., & Renn, O. (2009). On risk defined as an event where the outcome is uncertain. *Journal of Risk Research, 12*(1), 1–11.
Banham, R. (2004). Enterprising views of risk management: Businesses can use ERM to manage a wide variety of risks. *Journal of Accountancy, 197*, 65–71.
Beck, U. (1992). *Risk society: Towards a new modernity*. SAGE Publications.
Beck, U. (1999). *World risk society*. Polity Press.
Beck, U. (2006). Living in the world risk society. *Economy and Society, 35*(3), 329–345.
Bohnert, A., Gatzert, N., Hoyt, R. E., & Lechner, P. (2019). The drivers and value of enterprise risk management: evidence from ERM ratings. *The European Journal of Finance, 29*(5), 234–255.
Bonß, W. (1991). Unsicherheit und Gesellschaft – Argumente Für Eine Soziologische Risikoforschung. *Soziale Welt*, 258–277.
Bromiley, P., McShane, M. K., Nair, A., & Rustambekov, E. (2015). Enterprise risk management: Review, critique, and research directions. *Long Range Planning, 48*(4), 265–276.
Byrd, D. M., & Cothern, C. R. (2005). *Introduction to risk analysis: a systematic approach to science-based decision making*. Government Institutes, An Imprint of The Scarecrow Press.
Cabinet Office. (2002). *Risk: improving Government's capability to handle risk and uncertainty*. Strategy Unit Report.
Campbell, S. (2005). Determining overall risk. *Journal of Risk Research, 8*, 569–581.
COSO. (2017). *Enterprise risk management: Integrating with strategy and performance*. Accessed 11.06.2023, from www.coso.org/documents/2017-coso-erm-integrating-with-strategy-andperformance-executive-summary.pdf
D'Arcy, S. P., & Brogan, J. C. (2001). Enterprise risk management. *Journal of Risk Management of Korea, 12*(1), 207–228.
Denney, D. (2005). *Risk and society*. Sage Publication.
Douglas, M., & Wildavsky, A. (1983). *Risk and culture: an essay on the selection of technological and environmental dangers*. University of California Press.
Ewald, F. (1991). Insurance and risk. In G. Burchell, C. Gordon, & P. Miller (Eds.), *The Foucault effect: studies in governmentality*. Harvester Wheatsheaf.
Florio, C., & Leoni, G. (2017). Enterprise risk management and firm performance: The Italian case. *The British Accounting Review, 49*(1), 56–74.
Furedi, F. (2001). Korku Kültürü, *Risk Almamanın Riskleri*. Ayrıntı Yayınları
Giddens, A. (1991). *Modernity and self-identity: self and society in the Late Modern age*. Cambridge University Press.
Giddens, A. (1999). Risk and responsibility. *The Modern Law Review, 62*, 1–10.
Hanggraeni, D., Slusarczyk, B., Sulung, L. A. K., & Subroto, A. (2019). The impact of internal, external and enterprise risk management on the performance of micro, small and medium enterprises. *Sustainability, 11*(7), 2172. https://doi.org/10.3390/su11072172
Hopkin, P., & Thompson, C. (2022). *Fundamentals of risk management understanding, evaluating and implementing effective enterprise risk management*. Kogan Page Limited
ICAEW. (1999). *Internal control: Guidance or directors on the combined code [Turnbull report]*. Institute of Chartered Accountants in England and Wales.
Institute of Internal Auditors. (2004). *The role of internal auditing in enterprise risk management*. Accessed on 10.11.2022, from www.theiia.org
Institute of Internal Auditors. (2010). International professional practice framework (IPPF)
Institute of Risk Management. (2010). *A structured approach to enterprise risk management (ERM) and the requirements of ISO 31000*. IRM.
Institute of Risk Management. (2018). *Standard deviations: A risk practitioner's guide to ISO 31000*. Accessed on 15.09.2022, from www.theirm.org/media/6907/irm-report-iso-31000-2018-v2.pdf
ISO. (2009). ISO Guide 73:2009 Risk Management – Vocabulary. Accessed on 25.09.2022, from www.iso.org.
Jaaferi, A. (2001). Management of risks, uncertainties and opportunities on projects: time for a fundamental shift. *International Journal of Project Management, 19*, 89–101.

Jardine, C. G., & Hrudey, S. E. (1997). Mixed messages in risk communication. *Risk Analysis, 17*, 489–498.
Jurdi, D. J., & AlGhnaimat, S. M. (2021). The effects of ERM adoption on European insurance firms performance and risks. *Journal of Risk and Financial Management, 14*(11), 2–17.
Kalkan, M. E., & Deniz, V. (2013). Risk Kavramı Üzerine. *Mesleki Sağlık ve Güvenlik Dergisi*, 43–48.
Kaplan, S., & Garrick, B. J. (1981). On the quantitative definition of risk. *Risk Analysis, 1*, 11–27.
Kıral, H. (2023). *Kurumsal risk Yönetimi Ders Notları (Enterprise risk management lecture notes)*. Social sciences University of Ankara, Audit and Risk Management Master Program, Ankara.
Knight, F. (1921). *Risk, uncertainty and profit*. Riverside Press.
Kotb, M., & Ghattas, M. (2017). An overview of risk identification barriers with implementation of PMI standards in construction projects. *PM World Journal, 6*(10), 1–12.
Luhmann, N. (1991). *Soziologie Des Risikos*. W. de Gruyter.
Malik, M. F., Zaman, M., & Buckby, S. (2019). Enterprise risk management and firm performance: role of the risk committee. *Journal of Contemporary Accounting and Economics, 16*(1), 1–22.
Ni, H., Chen, A., & Chen, N. (2010). Some extension on risk matrix approach. *Safety Science, 48*, 1269–1278.
Olson, D. L., & Wu, D. (2010). *Enterprise risk management models* (2nd ed.). Springer-Verlag.
Pan, G., Zheng, L., Geng, Z., & Liu, M. (2023). Does enterprise risk management benefit manufacturing firms? Evidence from China. *Economıc Research-Ekonomska Istraživanj, 36*(2), 1–18.
Perry, J. G., & Hayes, R. W. (1985). Risk and its management in construction projects. *Proceedings of the Institution of Civil Engineers, 78*(3), 499–521.
Power, M. (2004). *The risk management of everything*. Demos.
Power, B. (2014). Writing good risk statements. *ISACA Journal, 3*.
Richard, L. (2003). *Management* (6th ed.). Thomson/South-Western West.
Rosa, E. A. (2010). The logical status of risk – To burnish or to dull. *Journal of Risk Research, 13*(3), 239–253.
Røyksund, M., & Flage, R. (2019). When is a risk assessment deficient according to an uncertainty-based risk perspective? *Risk Analysis, 39*(4), 761–776.
Slovic, P. (1999). Trust, emotion, sex, politics and science: Surveying the risk assessment battlefield. *Risk Analysis, 19*(4), 689–701.
TDK. (2021). *Türkçe Sözlük*. Türk Dil Kurumu Yayınları.
The Framework Regulation Guidelines. (2015). *Regulations relating to health, safety, and environment in the petroleum activities and at certain onshore facilities*.
Uzulans, J. (2018). Ontologıcal analysıs of the project Rısk management concept 'risk'. *Economics and Business, 32*, 21–35.
Van Loon, J. (2002). *Risk and technological culture: Towards a sociology of virulence*. Routledge.
Verbrugge, J., Smith, C., Niehaus, G., Briscoe, C., Coleman, W., Lawder, K., Ramamurtie, S., & Chew, D. (2003). Enterprise-wide risk management. *Journal of Applied Corporate Finance, 15*(4), 8–26.
Wassenius, E., & Crona, B. I. (2022). Adapting risk assessments for a complex future. *One Earth, 5*(1), 35–43.
Williams, M. J. (2008). (In) security studies, reflexive modernization and the risk society. *Cooperation and Conflict, 43*(1), 57–79.
Willis, H. H. (2007). Guiding resource allocations based on terrorism risk. *Risk Analysis, 27*(3), 597–606.
Zey, M. (1998). *Seizing the future: The dawn of the macroindustrial era* (2nd ed.). Transaction Publishers.

Mecbure Aslan is an internal auditor at the Internal Audit Department of the Ministry of Agriculture and Forestry in Turkey. She holds the certificates of CIA (Certified Internal Auditor), CGAP (International Government Auditor Certificate), and ISO 27001 LA. She worked as a culture and tourism expert at the Ministry of Culture and Tourism and as a youth and sports expert at the Ministry of Youth and Sports. She graduated from Hacettepe University, Faculty of Economics and Administrative Sciences, Department of Economics, and Anadolu University, Vocational School of Justice. She holds a master's degree in economics from Hacettepe University Department of Economics and a master's degree in public administration from Ankara Hacı Bayram Veli University (formerly Turkey and Middle East Institute of Public Administration). She is currently pursuing her PhD at the Social Sciences University of Ankara.

Chapter 5
Risk Assessment: Efficiency of Methods and Tools

Ali Erdem Saatçi

Abstract Reducing or minimizing the risk for a specific opportunity, which is the main purpose of risk management, only happens sometimes. This is often achieved through planned and designed measurements with well-chosen and efficient assessment tools. The only way for organizations to justify the belief that they are "very effective" in risk management, particularly in the risk assessment phase, is to have measured the risks efficiently. Thanks to the accurate and reliable information they provide, risk assessment tools steer the institutions towards making effective decisions. Risk assessment methods vary considerably between organizations. Some organizations prefer qualitative risk assessment methods, while others use quantitative methods. Some methods are more efficient than others. This study addresses the techniques and tools frequently used in the risk assessment process; their advantages and disadvantages; and how the concepts, published standards, and frameworks affect the process.

Keywords Risk management · Risk assessment · Risk assessment methods

5.1 Introduction

You want to take a short break from the challenging and intense pace of business life, and, to this end, you are planning to go on a journey. You map your travel route after making necessary plans and assessments. You decide on the places you want to see and visit, where to eat, and where you want to stay. Yet, when it's time to set off, you may blindfold yourself and start driving in the direction you think you should go, instinctively believing that it will be all right at night. Many of us are primarily unlikely to attempt something so bold. Still, we witness many organizations taking

A. E. Saatçi (✉)
Social Sciences University of Ankara, Ankara, Türkiye
e-mail: alierdem.saatci@student.asbu.edu.tr

H. Kıral (ed.), *Rethinking Enterprise Risk Management*, Accounting, Finance, Sustainability, Governance & Fraud: Theory and Application,
https://doi.org/10.1007/978-981-97-5983-5_5

such a "blind flight"[1] when it comes to risky activities in business life. If we start driving wearing a blindfold, the best-case scenario is to go in the wrong direction. In the worst case, we could have a fatal accident. Similar results are inevitable for the organizations if the risks are not duly and effectively analyzed and the obligations necessary for prioritization are not fulfilled while creating road maps.

Risks can appear anywhere at any time in our daily lives. You run into various risks when driving, riding a bike, exercising, investing, or even building relationships. Although risk often carries a negative implication, it can, under certain circumstances, yield beneficial outcomes. The important thing is to know how to react to risks when the time comes. This requires, of course, to identify and assess the risks beforehand. Otherwise, your path to the target will be blocked. To overcome this, it is necessary to clearly understand and comprehend risk identification and assessment. You can then apply these principles not only to corporate management but also to other activities in your daily life.

Risk management is an increasingly used strategy to increase security and credibility while reducing losses. Risks must be systematically identified, analyzed, and addressed to ensure informed decision-making. Achieving the goals and objectives is always ensured through an efficient risk assessment. Risk management provides a structured and systematic opportunity for the decision-making process (Moraru & Băbuţ, 2009). The value and power of the risk management approach lies in selecting efficient assessment methods and integrating these methods into the decision-making process as a coherent whole (Barb & Fita, 2019).

Risk assessment tools guide institutions to make effective decisions thanks to the accurate and reliable information they provide. The golden rule in a risk assessment is to ensure that the tools and methods used run properly and that the right tool and technique are chosen considering the purpose. Lack of adequate knowledge about the activities and/or processes of the organization may lead to a selection of wrong risk assessment tools, resulting in erroneous analyses and measurements. Hence, it is necessary to collect high-quality data and evidence using appropriate scientific methods. It is necessary to research everything impartially and in detail before making any decision or judgment. Identifying all difficulties professionally and with great precision is crucial for taking the right decision. Thus, it would be appropriate for managers to consider the following basic questions when determining risk assessment tools (Borghesi & Gaudenzi, 2012): "How do risk management and risk assessment function to enhance preparedness and minimize the impact of unforeseen events? In risk management, what are the priorities for risk assessment? To whom is the information obtained as a result of the assessment communicated? What roles are these tools expected to play? Are the features of risk assessment tools consistent with their purpose?"

There are many studies on risk assessment tools and methods in different fields in the literature. The present study's objectives include:

1. Examining prevalent risk assessment methods and tools

[1] In aviation, operating the aircraft in the dark or in fog using solely the flight instruments.

2. Analyzing practical implementation challenges
3. Evaluating method and tool efficiency
4. Addressing risks associated with the risk assessment process

A conceptual foundation is presented before these investigations. The study's findings and general evaluations are presented in the last part of it.

5.2 Risk Assessment

Risk assessment, a fundamental component of risk management, entails identifying and evaluating risks that could hinder an organization's goals (Djapić et al., 2013; Moeller, 2014). This process involves pinpointing, analyzing, and prioritizing risks to determine the most significant threats to an organization, project, or strategy (Hopkin, 2018).

Risk assessment definitions have been made by many standards and frameworks published on the international platform. However, these definitions need to be clarified and may lead to different problems for every organization. Therefore, it would be correct to define risk assessment as "a systematic, constantly developing and regularly conducted process that examines positive and negative risks, in other words, the threat and opportunity dimensions of risk, and prioritizes them by using one or more components of qualitative and quantitative methods to understand the impact of a risk on the organization."

Although the importance of corporate risk management and its added value is commonly acknowledged, it is tough to create a program that covers all organizations operating in different countries and sectors and can adapt to changing conditions. For institutions to have an effective risk management program, international commissions and organizations have established some standards and frameworks.

ISO 31000[2] (International Organization for Standardization) and COSO[3] Enterprise Risk Management (ERM) are the leading risk management standards and frameworks in the world today (Rubino, 2018). Although they are similar in scope, they differ from each other in terms of process and terminology. Risk assessment fundamentally involves the identification, analysis, and evaluation of potential risks according to the ISO 31000 Standard. This process is handled in a single step within the framework of COSO ERM and risk identification constitutes the previous component (Rubino, 2018).

[2] A comprehensive suite of risk management standards, codified as ISO 31000 by the International Organization for Standardization, offers a standardized framework for risk management practices.

[3] The Committee of Sponsoring Organizations of the Treadway Commission. Organizations sponsoring this Commission are the American Institute of Certified Public Accountants (AICPA), the Institute of Internal Auditors (IIA), the American Accounting Association (AAA), Financial Executives International (FEI), and the Institute of Management Accountants (IMA).

"Risk analysis" is sometimes used in lieu of risk assessment as a more comprehensive concept that includes elements related to risk management (Ansell & Wharton, 2002). Within certain risk management methodologies, risk analysis is considered a specific step in the broader risk assessment process (ISO/IEC, 2002). In the literature, the concept of risk assessment is apparently used interchangeably in different forms such as "*risk analysis*," "*risk estimation*" (Gadd et al., 2004), and "*risk measurement*" (Raz & Hillson, 2005). The diversity of these concepts and definitions leads to conceptual confusion and contradictions, and prevents the risk assessment process from operating efficiently in concrete uses (Assmuth & Hildén, 2008). On the other hand, a good reading and understanding of both frameworks is to the organization's benefit. However, despite the updates and improvements in the original versions, the best risk management practices make sense beyond these standards (Marks, 2015; Leech, 2018). The frequent conflation of risk definition, risk identification, and risk analysis highlights the interconnected and iterative nature of these processes, with fluid boundaries between them (Stulz, 2008).

In order to make an assessment on any subject, it is necessary to determine and define it in the first place. While the definition of risk tells us what the risk is, the risk assessment tells how the risk will affect the objectives (Marks, 2015). The tools and methods used to identify and evaluate the risks are different. Therefore, incorrect selection of identification and evaluation tools may lead to different results in practice.

Risk assessment methods vary greatly between institutions (Fraser & Simkins, 2010). Some institutions prefer a qualitative method, while others use quantitative methods. It is observed that some of the methods and tools used to evaluate risks of different types and sizes have recently increased in popularity and are frequently used by organizations. Believing that they produce more accurate results, the widespread use of mathematical models in recent years, especially those with complex tools, brings along some risks. The use of these methods by organizations that do not have the skills to use complex tools may lead to an ineffective result.

In order for the risk assessment process to work efficiently, there are a number of approaches that can be considered during the planning phase. Determining the optimal participants in the risk assessment process is crucial (Beasley et al., 2015). While top-down board-level assessments and bottom-up employee-driven approaches are both valid, incorporating diverse perspectives is key (Beasley et al., 2010; Hopkin, 2018). Balancing CEO input (critical for overall risk tolerance) with broader stakeholder feedback ensures comprehensive risk identification (Brady, 2015).

To ensure optimal efficacy, risk assessment methodologies must be strategically selected in accordance with prevailing organizational culture. The adoption of methods congruent with established communication channels and documentation practices promotes stakeholder engagement and ensures the generation of verifiable results for auditing purposes.

5.3 Risk Assessment: Efficiency of Methods and Tools

A key distinction between historical and contemporary risk management lies in the adoption of systematic assessment methodologies (Dionne, 2013). Advancements in probability theory and statistics during the seventeenth century facilitated the quantification of risk, allowing for more objective and structured analysis. However, these tools were only adopted for certain applications in certain industries, yet very slowly even then (Althaus, 2005). Quantitative methods were limited to the insurance and banking sector from the eighteenth century to the beginning of the twentieth century, and they were subsequently applied in financial markets and health, especially in the public sector (Merna & Al-Thani, 2011). The 1960s witnessed a surge in quantitative risk modeling, fueled by computer technology. Engineers and economists leveraged this capacity to develop probabilistic models accommodating uncertainty, supplementing traditional risk assessment methods (Dionne, 2013). Additionally, economic theory drew inspiration from game theory and decision theory, offering mathematical frameworks for joint decision-making under uncertainty (Althaus, 2005). This period also saw consulting firms introduce qualitative risk-scoring methods and tools like risk matrices (Marks, 2015).

Easy-to-use features of these methods and the pressure to adopt a standard risk assessment tool have led to the choice of the easiest method, regardless of its efficiency. As this approach has gained momentum in adoption, prudent managers have become increasingly interested in using a commonly used method. Societal and organizational responses to destabilizing events, such as natural disasters, economic instability, terrorism, and cybersecurity vulnerabilities, have often precipitated the mainstreaming of formal risk management practices in the pursuit of enhanced resilience (Hubbard, 2020).

Risk assessment methodologies exhibit significant cross-disciplinary variation. Data-driven fields like insurance and medicine rely on quantitative probability calculations, while engineering leverages fault tree analysis (Hubbard, 2020). Conversely, psychology and anthropology emphasize stakeholder perceptions and collective behavior (Douglas & Wildavsky, 1983; Slovic, 2000). To bridge knowledge gaps, these assessments often necessitate multidisciplinary working groups (Antosiewicz et al., 2020; Mayer et al., 2020; Nikas et al., 2020; Silaen et al., 2020; Taylor et al., 2020).

International standards organizations and management consultants mostly highlight qualitative assessment methods due to their simple use. These methods are generally used in cases where the current impact and probability are low or there is no quantitative data and experts to analyze this data (IIARF, 2003). Qualitative assessment is the expression of the potential impact level of risks and their probability of occurrence with the personal knowledge, experience, and judgment of the evaluators rather than numerical data-based methods and tools (Gupta & Thakkar, 2018). Risk matrices, where probability and impact are assessed and visualized, are a dominant risk assessment tool in ERM and various specialized domains like cybersecurity and project management (Gadd et al., 2004; Hubbard, 2020). Their widespread use extends across industries, including medicine, construction, aviation, agriculture, and mining (Bender, 2004; Hewett et al., 2004; McIlwain, 2006; Md-Nor et al., 2008; Malone & Moses, 2004).

Which methods and tools to use in risk assessment depends on the competent human resources in the organization, the current data set, the purpose of the assessment, time constraints, expectations, and the desired result. The organization completes the risk assessment process by taking into account all these factors (Sobel, 2015).

The most widely used qualitative assessment methods in practice are risk matrix (map), brainstorming based on expert opinions, Delphi analysis technique and interview, checklists, risk record, and other probability-impact tables. Key quantitative risk assessment methods, often leveraging statistical and probabilistic modeling, include Monte Carlo simulation, decision trees, sensitivity analysis, Markov analysis, Bayesian networks, and artificial neural networks (Merna & Al-Thani, 2011).

In 2017, KPMG and HDR consultancy firms conducted a survey with risk experts consisting of analysts, risk managers, CEOs, and employees at other levels working in 283 organizations of different sizes and operating in different sectors in 53 countries. The following results were obtained in the surveys conducted on how organizations and risk experts actually assess and manage risks, as well as on the efficiency and productivity of this process (Table 5.1).

Survey data underscores the dominance of risk matrices in risk assessment, with 41% of respondents (HDR/KPMG, 2017) employing this tool. Their popularity stems from ease of development and use, with 27% utilizing in-house matrices and 14% referencing established standards such as COSO, ISO, and NIST (Albery et al., 2016).

Other qualitative approaches such as questionnaires, expert opinions, checklists, and audit reports were found to be frequently used methods by 39% of the participants. These methods often involve assessing risks as high, medium, or low, based on impact and probability, as in the risk matrix. Risk assessment may incorporate weighted scoring systems where identified risk indicators receive individual scores and weights, with the product of these values then summed for aggregate risk calculation. On the other hand, it was determined that 20% of the participants preferred quantitative evaluation techniques, that the most commonly used ones were Monte

Table 5.1 Most commonly used risk assessment methods

Method	Ratio of participants
A standard-based risk matrix (ISO, COSO, NIST[a], etc.)	14
In-house developed risk matrix	27
Other qualitative scoring and ranking methods (expert opinion, survey, checklists, audit reports)	39
Quantitative methods (such as probability methods, math-based simulations, and statistical methods)	20

Source: HDR/KPMG (2017)

[a] The National Institute of Standards & Technology

Table 5.2 Pros and cons of risk assessment methods

Method	Sample method	Pros	Cons
Qualitative methods	*Expert opinion*	• Easy to understand and apply • Time- and cost-efficient • Strong interaction	• Subjective judgments • Past-oriented • Dominance of senior management
	Survey and checklists		
	Workshops and brainstorming		
	Risk matrix		
	Audit reports		
Quantitative methods	*Monte Carlo simulation*	• Can be widely used • Objective methods • Relatively accurate result	• Complicated and long process • Use mathematical methods based on sometimes unavailable data (Simulations)
	Fuzzy logic		
	Bayes networks		
	Fault-event tree analysis		
Comprehensive methods	*Fuzzy-AHP*	• High accuracy rate • Mixed method	• Complicated structure • Hard to apply • Using more data
	Delphi-AHP		
	Entropy-TOPSIS		

Source: This table generated by the author
AHP Analytical hierarchy process, *TOPSIS* Technique for order preference by similarity to ideal solution

Carlo simulations (85%) and statistical analysis of historical data (77%), and also, methods such as Bayesian statistics and networks (56%) or utility theory (17%) were used less frequently.

Table 5.2 shows the overall pros and cons of frequently used risk assessment tools. All organizations can develop their own scoring method. Almost all of them use tables showing impact and probability calculations at different scales (Brady, 2015). Qualitative methods are simpler to use and more time- and cost-efficient. The most important con is that it contains subjective judgments and is past oriented (Stulz, 2008). This may lead to erroneous assessments, because the human brain cannot remember past events as precisely and clearly as a computer does. A prevalent error in risk assessment is prioritizing high-probability, low-impact events over those with lower probability but significantly greater potential consequences (Pickering & Cowley, 2010). Furthermore, subjective risk perception varies between individuals, leading to divergent evaluations of the same risk factors (Stulz, 2008; Tversky & Kahneman, 1992).

The widespread belief that quantitative methods for risk management are impractical and difficult to use enables qualitative methods and scoring tools to be used in almost all areas (Ostrom & Wilhelmsen, 2019). This perceived advantage regarding qualitative methods is mostly the placebo effect[4] (Hubbard, 2020). Individuals are

[4]The placebo effect refers to the beneficial impact of an inactive treatment due to the patient's belief in its efficacy. Despite its psychological basis, this effect can manifest in measurable physiological changes, such as altered blood pressure or cholesterol levels.

inherently limited in their ability to accurately assess risk due to cognitive biases that compromise objectivity and rationality (Kahneman et al., 1982; Slovic, 1967). Evidence suggests widespread difficulty in understanding, trusting, and utilizing probability estimates for risk evaluation (Fischhoff et al., 1983; March & Shapira, 1987).

Quantitative risk analysis frequently employs Monte Carlo simulations, particularly when inputs are uncertain and expressed as probability distributions (HDR/KPMG, 2017; Wall, 1997; Wing Chau, 1995). This computational technique generates a range of potential outcomes, addressing input ambiguity. While some perceive insufficient data as a limitation (HDR/KPMG, 2017), modern statistical methods and skilled personnel can mitigate this challenge (Huang et al., 2004).

The insurance and finance sectors rely heavily on probabilistic risk modeling, characterized by the mathematical derivation of potential losses. Such methods demonstrate flexibility by accommodating both subjective inputs and objective data sources, such as historical records and empirical findings (Bedford & Cooke, 2001). The main strength of the probability approach is that it is a holistic quantitative approach that allows ranking subjects and outcomes, unambiguous handling of any uncertainties, and applying an optimization process (Apostolakis, 1990). The perception that statistical inferences necessitate extensive datasets is inaccurate. The judicious application of appropriate statistical methods can facilitate the extraction of meaningful insights, even when sample sizes are limited. For example, Bayesian statistical methods calculate and update probabilities using the available data set by means of Bayes' theorem (Bedford & Cooke, 2001).

While deterministic methods (e.g., sensitivity analysis, scenario analysis, network timing) lack the statistical foundation of probabilistic models, they can be integrated with mathematical or scientific techniques (Merna & Al-Thani, 2011). These approaches are attractive in contexts prioritizing straightforward analysis, offering clear and computationally efficient decision support (Kirchsteiger, 1999). Its weakest point is that it is based on experience and common sense specific to the organization and person (Davison & Vantine, 1998).

Emergence of new technologies leads to the fact that broader quantitative methods grouped together with mathematical methods have been combined with multi-criteria decision analysis and artificial intelligence models in risk assessment (Baryannis et al., 2019). Among these methods are fuzzy logic, analytical hierarchy process (AHP), artificial neural networks, Technique for order preference by similarity to ideal solution (TOPSIS), and VlseKriterijumska Optimizacija I Kompromisno Resenje (VIKOR). The strongest aspect of these methods is that they have a high accuracy rate (Tüysüz & Kahraman, 2006). These methods, which require technical competence, have some difficulties in practice because of their complex structure and need for more data. Qualitative methods, especially expert opinions, are used. However, a more complex method is used to determine whether this information based on expert opinions is internally consistent.

Multi-criteria decision-making (MCDM) methods provide a valuable tool kit for navigating complex business decisions characterized by uncertainty and conflicting objectives (Hahn, 2003). To enhance the accuracy and reliability of risk assessments, a multidimensional approach evaluating risks against multiple criteria is recommended (Tüysüz & Kahraman, 2006). These comprehensive assessments are based on methods from various fields of expertise (Van Vliet et al., 2020).

Hubbard (2020) critiques the widespread use of risk analysis methods lacking a theoretical foundation and empirical evidence of their efficacy in improving decision-making. He posits that many managers lack the expertise to evaluate available methods, further highlighting a dearth of objective performance measurement even under optimal conditions.

Subjective risk assessment methods are inherently vulnerable to cognitive biases that lead to systematic underestimation of risk (Gadd et al., 2004). Even quantitative approaches relying on historical data can yield unreliable inferences (Hopkins, 2004). The Dunning-Kruger effect highlights the disconnect between perceived and actual expertise, undermining the validity of intuitive judgments (Dunning, 2011; Kahneman & Klein, 2009). These limitations threaten the efficacy of any risk assessment process dependent on human judgment.

5.4 Risks of Risk Assessment Process

The absence of performance metrics for risk assessment methods, even within organizations adhering to sound practices, poses a critical challenge (Hubbard, 2020; Marks, 2015). This creates a conducive environment for the proliferation of ineffective methodologies. Their subsequent entrenchment, due to institutional inertia and designation as "best practices," can mask inherent weaknesses until significant adverse consequences emerge.

Despite expert recommendations for systematic, enterprise-wide risk management (Beasley et al., 2010), many organizations report inefficiencies in their risk assessment processes. Aon's 2017 survey highlights this disparity, revealing that only 40% and 33% of participating organizations employ systematic, enterprise-wide methods for risk identification and assessment, respectively.

On the other hand, the longitudinal case study on the applicability of organizational risk management and, in particular, the efficiency of the risk management process conducted by Arena et al. (2010) found that many organizations adopted a systematic model only as a compliance tool in theory; the risk assessment process has a static structure; and the communication and interaction between senior management, managers, and employees are not sufficient, therefore risk assessment techniques are not used efficiently.

Another risk encountered in risk assessments is the absence of an agreed definition of critical risks. Everyone has apparently different perspectives, definitions, and understandings of risks (Brady, 2015). In a rapidly changing and developing world, the constant and rapid change in risks causes the previous evaluations to lose their validity, and the likelihood of risks to occur and the impact they create to differ, which makes it difficult to evaluate using historical data and makes the existing data meaningless.

Each organization's risk assessment is actually a reflection of its own perspective, that is, corporate culture, risk appetite, risk tolerance, risk capacity, and experience and knowledge of corporate activities (Stulz, 2008; Özbek, 2012). The stronger the risk culture of the organizations, the more skilled the institutions are in terms of efficiently assessing and managing risks and maintaining their existence. On the other hand, if an organization is not very willing to take risks, it would prefer to reduce the uncertainties to a great extent and avoid risky transactions. On the contrary, if the organization's risk appetite is high, it would have a structure that is not uneasy despite the threats posed by the risk and sees a positive picture in terms of opportunities (Hillson & Murray-Webster, 2007).

Although concepts such as risk appetite and risk tolerance have been defined in the risk management literature, there is no defined approach with regard to how they should be measured (Kıral, 2018). Although a special document on risk appetite was published by COSO in 2020, there is still uncertainty about how risk appetite will be determined in practice, whether in a qualitative or quantitative manner (Kerstin et al., 2014). Therefore, insufficient cultural or conceptual understanding of the organization, function, or process for which the risk assessment is conducted may lead to some wrong steps, such as not including the right stakeholders in the assessment.

The results of erroneous but widely adopted methods and tools are of great importance for organizations that make critical decisions. Not only financial decisions, but also decisions about the whole economy, even human life, are heavily supported by the assessment and management of risks. If the risk analysis is not based on meaningful measurements, risk response methods will have to deal with the wrong problems as a result of the domino effect (Hopkin, 2018). Finally, an unsuccessful, inefficient risk assessment will not lead to achievement in improving processes, so the risk management effort will only turn out to be a waste of time and money.

While a 2012 Deloitte survey indicated high self-reported efficacy in risk management (72%), reliance on subjective assessment warrants scrutiny (Deloitte, 2017). The critical question remains: What demonstrable evidence supports the perceived success of risk management practices? If an organization is unable to answer this question, one should be skeptical about if the efforts to assess and manage the risks are working, or even focusing on the right risks. Nonetheless, it was found that 69% of the organizations participating in the HDR/KPMG (2017) survey did not measure whether risk management worked or not, and those who said they did measure risk could not go beyond the personnel survey on the efficiency of risk management (HDR and KPMG, 2017).

If risk assessment is undervalued by senior management, deemed as a low-level activity or a one-time effort, it may be a harbinger of failure. The survey conducted by the Economist Intelligence Unit (EIU) in 2017 found that the importance of risk assessment was not understood by the senior management at a rate of 21% and that risk assessment tools steered the strategic decision-making process by 47%.

In the surveys conducted by HDR/KPMG (2017), it was stated that 31% of respondents believed that the importance of risk assessment was not recognized by senior management and that risk assessment was used to provide "partial guidance" or "considerable guidance" in important decisions.

While ERM frameworks offer a holistic approach, their focus on business processes risks overemphasizing operational risks, potentially neglecting the integrated assessment of strategic risks (Borghesi & Gaudenzi, 2012). A comprehensive risk management approach necessitates the identification of adverse events with both strategic and operational implications (Brady, 2015), involving key stakeholders from entrepreneurs to management (Borghesi & Gaudenzi, 2012).

With the adoption of an approach of the ERM framework that includes all processes at the corporate level and is associated with strategic goals, ERM has turned into a structure that is uncertain and not well defined in terms of the tools used, and thus, risk assessment has become more difficult and subjective (Kıral, 2018). In addition, using a systematic framework can lead to overlooking the critical process owners and under-participation in risk assessment.

5.5 Conclusion

An old saying about management, often attributed to W. E. Deming, goes, "You can't manage what you can't measure." Similarly, a statement by author Dr. H. James Harrington, "If you can't measure something, you can't understand, if you can't understand it, you can't control it, if you can't control it, you can't improve it," emphasizes the basic principles of productivity in management and reveals the importance of assessment and measurement. Peter Drucker, a management guru, has described measurement as "the fourth essential element of the manager's job." Reducing or minimizing the risk for a specific opportunity, which is the main purpose of risk management, does not happen automatically. It is possible only through planned and designed measurements with well-chosen, efficient assessment tools.

The only way for organizations to justify the belief that they are "very effective" in the risk, assessment, and management phases is to have measured the risks efficiently.

The key criterion for organizations with varying structures across different sectors is to identify and create customized methods tailored to the organization's specific needs, considering the nature, scale, and complexity of the work, project, or investment, as well as the availability of resources, the maturity of human, time, and information technology systems, and the experience of analysts. This approach should be prioritized over relying on a standard risk assessment framework. To this end, it is necessary, first of all, to clearly understand and comprehend what the concepts of risk identification and assessment are.

Uncertainty in measuring concepts such as risk appetite, risk tolerance, and risk capacity, largely determined by the corporate culture, is one of the most significant obstacles to an effective risk assessment process. Creating an influential risk culture, determining what is acceptable and what is not, via strong internal and external communication to be established within the organization in a way that is specific to it is a critical step towards removing these obstacles.

Since organizations face more risks than they can control, they must prioritize these risks and make the right choice among them. Before making any decision or making a judgment, it is necessary to research everything objectively and in detail. In order to make the right decisions, it is inevitable to professionally identify all challenges with great precision. There is a need for a practical and sustainable risk assessment process, especially in a dynamic business environment where emerging risks can suddenly develop and cause dangerous effects for organizations. However, in practice, it is observed that the organizations are reluctant to make a dynamic risk assessment.

The real understanding of the value of risk management depends on the continuity of risk assessment activities. Risk reduction options such as investing in new cybersecurity controls, tighter control over the supply chain, diversifying production processes, increasing the number of auditors, and requesting new training are quite costly and not equally effective. However, this can be avoided by means of an efficient and dynamic risk assessment methodology and pinpoint detections. For example, more meaningful risk reports can be generated based on quantitative data that can provide more valuable information for management, by keeping an up-to-date risk list. Thanks to the comprehensive quantitative methods combined with multi-criteria decision analysis and artificial intelligence models, which have been frequently used in recent years, especially in the fields of financial and project risk management, the highly accurate numerical results obtained from the modeling help the organization take the right amount of risks and identify effective risk responses in the way to ensure its success in the short and long term.

The inclusion of effective measurement tools in the risk assessment process is of great importance for the sustainability of organizations in order to manage the future in a dynamic environment where technology is developing rapidly, uncertainties and complexities are increasing, and risks are constantly changing. Otherwise, your path to the target will be blocked, your journey will be interrupted, and your blind flight in the dark will result in the worst-case scenario.

References

Albery, S., Borys, D., & Tepe, S. (2016). Advantages for risk assessment: Evaluating learnings from question sets inspired by the FRAM and the risk matrix in a manufacturing environment. *Safety Science, 89*, 180–189. (SCI, SSCI).

Althaus, C. E. (2005). A disciplinary perspective on the epistemological status of risk. *Risk Analysis: An International Journal, 25*(3), 567–588. (SCI, SSCI).

Ansell, J., & Wharton, F. (Eds.). (2002). *Risk analysis and management*. Wiley.

Antosiewicz, M., Nikas, A., Szpor, A., Witajewski-Baltvilks, J., & Doukas, H. (2020). Pathways for the transition of the polish power sector and associated risks. *Environmental Innovation and Societal Transitions, 35*, 271–291. (SCI, SSCI).

Aon Corporation. (2017). *Global risk management survey*. Retrieved 06.06.2021, from https://www.aon.com/2017-global-risk-management-survey/
Apostolakis, G. (1990). The concept of probability in safety assessments of technological systems. *Science, 250*(4986), 1359–1364. (SCI, SSCI).
Arena, M., Arnaboldi, M., & Azzone, G. (2010). The organizational dynamics of enterprise risk management. *Accounting, Organizations and Society, 35*(7), 659–675. (SSCI).
Assmuth, T., & Hildén, M. (2008). The significance of information frameworks in integrated risk assessment and management. *Environmental Science & Policy, 11*(1), 71–86.
Barb, C. M., & Fita, D. N. (2019). A comparative analysis of risk assessment techniques from the risk management perspective. In MATEC Web of Conferences (Vol. 290, p. 12003). EDP Sciences. (SCI, SSCI)
Baryannis, G., Dani, S., Validi, S., & Antoniou, G. (2019). Decision support systems and artificial intelligence in supply chain risk management. In *Revisiting supply chain risk* (pp. 53–71). Springer.
Beasley, M. S., Branson, B. C., & Hancock, B. V. (2010). *COSO's 2010 report on ERM*. Committee of Sponsoring Organizations of the Treadway Commission.
Beasley, M., Branson, B., & Hancock, B. (2015). Report on the current state of enterprise risk oversight. The ERM Initiative at North Carolina State University, Raleigh, NC.
Bedford, T., & Cooke, R. (2001). *Probabilistic risk analysis: Foundations and methods*. Cambridge University Press. (SCI, SSCI).
Bender, W. J. (2004). Simplified risk assessment for construction clients. *AACE International Transactions, RI51*.
Borghesi, A., & Gaudenzi, B. (2012). *Risk management: How to assess, transfer and communicate critical risks* (Vol. 5). Springer Science & Business Media. (SSCI).
Brady, J. (2015). *Risk assessment: Issues and challenges*. Pharmaceutical Engineering.
Davison, M., & Vantine, W. (1998). Understanding risk management: A review of the literature and industry practice. In *Proceedings of ESA Risk Management Workshop* (pp. 253–256).
Deloitte Touche Tohmatsu LLC. (2017). *Global Risk Survey*. Retrieved 07.06.2021, from https://www2.deloitte.com/content/dam/Deloitte/lu/Documents/risk/us_en_globalrisksurvey8_23072013.pdf
Dionne, G. (2013). Risk management: History, definition, and critique. *Risk Management and Insurance Review, 16*(2), 147–166.
Djapic, M., Lukic, L., & Popović, P. (2013). Technical product risk assessment integration into the Enterprise risk management. *Tehnicki Vjesnik= Technical Gazette, 20*(4), 721–730. (SCI).
Douglas, M., & Wildavsky, A. (1983). *Risk and culture: An essay on the selection of technological and environmental dangers*. Univ of California Press. (SSCI).
Dunning, D. (2011). The Dunning–Kruger effect: On being ignorant of one's own ignorance. In *Advances in experimental social psychology* (Vol. 44, pp. 247–296). Academic Press. (SSCI)
Economist Intelligence Unit. (2017). *The Global Liveability Report*. Retrieved 07.06.2021, from https://www.eiu.com/n/campaigns/the-global-liveability-report-2017/
Fischhoff, B., Lichtenstein, S., Derby, S. L., Slovic, P., & Keeney, R. (1983). *Acceptable risk*. Cambridge University Press.
Fraser, J. R., & Simkins, B. (Eds.). (2010). *Enterprise risk management: Today's leading research and best practices for tomorrow's executives* (Vol. 3). Wiley.
Gadd, S. A., Keeley, D. M., & Balmforth, H. F. (2004). Pitfalls in risk assessment: Examples from the UK. *Safety Science, 42*(9), 841–857. (SSCI).
Gupta, V. K., & Thakkar, J. J. (2018). A quantitative risk assessment methodology for construction project. *Sādhanā, 43*(7), 1–16. (SSCI).
Hahn, E. D. (2003). Decision making with uncertain judgments: A stochastic formulation of the analytic hierarchy process. *Decision Sciences, 34*(3), 443–466. (SSCI).
Hewett, C. J. M., Quinn, P. F., Whitehead, P. G., Heathwaite, A. L., & Flynn, N. J. (2004). Towards a nutrient export risk matrix approach to managing agricultural pollution at source. *Hydrology and Earth System Sciences, 8*(4), 834–845. (SCI).

Hillson, D., & Murray-Webster, R. (2007). *Understanding and managing risk attitude*. Gower Publishing (SCI, SSCI).

Hopkin, P. (2018). *Fundamentals of risk management: Understanding, evaluating and implementing effective risk management*. Kogan Page Publishers.

Hopkins, A. (2004). *Quantitative risk assessment: A critique*. Working paper. Canberra National Research Centre for Occupational Health and Safety Regulation. Working Paper 25.

http://www.rmmagazine.com/articles/article/2015/05/01/-The-Benefits-of-a-Risk-Assessment-Dialogue- (Retrieved 07.06.2021)

Huang, Z., Chen, H., Hsu, C. J., Chen, W. H., & Wu, S. (2004). Credit rating analysis with support vector machines and neural networks: A market comparative study. *Decision Support Systems, 37*(4), 543–558. (SCI).

Hubbard, D. W. (2020). *The failure of risk management: Why it's broken and how to fix it*. Wiley.

Hubbard Decision Research (HDR) and KPMG. *Enterprise Risk Managament Survey*, (2017). https://www.probabilitymanagement.org/blog/2019/2/26/hubbardkpmg-enterprise-risk-management-survey (Retrieved on 05.06.2021)

ISO/IEC. (2002). https://www.iso.org/obp/ui/#iso:std:iso-iec:27002:ed-3:v2:en (Accessed on 05.11.2022)

Kahneman, D., & Klein, G. (2009). Conditions for intuitive expertise: A failure to disagree. *American Psychologist, 64*(6), 515. (SSCI).

Kahneman, D., Slovic, S. P., Slovic, P., Tversky, A., & (Eds.). (1982). *Judgment under uncertainty: Heuristics and biases*. Cambridge University Press.

Kerstin, D., Simone, O., & Nicole, Z. (2014). Challenges in implementing enterprise risk management. *ACRN Journal of Finance and Risk Perspectives, 3*(3), 1–14.

Kıral, H. (2018). Kurumsal Risk Yönetiminin Riskleri. *Denetişim, 18*, 5–14.

Kirchsteiger, C. (1999). On the use of probabilistic and deterministic methods in risk analysis. *Journal of Loss Prevention in the Process Industries, 12*(5), 399–419.

Leech, T. (2018). Reinventing ERM to support better decision making. *EDPACS, 58*(5), 1–4.

Malone, R. W., Jr., & Moses, K. (2004). *Development of risk assessment matrix for NASA*. Engineering and Safety Center.

March, J. G., & Shapira, Z. (1987). Managerial perspectives on risk and risk taking. *Management Science, 33*(11), 1404–1418. (SSCI).

Marks, N. (2015). *World-class risk management*. CreateSpace Independent Publishing Platform.

Mayer, J., van der Gaast, W., Bachner, G., & Spijker, E. (2020). Qualitative and quantitative risk assessment of expanding photovoltaics in The Netherlands. *Environmental Innovation and Societal Transitions, 35*, 357–368. (SCI, SSCI).

McILwain, J. C. (2006). A review: A decade of clinical risk management and risk tools. *Clinician in Management, 14*(4).

Md-Nor, Z., Kecojevic, V., Komljenovic, D., & Groves, W. (2008). Risk assessment for loader-and dozer-related fatal incidents in US mining. *International Journal Of Injury Control and Safety Promotion, 15*(2), 65–75. (SSCI).

Merna, T., & Al-Thani, F. F. (2011). *Corporate risk management*. Wiley.

Moeller, R. R. (2014). *Executive's guide to COSO internal controls-understanding and implementing the new framework*. Wiley.

Moraru, R. I., & Băbuț, G. B. (2009). *Risk management. Global approach-concepts, principles and structure* (in Romanian). Petroşani.

Nikas, A., Stavrakas, V., Arsenopoulos, A., Doukas, H., Antosiewicz, M., Witajewski-Baltvilks, J., & Flamos, A. (2020). Barriers to and consequences of a solar-based energy transition in Greece. *Environmental Innovation and Societal Transitions, 35*, 383–399. (SCI, SSCI).

Ostrom, L. T., & Wilhelmsen, C. A. (2019). *Risk assessment: Tools, techniques, and their applications*. Wiley.

Özbek, Ç. (2012). *İç Denetim Kurumsal Yönetim Risk Yönetimi İç Kontrol* (p. 1). Türkiye İç Denetim Enstitüsü Yayınları.

Pickering, A., & Cowley, S. P. (2010). Risk matrices: Implied accuracy and false assumptions. *ReSeaRcH & PRactice, 11*.

Raz, T., & Hillson, D. (2005). A comparative review of risk management standards. *Risk Management, 7*(4), 53–66.

Rubino, M. (2018). A comparison of the main ERM frameworks: How limitations and weaknesses can be overcome implementing IT governance. *International Journal of Business and Management, 13*(12), 203–214.

Silaen, M., Taylor, R., Bößner, S., Anger-Kraavi, A., Chewpreecha, U., Badinotti, A., & Takama, T. (2020). Lessons from Bali for small-scale biogas development in Indonesia. *Environmental Innovation and Societal Transitions, 35*, 445–459. (SCI, SSCI).

Slovic, P. (1967). The relative influence of probabilities and payoffs upon perceived risk of a gamble. *Psychonomic Science, 9*(4), 223–224.

Slovic, P. E. (2000). *The perception of risk*. Earthscan publications.

Sobel, P. J. (2015). *Auditor's risk management guide integrating auditing and ERM*. CCH Incorporated.

Stulz, R. M. (2008). Risk management failures: What are they and when do they happen? *Journal of Applied Corporate Finance, 20*(4), 39–48.

Taylor, R., Wanjiru, H., Johnson, O. W., & Johnson, F. X. (2020). Modelling stakeholder agency to investigate sustainable charcoal markets in Kenya. *Environmental Innovation and Societal Transitions, 35*, 493–508. (SCI, SSCI).

The Institute of Internal Auditors Research Foundation (IIARF). (2003). *Research opportunities in internal auditing, Sridhar Ramamoorti, internal auditing: History, evaluation, and prospects*. The Institute of Internal Auditors.

Tüysüz, F., & Kahraman, C. (2006). Project risk evaluation using a fuzzy analytic hierarchy process: An application to information technology projects. *International Journal of Intelligent Systems, 21*(6), 559–584. (SCI).

Tversky, A., & Kahneman, D. (1992). Advances in prospect theory: Cumulative representation of uncertainty. *Journal of Risk and uncertainty, 5*(4), 297–323. (SSCI).

Van Vliet, O., Hanger-Kopp, S., Nikas, A., Spijker, E., Carlsen, H., Doukas, H., & Lieu, J. (2020). The importance of stakeholders in scoping risk assessments—Lessons from low-carbon transitions. *Environmental Innovation and Societal Transitions, 35*, 400–413. (SCI, SSCI).

Wall, D. M. (1997). Distributions and correlations in Monte Carlo simulation. *Construction Management & Economics, 15*(3), 241–258.

Wing Chau, K. (1995). The validity of the triangular distribution assumption in Monte Carlo simulation of construction costs: empirical evidence from Hong Kong. *Constr Manag Econ, 13*(1), 15–21.

Ali Erdem Saatçi is a Social Sciences University of Ankara student in the Turkey Audit and Risk Management PhD Program. He graduated from Hacettepe University in Turkey, Faculty of Economics and Administrative Sciences, Department of Finance, with bachelor's and master's programs. His career began in finance and foreign trade. He is currently the Chief Audit Executive at Agricultural Credit Cooperatives of Turkey, where he started working as an assistant auditor in 2007.

Chapter 6
Beyond Fight or Flight: Alternative Risk Response Strategies

Mehmet Baha Karaçolak

Abstract The purpose of enterprise risk management (ERM) is to identify and implement strategies or actions in order to address and evaluate uncertainties, threats and possible opportunities that may affect the existence and continuity of the organization and to respond to risks as a result of this assessment. A well-implemented ERM model adds competitive value by providing reasonable assurance to the organization. The stage of developing a response to risks is the stage which, as a result, puts the organization into action. The organization's perspective and attitude towards risks are the main factors in determining risk response strategies. In this context, first of all, response strategies are determined separately for each risk. However, response strategies may differ for threats and opportunities. Once the response strategy has been decided, appropriate response actions are identified and combined into a risk response plan. This study searches whether the belief that risk strategies are limited to fight-or-flight motivation is accurate. To that end, the conceptual framework for responding to risks and alternative strategies other than fighting or avoiding risk are examined in detail. Thus, it has been revealed that the risks that are perceived only as a threat should also be considered in terms of the opportunities they may provide. It has been concluded that, contrary to the general belief, the strategies developed against risks are not only aimed at eliminating the threats caused by the risks, but they also differ in order to reveal the possible opportunities that these risks contain.

Keywords Enterprise risk management · Risk response strategies · Risk responses

M. B. Karaçolak (✉)
Social Sciences University of Ankara, Ankara, Türkiye
e-mail: mehmetbaha.karacolak@student.asbu.edu.tr

H. Kıral (ed.), *Rethinking Enterprise Risk Management*, Accounting, Finance, Sustainability, Governance & Fraud: Theory and Application,
https://doi.org/10.1007/978-981-97-5983-5_6

6.1 Introduction

In today's rapidly changing world, the number and variety of uncertainties that affect the assets and profitability of enterprises/organizations have increased. This increase has led to more competitive conditions, and it has become necessary to manage internal and external risks arising from uncertainties. Organizations use various risk management models in order to eliminate the risks they are exposed to and to make use of possible opportunities arising from risks.

The enterprise risk management (ERM) model, in which important risks are defined, assessed, managed and reported (Hunziker, 2019), brings together human resources, knowledge, process and technology, and strategic thinking competence (Marchetti, 2012) and creates value for its stakeholders and shareholders (Kucuk Yilmaz & Flouris, 2017; Quon et al., 2012). In other words, ERM is composed of various processes and tools that can evaluate opportunities that may arise from risks by managing the organizations' uncertainties (Monahan, 2012) and risks (Malik et al., 2020).

Businesses with an effective ERM in place within their organization are competitive in the long run compared to businesses that manage their risks with a non-holistic approach (Chew, 2008). Within the framework of national and international standards regarding ERM, there are three basic stages for the implementation process: (1) identifying risks, (2) analysing risks and (3) responding to risks (Raz & Hillson, 2005). At the stage of producing responses to risks, alternative response strategies are created by taking into account the costs and benefits of risks within the framework of the risk appetite and tolerance of the organization (Moeller, 2007, 2011).

Risk response strategies express what kind of an attitude will be developed towards risks in order to manage the risks identified and analysed. Management's appetite (Pehlivanlı, 2020) and tolerance (Greiman, 2013) for taking risks are the main factors in determining the attitude towards risk. Risk appetite and tolerance determine what kind of strategy to develop against risks. Response strategies are basically risk avoidance, transferring, mitigating and accepting risks (PMI, 2009).

After deciding on response strategies, risk responses are identified. Risk responses are control activities carried out within the framework of the preferred strategy for each risk. Alternative activities are determined in order to reduce threats and make use of opportunities when producing responses (Panthi et al., 2007).

Studies on risk response strategy and risk responses, in the literature, often aim to select a risk strategy or response among alternatives and put them in order and prioritize them. It is clear that those studies mostly focus on project risk management. ERM and project management disciplines follow identical steps when developing risk response strategies and response actions. In this respect, it is considered that the approaches and methods other than the work breakdown–based approach developed for project management can also be used in ERM studies. From this point of view, below is the literature within the scope of risk response strategy and determination, selection and prioritization of risk responses in project management.

Wu et al. (2018) classify approaches developed as based on methods in four main groups: regional-based, work breakdown–based, trade-off-based and optimization-based approaches. Regional-based approaches are used to show on two-dimensional diagrams the nature of control activities according to the area where the risk is located. In their study, Datta and Mukherjee (2001) created a two-dimensional matrix based on the externality of risks and their proximity in terms of time, to be used by the project risk manager when deciding on the risk response. Miller and Lessard (2001) developed a matrix for selecting responses to risks in large engineering projects, taking into account the nature of risk and controls on risk.

In the trade-off-based approach, the decision-maker chooses between parameters such as quality, time, effort and money. Kujawski (2002) worked on creating a risk response action set within the framework of the decision-maker's attitude towards risk, using Monte Carlo simulation. In the model they developed for the selection of optimal risk reduction strategies in construction projects by taking into account the complexity of the project and the interdependence of risks, Qazi et al. (2016) used the Expected Utility Theory, which is based on individuals' preference for the alternative they think will provide them with the most benefit under risk and uncertainty, and Bayesian networks approach, a method examining the relationship between variables by creating probabilistic conditions.

The optimization-based approach aims to find the best combination by considering various variables of control activities for risk reduction. Ben-David and Raz (2001) used optimization to create the most affordable combination of risk reduction activities based on the overlapping effects of multiple risk mitigation actions and secondary risk events. Fan et al. (2008) developed an optimization model using variables such as project size and complexity and found the response strategy with the least cost. The study of Zhang and Fan (2014) aimed to find the most appropriate solution strategy by building an optimization model on the factors of project cost, quality and project schedule. Zhang and Zuo (2016) used the MACBETH method, a technique that measures the decision maker's preference levels between options using verbal judgments to measure the interdependencies of the risks. In addition, they defined the risk aversion behavior of the decision maker using the utility function. Eventually, an optimization model including the evaluated risk dependencies and the decision maker's risk preferences was constructed. The model maximizes the decision maker's expected utility while considering budget constraints for the selection of risk response actions. Ptaszymska and Kuchta (2017) made improvements to the model developed by Zhang and Fan (2014) in order to optimize risk response strategies. Wu et al. (2019) developed an optimization model aiming to minimize the cost of risk response and the value exposed to risk in IT projects. Wang et al. (2019) aimed to optimize the simulation model developed for risk interactions to evaluate risk response decisions. Chu and Wang (2020) proposed a risk response strategy selection model based on the Gray K-shell algorithm which took into account the interrelationships of risk factors in projects. Since the work breakdown–based approach is built on project steps, approaches other than this can be evaluated within the scope of ERM studies.

Multiple-criteria decision-making techniques (MCDM) are also used to select risk response strategies. Multiple-criteria decision-making techniques are a set of methods that model the decision-making process in line with various criteria and relationships, and thus reach the most appropriate or best solution. Mousavi (2012) used the decision network, a method that shows possible solutions by branching from a point in the form of a tree structure, within the framework of various conditions in the selection of response strategies for major risks in mega projects, and the TOPSIS method, which is a MCDM method where alternatives are ranked by considering the ideal solution. Ghassemi and Darvishpour (2018) produced a three-step risk response strategy selection model which included the ANP, an MCDM technique that defines the directional relationships between criteria and options in a geothermal drilling project and ranks the alternatives from the most important to the least important within the framework of the decision-maker's assessments; DEMATEL, a method that weights the factors by using the causality relationships between the factors affecting a system; and fuzzy logic methods, a thinking approach that stretches the options that indicate certainty in classical logic and increases the options by adding uncertainty situations to the options. Zhang and Sun (2019) tried to develop a response strategy to prevent train accidents by using ANP and DEMATEL techniques in which various criteria were evaluated.

Another method is the case-based reasoning method. Fan et al. (2015) worked on developing response strategies with the case-based reasoning method. Case-based reasoning method is a problem-solving method where solutions of problems encountered in the past and similar to the current problem are used. Zhang et al. (2020) developed a method where alternative answers were formulated with the case-based reasoning method and which aimed to obtain the optimal response set with fuzzy optimization. The fuzzy optimization method is a method in which uncertainties are included, by means of a fuzzy logic approach, in the problems that can be solved using the optimization technique.

Roth et al. (2021) used structural modelling and Bayesian networks to develop and assess strategies for mitigating the effects of risks in the production planning process. Naji and Ali (2017) used fuzzy decision tree method to analyse risks arising from risk responses in construction projects. Fateminia et al. (2019) developed a model assessing the effectiveness of risk avoidance, risk neutrality and risk-prone response strategies using a fuzzy rule-based system that includes cost affordability, achievability and risk controllability variables. Razi et al. (2020) proposed a risk response and monitoring strategy based on deriving risk index and the obtained risk index in Public–Private Partnership (PPP) residential construction projects.

This study aims to provide the reader with a broad perspective by examining in detail the process of producing risk response strategies in the implementation of ERM. In this context, we will address the risk attitude, which is the main determinant when formulating risk response strategies, and the appetite and tolerance of the organization towards risk-taking. The generic risk strategies, which are the reflections of risk-taking tendencies or avoidance attitudes, will be elaborated and the studies within the scope of the relevant standards and literature on the selection of these strategies will be mentioned. The process will be concretized by providing the reader with information about risk responses, commonly called control activity in public administration and action in private sector, and about the risk response plan, which is created within the framework of risk response strategies.

To that end, the basic concepts related to the attitudes of organizations towards risk-taking will be discussed in the first part of the study. In the second part, the risk response strategies shaped around the abovementioned attitudes will be provided, and in the third part, the methods used when selecting the response strategies will be explained. In the last section, the issue of producing risk responses within the framework of preferred risk response strategies will be elaborated. This will provide the reader with a general framework for formulating risk responses.

6.2 Conceptual Framework

First, we should explain the motivations behind the process in order to explain the process of identifying responses by using risk response strategies. When selecting the approaches developed against risk in organizations, the risk appetite and tolerance of the organization and the risk attitude of individuals and groups responsible for the management stand out along with the corporate risk culture.

6.2.1 Risk Culture

The perspectives of individuals and groups who have managerial responsibility and decision-making positions on risk-taking are an important factor in formulating risk strategies. Risk culture can be expressed as institutional attitudes, norms and behaviours related to risk-taking and risk awareness (Yusuf et al., 2020).

The cultural structure of the organization, the way of doing business, the practices from the past and the attitudes of the senior management towards risk shape the risk-taking behaviours of the organizations, management and employees. Banks (2012) defines risk culture as "inner sensitivity that reflects the knowledge and respect for risk that is reflected in the daily thoughts and actions of all employees of an organization". The reflections of this culture become evident in the behaviour of the employees (Lam, 2017) and the way they do business and take decisions (Chappell, 2014).

Establishing an effective ERM depends on defining a desired risk culture within the organization (Duckert, 2011). A successful risk culture should be specific to the organization (Carrel, 2010) and in harmony with the objectives of the organization (IRM, 2012).

The development of a strong and proactive risk culture in the organization will increase the willingness to take risks. Likewise, an increase in risk appetite will contribute to the establishment of a corporate risk culture understanding (Laycock,

2014). In this respect, it can be said that risk culture and risk appetite are the phenomena that feed each other.

6.2.2 Risk Appetite

Risk appetite is "the upper limit of the risk that the organisation is willing to take" within the framework of its goals and strategies (de Getz, 2017). Risk appetite is the amount of risk the organization is willing to take actively on a risk-gain basis. Risk appetite can be expressed qualitatively or quantitatively (Crickette et al., 2012). Mentioned appetite is for obtaining a value in return (AICPA & Cho, 2018; Hopkin, 2017).

Pritchard (2015) defines risk appetite as "the level which one can digest" or "tolerate" certain types or degrees of risk, and Chapman (2012) defines it as "the amount of risk that the business is ready to tolerate at any given time". A high-level risk appetite in an organization means that risk is consciously accepted, a medium-level risk appetite indicates that as much of the risk is accepted as needed and a low-level appetite indicates that the risk is avoided as much as possible (de Getz, 2017; Louisot & Ketcham, 2014).

The concept of risk appetite is also frequently used in financial markets and expresses the willingness of the investor to undertake the financial risk with the expectation of a possible gain (ECB, 2007).

6.2.3 Risk Tolerance

The Committee of Sponsoring Organizations of the Treadway Commission (COSO) defines risk tolerance as an acceptable level of deviation in order to achieve a goal (AICPA & Cho, 2018). It shows the level of residual risk undertaken by the organization after the responses to risks (de Getz, 2017; Louisot & Ketcham, 2014).

In determining risk tolerance levels, it is important for the organization to evaluate (1) risk attitude, (2) goals and objectives, (3) capacity to manage risk, (4) ability to tolerate a possible loss and (5) cost-benefit balance stemming from risk management (Fraser & Simkins, 2010). Risk appetite is the total value of the portion of an organization's resources that can be risked. Risk appetite can be considered as a kind of investment to seize the opportunity (Hopkin, 2017). The relationship between the concepts of risk appetite, tolerance and capacity is depicted in Fig. 6.1. Exceeding the appetite threshold can be considered as a signal for the implementation of control activities. Exceeding the tolerance threshold necessitates the implementation of control activity.

Risk appetite is a strategic choice while tolerance is a tactical choice (Protiviti, 2006). In risk capacity, there is no choice or preference. It represents the total risk load that the organization can bear. Risk capacity is the maximum amount of risk

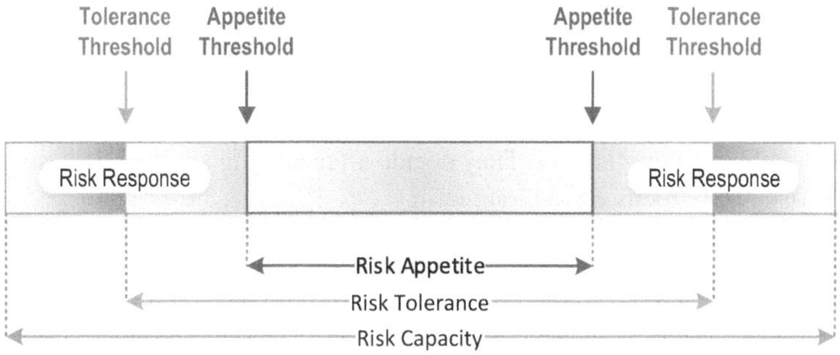

Fig. 6.1 The relationship between risk appetite, tolerance and capacity. Source: Inspired by Wu (2019)

that the organization can take in line with its goals (COSO, 2018; OGC, 2014). However, the organization does not tend to use all of this capacity or test this competence in ordinary situations. Risk capacity is an absolute limit (Banks, 2012).

6.2.4 Risk Attitude

Risk attitude is a positive, negative or neutral approach developed towards risk as a result of risk assessment (Lark, 2015; Louisot & Ketcham, 2014). As is the case in individuals, organizations also have different risk attitudes. This difference in risk attitudes may lead to different behaviours against risks (Wauters et al., 2014).

Factors such as the management's approach to risk, the industry and the market in which the organization operates in have a role in shaping the risk attitudes of organizations (Hopkin, 2017). PMI[1] states that, in addition to other factors, the risk attitudes of individuals or organizations are affected by three basic factors: risk appetite, tolerance and tolerance threshold (PMI, 2013). Risk attitude can be considered as a function of risk appetite, tolerance and tolerance threshold.

Individuals may exhibit different risk attitudes under different risk conditions. Hillson (2009) groups the attitude patterns towards risks as (1) risk aversion, (2) risk seeking, (3) risk tolerance and (4) risk neutrality. Moran (2014) explains these attitudes as follows.

- Individuals and groups with a risk-avoidant attitude do not like uncertainty and do not want to take risks in uncertain situations. Thus, they ignore possible opportunities that risks may bring. Risk-avoidant individuals tend to overreact to threats and rather underreact to opportunities and almost ignore them.

[1] PMI is an acronym used to refer to Project Management Institute, a globally known and recognized organization.

- Risk-tolerant individuals and groups are indifferent to risks and tend to ignore and disregard the risks. They fail to appreciate the seriousness of opportunities and threats.
- Risk-neutral individuals and groups calculate the possible returns and costs of the risk before taking the risk. They decide after making an objective assessment of the risk. They focus on the long term.
- Individuals and groups with a risk-seeking attitude do not hesitate to take action and want to make use of possible opportunities. They tend to underestimate the threats and exaggerate opportunities.

6.3 Risk Response Strategies

Risk response strategies are the formalized form of the risk attitude towards the identified risk. The attitudes of individuals and groups towards risk shape the perspective about risk throughout the organization. Risk response is the action taken for risks in line with the decided response strategies. Different risk attitudes affect the development and implementation of risk strategies and responses in different ways. Mentioned effects are provided in Table 6.1 (Hillson, 2009).

Table 6.1 clearly shows that the level of aggression in the strategies preferred in the formulation of response strategies is highest in risk-avoidant and risk-seeking individuals, and lowest in risk-tolerant individuals. It can be said that risk-neutral individuals are partially aggressive in their strategy selection.

Table 6.1 Effects of different risk attitudes on the Corporate Risk Management (CRM) implementation processes

Implementation step	Risk attitudes			
	Risk avoidant	Risk tolerant	Risk neutral	Risk-seeking
Formulating risk response strategies	Tend to ignore/ accept opportunities by choosing proactive and aggressive response strategies for threats	Tend to ignore the risks and accept them as they are	Aggressive against imminent risks, tend to accept long-term ones (temporal closeness)	Tend to ignore/accept the threats by choosing proactive and aggressive response strategies for opportunities
Implementing risk response strategies	Not focusing on actions for opportunities, consciously preferring measures to avoid and reduce risk	Ignoring risk responses and focusing on the business/ process with risk itself	Focusing on responses to imminent risks	Ignoring the activities against threats and consciously preferring the activities which will enable them to make use of the opportunities

Source: Hillson (2009)

The development of response strategies for risks is carried out through one or more of the options provided below (Lark, 2015).

- Reviewing, ending or not starting at all the action or situation that causes the risk, if it can be intervened
- Accepting the risk to seize an opportunity that the risk brings along
- Changing the probability of occurrence of the risk or the effect of its consequences
- Transferring the risk to other parties
- Acknowledging the existence of the risk after being informed about it

There is no uniformly agreed definition of the terms "risk response strategy", "risk response" and "risk treatment" in the literature. These concepts differ in terms of meaning, action or process they refer to in different studies, standards and frameworks (see Table 6.2).

As indicated in Table 6.2, the meanings attributed to the concepts of risk treatment, risk response strategy and risk response differ in various sources. However, overall, it is understood that risk treatment refers to risk response strategy and risk responses; risk strategy refers to approaches such as avoidance and reduction; and risk response/response action and control activity refer to the actual practices carried out against the risk.

In this study, risk response strategy is used to refer to the attitude towards risk, and the concepts of control activity, response and measure are used to refer to the actions developed and implemented within the framework of these strategies.

Table 6.2 The meaning of risk treatment, response strategy and response concepts in various studies

Study	Use
Robertson (2005)	Risk response and risk treatment are synonymous and refer to both strategies and control activities
Banaitiene (2012), Cendrowski and Mair (2009), Chapman (2012), COSO (2018), Greiman (2013), Hillson (2003), Marchetti (2012), Passenheim (2013), PMI (2013), Protiviti (2006), Raczkowski (2017), Steinberg (2011)	Risk response strategies refer to approaches such as avoidance and reduction; risk response/response action refers to control activities
Bissonette (2016), BSI (2011), Cooper et al. (2005), Green (2016), ISO (2009), Lark et al. (2015), McLaughlin (2006), Yoe (2019)	Risk treatment refers to both avoidance and reduction approaches and control activities
Pinto (2015), Scherling (2016)	Risk treatment refers to approaches such as avoidance and reduction while control activities refer to risk measures

Source: Generated by the author

6.3.1 Risk Response Strategies in Risk Management Standards and Frameworks

BS 31100 (2011), ISO 31000 (2009) and AZ/NZS 4360 (2004) risk management standards and COSO (2018), PMI Project Management (2009), PRINCE2 (Projects IN Controlled Environments), Orange Book[2] (The Orange Book, 2020), APM[3] Project Management (2017) and M_o_R (Management of Risk Guidance for Practitioners, 2010) frameworks were examined to explain risk response strategies. Different terminologies are used in the said documents for the strategies, although they are essentially the same. Response strategies for threats and opportunities included in the abovementioned documents are presented in Tables 6.3 and 6.4, grouped thematically in terms of their meaning, action or process.

The strategies in the standard and framework documents examined within the scope of the study are apparently grouped under seven themes: avoidance, reduction, acceptance, return, emergency and contingencies, transfer and sharing.

Return plans step in when the emergency and contingency plan does not produce the desired result or becomes ineffective. A return plan is a backup of emergency and contingency plans. In the PRINCE2 and APM frameworks, return planning is expressed as a response strategy.

Table 6.3 Risk response strategies for threats included in standard and framework documents[a]

	Thematic strategy groups						
Standard/framework	Avoid	Reduce	Accept	Emergency and contingency	Return	Transfer	Share
COSO (2018)	Avoid	Reduce	Accept			Share	
BS 31100 (2011)	Avoid	Change	Retain			Share	
ISO 31000 (2009)	Avoid	Reduce	Retain			Share	
PMI (2009)	Avoid	Mitigate	Accept			Transfer	
PRINCE2 (2017)	Avoid	Reduce	Accept		Return	Transfer	Share
Orange Book (2020)	Avoid	Mitigate	Accept			Transfer	
APM (2017)	Avoid	Reduce	Accept		Return	Transfer	
AZ/NZS 4360 (2004)	Avoid	Reduce	Retain			Share	
M_o_R (2010)	Avoid	Reduce	Accept	Emergency and contingency		Transfer	Share

Source: Adapted from Denney (2020)

[a] Risk response strategies are not clearly named in ISO 31000 and the Orange Book. Strategies are named by the author as they are commonly accepted, taking into account the explanations in the risk response options section

[2] The Orange Book is a risk management framework prepared by the UK Government to explain the principles and concepts related to risk management.

[3] APM is an acronym used to refer to the Association for Project Management, a globally known and recognized organization in the field of project management.

Table 6.4 Risk response strategies for opportunities in standard and framework documents

	Thematic strategy groups			
Standard/framework	Exploit	Enhance	Accept	Share
COSO (2018)	Follow			
BS 31100 (2011)	Seek	Change		
ISO 31000 (2009)	Follow			
PMI (2009)	Exploit	Enhance	Accept	Share
PRINCE2 (2017)	Exploit	Enhance	Reject	Share
The Orange Book (2020)	Follow			
APM (2017)	Exploit	Enhance	Accept	Share
AZ/NZS 4360 (2004)	Seek	Enhance	Accept	Share
M_o_R (2010)	Exploit	Enhance		

Source: Adapted from Denney (2020)

In the framework of M_o_R, it is mentioned that while losses arising from possible risks are transferred, possible opportunities can also be transferred, although it is not very common. The know-how and patents of products, methods, etc. obtained as a result of the R&D activities carried out by the manufacturer in order to manufacture a high-risk part with the desired qualities through outsourcing can be given as examples of the transfer of opportunity.

Transfer and sharing strategies are separated in PRINCE2 and M_o_R frameworks. In the aforementioned frameworks, the sharing strategy refers to the implementation of practices such as partnership and cooperation in order to share the possible consequences of the assumed risk between the parties.

The replace strategy in BS 31100 and the exploit strategy in the M_o_R approach are response strategies for both threats and opportunities. Since the strategies for threats and opportunities are shown in separate tables in Tables 6.3 and 6.4, the mentioned two strategies are included in both tables.

Return is included as a response strategy in the PRINCE2 and APM frameworks and emergency and contingency planning are included as response strategies in the M_o_R frameworks, unlike other standards and frameworks. In ISO 31000, secondary risks are covered implicitly as monitoring of residual risks and taking action when necessary, while the aforementioned plans are not mentioned in COSO. It is clear in Table 6.4 that risk response strategies for opportunities are grouped under four themes: exploitation, reproduction, acceptance and sharing.

The Committee of Sponsoring Organizations of the Treadway Commission's follow strategy and seek strategy as included in BS 31100 and AZ/NZS 4360 standards imply that certain risk responses can be implemented because responses to risks have the potential to bring new opportunities. Producing the relevant response in order to obtain the opportunity is only possible with the occurrence of the risk. Mentioned documents makes no reference to increasing the probability and impact values of the risk that will mediate the emergence of the opportunity. However, these strategies are indicated among the strategies under the exploit theme due to the strong desire for risk to occur.

The BS 31100 and ISO 31000 standards and the Orange Book do not differentiate between exploit and enhance strategies, rather emphasize overall increasing probability in order to seize the opportunity. In enhance strategies, the probability and effect are increased in order to obtain the opportunity, while in exploit themed strategies, only the probability value of the risk is increased in order to obtain the opportunity absolutely. This difference is considered in the PMI, PRINCE2, APM and M_o_R approaches, and exploit and enhance are expressed as two different strategies. And only the enhance strategy is mentioned in the AZ/NZS 4360 standard.

The reject strategy of the PRINCE2 framework refers to not taking any action despite the presence of opportunity. It is essentially a passive accept strategy. Share strategies refer to partnership and cooperation to confront risks with a view to increasing the chances of seizing opportunities.

It has been emphasized many times in COSO, ISO 31000 and Orange Book that risks can have positive outcomes besides threats and that risks have the potential to create opportunities. However, risk response strategies for opportunities were not diversified in line with the emphasis made and remained limited to the exploit strategy. It can be thought that the COSO framework was written with a rather protective approach since it is needed as a result of major scandals. However, the repeated mention of the concept of opportunity invalidates the belief that COSO is more inclined to highlight threats compared to opportunities, stemming from its conservative and protectionist nature. Therefore, it can be concluded that not enough attention is attached to strategies for opportunities in these three documents, including the COSO.

6.3.2 Risk Response Strategies

Risk response strategies are approaches defined to express that there is a conscious awareness of risks and a risk-specific attitude is developed in the organization. Cooper et al. (2005) classified risk response strategies as (1) avoid and prevent loss, (2) reduce, (3) share, (4) underwrite and (5) maintain. There are seven response strategies in the study by Goncalves and Heda (2014), namely avoid, transfer and reduce strategies to respond to threats as well as exploit, share, enhance or enrich strategies to seize the opportunities and accept strategy which can be included in both groups. Greiman (2013) and Borghesi and Gaudenzi (2013) classify strategies as avoid, prevent, reduce, separate, copy and transfer strategies.

There are also studies, in the literature, which use the concepts of positive or negative risks, considering the possible opportunities that the risks will provide and the possible dangers they will cause (Denney, 2020). In terms of their effects, it has been stated that the avoid, transfer, share and remove strategies for risk have a negative character, while the maintain and diversify strategies have a positive character (Strelnik, 2016).

Ahmadi-Javid et al. (2020) evaluated risk strategies according to their proactive and reactive nature. He has grouped the following strategies as proactive strategies:

avoid, reduce and transfer strategies for negative risks (threats) and exploit, enhance and share strategies for positive risks. It has been emphasized that the accept strategy for negative risks (threats) has a reactive nature. Strelnik (2016) defined the strategies implemented before the risk has occurred as proactive, and the strategies implemented after the occurrence of the risk and its effects as reactive strategies.

Accept strategies are strategies that come into play following the occurrence of the risk. An active accept strategy includes actions to ensure business continuity after the risk has occurred. In the passive acceptance strategy, the risk that has occurred is treated as if it has never happened and no action is taken regarding the effects of the risk.

Regardless of whether it is implemented before or after a risk occurs, the strategies applied are active if the response to the risk, in the form of either action or inaction, is defined before the risk occurs. In this respect, accept strategies, be it whether active or passive acceptance, are active because they are defined before the risk occurs. Strategies developed for undefined risks, about which no information is known until they occur, are passive in character. Therefore, whatever the situational strategies may be, they are passive in character.

Response strategies for risks in different studies, standards and frameworks on risk management are provided in Fig. 6.2. The following subsections address the risk response strategies included in the largest set, taking into account the different classifications in various sources.

Tables 6.3 and 6.4 display emergency and contingency planning and return planning as response strategies. However, since the aforementioned planning studies are not considered as independent strategies by international standards, they are not shown as separate strategies in Fig. 6.2, and they are not included as separate strategies in the following sections where response strategies are elaborated.

6.3.2.1 Risk Strategies for Threats

As displayed in Fig. 6.2, avoid, reduce, transfer, active and passive acceptance, share, separate, copy and diversify are strategies for threats and are proactive in character. Accept strategies are reactive strategies.

Avoid/Terminate Strategy

Risk avoidance refers to never starting an activity that may create risk (Spedding & Rose, 2008) or ending an existing risky activity (COSO, 2004). An example of a risk avoidance strategy is that an enterprise terminates its operations in a certain geographical area, or that a company planning to establish a nuclear power plant abandons this plan when it takes into account the existing human resources, experience and limited capital.

This strategy is expressed as a single strategy in the form of risk avoidance and risk termination in the COSO (2018) framework and BS 31100 (2011) and ISO 31000 (2009) risk management standards. Organizations preferring this strategy prioritize risk avoidance over the potential opportunities that risk will bring when

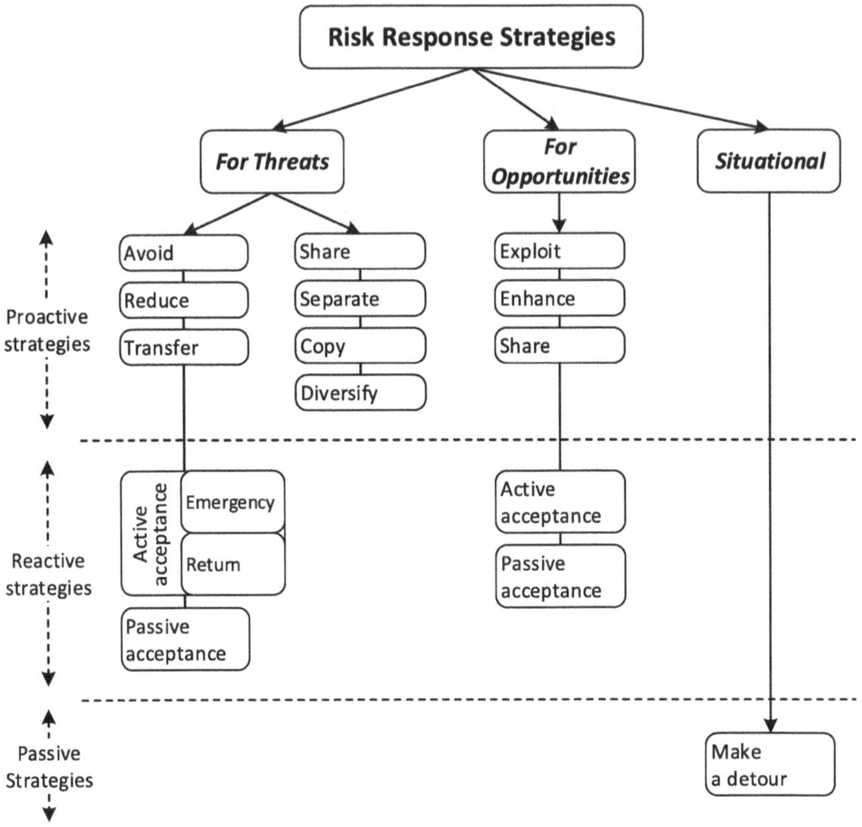

Fig. 6.2 Risk response strategies (strategies for threats are divided into two branches for ease of display). Source: Generated by the author

producing a response to the risk. With a proactive approach to ensure this, measures to avoid risk are preferred (Hisrich & Ramadani, 2017). The difficulty in implementing the avoidance strategy is that the strategy is generally preferred after experiencing the risk along with its negative consequences (Moeller, 2011). Choosing a risk avoidance strategy may require changes to the entire business plan.

Reduce Strategy
The risk reduction strategy refers to reducing the severity of the loss that may occur if the risk occurs (Spedding & Rose, 2008). In a reduce strategy, measures are developed to reduce both the probability of the risk and its impact (COSO, 2004). Thus, the size of the risk is changed (Hillson, 2003). For example, turning to robot technology is a reduce strategy in order to reduce possible occupational safety risks that may arise from the human factor. Many controls already carried out in day-to-day operational work are the result of risk reduction strategies.

Transfer Strategy
Transferring the risk means transferring the responsibility to the other party, such as insurance companies, in case of the occurrence of the risk (Hisrich & Ramadani, 2017). Insuring the factory against the risk of fire is an example of this strategy.

Outsourcing for sensitive businesses requiring expertise is also a transfer strategy. Hedging in financial transactions is a transfer method as well (Spedding & Rose, 2008).

Transferring risk also has a cost. By paying this price, the organization buys the compensation for the loss that will occur in case of the occurrence of the risk. Cost-benefit analysis is important in making this decision. This strategy is preferred in cases where the cost of the loss to occur in the event of the occurrence of the risk is higher than the cost of the transfer (Bozkurt, 2010). The transfer of risk to the other party does not cause any change in the nature of the risk (Passenheim, 2013). The probability of occurrence of the risk and the impact value are the same. The risk here is assuming of it by the other party often through a contract.

Accept Strategy

The acceptance strategy refers to accepting the risk and its consequences. In this strategy, no measures are taken to reduce the possibility or impact of the risk (Spedding & Rose, 2008). In other words, it is an inertial strategy (Moeller, 2011). An example of a risk avoidance strategy is accepting the risk of robbery rather than installing an alarm system at costs that exceed the total cost of the merchandise in a small flower shop (Hisrich & Ramadani, 2017).

The probability and impact of the risk and the risk tolerance of the organization are evaluated together when making the decision to accept the risk (Moeller, 2011). The cost-benefit balance of the measures to be taken to avoid or reduce the risk is also important when selecting this strategy. It is a risk strategy that can be applied to relatively simple and small-scale risks where the cost of remediation is higher than the benefit or harm to be caused by the risk (Spedding & Rose, 2008).

In the acceptance strategy, making a financial provision for possible low-scale losses that will occur in the event of the occurrence of the risk makes it easier to ensure business continuity by using this provision for losses (Passenheim, 2013). This method is called the active acceptance strategy. As for the passive acceptance strategy, the risk is completely ignored and nothing is done against the possibility of its occurrence (Cretu et al., 2011).

Preferred response strategies for threats aim to reduce or eliminate the likelihood, impact, or both of risks. However, a risk that is already known and defined in the risk inventory may occur and/or the measures taken may not have the desired effect. In such cases, emergency planning and return planning methods can be used to reduce the negative impact and ensure business continuity. The first of these is "emergency and contingency planning" regarding the preparation made before the occurrence of the accepted risk. Emergency plans are included in the active acceptance strategy (Keshk et al., 2018). The other one is the plan known as "return plan" or "Plan B", which is prepared for secondary risks that may arise due to the inadequacy of the emergency plan or stem from the measures in the emergency plan (Chung, 2017).

Share Strategies

Risk-sharing strategy is a strategy that involves more than one party and is built on costs. If the cost of the action subject to the risk is lower than the planned costs, the loss is shared when it is more than the gain arising from the difference (Turley, 2010). R&D studies, joint ventures to expand the market (Taplin, 2005) or the creation of partnerships such as consortiums for very high-cost projects can be given as examples of risk sharing.

It is a strategy that addresses both opportunities and threats. It is highly preferred in supply chain processes. It is the same as the transfer strategy in standards and frameworks except for PRINCE2 (2010) and M_o_R (2010).

The contract between the parties does not transfer the risk itself from one to the other, rather it aims to ensure that the risk is shared between the parties (Cooper et al., 2005). As for the sharing strategy, a possible harm is transferred from the individual to the group (Moosa, 2007). This way, the possible consequences of the risk are distributed among the parties (Bekefi et al., 2008).

Unbundle Strategy

As for the unbundle strategy, the effect of possible loss on other assets is isolated. The unbundle strategy aims at preventing the concentration of physical and human resources and work in a single location, in the market or on a work or project. The concentration of all assets at a single point will cause a possible loss to have a severe impact in the event of the occurrence of the risk (Borghesi & Gaudenzi, 2013). Unbundling is a strategy to reduce risk by separating the corporate assets, business segments or debts of businesses (Hidayat, 2016). This strategy can be used against disasters such as fire and flood and location-based risks.

Copy Strategy

As for the copy strategy, critical information, resources and competencies are backed up (Borghesi & Gaudenzi, 2013). It is similar to the unbundle strategy in that it reduces reliance on a single entity. Backing up electronic information on different servers and adopting shadow personnel practice can be given as examples of this strategy.

Diversify Strategy

The diversify strategy aims to reduce the severity of the loss caused by singularity by expanding the possible losses to various projects, businesses, products, markets and locations (Borghesi & Gaudenzi, 2013). The possible impact of the risk is distributed to different operations and units, thereby reducing the impact value (Spedding & Rose, 2008). While the unbundle strategy aims to reduce the loss by isolating the possible effect of the risk, the diversify strategy aims to reduce the loss by spreading the possible effect.

6.3.2.2 Risk Response Strategies for Opportunities

As can be seen in Fig. 6.2, exploit, enhance and share strategies for opportunities are proactive strategies, while the accept strategy is reactive. Opportunity strategies are acceptance strategies. When considering these risk strategies, it should be kept in mind that risk is not always an event producing negative results and that risk can lead to positive results. Positive risk actually means the realization of a chance.

Exploit Strategy

Exploit strategy aims at increasing the probability of occurrence of risks with high potential opportunities (Cretu et al., 2011). In terms of its purpose, it is the opposite of the avoidance strategy (Şakar, 2020).

Exploit strategy requires time and financial resources, and it is aimed to achieve greater gains with the cost incurred. In order to reach the opportunity faster, resources are transferred to the relevant direction. This strategy can be preferred for risks that may have positive effects based on its results (PMI, 2013). For instance, it has been announced that the company can get paid earlier if the project currently being undertaken can be completed quickly. In order to seize this opportunity, the company has decided to hire a few more staff at additional expense.

Enhance Strategy

The enhance strategy focuses on increasing the realization probability of the opportunity. The speed and chance of obtaining the opportunity are increased by enhancing the probability of the risk.

It is similar to the exploit strategy in terms of increasing the probability of the risk. The enhance strategy aims to realize the opportunity by increasing the probability of its occurrence. Yet the opportunity may not come true. In the exploit strategy, on the other hand, the focus is on increasing the probability of occurrence of the risk in order to absolutely obtain the opportunity. It is an aggressive method compared to the enhance strategy (Hutchings, 2017). If an analogy is made, the enhance strategy is the opposite of the reduce strategy while the exploit strategy is the opposite of the avoid/terminate strategy (Usmani, 2020).

Share Strategy

The purpose of risk sharing is to create opportunity (Banaitiene, 2012). Cooperation should be made with the other party by waiving a part of the opportunity in order to increase the probability of obtaining the opportunity provided by the risk. It is a win–win situation (Cretu et al., 2011). For instance, undertaking a job that requires technical competence together with a stakeholder who is competent and experienced in this field will reduce the risk (Şakar, 2020).

The size of the opportunity plays an important role in the choice of strategy. The enhance strategy is preferred for large opportunities while the accept or exploit strategy is preferred in the event of small or relatively insignificant opportunities.

Accept Strategy

This strategy recognizes the consequences of risk as well as its opportunities. In the passive acceptance strategy, there is no intention of any action in case the opportunity comes true. In the active acceptance strategy, there are actions that are intended to be performed in case the opportunity occurs (Pritchard, 2015).

6.3.2.3 Situational Risk Response Strategies

Sometimes, instant risks that are not defined in the risk inventory may occur. Until the occurrence of the risks in question, there is no information about them, and they happen unexpectedly. "Detour" strategy, a.k.a. "bypass" strategy, which includes unplanned measures against such risks, is implemented (Konyalı, 2016). Walk around is a passive approach to recovering from the current situation after the risk has occurred.

6.3.3 Selecting Risk Response Strategies

The process of determining the risk response should consist of two separate stages, namely identifying strategies and defining control activities within the framework of these strategies (Hillson, 2003). As for the selection of risk response strategies, a strategy should be chosen that is appropriate to the nature of each risk and the organization's attitude towards risk. In order to achieve this, strategy alternatives need to be analysed in depth.

Management builds its strategy in line with one or a combination of response strategies for each of the risks. The compliance of the strategy with the risk appetite of the organization (Moeller, 2011), the efficiency of the strategy in terms of cost-benefit (Yoe, 2019) and the possible control activities to be determined subsequently (Pinto, 2015) should be considered when selecting a strategy.

Hillson (2009) stated that when selecting a strategy, importance should be attached to the adequacy of resources, the cost-effectiveness of taking the risk, the probability and magnitude of the impact, and the potential of the response to cause secondary risks. Protiviti (2006), on the other hand, states that the strategy's compliance with and the impact on the goals and objectives of the organization, the risk management competence of the organization, the validity/impact period of the risk, the opportunity cost of taking immediate action when compared to waiting, the magnitude of residual risks, and the compliance with the response strategies chosen for other risks are factors that should be considered by the management when developing alternative strategies. Selecting of risk response strategy is influenced by the organization's risk appetite and tolerance, risk culture, and management's expertise and experience (Gericke et al., 2009).

6.4 Risk Responses

Identifying response strategies for risks is followed by identifying risk response actions and formulating a plan. Risk response actions are also called control activities.

6.4.1 What Is Risk Response?

Risk response is the actions planned and performed against risks in line with the determined risk strategies. Risk response may be referred to as control activities, activity or action. The risk response process consists of selecting and implementing alternatives using the options to implement a new activity or modify an already implemented control activity to change the possible consequences of risks (Lark, 2015).

If the residual risks have exceeded the risk tolerance level that the organization can accept, the management selects an appropriate response or set of responses from among the alternatives to bring the risks below the tolerance level (AICPA, 2018). The risk response process includes the identification and selection of alternative control activities and the implementation of the selected control (Fraser & Simkins, 2010).

The management analyses the entire portfolio to ensure that the total impact of risks in the risk portfolio does not exceed the organization's overall risk tolerance level. While determining the appropriate risk response, evaluations are made in terms of the cost-benefit for the proposed alternatives and the amount of resources needed to reduce the risk.

6.4.2 Types of Risk Responses

The purpose of risk responses is primarily to ensure that the risk does not occur. If the organization fails to prevent the risk and thus the risk occurs, minimizing the impact of the risk is the secondary objective. To that end, four different basic risk responses are applied: guiding, preventive, detective and corrective (Robertson, 2005).

Directive controls are applied to display threat avoidance behaviour and to achieve a certain result. The instructions, procedures and actions defined for the execution of the business process have a guiding nature (Chapelle, 2019) and undertake the task of guidance (Koletar, 2011).

Preventive control activities are activities aimed at eliminating the possibility of the occurrence of the risk (Gericke et al., 2009). These controls deal with possible problems likely to be encountered in the future and aim to maintain the continuity of the operating system, process or business in the same way as they are.

Assessments included in the literature on what detective control activities are differ (Chapelle, 2019). According to Moran (2014), detective control activities step in during or immediately after a risk occurs, and thus help reduce the effects of the risk by detecting the risk at the first moment. In this context, the smoke detector is a detective control activity.

On the other hand, Lam (2017) and Robertson (2005) define these controls as controls designed to detect possible negative consequences before the risk occurs.

In line with this definition, the commissioning of early warning systems against possible hacking is a detective control activity.

Corrective activities are activities aimed at eliminating the impact of the occurred risk (Gericke et al., 2009). They aim to solve the problems at that point. Activities such as taking backups and creating plans to ensure business continuity are corrective control activities.

Anderson (2014) mentions complementary control activities in addition to the abovementioned four types of activities. These activities are controls that are not sufficient on their own, but will help reduce risk when used in conjunction with other control activities.

Olawale and Sun (2010) add organizational controls to the controls mentioned above. Organizational control activities are those that originate from the culture and customs of the organization. A culture of working together and making collaborations can be an example of organizational control activities.

Implementation of the principle of separation of duties in critical business processes is an example of preventive control activities; recovery activities to ensure business continuity are examples of corrective control activities; security policy measures are examples of guiding control activities and applications for monitoring purposes are examples of detective control activities (Moran, 2014).

Gericke et al. (2009) make a classification based on the planning and execution time of the control activity. Proactive control activities are those that are planned before the risk occurs and that are carried out before or after the event to mitigate possible impact. Reactive control activities are the activities planned after the occurrence of the risk and carried out to mitigate the impact.

Engemann and Henderson (2012) group control activities according to the order in which they are performed. Accordingly, preventive actions against the occurrence of the risk are prioritized. However, this is followed by detective activities predetermining the possibility of the occurrence of the risk considering that the possibility increases due to insufficient preventive activities. In the final stage, once the risk occurs, corrective actions are taken to mitigate the impact.

6.4.3 Assessing Response Alternatives and Selection

After determining the control activities for the risks, it is important which activities to choose against the risks posing a threat. Residual risks are analysed and responses are produced so that the organization stays within the framework of its risk appetite and tolerance. The purpose of the responses is to take the residual risk below the tolerable level. Management can consider past experiences and possible future scenarios when analysing responses (COSO, 2004).

In order to select the control activity, Hopkin (2017) establishes a relationship between risk response strategies and control activity types, taking into account the impact and probability values, as seen in the matrix in Fig. 6.3.

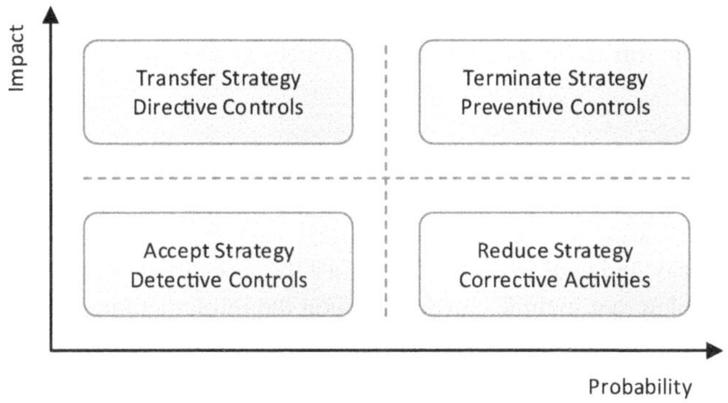

Fig. 6.3 Selecting controls according to strategies. Source: Hopkin (2017)

According to this matrix, (1) terminate strategy and mostly preventive control activities should be implemented in cases where the probability and impact of the risk is high, (2) transfer strategy and mostly guiding control activities should be implemented in cases of low probability and high impact, (3) reduce strategy and mostly corrective control activities should be implemented in cases of high probability but low impact, and (4) accept strategy and mostly detective control activities should be implemented where both the probability and the impact are low.

When developing control activities for opportunities and threats, the ability of these activities to produce the expected impact should be considered. Pojasek (2017) lists the criteria that can be used to evaluate the effectiveness of the response as follows: (1) First of all, the response must be proportional and appropriate to the size of the risk. (2) The money, effort and time spent to respond should not exceed the loss caused by the risk. (3) In terms of the urgency of the risk response, the timing of the response should be appropriate to the circumstances. (4) The response must be practical and realistic in terms of the capacity and competence of the organization. (5) A single employee should be identified as the main responsible person for the response. (6) The views of the stakeholders should also be taken into account in producing the response within the framework of the size of the risk. Hillson (2003) stated that the responses should be evaluated in accordance with these criteria in terms of their expected impact before they are implemented since a resource will be used, namely effort, time and money.

6.4.4 *When to Take Action?*

Actions developed against risks are implemented within the framework of the position of the impact or probability values of the risks to the risk thresholds defined by the organization. The first of these thresholds is the risk appetite value. Exceeding risk appetite can be considered as the first signal for the organization to create a risk response. At this point, an action can be defined and implemented. The second threshold is the risk tolerance value. If the tolerance value is exceeded, the organization must take action and implement a control activity (Benjamin, 2017).

6.4.5 Developing and Implementing Risk Response Plans

When the strategy and control activities against the risks are determined, it is necessary to draft a plan that includes information on the implementation of these activities. When drafting a risk response plan, some factors should be taken into account in order to ensure the expected impact and investment in responses (Zhang & Guan, 2021).

The event that will trigger the occurrence of the risk and the risk owner, who will be responsible for monitoring this event and activating this emergency plan when the risk occurs, should also be included in the plan (Kendrick, 2015). The plan should include identified risks, responsibilities, risk analyses and risk responses along with the implementation dates and contingency plans. AZ/NZS (2005) and Keyes (2018) add to these the performance expected from the response in terms of effectiveness, feasibility and reliability. Yoe (2019) states that the reason for choosing the response, limitations to the application, resources, and details about reporting and monitoring should also be included in the plan. The secondary risks, possible opportunities and threats that the activities planned to be included in the plan will create when they are carried out should also be defined when drafting the plan (OGC, 2014). The stage of implementing and monitoring of control activities begins once the risk response plan is prepared and approved by the senior management.

6.5 Conclusion

This study discusses the accuracy of the perception that the response strategies in risk management are developed for defence purposes as a result of focusing only on the threat dimension of the perceived risk by making an analogy with the fight or flight response. In the first place, the equivalents of sociological and psychological concepts of risk in ERM are discussed, and attitudes that prevent enterprises/organizations from taking risks or lead them to risk are examined. In the second stage, the effects of these risk attitudes on strategy formation and possible strategies are addressed. In the last part, the responses and their qualities that enable the execution of response strategies are emphasized. Completeness is achieved in the process from attitude and thought to action by elaborating the aforementioned three stages.

At this stage, fight or flight strategies for risk correspond to risk reduction and risk avoidance strategies with their generic names. Both strategies are strategies developed against threats. The common perception that an unfavourable outcome will occur regarding the risks involuntarily leads the minds to take a protective position, which causes our perspective on risk to evolve into a negative perception over time and become fixed this way.

However, it is a fact that risks have the potential to cause a threat due to their consequences, as well as to open a door to an opportunity. In some studies on this subject, risks are classified as risks with negative and positive characteristics. However, the fact that the established perception focuses only on the negative dimension of risk prevents making use of the opportunity part.

Strategies currently in use indicate that this perception is wrong. As a matter of fact, there are other strategies for threats other than reduce and avoid, as well as strategies such as enhance, exploit and share for seizing opportunities. The fact that the awareness and practical use of strategies for opportunities is relatively limited compared to the strategies for threats can be considered as the reason for misperception. Therefore, it can be said that risk response strategies have gained new dimensions beyond fight or flight behaviours.

On the other hand, it is apparent, throughout the study, that different thoughts and interpretations have been developed for some concepts related to the field of ERM. The first one is that the concepts of risk appetite and tolerance are often misunderstood and misdefined. However, appetite refers to the willingness to be active in terms of the opportunity to be obtained as a result of the occurrence of the event, and risk tolerance refers to the endurance level which it can bear or stand against in line with the existing control activities in relation to the threats that may arise as a result of the occurrence of the event. Once the appetite level is exceeded, the tolerance field begins. Exceeding the tolerance requires taking measures against the damage the event will probably cause.

Another point is that there is a differentiation in the literature regarding the concepts of risk response strategy, risk treatment and risk response. Risk response strategies should be defined as formed and generic versions of risk attitude while risk responses should be defined as actions taken to implement strategies. The concept of risk treatment can be considered as an umbrella concept that includes both strategies and response actions.

It is observed that even the response strategies within the same thematic group in the international standards and frameworks discussed for the purpose of explaining risk response strategies differ in terms of both terminology and meaning, action or process. For instance, emergence and contingency planning is also addressed in the change strategy in BS 31100, the accept strategy in the PMI and the mitigate strategy in the Orange Book. Emergency and contingency planning is considered as a response strategy within the framework of M_o_R, and it is explained under a separate heading in the AZ/NZS 4360 standard, other than response strategies. However, the strategies are expected not to be that different in terms of their content in the standards and frameworks in question which have the same purpose. It is important to reveal the thought and understanding underlying this difference apparent in the mentioned documents.

Consequently, the facts that the risks can have negative or positive results, generic threat and opportunity strategies have been developed for these results and the strategies go beyond the dimension of fight or flight, yet the opportunity dimension is not sufficiently focused on due to the negative character of the established perceptions of risk and that the strategies for opportunities are rarely used in practice are considered to be the reasons for ignoring these strategies. On the other hand, it is observed that common mistakes are encountered in the interpretation of risk appetite and tolerance, and there are differences in the use of risk treatment, risk response strategies and risk response concepts in the literature and in various standards and frameworks.

References

Ahmadi-Javid, A., Fateminia, S. H., & Gemünden, H. G. (2020). A method for risk response planning in project portfolio management. *Project Management Journal, 51*(1), 77–95. https://doi.org/10.1177/8756972819866577

AICPA. (2018). *Practice aid—Enterprise risk management—guidance for practical implementation and assessment, 2018*. Place of publication not identified. Wiley. https://onlinelibrary.wiley.com/doi/book/10.1002/9781119572794 (Accessed on September 15, 2024)

AICPA, & Cho, S. (2018). *Practice Aid—Enterprise Risk Management—Guidance For Practical Implementation and Assessment, 2018. Place of publication not identified*. Wiley. https://doi.org/10.1002/9781119572794. (Accessed on September 15, 2024)

Anderson, E. (2014). *Business risk management: Models and analysis*. Wiley (Anderson)

APM (2017) Managing risk and issues—The Projex Academy | PRINCE2 PMP APM LEAN6SIGMA. (t.y.). Retrieved 15.06.2021., from https://www.projex.com/apm-managing-risk-and-issues

AZ/NZS. (2005). *Risk management guidelines: Companion to AS/NZS 4360:2004: handbook*. Standards Australia International.

Banaitiene, N. (Ed.). (2012). Risk management—Current issues and challenges. *InTech*. https://doi.org/10.5772/2568

Banks, E. (2012). *Risk culture*. Palgrave Macmillan UK. https://doi.org/10.1057/9781137263728

Bekefi, T., Epstein, M. J., & Yuthas, K. (2008). *Management accounting guideline managing opportunities and risks*. The Society of Management Accountants of Canada, the American Institute of Certified Public Accountants and The Chartered Institute of Management Accountants.

Ben-David, I., & Raz, T. (2001). An integrated approach for risk response development in project planning. *Journal of the Operational Research Society, 52*(1), 14–25. https://doi.org/10.1057/palgrave.jors.2601029

Benjamin, A. S. (2017). *Enterprise risk and opportunity management: Concepts and step-by-step examples for pioneering scientific and technical organizations. Wiley finance*. Wiley.

Bissonette, M. (2016). *Project risk management: A practical implementation approach*. Project Management Institute, Inc.

Borghesi, A., & Gaudenzi, B. (2013). *Risk management how to assess, transfer and communicate critical risks*. Perspectives in Business Culture. Milano: Springer Milan. https://doi.org/10.1007/978-88-470-2531-8

Bozkurt, C. (2010). Risk, Kurumsal Risk Yönetimi Ve İç Denetim. *Denetişim, 4*, 17–30.

BSI. (2011). *Risk management*. Code of practice and guidance for the implementation of BS ISO 31000: BSI British Standards. https://doi.org/10.3403/30228064

Carrel, P. (2010). *Handbook of risk management: Implementing a post crisis corporate culture* (1. bs.).

Cendrowski, H., & Mair, W. C. (2009). *Enterprise risk management and COSO: A guide for directors, executives, and practitioners*. Wiley.

Chapelle, A. (2019). *Operational risk management: Best practices in the financial services industry. The Wiley finance series* (1st ed.). Wiley.

Chapman, R. J. (2012). *Simple tools and techniques for enterprise risk management: Chapman/simple*. Wiley. https://doi.org/10.1002/9781118467206

Chappell, C. (2014). *The executive guide to enterprise risk management*. Palgrave Macmillan UK. https://doi.org/10.1057/9781137374547

Chew, D. H. (Ed.). (2008). *Corporate risk management*. Columbia University Press.
Chu, Y., & Wang, Z. (2020). Research on project risk response strategy selection based on grey K-shell algorithm. *Grey Systems: Theory and Application, 10*(4), 425–438. https://doi.org/10.1108/GS-10-2019-0043
Chung, E. (2017). *Project risk management: Contingency plan vs fallback plan for PMP exam*. Updated PMP, PMI-ACP & ITIL exam tips 2021. https://edward-designer.com/web/project-risk-management-contingency-plan-vs-fallback-plan-for-pmp-exam/ (Accessed on September 15, 2024)
Cooper, D. F., Grey, S., Raymond, G., & Walker, P. (2005). *Project risk management guidelines: Managing risk in large projects and complex procurements*. Wiley.
COSO (Ed.). (2004). Enterprise risk management - Integrated framework: Executive Summary. IIA (C. 2).
COSO. (2018). *Enterprise risk management—integrating with strategy and performance*. Committee of Sponsoring Organizations of the Treadway Commission.
Cretu, O., Stewart, R., & Berends, T. (2011). *Risk management for design and construction*. Wiley, RSMeans.
Crickette, G., Demian, R., Fox, C., Hach, J., Makomaski, J., Mazumdar, R., & Arbasetti, K. (2012). *Exploring risk appetite and risk tolerance*. Risk Management Society.
Datta, S., & Mukherjee, S. K. (2001). Developing a risk management matrix for effective project planning—An empirical study. *Project Management Journal, 32*(2), 45–57. https://doi.org/10.1177/875697280103200206
de Getz, L. V. (2017). Resolving the disconnect between risk appetites, tolerances, exposures and monitoring measurements. *Journal of Securities Operations & Custody, 9*(4), 18.
Denney, V. P. (2020). Exploring the upside of risk in project management a phenomenological inquiry, 23.
Duckert, G. H. (2011). *Practical enterprise risk management: A business process approach*. Wiley.
ECB (European Central Bank): "Measuring Investors' Risk Appetite", 2007 (Online). Retrieved 10.06.2021, from https://www.ecb.europa.eu/pub/pdf/fsr/art/ecb.fsrart200706_04.en.pdf?d8388b4ee800bcbd51279d31db0b336d
Engemann, K. J., & Henderson, D. M. (2012). *Business continuity and risk management: Essentials of organizational resilience*. Rothstein Associates.
Fan, M., Lin, N.-P., & Sheu, C. (2008). Choosing a project risk-handling strategy: An analytical model. *International Journal of Production Economics, 112*(2), 700–713. https://doi.org/10.1016/j.ijpe.2007.06.006
Fan, Z.-P., Li, Y.-H., & Zhang, Y. (2015). Generating project risk response strategies based on CBR: A case study. *Expert Systems with Applications, 42*(6), 2870–2883. https://doi.org/10.1016/j.eswa.2014.11.034
Fateminia, S. H., Seresht, N. G., & Fayek, A. R. (2019). Evaluating risk response strategies on construction projects using a fuzzy rule-based system. In *36th international symposium on automation and robotics in construction, sunulmuş bildiri*, Banff. https://doi.org/10.22260/ISARC2019/0038
Fraser, J. R. S., & Simkins, B. J. (Eds.). (2010). *Enterprise risk management. The Robert W. Kolb series in finance*. Wiley.
Gericke, K., Klimentew, L., & Blessing, L. (2009). Measure and failure cost analysis selecting risk treatment strategies, 12.
Ghassemi, A., & Darvishpour, A. (2018). A novel approach for risk evaluation and risk response planning in a geothermal drilling project using DEMATEL and fuzzy ANP. *Decision Science Letters*, 225–242. doi:https://doi.org/10.5267/j.dsl.2017.10.001
Goncalves, M., & Heda, R. (2014). *Risk management for project managers: Concepts and practices. The technical manager's survival guides*. ASME Press.
Green, P. E. J. (Ed.). (2016). Enterprise risk management: A common framework for the entire organization.

Greiman, V. A. (2013). *Megaproject management: Lessons on risk and project management from the big dig*. Wiley. https://doi.org/10.1002/9781118671092
Hidayat, S. (2016, April 22). 10. *Risk management process*. https://seprianhidayatamin.org/2016/04/22/10-risk-management-process/ (Accessed on September 15, 2024)
Hillson, D. (2003). *Effective opportunity management for projects (0 bs.)*. CRC Press. https://doi.org/10.1201/9780203913246
Hillson, D. (2009). *Managing risk in projects. Fundamentals of project management*. Gower.
Hisrich, R. D., & Ramadani, V. (2017). *Effective entrepreneurial management*. Springer Texts in Business and Economics. Springer International Publishing. https://doi.org/10.1007/978-3-319-50467-4
Hopkin, P. (2017). *Fundamentals of risk management: Understanding, evaluating and implementing effective risk management* (4th ed.). Kogan Page.
Hunziker, S. (2019). *Enterprise risk management: modern approaches to balancing risk and reward*. Springer Fachmedien Wiesbaden. https://doi.org/10.1007/978-3-658-25357-8
Hutchings, A. (2017). *Difference between enhancing and exploiting a risk*. ProjectManagement.com. https://www.projectmanagement.com/discussions/discussionsTopicContainer.cfm?ID=74144&thisPageURL=/discussion-topic/74144/Difference-between-Enhancing-and-Exploiting-a-risk#_=_ (Accessed on September 15, 2024)
IRM. (2012). *Risk culture under the microscope guidance for board*. Institute of Risk Management. https://primo-europe.eu/risk-culture-under-the-microscope-guidance-for-boards/ (Accessed on September 15, 2024)
ISO. (2009). *ISO 31000 risk management—principles and guidelines*. International Organization for Standardization.
Kendrick, T. (2015). *Identifying and managing project risk: Essential tools for failure-proofing your project* (3rd ed.). American Management Association.
Keshk, A. M., Maarouf, I., & Annany, Y. (2018). Special studies in management of construction project risks, risk concept, plan building, risk quantitative and qualitative analysis, risk response strategies. *Alexandria Engineering Journal, 57*(4), 3179–3187. https://doi.org/10.1016/j.aej.2017.12.003
Keyes, J. (2018). *The CIO's guide to risk*. CRC Press, Taylor & Francis Group.
Koletar, J. W. (2011). *Rethinking risk: How companies sabotage themselves and what they must do differently*. American Management Association.
Konyalı, V. (2016, November 12). Risk Yanıt Stratejileri. Retrieved from https://vkegitimvedanismanlik.wordpress.com/2016/10/25/risk-yanit-stratejileri-durumsal-yanit-plani-b-plani-etrafindan-dolasma-plani/ (Accessed on June 05, 2021).
Kucuk Yilmaz, A., & Flouris, T. (2017). Corporate risk Management for International Business. In *Accounting, finance, sustainability, governance & fraud: Theory and application*. Springer Singapore. https://doi.org/10.1007/978-981-10-4266-9
Kujawski, E. (2002). Selection of technical risk responses for efficient contingencies. *Systems Engineering, 5*(3), 194–212. https://doi.org/10.1002/sys.10025
Lam, J. (2017). *Implementing enterprise risk management: From methods to applications*. Wiley.
Lark, J. (2015). *ISO31000: Risk management: A practical guide for SMEs*.
Lark, J., Nikonov, V., International Organization for Standardization, International Trade Centre UNCTAD/GATT, ve United Nations Industrial Development Organization. (2015). ISO31000: Risk management: A practical guide for SMEs.
Laycock, M. (2014). *Risk management at the top: A guide to risk and its governance in financial institutions*. Wiley.
Louisot, J.-P., & Ketcham, C. (Eds.). (2014). *ERM, enterprise risk management: Issues and cases. The Wiley finance series*. Wiley.
Malik, M. F., Zaman, M., & Buckby, S. (2020). Enterprise risk management and firm performance: Role of the risk committee. *Journal of Contemporary Accounting & Economics, 16*(1), 100178. https://doi.org/10.1016/j.jcae.2019.100178
Marchetti, A. M. (2012). *Enterprise risk management best practices: From assessment to ongoing compliance. Wiley corporate F&A series*. Wiley.

McLaughlin, T. A. (2006). *Nonprofit strategic positioning: Decide where to be, plan what to do*. Wiley.
Miller, R., & Lessard, D. (2001). Understanding and managing risks in large engineering projects. *International Journal of Project Management, 7.*
Moeller, R. R. (2007). *COSO enterprise risk management: Understanding the new integrated ERM framework*. Wiley. https://doi.org/10.1002/9781118269145
Moeller, R. R. (2011). *COSO Enterprise risk management: Establishing effective governance, risk, and compliance processes*. Wiley. https://doi.org/10.1002/9781118269145
Monahan, G. (Ed.). (2012). *Enterprise risk management: A methodology for achieving strategic objectives*. Wiley. https://doi.org/10.1002/9781119197546
Moosa, I. A. (2007). *Operational risk management*. Palgrave Macmillan UK. https://doi.org/10.1057/9780230591486
Moran, A. (2014). *Agile risk management*. SpringerBriefs in Computer Science. Springer International Publishing. https://doi.org/10.1007/978-3-319-05008-9
Mousavi, S. M. (2012). A multi-criteria decision-making approach with interval numbers for evaluating project risk responses. *International Journal of Engineering, 25*(2 (B)), 121–129. https://doi.org/10.5829/idosi.ije.2012.25.02b.05
Naji, H. I. & Ali, R. H. (2017). Fuzzy decision tree of risks assessment generated from risk response, *12*(20), 9.
OGC. (2014). *Management of risk guidance for practitioners*. TSO (The Stationery Office).
Olawale, Y. A., & Sun, M. (2010). Cost and time control of construction projects: Inhibiting factors and mitigating measures in practice. *Construction Management and Economics, 28*(5), 509–526. https://doi.org/10.1080/01446191003674519
Panthi, K., Ahmed, S. M., & Azhar, S. (2007). Risk matrix as a guide to develop risk response strategies. In *Proceedings of 43 rd ASC National Annual Conference (s. 12). ASC National Annual Conference*, Presented paper.
Passenheim, O. (2013). *Enterprise risk management*.
Pehlivanlı, D. (2020). *Kurumsal Risk Yönetimi*. MÜSİAD.
Pinto, C. A. (2015). *Operational risk management*. Momentum Press. https://search.ebscohost.com/login.aspx?direct=true&scope=site&db=nlebk&db=nlabk&AN=1048971
PMI (Ed.). (2009). *Practice standard for project risk management*. Project Management Institute.
PMI (Ed.). (2013). *A guide to the project management body of knowledge (PMBOK guide)* (5th ed.). Project Management Institute, Inc.
Pojasek, R. (2017). *Organizational risk management and sustainability: A practical step-by-step guide*. CRC Press. https://doi.org/10.1201/9781315370620
Pritchard, C. L. (2015). *Risk management: concepts and guidance*.
Protiviti. (2006). *Guide to enterprise risk management frequently asked questions*. Protiviti.
Ptaszymska, E., & Kuchta, D. (2017). *Modified optimization model for selecting project risk response strategies*. Operations Research and Decisions. https://doi.org/10.5277/ORD170205
Qazi, A., Quigley, J., Dickson, A., & Kirytopoulos, K. (2016). Project complexity and risk management (ProCRiM): Towards modelling project complexity driven risk paths in construction projects. *International Journal of Project Management, 34*(7), 1183–1198. https://doi.org/10.1016/j.ijproman.2016.05.008
Quon, T. K., Zeghal, D., & Maingot, M. (2012). Enterprise risk management and firm performance. *Procedia—Social and Behavioral Sciences, 62*, 263–267. https://doi.org/10.1016/j.sbspro.2012.09.042
Raczkowski, K. (Ed.). (2017). *Risk management in public administration*. Springer International Publishing. https://doi.org/10.1007/978-3-319-30877-7
Raz, T., & Hillson, D. (2005). A comparative review of risk management standards. *Risk Management, 7*(4), 53–66. https://doi.org/10.1057/palgrave.rm.8240227
Razi, P. Z., Ali, M. I., & Ramli, N. I. (2020). Incorporation of risk index for risk response and risk mitigation strategies of public-private partnership (PPP) housing construction project in Malaysia. *IOP Conference Series: Materials Science and Engineering, 712*, 012031. https://doi.org/10.1088/1757-899X/712/1/012031

Robertson, J. (2005). *Risk and control strategy*. CIMA Pub. http://site.ebrary.com/id/10187299 (Accessed on September 15, 2024).

Roth, S., Kalchschmid, V., & Reinhart, G. (2021). Development and evaluation of risk treatment paths within energy-oriented production planning and control. *Production Engineering, 15*(3–4), 413–430. https://doi.org/10.1007/s11740-021-01043-5

Şakar, S. (2020, 15 September). *Projelerde Olumlu Riskler (Fırsatlar) ve Yanıt Stratejileri*. Savaş Şakar. https://www.savassakar.com/projelerde-olumlu-risklerfirsatlar-ve-yanit-stratejileri/ (Accessed on September 15, 2024).

Scherling, M. (2016). Practical risk management for the CIO

Spedding, L. S., & Rose, A. (2008). *Business risk management handbook: A sustainable approach*. CIMA.

Steinberg, R. M. (2011). *Governance, risk management, and compliance: It can't happen to us—avoiding corporate disaster while driving success*. John Wiley & Sons, Inc. https://doi.org/10.1002/9781118269190.

Strelnik, M. (2016). Corporate restructuring as a risk treatment method. *Verslas: Teorija ir praktika, 17*(3), 225–233. https://doi.org/10.3846/btp.2016.658

Taplin, R. (Ed.). (2005). *Risk management and innovation in Japan, Britain and the United States. Routledge studies in the growth economies of Asia*. Routledge.

Turley, T. (2010). *The PRINCE2 training manual.pdf*. Office of Government Commerce.

Usmani, F. (2020, July). Enhance risk response vs exploit risk response strategies—PM study circle. *The PM Study Circle*. Retrieved 19.05.2021, from https://pmstudycircle.com/2012/02/enhance-risk-response-vs-exploit-risk-response-strategies/

Wang, L., Goh, M., Ding, R., & Pretorius, L. (2019). Improved simulated annealing based risk interaction network model for project risk response decisions. *Decision Support Systems, 122*, 113062. https://doi.org/10.1016/j.dss.2019.05.002

Wauters, E., van Winsen, F., de Mey, Y., & Lauwers, L. (2014). Risk perception, attitudes towards risk and risk management: Evidence and implications. *Agricultural Economics (Zemědělská ekonomika), 60*(9), 389–405. https://doi.org/10.17221/176/2013-AGRICECON

Wu, W. (2019, November 6). *Risk capacity and risk appetite*. Wentz Wu. Accessed on May 15, 2021, from https://wentzwu.com/2019/11/06/risk-capacity-and-risk-appetite

Wu, D., Li, J., Xia, T., Bao, C., Zhao, Y., & Dai, Q. (2018). A multiobjective optimization method considering process risk correlation for project risk response planning. *Information Sciences, 467*, 282–295. https://doi.org/10.1016/j.ins.2018.07.013

Wu, D., Zhu, X., Wan, J., Bao, C., & ve Li, J. (2019). A multiobjective optimization approach for selecting risk response strategies of software project: From the perspective of risk correlations. *International Journal of Information Technology & Decision Making, 18*(01), 339–364. https://doi.org/10.1142/S0219622019410013

Yoe, C. E. (2019). *Primer on risk analysis: Decision making under uncertainty* (2nd ed.). CRC Press.

Yusuf, I. A., Amadi, A. N., & Salaudeen, M. B. (2020). Effects of risk culture and appetite on effective risk management in Nigerian Banks: Case Study of United Bank for Africa Plc, *6*, 8.

Zhang, Y., & Fan, Z.-P. (2014). An optimization method for selecting project risk response strategies. *International Journal of Project Management, 32*(3), 412–422. https://doi.org/10.1016/j.ijproman.2013.06.006

Zhang, Y., & Guan, X. (2021). Budget allocation decisions for project risk response. *Kybernetes*, ahead-of-print(ahead-of-print). https://doi.org/10.1108/K-03-2020-0188

Zhang, H., & Sun, Q. (2019). An integrated MCDM approach to train derailment risk response strategy selection. *Symmetry, 12*(1), 47. https://doi.org/10.3390/sym12010047

Zhang, Y., & Zuo, F. (2016). Selection of risk response actions considering risk dependency. *Kybernetes, 45*(10), 1652–1667. https://doi.org/10.1108/K-05-2016-0096

Zhang, Y., Zuo, F., & Guan, X. (2020). Integrating case-based analysis and fuzzy optimization for selecting project risk response actions. *Physica A: Statistical Mechanics and its Applications, 545*, 123578. https://doi.org/10.1016/j.physa.2019.123578

Mehmet Baha Karaçolak is a PhD student at the Department of Audit and Risk Management at the Social Sciences University of Ankara in Turkey. Including four years of managerial position, he has experience in strategic management and enterprise process, risk and performance management, organizational development, budgeting, data analysis, and reporting for 12 years. He has been working on accounting for public debts and receivables, swap transactions, and data analysis and reporting for five years at the Ministry of Treasure and Finance. His main scientific research areas cover risk management, risk psychology, strategic management, and decision-making.

Chapter 7
Analysis of Recording, Monitoring and Reviewing Risks in Enterprise Risk Management

Esra Güneş and Caner Erşan

Abstract The success of enterprise risk management can be ensured through the effective design and implementation of all components of enterprise risk management processes. This study analyses the activities of recording, monitoring and reviewing risks, among the most important steps of the enterprise risk management process. The methods presented in the most widely used risk management standards and frameworks in organisations were researched to determine the current situation. In this context, risk management approaches applied in project management standards were also included in the scope of the study in order to indicate different understandings in risk management. Although these methods are essentially designed to serve the same purpose, the differences and shortcomings in the way risks are recorded, monitored and reviewed are noteworthy. There is a need for a common language and new regulations on how the processes of recording, monitoring and reviewing risks should be implemented in organisations. This study provides opinions and suggestions on how to improve the effectiveness of these processes.

Keywords Risk management · Risk register · Risk monitoring · Risk review

E. Güneş
Turkish National Agency, Social Sciences University of Ankara, Ankara, Türkiye
e-mail: esra.gunes2@student.asbu.edu.tr

C. Erşan (✉)
Republic of Turkey Ministry of Agriculture and Forestry, Directorate General of State Hydraulic Works, Social Sciences University of Ankara, Ankara, Türkiye
e-mail: caner.ersan2@student.asbu.edu.tr

H. Kıral (ed.), *Rethinking Enterprise Risk Management*, Accounting, Finance, Sustainability, Governance & Fraud: Theory and Application,
https://doi.org/10.1007/978-981-97-5983-5_7

7.1 Introduction

Organisations should adopt enterprise risk management (ERM) in order to adapt to change and be prepared for the uncertain (Fraser et al., 2021). Risk management is generally implemented in four steps. These are (1) identification of risks, (2) assessment of risks, (3) prioritisation of risks and preparation of risk response plan and (4) monitoring of risks (Moeller, 2011). It is important for the effective execution of the risk management process to record identified risks. Recording the risks provides many benefits, such as creating a list of the risks identified in organisations, identifying the risk responsible for each risk, understanding the cost to the organisation of responding to the risks and the consequences of the risk if it occurs. Considering that risks can sometimes create opportunities rather than negative consequences, a risk recording can also provide users with a list of risks that turn into opportunities. Recording, monitoring and reviewing risks ensures that all stakeholders have confidence in risk management processes.

The purpose of this study is to examine in detail the activities of recording, monitoring and reviewing risks in the enterprise risk management process using different approaches in international standards and frameworks and to provide suggestions for increasing the effectiveness of these activities. The second part of the study analyses the literature on the processes of recording, monitoring and reviewing risks. In the third part, the current situation was determined after analysing the processes of recording, monitoring and reviewing risks in risk management standards, frameworks and project risk management approaches. In the conclusions and evaluations section, the findings obtained as well as the opinions and suggestions for increasing the effectiveness of risk recording, monitoring and reviewing activities are explained and general evaluations are provided.

7.2 Literature Review

Stating that recorded risks will be an inventory of the information required for risk management, Hopkin and Thompson (2022) emphasised the importance of recording risks. The purpose of risk recording is to create a record of the significant risks that have been identified and the control activities that are currently in place. Analysing risk register and similar concepts in project risk management studies in the literature through qualitative methods, Uzulans (2019) found that the terms *"risk register"*, *"risk form"* and *"risk log"* were frequently used in project risk management. The author also emphasised that risk register is a part of the risk management plan and is an important project risk management document.

O'Har, Senesi and Molenaar (2017) stated that a risk register is a document elaborating the risks identified at the entity or programme level in the organisation. The authors also expressed that the risk register to be created for each risk should include a description of the risk, the likelihood of occurrence of the risk and its impact on the objectives, proposed risk responses, remaining risk exposure and risk owners. Dunovic et al. (2013) argue that risk registers, as a document containing risk information and as a management tool, are at the centre of the risk management process. According to Tzanakakis (2021), the risk register is a tool that helps to monitor and address issues as they arise.

Risk registers facilitate risk analysis and monitoring at all levels of the organisation. The risk register can be used to determine whether residual risks are at the agreed risk appetite level. If the residual risk exceeds that level, it is determined which mitigating actions should be taken in addition to the controls in place. Risk registers need to be updated to support decision-making processes with risk assessment data and mitigating actions need to be tracked by risk owners (UNICEF, 2022). A risk register is a highly effective tool to ensure that everyone involved in the project can consciously assess and manage risks as part of the decision-making process. It also provides a better understanding of risks and documentation of risk reduction and mitigation plans within the project itself (Patterson & Neailey, 2002).

Responding to risks are not a one-off action. Risks are constantly changing as the external environment and internal systems change. Therefore, efforts to analyse, classify, assess and measure risk should be regularly monitored. Regular risk monitoring would ensure that risks are reassessed to reassure ERM practitioners that risks remain within the risk appetite (Hopkin & Thompson, 2022). Monitoring and reviewing risks involves identifying, analysing and assessing risks and periodically reviewing responses to risks. The results of the review process are reported to ensure continuous monitoring of risks and to recognise significant changes that may occur (Sârb et al., 2020). It also allows the evolution of risks to be tracked over time. Monitoring, reviewing and reporting are fundamental and integral steps of the risk management process and are performed throughout the risk management process (Dias et al., 2011).

The above-mentioned studies emphasise that the processes of recording, monitoring and reviewing risks are important and integral parts of the risk management process. Correctly defining the scope of these processes and implementing them effectively help organisations better understand the risks they face and improve their ability to manage them. The processes of recording, monitoring and reviewing risks are mutually supportive activities. Recording risks facilitates the traceability and review of risks, while monitoring and review ensure that risk registers are kept up to date.

7.3 Recording, Monitoring and Reviewing Risks

In the risk management process, risk recording refers to the identification and systematic recording of risks, and a risk register is an official document containing the risks identified by an organisation in relation to a specific project or activity. Risk register ranks the risks according to their severity and indicates the areas that will be affected if the risk occurs, the persons responsible for the risk and summaries of action plans. According to Moeller (2011), the risk register is the primary output of the risk identification process and is a document that lists potential responses to identified risks.

Another important step in the risk management process is the monitoring and review of risks. Before moving on to the processes of monitoring and reviewing risks, it is important to clarify the difference between the concepts of monitoring and reviewing. Monitoring is the routine checking of actual performance against expected performance. Review, on the other hand, is period checking of the current situation against internal and external factors that may affect the processes. Continuous or periodic review of risks by organisations, including monitoring activities, enables the necessary interventions and corrections to be made in a timely manner.

This study analyses the processes of recording, monitoring and reviewing risks in risk management standards and frameworks. Approaches to recording, monitoring and reviewing risks in project management standards are also included in the scope of the review.

7.3.1 Recording Risks in Standards and Frameworks

Published standards and frameworks on risk management do not include the process of recording risks as a major component but define it as a process associated with all stages of the risk management process. In this context, risk recording is a repository of information to be used in making corrections for the past and implementing future strategies.

In the tenth principle of the performance component of the COSO[1] ERM framework, which is the most widely used in organisations to implement enterprise risk management, the identification of risks is defined as a process to be carried out immediately after the identification of possible risks. According to COSO (2017), organisations must identify events that may affect their strategy and business objectives or turn into opportunities. The identified risks are included in a risk inventory. This inventory includes the impact of each risk, actions to mitigate the risk and the owner of the risk.

Risk identification within the COSO framework recommends starting with a standardised inventory of identified and documented risks to the organisation using an organisation's risk taxonomy. A risk inventory, sometimes referred to as a risk register, enables the development of a common language for risks across the organisation and a more systematic and consistent addressing of risks across the organisation (AICPA & CIMA, 2018).

The International Organization for Standardisation (ISO) defines risk register in its Risk Management Terms Guide (Guide73, 2009b) as "*a record of information*

[1]COSO stands for Committee of Sponsoring Organizations of Treadway Commission.

about identified risks". ISO 31000 standards published in 2009 and 2018 include regulations for documenting and reporting the risk management process and results as a whole. From this point of view, ISO aims to record risk management processes as a whole and to provide a flow of information throughout the organisation through reporting of the results obtained by recording. Similarly, the Australian and New Zealand Risk Management Standard AZ/NZS 4360 (2004) refers to the whole risk management process for recording. The standard also emphasised that each stage of the risk management process should be properly recorded and that risk analysis and results, as well as risk decisions and justifications, should be included in the records made.

Organisations should identify risk sources, impact areas, events and their causes and potential consequences. They should generate a comprehensive list of risks based on the events that could prevent, delay or accelerate the achievement of objectives. Comprehensive identification is critical because a risk not identified at this stage cannot be included in subsequent analyses (ISO 31000, 2009a).

The Institute of Risk Management (IRM),[2] in its Guide on ERM, stated that the recording of risks should be in the form of "*recording risk assessments*". For the risks defined according to the Guide, impact and probability values, prioritisation of risks and the controls determined should be recorded in a spreadsheet or a computer-based system. The risk register should not be a static report recording the specific risks faced by the organisation. The risk register should be seen as a risk action plan that includes current controls as well as details of planned future activities (Airmic & IRM, 2010).

The Orange Book[3] (2020) states that risk assessment results should be recorded and risk information should be communicated within the organisation. The risks encountered should be regularly reviewed for significance and revised as necessary. The Management of Risk Guidance for Practitioners (M_o_R)[4] framework explains the recording of risks with a series of documents under the title of risk management approach. These consist of "*risk management policy*", "*risk management process guide*" and "*risk management strategies*". The additional document recommended to underpin these three documents is the "*recording of risks and issues*" document within the M_o_R framework. The risk register, which provides instant information at any time, includes risk prioritisation, the strategy to be chosen by the risk owner for each risk and the responses to the risk (M_o_R, 2010).

It has been observed that project management standards also include recording of risks. In project risk management, the transfer of information between project phases is possible through risk registers. A risk register (log) prepared for project risk management is a memory record in the project management process of the

[2] IRM stands for Institute of Risk Management, which is a professional body for enterprise risk management in the UK.

[3] The Orange Book is a risk management framework prepared by the UK Central Government to set out the key principles and concepts underlying effective risk management.

[4] M_o_R (Management of Risk Guidance for Practitioners) is a risk management guide prepared by AXELOS (Joint Venture of the UK Cabinet Office).

organisation. The document prepared to record the risks is the risk register, while the document prepared to record the problems is the issue log. There are differences between the two documents. Deviations, delays, unforeseen events in the project plan turn into problems and these are recorded in the issue log. These records allow corrections to be made by looking at past records in cases such as time and budget deviations in the project. Risk registers are risk lists that record events that may have an impact on the objectives of the project, with a view to identifying the risks before they occur, determining necessary risk responses and monitoring risks.

In its implementation standard guide for project risk management published in 2009, the Project Management Institute (PMI) defined the risk register as a document containing the results of qualitative risk analysis, quantitative risk analysis and risk response planning. The risk register details all risks, including the identification of risks, subcategories, causes, likelihood of occurrence, impact on objectives, responses to risks and risk owners.

The risk management process should be iterative to reflect the dynamic nature of project work. This requires managing emerging risks and reflecting new information in existing risk analyses and estimates. A risk register is used to document risks, analyses and risk responses. It also assigns clear ownership of actions. Risk register is a document that lists identified risks, risk events and a plan of corresponding responses (APM, 2019).

The PRojects IN Controlled Environments (PRINCE2)[5] method describes the risk register in a similar way to the M_o_R framework. This method includes an issue log in addition to the risk register and relates the "*risk management approach*" to the "*risk register*". The risk management approach describes how risk will be managed in the project, processes, procedures, techniques, standards and responsibilities. The risk register is used to collect information on all threats and opportunities identified with the project. Both of these documents should be drawn up at the start of a project process. PRINCE2 recommends that risks should be recorded as soon as they are identified, using a spreadsheet or a dedicated IT system (AXELOS, 2017).

The risk register is one of the most important project documents used in conjunction with the issue log for risk identification and implementation of risk responses. The risk register may include a short risk title, risk category, current risk status, risk triggers (events or conditions indicating that a risk is about to occur) and timing of affected activities. A risk register should be created using a risk database for all identified project risks (PMI, 2017).

The main output of the risk identification process is the risk register. This register contains an appropriately structured risk definition and the assigned risk owner for each risk. Risks on the project are prioritised according to their likelihood of occurrence and their potential impact on the project objectives. This information is kept

[5] PRINCE2 (PRojects IN Controlled Environments) is a widely recognised project management method used by a wide range of industrial organisations around the world.

in the risk register, which can be easily updated to reflect new information (PMI, 2009).

Looking at the published standards and frameworks for the systematic implementation of risk management in organisations, as shown in Table 7.1, there are differences between the form, scope and related components/documents of risk registers. While Orange Book, ISO 31000 and AZ/NZS 4360 standards emphasise the recording of risk management processes as a whole, COSO ERM, IRM, M_o_R and project risk management standards state that a risk register should be created for each identified risk. This resulted in two different situations: recording risk management processes and creating a risk register for identified risks.

Table 7.1 Recording of risks in standards and frameworks

Standards and frameworks		Form and scope of record	Related component(s)/ document(s)
Risk management	The Orange Book (2020)	Recording of risk assessment results	Risk identification and risk assessment
	ISO 31000 (2018) and (2009)	Recording of risk management processes	Risk management process
	COSO (2017)	Creating a risk inventory for all events that may have an impact on strategy and business objectives	Performance component, principle of risk identification
	M_o_R (2010)	Creating a risk register for all identified risks using a table or a risk database	Issue log, risk management policy, risk management process guide, risk management strategies
	AZ/NZS 4360 (2004)	Recording all stages of the risk management process	Risk management process
	IRM (2002)	Displaying all identified risk information in the risk identification table	Risk analysis, risk identification
Project management	APM (2019)	Creating a risk register, risk repository or risk register for all identified project risks	Risk analysis, risk responses
	PMBOK (PMI, 2017)	Creating a risk register for all identified project risks using the risk database	Issue log, project documents
	PRINCE2 (AXELOS, 2017)	Creating a risk register for all identified project risks using a spreadsheet or a dedicated IT system	Issue log, daily log, risk management approach
	PMI (2009)	Creating a risk register for all identified project risks	Communication plans, risk status reports

Source: Created by the authors

7.3.2 Monitoring and Reviewing of Risks in Standards and Frameworks

One of the main components of the risk management process in enterprise risk management standards and frameworks is the monitoring and/or review of risks. There are significant differences between standards and frameworks on how monitoring and reviews should be carried out. The enterprise risk management standard ISO 31000 (2018), which is widely used around the world in enterprise risk management, explains the purpose of monitoring and review activities as ensuring and improving the quality and effectiveness of process design, implementation and results. According to ISO 31000, the results of monitoring and reviews should be used in the measurement of the organisation's performance management and reporting activities. The ISO 31000 Standard takes a holistic approach to the monitoring and review activities of the risk management process. It applies the risk monitoring and review process integrated with all other processes. It uses the information obtained from these processes as an input to the monitoring and review of the entire ERM framework. This provides the necessary feedback for continuous improvement. This feedback contributes significantly to the continuous improvement of the risk management process.

COSO (2013) included monitoring activities as the main component in its internal control framework. In its 2017 ERM framework, it explained the review and revision component with three basic principles. The first is the review of significant changes that may occur in the internal and external environment that will have an impact on the organisation's achievement of its strategy and business objectives. The second is to review and/or revise the objectives and risks that will affect performance. The third and final principle is to follow the improvements in ERM in order to increase ERM efficiency and continuous improvement. COSO explains review as recognising changes, making corrections in this direction and getting opportunities for improvement of the entire ERM.

According to the Orange Book (2020), risk monitoring should take place before, during and after the implementation of responses to risks. The results of monitoring should help to understand whether the risk profile has changed and to what extent the designed controls are working to achieve organisational objectives. The results of monitoring and review should be incorporated into performance management measurement and reporting activities. The risk management framework should also be reviewed periodically.

The probability and impact factors that affect the level of a risk may change, as may factors that may affect the appropriateness or cost of response options to the risk. Therefore, the risk management cycle should be repeated regularly (AZ/NZS 4360, 2004).

Risk monitoring within M_o_R covers all identified risks. Monitoring is a process of observation. It is neutral as it is outside the realised activity. Monitoring is necessary to check whether the identified risk interventions have been implemented. In addition, risk monitoring should include reconsideration of threats and opportunities that may arise over time. Within the framework of M_o_R, risk review is integrated into all processes with the main component that is "*integrating and reviewing risk management*".

When the activities of monitoring and reviewing risks in project management standards are analysed, it is clear that PMI associates the recording of risks with the process of monitoring risks as part of the project management plan. The risk monitoring process is carried out during the execution of the intervention planning for risks, identification and analysis of risks processes, based on the information included in the risk register. Information about the intervention for each risk is recorded in the risk register and updated regularly. At the end of the project, the project manager should ensure that for each risk in the risk register, a statement of risk closure is made with one of the following options, for instance, (a) did not occur; (b) did occur and the contingency plan was activated; or (c) did occur and had an impact on the project scope (time, cost and quality).

The PRINCE2 method specifies that the review of risks in project management should be done through the "*risk management approach*" and the "*risk register*" document. The risk management approach should specify how and when the risk register will be reviewed and updated. The risk management approach should be reviewed and updated on a regular basis.

The PMBOK guide explains that the monitoring of project risks should take place through a three-part structure: (1) Inputs are "*project management plans*"[6] and "*project documents*".[7] (2) Tools and techniques used in risk monitoring are "*data analysis, audit and review*" meetings. (3) Outputs are "*evaluation of risk management performance, requests for changes to risk monitoring processes and updates to the project management plan*".

The differences in the scope of monitoring and review activities in standards and frameworks are striking. In risk management standards and frameworks, monitoring and/or reviews are the main components of the risk management process. In the Orange Book, the scope of the monitoring component is defined as before, during and after risk responses. In the ISO 31000, IRM and AZ/NZS 4360 standards, monitoring and review components are defined to cover risk management processes. COSO ERM (2017) and M_o_R frameworks do not include any monitoring component. In COSO ERM, the review and revision component specifically addresses performance objectives. M_o_R, on the other hand, focuses on the entire scope of risk management with the embedding and review component. In project management standards, monitoring and review activities are carried out through documents such as risk management plans, risk registers and risk management approach. The scope differences in standards and frameworks are shown in Table 7.2.

[6] Project management plans are the plans that describe how and when risks should be reviewed, which policies and procedures will be followed and the roles and responsibilities in the monitoring process.

[7] Project documents are the documents including issue logs recording issues in the monitoring process, updated risk registers, risk reports with details of significant risks and detailed information such as risk responses.

Table 7.2 Monitoring and review of risks in standards and frameworks

Standards and frameworks		Components/ activities	Scope
Risk management	The Orange Book (2020)	Monitoring	Before, during and after implementing the risk responses
	ISO 31000 (2018) and (2009)	Monitoring and review	Risk assessment processes, control processes, risk response plans, risk management framework
	COSO (2017)	Review	Risk and performance, business objectives, strategy, culture, ERM improvements
		Revision	Performance targets, risk appetite, risk responses
	M_o_R (2010)	Embedding and review	Risk management
	AZ/NZS 4360 (2004)	Monitoring and review	Management plan, actual events, progress on risk response plans and their results
	IRM (2002)	Monitoring and review	Risk management processes
Project management	APM (2019)	Monitoring the progress	Changes in the risk profile
	PMBOK (PMI, 2017)	Monitoring and updates	Risk management performance
	PRINCE2 (AXELOS, 2017)	Review and updates	Risk register, risk management approach
	PMI (2009)	Monitoring and control	Risk management plans, residual risk, risk registers, risk responses

Source: Created by the authors

In the risk management standards and frameworks analysed, the position and functioning of monitoring and review components in the risk management process differ. As shown in Table 7.3, the IRM, ISO 31000 and AZ/NZS 4360 standards include monitoring and review components, while the M_o_R framework includes embedding and review components under a single component. Similarly, the COSO ERM framework includes review and revision under a single component. The Orange Book only includes the monitoring component.

7.4 Conclusion and Assessment

The Latin saying "*Verba volant, scripta manent; spoken words fly away, written words remain*" and the motto of the ISO quality system "do what you write, write what you do" are examples that serve to emphasise the importance of recording the transactions in writing. Organisations should identify potential risks that may have an impact on their objectives and record them in writing. This recording process is

Table 7.3 Monitoring and review components in risk management standards and frameworks[a]

	Components				
	monitoring	Review	Embedding and review	Monitoring and review	Revision
The Orange Book (2020)	Implementing risk responses	*Risk management framework*	–	–	–
ISO 31000 (2009) (2018)	–	–	–	Risk assessment and control processes, risk response plans, risk management framework	–
COSO (2017)	–	Risk and performance, business objectives, strategy, culture, ERY improvements	–	–	Performance objectives, risk appetite, risk responses
M_o_R (2010)	*Identified risks*	–	Risk management approach	–	–
AZ/NZS 4360 (2004)	–	*Risk management culture, organisational maturity, regulatory compliance, resource constraints*	–	Management plan, actual events, risk response plans and results, actual progress against risk response plans	–
IRM (2002)	–	–	–	Risk management processes	–

Source: Created by the authors
[a]Expressions in italics in the table are not expressed as main components in standards and frameworks but are presented as recommendations.

much more than just preparing a list of risks. The risk register is the most important written document that serves as the output of the risk identification process and the input of all other processes; as a result of situations arising from changes in risks, retrospective corrections can be made and future measures can be taken. Once the risks have been identified and recorded, they are evaluated and the actions to address them are determined. In order for organisations to understand what these efforts have changed and how they affect the organisation, the risks recorded should be monitored and reviewed.

Looking at the frameworks and standards published in risk management and project management, there are different understandings of how to record risks. COSO ERM, one of the risk management frameworks, states that a risk inventory should be created for all events that will have an impact on strategy and business objectives. Similarly, the IRM framework states that a risk identification table should be created containing information on all identified risks. According to the M_o_R framework, a risk register should be created for all identified risks using a table or a risk database. In the COSO ERM, IRM, M_o_R, PRINCE2, PMI, PMBOK and APM standards, the scope of risk registers is defined as all risks identified throughout the organisation/project and the elements that a risk register should contain are specified. Other standards and frameworks (ISO 31000, the Orange Book, AZ/NZS 4360) points at risk management processes for the scope of recording (see Table 7.1).

The study found that there are significant differences in standards and frameworks for what risk registers should look like and what they should cover and that there is no common language for recording risks. In this context, the recommendations that are considered to help improve the effectiveness of the risk recording process are set out below:

- The information in the documents or lists used to record the risks should be accurate, up to date and at the appropriate level of detail. In addition, the use of technology to manage comprehensive and complex risk register lists is important in terms of increasing time and manageability. This can ensure that the risk register is a real-time tool (Hopkin & Thompson, 2022). In particular, the organisations under regulatory pressure tend to create comprehensive risk registers. Both creating and updating comprehensive risk registers becomes a workload and the risk monitoring process becomes difficult (Fraser & Simkins, 2016). Correctly defining the scope of risk registers plays an important role in increasing the effectiveness of the recording process.
- Risk recording, monitoring and review activities should be more closely linked. Because risk registers and monitoring and review process are directly related. The data in risk registers should be used as a database for monitoring and reviewing risks. This link, which is not included in risk management standards and frameworks, is explained in detail in project risk management approaches.
- There is no fixed risk recording method defined for an organisation. Depending on the size of the organisation, the way of documenting the recording process may vary. Organisations should determine how risk registers will be created, whether electronically or in writing, and how they will be designed for business processes that are being transformed by digitalisation.
- Organisations should systematically record all risks to be identified in order to accurately assess risks for decision-making. A well-structured and effective risk recording should provide decision-makers with a summary of all information in the risk assessment, risk analysis and risk response processes.

The study found that standards and frameworks have different understandings and methodologies for monitoring and reviewing risks, as is the case for recording risks. COSO has not included explanations on risk monitoring in its new ERM framework published in 2017. It refers readers to the COSO internal control framework as a source for monitoring. In the COSO ERM, the revision component is included instead of the monitoring component. One of the main components of the M_o_R framework is the review and embedding component. Risk monitoring is also recommended in the M_o_R approach. The COSO ERM and M_o_R framework differ from other standards and frameworks by using different terminology such as revision and embedding.

Among the risk management standards and frameworks, COSO ERM, ISO 31000, Orange Book and M_o_R have similar statements on the need to review the risk management framework applied by the organisations as a whole. Although the Orange Book does not include a review component in the risk management process, it does state that the risk management framework should be reviewed. The COSO ERM framework emphasises the importance of reviewing the entire ERM framework to improve ERM. The M_o_R framework, on the other hand, states that the review and embedding of the risk management approach into the organisation should be carried out together and that the risk management approach embedded into the organisation should be reviewed. According to the ISO 31000 Standard, the risk management framework should be monitored and reviewed (see Table 7.3).

In project risk management approaches, monitoring and review activities are based on risk management plans, performance results and changes in the risk profile. PRINCE2 and PMBOK's use of "*update*" and PMI's use of "*control*" concepts distinguish them from other methods. Risk register is the most important tool used in project risk management methods for monitoring and reviewing risks. For PRINCE2, the risk register is the second most important document for monitoring risks after the risk management approach document. PMI has linked the recording of risks directly to the monitoring activities.

Considering the current state of risk management standards and frameworks, the following recommendations are considered to contribute to increasing the effectiveness of risk monitoring and review processes in organisations:

- Changes in the environment in which organisations operate may introduce a new risk or increase the potential impact of an existing risk. In this case, the results of monitoring and reviews should mobilise risk management practitioners to re-evaluate the risk and possibly modify the risk inventory. For example, the recent water shortage in South Africa has had rapid and severe impacts. Although manufacturing companies have recognised that their operations in South Africa are dependent on water, they may not have identified water scarcity as a significant risk. As water shortage increases, organisations can raise the priority of the risk, develop water use reduction programmes and business continuity plans and establish indicators to monitor water use and reserve levels (COSO & WBCSD, 2018).
- It is important to clearly define responsibilities and tasks for monitoring and review processes. In addition, software based on key performance measures can be used to design an effective risk monitoring process (Kerstin et al., 2014).
- Monitoring and review processes can be used to monitor stakeholders' feedback and complaints. Particularly in organisations where stakeholder satisfaction is important, the process becomes even more important to ensure that any dissatisfaction is addressed in a timely manner (Yap & Yap, 2018).

- It is not enough for monitoring and review to be process-oriented. They should also cover the current status and development of a risk management framework that organisations have put in place.
- The results of monitoring and review should be recorded and reported appropriately as they may be a performance indicator for senior management when evaluating risk management activities.

Consequently, a risk register should include the definition of risks, time of occurrence, impact and likelihood values, ranking of importance, inherent risk and residual risk levels, the level of risk appetite of the organisations, response plans (controls) for risks and information on the persons responsible for the risk. This register should be designed as a dynamic and continuously updated tool and play a critical role in tracking risks and sharing risk information across the organisation. Given that organisations face ever-changing and diversifying risks as a result of increasingly complex business processes, the information in the risk register can easily identify which risks are more important, which risks are no longer a threat or which risks have the potential to turn into opportunities. Therefore, risks should be properly recorded, monitored and reviewed in order to provide a holistic perspective and to ensure the continuity and improvement of the risk management system.

References

AICPA, & CIMA. (2018). *Practice aid enterprise risk management: guidance for practical implementation and assessment*. Association of International Certified Professional Accountants.

Airmic, A., & IRM. (2010). *A structured approach to Enterprise Risk Management (ERM) and the requirements of ISO 31000*. The Public Risk Management Association. 11. Retrieved 11.04.2023, from https://www.ferma.eu/app/uploads/2011/10/a-structured-approach-to-erm.pdf

APM. (2019). *Body of knowledge association for project management* (7th ed.).

AXELOS. (2017). *Managing successful projects with PRINCE2*. PRINCE2 6th Edition. TSO (The Stationery Office).

AZ/NZS 4360. (2004). *Risk management*. Standards Australia International, Ltd. Standards New Zealand.

COSO. (2017). *Enterprise risk management: integrating with strategy and performance - Executive summary*. Committee of Sponsoring Organizations of the Treadway Commission.

COSO, & WBCSD. (2018). *Applying enterprise risk management to environmental, social and governance-related risks*. Retrieved 15.03.2023, from https://wbcsd.my.salesforcesites.com/CampaignSubscriptionPage?id=7010N0000011RPE

Dias, S., Le Guen, Y., Poupard, O., & Shtivelman, V. (2011). Risk assessment of MUSTANG project experimental site–Methodological development. *Energy Procedia, 4*, 4109–4116.

Dunovic, I., Radujkovic, M., & Vukomanovic, M. (2013). Risk register development and implementation for construction projects. *Gradivinar, 65*(1), 23–25. Retrieved 04.04.2023, from http://casopis-gradjevinar.hr/assets/Uploads/JCE_65_2013_1_4_722_EN.pdf

Fraser, J. R., & Simkins, B. J. (2016). The challenges of and solutions for implementing enterprise risk management. *Business Horizons, 59*(6), 689–698. https://doi.org/10.1016/j.bushor.2016.06.007

Fraser, J. R., Quail, R., & Simkins, B. (2021). *Enterprise risk management: Today's leading research and best practices for tomorrow's executives*. Wiley.

HM Government. (2020). *The Orange book management of risk—principles and concepts*.

Hopkin, P., & Thompson, C. (2022). *Fundamentals of risk management: understanding, evaluating and implementing effective risk management*. Kogan Page Ltd.

IRM. (2002). *A risk management standard*. https://www.theirm.org/media/4709/arms_2002_irm.pdf (Accessed on September 15, 2024)

ISO. (2009a). *ISO 31000 Risk management—Principles and guidelines*.

ISO. (2009b). *ISO Guide 73:2009, Risk management—Vocabulary*.

ISO. (2018). *ISO 31000 risk management—Principles and guidelines*. International Organization for Standardization.

Kerstin, D., Simone, O., Nicole, Z., & Lehner, O. M. (2014). Challenges in implementing enterprise risk management. *ACRN Journal of Finance and Risk Perspectives, 3*(3), 1–14.

M_o_R. (2010). *Management of risk: Guidance for practitioners*.

Moeller, R. R. (2011). *COSO Enterprise risk management: establishing effective governance, risk, and compliance processes* (Cilt 560) (2nd ed.). Wiley.

O'Har, J., Senesi, C., & Moleneaar, K. (2017). Development of a risk register spreadsheet tool for Enterprise and program-level risk management. *Transportation Research Record: Journal of the Transportation Research Board, 2604*, 19–27.

Patterson, F. D., & Neailey, K. (2002). A risk register database system to aid the management of project risk. *International Journal of Project Management, 20*(5), 365–374.

PMI. (2009). *Practice standard for project risk management*. Project Management Institute.

PMI. (2017). *A guide to the project management body of knowledge (PMBOK guide)*. Newtown Square: Pennsylvania: Project Management Institute, Inc.

Sârb, A., Burja Udrea, C., Itul, L., & Popa, M. (2020). The improvement of a quality management system by applying risk management. *Annales Universitatis Apulensis-Series Oeconomica, 22*(2).

Tzanakakis, K. (2021). *Managing risks in railway system. A practice-oriented guide*. (Cilt 18). Springer. https://doi.org/10.1007/978-3-030-66266-0

UNICEF. (2022). *Internal audit of enterprise risk management*. Office of Internal Audit and Investigations. UNICEF. Retrieved 07.04.2023, from https://www.unicef.org/auditandinvestigation/media/1736/file/2022%20OIAI%20Audit%20of%20Enterprise%20Risk%20Management.pdf

Uzulans, J. (2019). The project risk registers analysis based of the project risk management notion 'risk register'. *Project Management Development–Practice and Perspectives*, 25–29.

Yap, A. H., & Yap, S. (2018). COSO enterprise risk management: Small-medium enterprises evidence. *Asia-Pacific Management Accounting Journal, 13*(2), 83–111.

Esra Güneş is a PhD student in the Audit and Risk Management Program at the Social Sciences University of Ankara. She is an electrical and electronics engineer with a master's degree in information systems. She is working as an IT expert at the Turkish National Agency.

Caner Erşan is a mechanical engineer. He has worked as chief engineer in the General Directorate of State Hydraulic Work in Turkey. Also, he has taken on additional duties related to risk management, internal control, and strategic plan studies in the same company. He has a public internal auditor certificate approved by the Ministry of Finance. In addition, he has also graduated from the Internal Audit and Internal Control Master's Program at Ankara University and wrote a thesis on internal audit and risk management. He is a PhD student in the Audit and Risk Management Program at the Social Sciences University of Ankara.

Part IV
To Improve the Effectiveness of ERM

Chapter 8
Barriers to Effective Risk Communication

Murat Soner

Abstract It is a fact that studies on enterprise risk management mostly focus on risk management processes and risk identification. However, since the measures proposed in the studies are insufficient to prevent large-scale crises, the need for studies that differ from the existing studies and contribute to risk management is felt more and more every day. Research conducted for this purpose reveals that studies on risk communication are insufficient at the enterprise level and that existing studies focus on public health and environmental issues. For this reason, it is aimed to put forward a study that can guide enterprise governments and to support the study with examples to be presented. Within the scope of the study, risk communication definitions, necessity, approaches, and methods were examined, and obstacles and solutions to communication were tried to be identified.

Keywords Risk communication · Communication approaches · Communication barriers

8.1 Introduction

In premodern times, since risks were simpler and more predictable and their impact area was limited to the regions where the risk occurred, efforts to combat risk were mostly provided by individual behaviors and short-term measures. However, as a result of globalization, industrialization, science and technology, and advances in nuclear energy, risks have become more difficult to define, their spheres of influence have expanded, and new risk structures have been introduced into life (Hampel, 2006). The effects of the nuclear bomb dropped on Japan during World War II, the terrorist attack on the United States on September 11, 2001, and the Covid-19

M. Soner (✉)
Social Sciences University of Ankara, Ankara, Türkiye
e-mail: murat.soner@student.asbu.edu.tr

H. Kıral (ed.), *Rethinking Enterprise Risk Management*, Accounting, Finance, Sustainability, Governance & Fraud: Theory and Application,
https://doi.org/10.1007/978-981-97-5983-5_8

pandemic that emerged in China in 2019 and affected the whole world are examples of the security and health risks brought about by these advances (Bourrier & Bieder, 2018). In addition, beyond their global impact, they have crossed temporal boundaries and become a threat to the next generations, which has shown that individual struggle is not enough and the need to fight risks enterprisely has come to light. These needs have led to the emergence of enterprise risk management and made it an indispensable element of strategic planning. However, risk management mechanisms created with great expectations have been insufficient against new risks and their existence and effectiveness have been questioned, especially due to the inability to prevent financial crises (Kıral, 2018). An analysis of the studies conducted to address these problems reveals that direct factors for identifying and managing risks have been investigated more and many additional measures have been proposed, including the reorganization of the management structure. On the other hand, it is a fact that the effectiveness of risk communication, which contributes to the struggle of enterprise governments against risks, is ignored in the same studies and even left to the awareness and belief of enterprise managers. In the survey study conducted by Erdem (2014), only 10% of the employees stated that there is risk communication within the organization, which reveals the rightness of this determination. For this reason, it is considered that the existence and effectiveness of risk communication should be included in the studies to be conducted.

The purpose of this study is to examine the necessity of risk communication and the obstacles to effective risk communication and to offer solutions for effective risk communication in the organization. In addition, in order to support the study, in-house examples as well as determinations suitable for external communication stakeholders are also included. The study consists of seven chapters. In the following section, risk communication is defined by discussing national and international studies. In the third section, the necessity of risk communication is evaluated, and in the fourth section, risk communication approaches and methods are examined. In the fifth section, individual and organizational barriers are interpreted and in the sixth section, suggestions are made to establish effective communication. In the conclusion section, the findings and evaluations throughout the study are included.

8.2 What Is Risk Communication?

It is possible to talk about a consensus on the necessity of risk communication in academic studies. However, it is seen that the studies are limited to this common point and there are divergences on its definition. For example, risk communication is defined by the World Health Organization (2021) as the exchange of advice and ideas among stakeholders facing hazards, and by the National Research Council (1989) as an interactive process based on the exchange of opinions and information. Boholm (2008) defines risk communication as a point of intersection between governments and the implementation of their policies, as well as a means of educating the public about risk management and motivating expected behaviors through information and information activities, and Trautman (2001) defines it as an open process where different ideas based on science can be expressed. Da Cunha and De Andrade (2016) highlight the resource aspect of risk communication and emphasize that it brings audiences closer to understanding the technical characteristics of the risks they will be exposed to. Covello et al. (1986), on the other hand, emphasize that risk communication aims to provide stakeholders with information exchange, behavior change, ways to prevent diseases, and participation in solving the problem. Risk communication is defined by Turancı (2017) as the exchange of risk information that requires a certain literacy and the ability to analyze and synthesize during communication, and by Güler and Çobanoğlu (1997) as an interaction that aims to inform and raise awareness with the participation of the public.

On the other hand, although COSO (2004) does not provide a clear definition of risk communication, the necessity of risk communication can be found in other definitions. For example, in the COSO Enterprise Risk Management (ERM) definition, it is stated that risk management is affected by all employees of the organization. With this statement, it is understood that all stakeholders within the organization should participate in risk management processes and communicate with each other in order to manage these processes effectively. In the Enterprise Risk Management Strategy and Integration with Performance update published in 2017, which is also among the components of the same model, it is envisaged that effective communication can be achieved by communicating information horizontally and vertically throughout the organization.

When national legislation is analyzed, it is seen that the issue of risk communication is not explicitly mentioned, but similar statements are made about its necessity. For example, the Law No. 5018 on Public Financial Management and Control and the Procedures and Principles on Internal Control and Preliminary Financial Control, which constitute the basis for internal control and risk management activities in public institutions and organizations, do not explicitly mention risk communication. On the other hand, in the Communiqué on Public Internal Control Standards, it is emphasized that an effective and continuous communication system should be established to transfer information. Similarly, in the Public Internal Control Guidelines, it is stated that for effective communication, information should be communicated to all internal and external stakeholders and feedback should be received. Beyond the fact that these explanations are basically about the internal control system of the organization, inferences can be drawn about what risk communication is based on the fact that risk communication is an element of this system.

Considering the abovementioned explanations and implications, it is possible to provide a new definition for risk communication as "*the active participation of stakeholders in risk management processes by obtaining simultaneous and up-to-date data on risks by informing all stakeholders about potential hazards.*"

8.3 Why Is Risk Communication Necessary?

While the expected consequences and effects of an action taken a century ago were similar, the opportunities offered by science and technology bring new risks into our lives. An example of these new risks is when a person undergoing chemotherapy for cancer treatment also faces dangers such as infertility and kidney problems (TSV, 2021). In addition to the opportunities offered by the modern age, the number of unknowns, such as the unpredictability of the changes that may occur in our lives in the next year and the incalculability of the risks that the next generation may face as a result of global warming, are increasing day by day and exceed the limits of human perception and abilities (Giddens, 1991; Beck, 1996).

In order to cope with these uncertainties, individual efforts are insufficient and there is a need for all stakeholders who will be affected by risks to act together within an organizational structure. However, academic studies draw attention to the fact that this unity, which is also referred to as enterprise risk management, cannot be achieved only by the efforts of the managers or boards of directors of the organization. However, these criticisms expressed in these studies do not question the existence of enterprise risk management but point to the need to investigate how to combat risks in the most effective way. As a matter of fact, it should be accepted that this struggle, which is full of uncertainties, can only be possible by being planned by an enterprise structure, informing all internal and external stakeholders about risk management processes and contributing to risk communication.

8.4 What Are Risk Communication Approaches and Models?

The historical beginnings of risk communication date back to the early ages when risks existed in human life. Risk information written on cave walls in primitive life forms was transmitted through smoke as a result of the discovery of fire, and with the changes of the age, it was made available to wider masses through means such as messengers, letters, telephone, radio, television, and social media, respectively. In addition, with its inclusion and institutionalization in risk management processes, its place in academic studies based on state and public relations has gradually increased in recent years.[1] Contrary to the divergence on communication approaches and models in these studies, there is a common understanding of its necessity. In the crisis communication approach, which is one of these approaches, it is considered mandatory to use all means to motivate the target to action, and the communication structure is built on an ongoing or possible situation. In the mental model approach, the use of artificial intelligence and cognitive psychology is preferred to understand how the target understands the risks (Bourrier & Bieder, 2018; Lundgren &

[1] It was obtained from the data on https://books.google.com/ngrams.

McMakin, 2013). In the Scientific-Technical Approach, which is one of the other approaches, the source is considered more important and the purpose of communication is to inform, change risky behavior, and persuade the target. In the Social-Cultural Approach model, priority is given to the target in communication and it is assumed that all parties are in a dynamic structure from the first stage to the last stage. In contrast to these two approaches, the Synthesis Approach, which adopts a holistic approach, emphasizes the need to ensure a sustainable relationship between the target audience and the source and to organize the message and channels in accordance with the target audience (Yakut, 2008; National Research Council, 1989).

Over time, there has been a need to develop models that support these approaches to explain risk communication, and for this reason, some models have been proposed. However, it is a fact that these models are limited to the conditions of the time when they were proposed and cannot adapt to the needs of subsequent periods. For this reason, it would not be wrong to say that models and approaches that are insufficient for the requirements of the age and the complex structure of risks will gradually decrease and will remain only in the archives of academic studies. For example, the model put forward by Shannon and Weaver in 1948, which ignores human emotion and assumes that the message is conveyed in one direction, is gradually decreasing in use (Lundgren & McMakin, 2013; İplikçi, 2015). On the other hand, findings and criticisms in the context of these inadequacies can also be found in academic studies. For example, Alaszewski (2005) criticizes the rational risk communication model with the idea that there is no single truth in the content of risk information and that the target audience will prefer the source they trust. Bourrier and Bieder (2018), on the other hand, criticize crisis communication for being limited within the framework of current or predicted events and not adequately addressing the uncertainties inherent in risk.

In conclusion, there is a need for a new communication model that can support the common understanding reached by the authors on the necessity of risk communication and adapt to the changing nature of today's risks. It is predicted that the understanding and model that will meet this need will be the "*Situational Approach Model*," as shown in Fig. 8.1, where the best aspects of all other approaches and models can be used and reorganized according to the needs of the age.

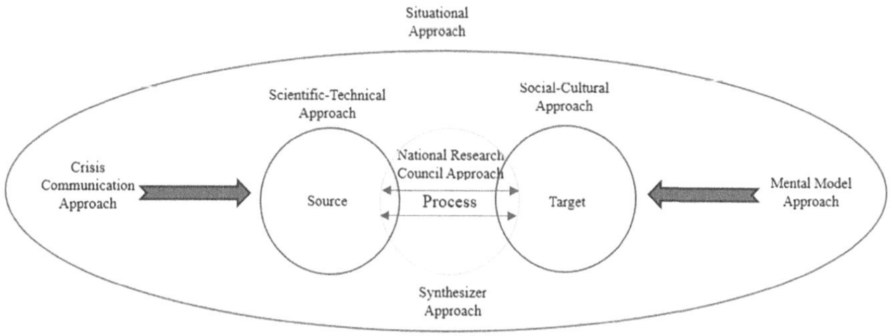

Fig. 8.1 Situational approach model. Source: Created by the author

8.5 What Are the Barriers to Risk Communication?

Risk communication applied in enterprise structures is formal when it is carried out in accordance with a certain structure and methods, and informal when it is applied in the form of experience transfer, conversation, etc., without any conditions. When academic studies in the field of risk communication are examined, it is seen that there is no categorical classification and naming standardization due to the common effects of some obstacles as well as conceptual distinctions.

Yeniçeri and Demirel (2007) state that beyond categorizing the barriers to communication processes as organizational and individual barriers, demographic differences such as gender and age should also be taken into account. Covello et al. (1986) categorize communication barriers as barriers arising from the message, from the source, from the communication channel, and from the receiver. Lundgren and McMakin (2013) examined organizational and emotional barriers as communicator-related barriers, and empathy, mistrust, learning disability, and hostility as listener-related barriers. In addition, it is thought that in some studies, it is expressed as unwillingness to listen, in others as indifference, and trust is related to the formation of risk perception (Hampel, 2006). Enterprise communication barriers and individual communication barriers are shown in Table 8.1. Contrary to the differences in classification and naming, it is accepted that there is a linear relationship between organizational barriers and individual barriers, and that definitions such as time management and technical barriers have common effects on both individual and organizational barriers.

Table 8.1 Risk communication barriers

Enterprise communication barriers	Individual communication barriers
Enterprise awareness	Trust
Communication approaches	Risk perception
Bureaucratic structure	Social environment
Technical barriers	Technical barriers

Source: Prepared by the author

8.5.1 Enterprise Communication Barriers

It is considered that the explanations expressed with different definitions in academic studies can be examined under the headings of enterprise awareness, communication approaches, bureaucratic structure, and technical barriers within the enterprise communication barriers as shown in Table 8.1.

8.5.1.1 Enterprise Awareness

The lack of awareness and belief in the necessity of communication by organization managers is one of the main obstacles to the development of risk communication. Due to this lack of belief, there are contradictions between how risk communication is defined and how it is practiced. Although definitions emphasize two-way dialogue processes, risk communication is currently practiced more for the purpose of educating employees and enabling them to make decisions about risks (Arwa, 2014). In addition, it is observed that the largest share of energy and financial resources in enterprise risk management is spent on identifying and calculating risks, while adequate equipment and personnel are not allocated for risk communication (Lundgren & McMakin, 2013). In addition, it is seen that the responsibility for unsuccessful risk management results is placed on communication stakeholders and managers often cut interactive communication and use only information gathering for the needs of the organization.

Another factor counted in enterprise awareness is other confidentiality policies that do not consider stakeholders valuable to organizations, assume that their concerns are meaningless and that they cannot understand scientific data (Trautman, 2001), and restrict information sharing based on mistrust. The phrase "*You can't understand!*" (Lundgren & McMakin, 2013) used by a manager toward an employee and the confidentiality statements such as "*This is a trade secret, it cannot be disclosed,*" which are more common in financial companies, are examples of this barrier structure. Indeed, the findings of the study conducted by Erdem (2014) reveal the accuracy of these evaluations. In this study conducted on employees in Regional Development Agencies for the European Union (EU) harmonization process, it was found that almost half of the employees answered no to the question "*Are you aware of the risks related to your job?*"

8.5.1.2 Communication Approaches

Communication studies conducted with the assumption that a single communication model will be effective by ignoring the demographic characteristics of the target audience are defined within this obstacle. It is seen that the effectiveness of communication policies that continue to use the same communication tools without feedback from the target audience is gradually decreasing. The findings of a 2015 study on a nuclear facility in Brazil are an example of this definition. It was found that the sounding of the siren on the 10th of every month to raise awareness among the local population and to announce an emergency warning has become less perceptually effective and ordinary over time, and even the next generation has different answers about what it means. These findings suggest that the constant repetition of risk information through the same medium without feedback does not have the expected effect (Da Cunha & De Andrade, 2016).

On the other hand, time planning failures for risk management are another barrier to communication. The creation of risk plans and schedules requires good organization-wide time planning and adequate information flow. As a result of the lack of these elements, risk management processes cannot be carried out properly, and the expected benefit in risk communication cannot be obtained as a result of the changes made in the meeting dates where the processes will be planned are not notified to the stakeholders on time and the participation remains at a minimum level (Lundgren & McMakin, 2013).

8.5.1.3 Bureaucratic Structure

Another obstacle to effective risk communication is that communication efforts about potential risks are restricted by bureaucratic processes. As a result of the unnecessary increase in review and approval processes by the management in an effort to protect the existence of the organization, employees often prefer inaction and prevent accurate information from reaching the management (Lundgren & McMakin, 2013).

Similarly, the fact that public relations representatives assigned for public disclosure prefer unilateral communication due to limitations on their authority and use statements such as "*I am not authorized to explain this*" in response to questions poses an obstacle to effective external communication. Therefore, it is concluded that the knowledge of the people assigned for risk communication and their command of the enterprise culture directly affect the effectiveness of risk communication (Lundgren & McMakin, 2013).

8.5.2 Individual Communication Barriers

It is considered that lack of trust or overconfidence in the source, differences in risk perception toward the risk message communicated, the effects of the social environment in which the individual is involved, and technical barriers to the means of communication can be examined within individual barriers as shown in Table 8.1.

8.5.2.1 Trust

Individuals need information in order to sustain their social and business life, and they need a source they can trust for this information such as family, friends, counselors, scientists, and authorities. Lack of trust between the target and the source, which cannot meet this need, harms not only the effectiveness of communication but also the effectiveness of the means of communication and the risk information transmitted through these means. For this reason, managers must also meet the trust expectations of employees in the decisions they take within the framework of their activities. For example, if an operational change required as a result of a risk assessment is not adequately communicated, employees may think that this change is only focused on production and profit and may worry that their expectations are ignored. As a matter of fact, it would not be wrong to say that if internal communication problems increase, employees' trust in management will be damaged and their work performance within the organization will decrease. Similarly, messages that evaluate only the economic dimensions of a national-level issue and ignore its legal or environmental impacts cause distrust among environmentally sensitive audiences (Trautman, 2001). Moreover, when the same data are not presented at an adequate level due to technical inadequacies or the influence of political groups but are communicated in the context of perception management and these data are refuted from different sources, trust gaps are created and these trust gaps are quickly met by informal relationship stakeholders (Covello et al., 1986). The public distrust caused by the idea that numerical data was not shared transparently at the beginning of the fight against the Covid-19 pandemic and the resulting effort to meet the needed risk information from social platforms is an example of this definition.

On the other hand, the term trust barrier between the source and the target indicates that not only the lack of this feeling but also its high level can be an obstacle in the healthy communication process. The excessive weakness of trust between the source and the individual and the relationship of manipulation draws attention to a concept that has been the subject of scientific research in recent years as "post-truth" and is expressed in terms such as beyond the truth or fake reality. The concept is based on elements such as fascination, mystery, fear, or interest in the unknown, with the aim of mobilizing the target audience to trust information that does not actually exist. The weakness of overconfidence, the use of which is more prevalent in the political discourse of policymakers and the financial advice of commercial actors, sometimes prevents the verification of risk information from other sources and makes individuals vulnerable to manipulation to the extent that it can profoundly affect their lives. The news about the end of the world on December 21, 2012, according to the Mayan Calendar, can be cited as an example of this definition (Özkan, 2019; Rose, 2017). The fact that studies have shown that people trust rumors spread by word of mouth more than experts (National Research Council, 1989) reveals how open they are to these directions. As a result of these evaluations, the importance of the responsibility of trust on stakeholders is once again understood and it is concluded that its subjective weight on communication processes is higher than other obstacles.

8.5.2.2 Risk Perception

The term "*risk*," which constitutes the basic element of risk communication, does not mean the same thing for experts and nonexperts. While experts seek concrete evidence as risk perception, others see uncertainty as more valuable (Hampel, 2006) and adopt optimistic approaches based on faith and fate (Covello et al., 1986). For example, experts' "*there is no proof of this*" is met with "*there is no proof that there is no proof of that*" by employees, which is an example of differences in risk perception. Risk assessment and analysis is quantitative in nature. However, as experts focus more on actual data, they may overlook the risk perceptions and judgments of employees. Risks that are highly probable for experts may seem impossible for employees. As a result, audiences who are not aware of the probabilities and effects of risks may exhibit reluctant and indifferent behaviors in risk communication (Turancı, 2017; Lundgren & McMakin, 2013). In addition, it is a fact that communication processes in which the target audience is not sufficiently analyzed cause differences in perception. The fact that women feel more anxiety than men in reactionary approaches to safety concerns and the possibility of getting cancer can be shown as an example within the framework of the effect of gender difference on risk perception (Spence et al., 2015).

The purpose of communicating risk information is to bring about changes in individuals' lives in the direction of security. However, human beings cannot respond to these changes at the expected speed due to their nature. In fact, resistance emerges as the first reaction. It is seen that when a dangerous situation is detected in the production unit of a factory and communicated to the employees, responses such as "*I have been doing this for 20 years, nothing will happen!*" are encountered. Similar expressions of resistance are also encountered in public communication processes. For example, responses such as "*My grandfather used to drink from this well, nothing will happen!*" can be given as an example (Lundgren & McMakin, 2013). The fact that the number of families who do not want to have their children vaccinated increased from 183 to 12,000 between 2011 and 2016 in a study conducted to determine the opposition to vaccination across our country is an example of the fact that the act of resistance will gradually increase as a result of not eliminating the perception difference (Gür, 2019).

8.5.2.3 Social Environment

The concept used as the social environment defines the sociological and psychological structure formed as a result of the effects of media and social networks, which have evolved in parallel with the development of technology, on the attitudes and behaviors of family, employees, and society (Bourrier & Bieder, 2018). In the context of psychological factors, for the existence of effective communication, it is not enough to convey risk information to the target in a healthy way; it must pass through the filter of individual values, beliefs, and feelings that lead the individual to different communication behaviors (Lundgren & McMakin, 2013). Within the framework of sociological factors, family environment, work environment, and friendship environment are evaluated. The uneasy work environment within the organization, lack of trust in coworkers, or the expectation of acceptance from coworkers and the fear of humiliation due to mistakes to be made create social pressure on individuals, and as a result, it is seen that individuals only participate in mandatory communication processes instead of interactive communication processes.

8.5.3 Technical Barriers

This barrier, which is also considered as technological barriers in some studies, can be examined among both individual and organizational barriers as shown in Table 8.1. Communication effectiveness may decrease because technological changes do not find enough space in enterprise organizations or because the communication structure is completely surrendered to technological change, and the lack of adaptation to this change in employees causes loss of motivation. For example, in a communication model where e-mail system is used extensively, it is inevitable to experience a dialogue deprived of the advantages specific to the telephone communication structure. In the telephone communication structure, interactive information transfer takes place and previously unforeseen risk information details or solutions can be reached. In contrast, in the e-mail system, the parties cannot follow the communication simultaneously and the actual risk information may not be conveyed properly due to correspondence procedures (Boiarsky, 2016). Counterexamples of the benefits and drawbacks in this comparison can also be found. For example, in telephone communication, important details may be overlooked or forgotten as a result of not recording risk information, whereas in e-mail communication, all messages can be tracked in accordance with the time flow.

Another factor evaluated within the framework of technical barriers is that not all employees in the organization are of the same generational structure and therefore cannot adapt to communication tools equally. In the context of internal communication, the adaptation problems of Generation X and Y employees and the problems of harmonization with Generation Z employees are among the issues that need to be solved with activities such as in-house training for the managers of the organization. It can be mentioned that similar solutions are also needed for external communication stakeholders. For example, Da Cunha and De Andrade (2016) point out that the use of communication tools is not at the same level between generations. In addition, it was emphasized that the effectiveness of the calendars distributed about the actions to be taken in dangerous situations that may occur in the nuclear facility on the people of the region was low due to the illiteracy of almost half of the people. In the same study, it was determined that the mechanism through which the people of the region received the most information about the nuclear facility was television. These findings indicate that administrations should update their external communication tools in line with the target audience and the age.

8.6 How to Ensure Effective Risk Communication?

There is no single way to ensure risk communication in enterprise governance. Establishing risk communication and whether it continues in the desired way or not is a variable structure. Therefore, its model and structure are determined by experiences and time, including the enterprise culture (Hampel, 2006). For an effective communication structure, it is first necessary to recognize that the desired outcome is not the only measure of success (Trautman, 2001). At the beginning of communication processes, it is necessary to take into account that insecurity and uneasiness will be more dominant due to the fact that the participating employees have their own value judgments and concerns, and there is a need to be willing for continuity in the communication process (Covello et al., 1986).

Risk blindness is inevitable in risk management where the same approaches are constantly adopted. Therefore, it is thought that effective risk communication can be achieved by bringing together many technical and nontechnical elements instead of experts with a single point of view (Arwa, 2014). Thanks to this understanding, communication will be based on scientific evidence as well as expressing different ideas and opinions, bringing management one step closer to making the right decision (Trautman, 2001).

Creating a common risk perception among employees is very important for risk communication. For this purpose, common language, understanding, values, and experiences are among the requirements for successful communication (Hampel, 2006). In order to guide employees' risk perception, it is useful to consider demographic diversity such as gender differences (Spence et al., 2015) and to include previously unknown concepts and expressions of concern in message content to eliminate perception gaps and keep risk interest at a high level (Trautman, 2001).

It is also true that alternative practices such as organizing workshops, publishing information brochures, and sharing warning messages on enterprise network platforms will be useful in raising risk awareness. In addition, it is assessed that employees should be encouraged to actively participate in all risk management processes starting from the risk strategy determination stage by increasing their sense of trust in the management of the organization and ensuring risk communication ownership. Approaches that focus only on the informational aspect of enterprise risk communication processes should be abandoned and efforts to improve employees' risk literacy should be included in management plans (Turancı, 2017). Before time and resource planning, target audience analysis should be done well and risk communication efforts should be directed in a way to eliminate feelings of apathy among employees (Lundgren & McMakin, 2013).

The quality of alternative channels for communicating risk information increases the accuracy of risk information (Yeniçeri & Demirel, 2007). For this reason, it is envisaged that it would be beneficial to include communication tools suitable for the development of technology in the process in a planned manner and to increase the utilization rates of these elements through activities such as in-house training. For this purpose, it is possible to prevent risk misconceptions that may occur due to risk messages transmitted simultaneously by categorizing communication channels and elements as good, medium, or poor (Arwa, 2014). In addition, it is believed that in order to ensure the effectiveness of risk communication, it would be beneficial to schematically determine the end-to-end communication networks and to increase the awareness of the personnel toward these networks and to test these networks periodically.

On the other hand, in vertical communication structures, which are more common in hierarchical organizations, risk information should not be changed and trivialized in the process of presenting the real information about the risk to senior management, and risk perception should not be changed by adding additional measures and instructions in the downward communication process. Ensuring the effectiveness of risk communication should not be a mere arbitrariness for the managers of the organization and should be made mandatory through legislative arrangements. Within the regulations to be made, the structure, obligations, and communication periods of communication channels should be determined and included in audit plans.

8.7 Conclusion

Since the concept of risk management has an interdisciplinary structure and has a place in many fields such as finance, health, security, and environment, the need for qualified academic studies on risk communication is felt more and more every day. In the academic studies reviewed, it is seen that beyond accepting the necessity of communication, these spatial differences are also reflected in the definitions of what risk communication is.

In the studies conducted in the field of risk communication, it has been observed that risk communication models have changed in accordance with the spirit of time and the necessity of the age. It has been determined that the understandings that initially emphasized the notification aspect of communication and considered the source more valuable have started to attach importance to the effectiveness of communication over time and focus on all elements of communication.

In the context of risk communication barriers, it was observed that there were divergences in the classification and explanation of individual and organizational barriers. On the other hand, it was evaluated that the biggest obstacle to be overcome for enterprise managers is enterprise awareness within the framework of the necessity of communication and the elimination of trust deficiencies within the framework of ensuring the participation of individuals in communication. In institutions where bureaucratic processes are preferred, employees show reluctance to participate in communication, and the effectiveness of communication tools planned by ignoring the demographic characteristics of the target audience in communication processes carried out at the public level decreases over time. It is understood that risk messages lacking objective qualities may cause misperceptions in risk perceptions, and the resulting trust gaps may be used for malicious purposes by nonexpert sources.

In addition, it is envisaged that dangers such as risk blindness that may occur in the risk management process in which only experts will participate can be minimized with the participation of nonexpert stakeholders. In addition, although communication processes supported by technological means are beneficial, it was mentioned that their excessive use may cause adaptation problems in employees.

As a result of the study, it has been seen that the communication outcome should not be the primary goal and the existence and quality of the communication process should be given importance. However, it is understood that establishing effective risk communication is not a choice but a necessity for enterprise governments. On the other hand, it is concluded that there is no standard communication model that can be applied in every organization and that the best model can be reached as a result of time and experience, provided that organizational cultures are taken into account.

References

Alaszewski, A. (2005). Risk communication: İdentifying the İmportance of social context. *Healthy, Risk & Society, 7*(2), 101–105.

Arwa, J. (2014). The end of risk communication. *Journal of Risk Research, 17*(10), 1245–1249.

Beck, U. (1996). *Risk society: Towards a new modernity.* Sage Publications.

Boholm, A. (2008). New perspectives on risk communication: uncertainty in a complex society. *Journal of Risk Research, 11*(1–2), 1–3.

Boiarsky, R. C. (2016). *Risk communication and miscommunication.* University Press of Colorado.

Bourrier, M., & Bieder, C. (2018). *Risk communication for the future: Towards smart risk governance and safety management.* Springer International. https://doi.org/10.1007/978-3-319-74098-0

COSO. (2004). *Enterprise risk management.* Retrieved 10.04.2021, from http://coso.org

Covello, V. T., Winterfeld, D. V., & Slovic, P. (1986). Risk communication: a review of the literature. *Risk Abstracts, 3*, 171–182. https://www.researchgate.net/publication/285817518

Da Cunha, R. D. S., & De Andrade, D. A. (2016). Risk communication and external emergency plan in Angra dos Reis, Brazil. *World Journal of Nuclear Science and Technology, 6*, 301–308.

Erdem, E. (2014). Kurumsal Risk Yönetiminde Çalışanların Risk Algısı: Bir Kalkınma Ajansı Örneğinde. *Yüksek Lisans Tezi,* Gazi Ünv.Sos.Bil.Ens., Ankara.

Giddens, A. (1991). *The consequences of modernity.* Stanford University Press.

Güler, Ç., Çobanoğlu, Z. (1997). *Risk İletişimi ve Risk Yönetimi.* Ankara: Çevre Sağlığı Temel Kaynak Dizisi No.47. Retrieved 15.04.2021, from https://sbu.saglik.gov.tr/Ekutuphane/kitaplar/css47.pdf

Gür, E. (2019). Vaccine hesitancy-vaccine refusal. *Turkısh Archives of Pediatrics, 54*(1), 1–2.

Hampel, J. (2006). Different concepts of risk- a challenge for risk communication. *International Journal of Medical Microbiology, 296*(40), 5–10.

İplikçi, H. G. (2015). İletişimde Temel Modeller ve Kitle İletişim Modelleri. *Sosyal ve Beşeri Bilimler Dergisi, 7*(2), 15–25.

Kıral, H. (2018). *Kurumsal Risk Yönetiminin Riskleri.* Denetişim Dergisi, Sayı 18, s.5–18.

Lundgren, R. E., & McMakin, A. H. (2013). *Risk communication, a handbook for communicating environmental, safety, and health risk* (5th ed.). Wiley-IEEE Press.

National Research Council. (1989). *Improving risk communication, Committee on risk perception and communication.* National Academy Press.

Özkan, Ö. (2019). *Gerçeklik Sonrası (Post Truth) Zamanda Söylentinin Medyada Gerçek Gibi Sunulması: Maya Takvimi-Kıyamet Konusu*. Selçuk Üniversitesi İletişim Fakültesi Akademik Dergisi, s.64–91. https://www.researchgate.net/publication/330739745

Rose, J. (2017). Brexit, Trump ve post-truth politics. *Public Integrity, 19*(6), 555–558. https://doi.org/10.1080/10999922.2017.1285540

Spence, P. R., Lachlan, K. A., Westerman, D., Lin, X., Harris, C. J., Sellnow, T. L., & Sellnow-Richmond, D. D. (2015). Exemplification effects: Responses to perceptions of risk. *Journal of Risk Research*, 1. https://doi.org/10.1080/13669877.2015.1100658

Trautman, T. D. (2001). Risk communication- the perceptions and realities. *Food Additives and Contaminants, 18*(12), 1130–1134.

TSV. (2021). https://www.saglik.org.tr/makale-haber/kemoterapi-nedir-kanser-tedavisinde-nasil-uygulanir

Turancı, E. (2017). *Risk iletişimi Stratejileri Açısından Bilgi ve Bilgi Okuryazarlığı: Sağlık Haberlerine ve Sağlık Çalışanlarına Yönelik Araştırma, Doktora Tezi,* Gazi Ünviversitesi Sosyal Bilimler Enstitüsü.

WHO, Risk Communication. Retrieved 30.04.2021., from https://www.who.int/risk-communication/background

Yakut, İ. (2008). *İletişim Bilimi Perspektifinden Risk İletişimi Stratejileri*. Umuttepe Yayınları.

Yeniçeri, Ö., & Demirel, Y. (2007). Örgüt İçi Bilgi Paylaşımına Yönelik Bireysel ve Örgütsel Engeller Üzerine Bir Araştırma. *Selçuk Ünv Karaman İİBF Dergisi, 12*, 221–234.

Murat Soner is a PhD student at the Social Sciences University of Ankara, Department of Audit and Risk Management. He is also an officer in the Ministry of National Defense. He has been a manager at different levels within the Ministry of National Defense since 1999. In 2006, he completed his bachelor's degree in public administration, and in 2013, he completed his master's degree in private law. In addition to his risk communication studies, he continues to work on the relationship between enterprise risk management and strategic management. He has two published articles in this field and one article in the process of publication.

Chapter 9
Reputation Risk: Does an Increase in Reputation Risks Damage the Reputation of Risk Management?

Yasemin Gök

Abstract Intangible values such as reputation can create a strong perception on the public as much as material values. Various factors, be it internal or external, that can destroy reputation or cause loss of reputation are perceived as risks to reputation. Reputation risk, expressed as expectation gap, also indicates the effectiveness of risk management. After all, risk management effectiveness is related to our capacity to deal with reputation risks. In the context of reputation management, everything that has an impact on corporate reputation is perceived as a reputation risk. But can this lead to risk management of everything under reputation management and failure to manage anything? In this context, the aim of this study is to find an answer to the question, "Does the reputation of risk management decrease as the risks of reputation increase?" All in all, the perception, identification, definition, assessment, and effective management of risks to reputation will reveal the effectiveness of risk management. However, it should be noted that the approach of risk management of everything will lead to risk management of nothing.

Keywords Reputation risk · Reputation risk management · Reputation of risk management

9.1 Introduction

The concept reputation is associated with the meanings of being respected, reliable, and valuable in the dictionary of Turkish Language Association. It is apparent that reputation, which includes the feeling of trust and commitment without doubt, is closely related to how individuals, organizations, societies, and even countries are perceived and evaluated by others. From this point of view, reputation actually

Y. Gök (✉)
Social Sciences University of Ankara, Ankara, Türkiye
e-mail: yasemin.gok@student.asbu.edu.tr

H. Kıral (ed.), *Rethinking Enterprise Risk Management*, Accounting, Finance, Sustainability, Governance & Fraud: Theory and Application,
https://doi.org/10.1007/978-981-97-5983-5_9

includes perception in a way, and therefore it can be shaped by the perceptions. As a matter of fact, Gonzalez (2015) states that in terms of its literal meaning in Oxford Dictionary, reputation is defined as beliefs or opinions generally held about a person or something, which implies that reputation is based on perception, not reality. Likewise, according to Gaultier-Gaillard and Louisot (2006), reputation is a social construct that directly affects the market value of the organization and can turn into an important economic value as an intangible asset, relying on individual beliefs and perceptions. From this point of view, reputation is a social construct based on how you appear in the eyes of others and arises from the desire to have good impressions on others (Cañigueral & de Hamilton, 2019).

According to Walter (2016), reputation is a competition tool quite important in various fields such as education, business world, online communities, and social status, and when considered as a social evaluation tool, it can also be defined as the belief, opinion, or judgment of the public toward a person, group of people, or an organization. According to Charles Fombrun (1996), a famous author developing the reputation coefficient scale, reputation is a perceptual representation of an organization's past actions and possible future prospects, its chances of success, and is the overall appeal or image of the organization that reflects all its key components when compared to other leading competitors (Kwon & Rupp, 2012; Çillioğlu Karademir & Şimşek, 2013). Although it seems to be an intangible asset, reputation is actually considered as a material element in determining the organization's place in the market, because having a strong reputation will lead to more competitiveness and become more attractive to others (Çillioğlu Karademir & Şimşek, 2013). As a result, intangible values such as reputation can create a strong perception on the target audience or public opinion, as well as tangible values.

According to Kıyat and Sütçü (2013), who evaluate reputation in terms of corporate identity and image, reputation is expressed as the trust and respect by the society toward individuals or organizations. In addition, researchers state that corporate identity is related to the creation of corporate image (image), while corporate reputation is the sum of this corporate image (image) created by internal and external stakeholders such as communities, investors, consumers, and employees. It is also stated that the perceptions of these groups play an important role in the creation and measurement of corporate reputation.

According to Aula and Heinonen (2016), reputation is the mutual communication between how the organization sees itself and how it is perceived, as it is formed on the basis of experiences and comments about the organization. In addition, reputational problems are defined depending on how dominant or not the perceptions of reality-based first-hand experiences are (Aula & Heinonen, 2016). As stated by Kıyat and Sütçü (2013), while according to economists, reputation indicates the possible behavior of an organization, according to strategists, the reputation of an organization is a competitive advantage against competitors. According to accountants, reputation is an intangible corporate value that can go up and down in the market, while according to marketers, reputation is perceptual assets with the power to attract target audience or permanent customers (Kıyat & Sütçü, 2013).

Since it reflects the perspective and natural attitudes and behaviors of others, reputation apparently determines the position of individuals, organizations, societies, or countries in the environment in which they are located and can be a measure of the impact it will create in the environment, i.e., power. The effect of such position and power achieved will provide not only competitive advantage but also the power to direct some circles.

Defining reputation within the scope of six basic ideas regarding reputation management, Liehr-Gobbers and Storck (2011) consider reputation as an element that primarily depends on the behavior of various stakeholder groups and directs corporate values. Eisenegger (2009) states that reputation performs a basic guiding function in society. However, in the process, there may be some risks that will negatively affect and change these attitudes and behaviors formed as a result of others' perspectives. For example, external social phenomena that can have a serious impact on the organization, society, or the position of the country can exacerbate small problems and cause them to turn into huge problems.

Reputation-related risks, generally referred to as reputational risks, are characterized as potential loss or damage to reputation or internal and external risks that will destroy reputation. Such risks can be considered as potential losses in financial capital, social capital, or market share that may arise due to damage to the organization's reputation in the corporate sense. Since reputation risks are generally considered as "speculative risks,[1]" they must be evaluated in terms of both opportunity or gain and loss or damage (Herkenhoff, 2009, p. 197). According to Glickman (2014), reputational risks are both more threatening and more difficult to manage systematically compared to other types of risks as they can be quite destructive in terms of their consequences or reduce reputation. Due to the lack of a clear definition of the risks related to reputation and insufficient evidence, defining the value of any reputation, source, and extent of the damage to this reputation and risks related to reputation are quite challenging (Walter, 2016).

In fact, although reputation and reputational risks emerged in the early 1960s in economics, studies on the concept of reputation are only in the late 1990s (Gaultier-Gaillard & Louisot, 2006). Power (2004) stated that reputation risk emerged in 1995, as in operational risks. According to the statements of Çillioğlu Karademir and Şimşek (2013), there has been a need to be respected by others and earn reputation throughout the history, but the concept of corporate reputation has been focused on in the literature since the 1990s with studies on public organizations in various sectors and businesses in the private sector. As Soprano et al. (2009) point out, the key element of reputational risks is the level of credibility of an organization, individual, society, or country; product and service quality, managerial justice, or, more

[1] Speculative risks: category of risk that, when assumed, results in an uncertain degree of gain or loss (Finansal Ansiklopedi, 2021). Speculative risks indicate a situation where there is a possibility of losing as well as winning, with the possibility of losing, not losing or winning. Pure risks, on the other hand, are those with no possibility of gain but only possibility of loss. Financial and operational risks can be classified as pure and speculative risks (Outreville, 1998; Banks, 2008).

generally, impact of a specific event that may adversely affect the perception of trust or confidence.

Considering the above explanations in general, it is clear that the most important value that individuals and organizations, societies, and countries can have is their reputation. For this reason, identifying and managing all kinds of risks that will reduce reputation is deemed as one of the important responsibilities that can only be addressed strategically. The studies conducted on this subject state that corporate risk management is quite important in identifying and managing such risks, and such risks left unmanaged may probably result in an increase in reputational risks. It is stated that risk management is necessary in order to understand this uniquely complex structure of reputation and to identify threats to reputation (Szwajca, 2018). However, it should be taken into account that risk management can also cause risks itself.

In this case, does the reputation of risk management decrease as reputational risks increase? Or will the risks arising from risk management further reduce the reputation of risk management? This will continue to be a matter of curiosity. In fact, the efforts aiming to reduce the risk perception by increasing the level of reputation are important in terms of keeping and directing the attitudes and behaviors of the target group or the public. Considering the relationship between reputation and risk at first glance, it is expected to increase the effectiveness of risk management as the risks to reputation are determined and controlled. Naturally, it can be, consequently, predicted that reputation of risk management will be expected to increase as trust and credibility in risk management will increase. But the most critical thing in this process is how to explain risk management reputation because the question is: Will it be possible to identify the risk management reputation by "the difference or gap between expected value and actual value" as in the case in reputation risk? Or by the difference between its actual size and its perceived size? It is also important to explain what kind of factors may affect the effectiveness of risk management.

In the light of the information obtained in this part on reputation risk, "Does the increase in reputation risks really reduce the reputation of risk management?" Along with the effort to answer this question, we will explain exactly what it means. In this context, the study consists of three parts. The first part includes the introduction part which presents general information about the concept of reputation and the purpose of the study. In the second part, the literature is reviewed in terms of reputation risk and its scope, the risks related to reputation, the relationship between reputation risk and risk reputation, and the types of reputation risks in terms of risk-based audit practices. In the last part, possible answers to the question, "Does the reputation of risk management decrease as the risks of reputation increase?" are given in the light of the information obtained within the scope of this study.

9.2 Reputation Risk: Definition and Scope

The increase in social media tools and the ongoing globalization as a result of developments in communication technologies in the twenty-first century mean more competition. This shows that reputation and reputational risks have become even more important (Eckert, 2017). Similarly, it is stated that globalization leads to the emergence of an increasingly competitive market and reputation becomes more valuable and important, and as a result, a strong reputation is considered as an important and sustainable source of distinctive superiority (Tucker & Melevar, 2005). Despite absence of consensus in reputation management for defining and evaluating reputation and reputation risk, it is argued that a positive and strong reputation means an important competitive power (Eckert, 2017).

Reputation risk is understood as a source of strategy and a complex structure. In order to manage and work on reputation risk, reputation risk must first be understood and defined. Otherwise, reputation risks cannot be identified or evaluated (Swanepoel et al., 2017). As stated in the introduction, some differences in the definitions and conceptualizations of reputation in various fields such as economics, marketing, and accounting (Kıyat & Sütçü, 2013) indicate that there is no common approach to measurement of reputation and that there are various measurement methods and tools for reputation (Deren van het Hoff, 2013).

Considering the definitions of and explanations on the concept of reputation risk, it is apparently associated with risks to reputation, which lead to changes in attitudes and behaviors depending on the change in perception, eventually have a material effect and include results related to trust, honesty, and reputation. So how are reputation risk or reputational risks mostly defined?

Reputation risk can be defined as a situation, event, or actions that can have a positive or negative impact on the reputation of an organization (Gaultier-Gaillard et al., 2009). However, in general, reputation risk, with a largely negative definition, can be defined as a situation or events affecting an organization, weakening or strengthening its reputation and trust in the organization. The occurrence of a reputation risk may cause some loss or damage, as well as considerably weaken the legitimacy of the organization (Aula & Heinonen, 2016).

According to Scott and Walsham (2005), who reconceptualize reputation risk by considering the concepts of reputation, trust and risk, reputation risk is defined as "the potential to negatively associate actions or events with outcomes that affect aspects of an organization that people value, i.e., reputable action." In general, reputation risks may arise due to an event or circumstances that change stakeholders' perceptions, lead to behavioral change, and ultimately result in financial consequences. In addition to an organization's own actions and external events, reputation risks can also arise from relationships with other parties (Heidinger & Gatzert, 2018). In short, reputation risk is also defined as risks arising from negative perception by the public.

In the definitions made by Eckert (2017) on reputation risk, the concept is classified under three categories through creating a causal link. Accordingly, risks that may lead to negative perceptions on the stakeholders of the organization, possibly cause some changes in the behavior of the stakeholders and cause a financial loss or damage as a result, are defined as reputational risks.

As a result of the literature review on reputation risk, we come across with the concept expressed in different forms in English, namely, "reputation risk," "reputational risk," and "risk to reputation." According to Gaultier-Gaillard and Louisot (2006) , there is no such thing as "reputational risk", only "risks to reputation" exists. Because the concept of "reputational risk" is suitable for a concept that covers all risks that may affect reputation, regardless of source, but the source in question may be noncompliance with the legislation, decrease in data security, unexpected profit warning, or unethical behavior. Since reputation is a social construct (Gaultier-Gaillard & Louisot, 2006), reputation risk will also include a social construct in line with relevant expectations and is therefore the aggregate of expectations, perceptions, and statements.

It's really hard to say what the reputation risk is. While Honey (2009) generally defines reputation risk as uncertainties surrounded by situations where a strong and good reputation may somehow be tarnish and lost, Rayner (2003) states that there is no such thing as reputation risk; there is only risk to reputation, which is a situation, event, or action that covers any risk that may affect reputation, like Gaultier-Gaillard and Louisot (2006) mentioned above. Rayner (2003) also states that the source of risk affects both brand value and corporate reputation, and once the risk occurs, trust toward the organization can sometimes decrease. It is stated that Ross (2005) and Tonello (2007) have a similar point of view (Szwajca, 2018). Accordingly, Tonello (2007) evaluates that the source of reputation risk may be the cause or effect of another type of risk, and as a result, reputation risk is considered as the risk of risks. Ross (2005) states that many types of risk include reputation risk, which requires a different implementation, and will therefore have more serious effects in the long run than risks arising directly from the event itself (Szwajca, 2018).

Reputation risk, unlike other types of financial risk, cannot be reduced to a minimum tolerance level considering the possibility of making a higher profit. However, due to its emergence, reputation risks emerge as a type of risk that should be avoided due to its huge and often difficult-to-manage economic and social effects (Dell'Atti et al., 2016). Power (2004) points out that the secondary effects of a risk event refer to the risk of risks, and in some cases, reputation risk management concerns may sometimes call for risk aversity, but in reality, this is associated with responsibility aversity, not risk aversity (Power, 2004).

Given the above explanations, the extent of reputation risks generally appears to be the result of any adverse or potentially infringing or negligent event, regardless of whether the individual, organization, society, or country is directly responsible for the event in question. In fact, examining the events associated with reputation risks, it is clear that there are generally ethical violations, reliability issues, collateral issues, inadequacy in sustainability, low quality, deficiencies, or unethical innovations. Reputation of an organization is, indeed, recorded as an intangible asset in financial records. Therefore, it is clear that any damage to the reputation of an organization will have financial consequences.

9.3 Types and Sources of Reputation Risks

Larkin (2003) states that risks to reputation, which is a constant issue in reputation management, are very complex and diverse. The most common types of risk to reputation are inadequacy of product or service, lack of guarantee, misbehavior, unfair employment practices, damage health, safety or the environment, inconsistency in practices or policies, poor governance or ethics, interference in legislation, threat of litigation, competitor targeting, and negative stakeholder perception (Larkin, 2003).

In general, the formation of reputation risks is quite extensive in terms of various demands and needs. However, the technical and human risk categories confirm the thesis that reputation risk is the risk of risks and ultimately affect the reputation of the organization. Such technical and human risks include risk of harm, risk of distorting and leaking content presented and transmitted (content risk), risk of fraud, abuse, and illegitimacy risk (compliance risk). All these risk sources and dynamics make reputation risk an imperative task for internal auditors and risk managers (Szwajca, 2018). When reputation is considered as the sum of past and present perceptions and ideas about the organization that is often in the consciousness of stakeholders, it is apparent that the basic elements should be comprehended (Gaultier-Gaillard & Louisot, 2006).

With the developments in risk management practices since the beginning of the 1990s, risk management has been defined together with internal control more frequently, which has led to risk-based regulations coming to the fore. Power (2004) explains the reason for this as follows: The rise of risk management is an effective response to the fact that the world is getting riskier, i.e., more dangerous. As a matter of fact, countries with developed economies, despite being quite safe, may also face some "man-made risks"[2] due to the negative effects of advances or developments in the field of communication and technology. Although risk management of all things reflects increased attention to primary risks (health, financial, and bodily risks), in fact, reputation is largely characterized by secondary risk management.

From the point of view of Ulrich Beck, the author of the *Risk Society*, the reason for the increase in risks to reputation is the fact that the power shifts from organizations to unpredictable consumers (Power, 2004). In fact, most of the societies are aware of this. According to Power (2004), societies have no choice but to organize in the face of risk. Internal control should be provided in all areas of organizational life and every issue needs to be addressed as a part of risk management. While risk management of everything reflects the growing interest in primary (health,

[2] Man-made risks can also be defined as human risks. Human risks are one of the largest risk categories that organizations face, and they are risks that occur when people do what they should not do or do not do what they should do (Human Risk, 2020). Human-induced risks include risks arising from human error. Such risks are risks arising from human deficiencies caused by people's insufficient knowledge or skills, or from human faults stemming from an employee's willful violation of corporate policy or the law, or from a failure of the organization's human resource management process (Bombiak, 2017).

financial, and bodily risks) risks very well, in fact, reputation is also and to a large extent characterized by secondary risk management. The underlying problem of risk management of everything is the ongoing change in society in the balance between the management of primary and secondary risks, and quite high growth especially in secondary risks. Of course, primary risks are identical to secondary risks although the distinction between primary and secondary risk is often argued as artificial risks for organizations whose existence are largely intangible and reputation based. Risk management of everything is characterized by the emergence of secondary, i.e., reputational risk management because if everything has an impact on corporate reputation, then reputational risk management requires risk management of everything. Therefore, the rise of reputation risk management is not only a product of the emergence of the new economy but also a requirement of managing intangible assets (Power, 2004). After all, all kinds of developments and changes in the twenty-first century cause our world to become riskier and more dangerous, as Power (2004) states, and the most effective response to this can be given through effective risk management.

Studies on reputation risks indicate that it is difficult to manage such risks since reputation risk is a qualitative risk rather than a quantitative one. Given the preferred managerial approaches in case of reputation risks, it is clear that reactive approaches are mostly relied on because the proactive approach measures are quite costly in general. As a result, reactive approaches, compared to proactive approaches, clearly cannot provide an ongoing risk definition structure for identifying and controlling potential events that may lead to reputation risk. Thanks to holistic, proactive, and systematic reputation risk management, stakeholders' trust and credence are created and investments and public loyalty are increased, which in turn, reduces regulatory response (Szwajca, 2018). As a result of the research conducted by Groza et al. (2011), it is stated that proactive approaches are more strategic and value oriented compared to reactive approaches. In fact, it is predicted that the proactive approach can lead to a more positive perceived reputation than the reactive approach (Rim & Ferguson, 2017).

Possible consequences of situations and events involving reputational risks are addressed through proactive or reactive approaches in reputation management as is the case in risk management. In fact, reputation and reputation management are apparently systematic elements within the structure of risk management. According to Hume (2016), Professor Elisa Juholin, studying on corporate promotion and current media strategies, has identified four possible strategies implemented by organizations: proactive, active, reactive, and passive. Accordingly, the proactive promotion strategy is credible and open to the public, and this strategy also ensures public visibility by presenting reports on negative issues. An active promotion strategy shares corporate stories and ideas with the media, whereas the reactive promotional strategy only takes action when requested by the media. In the passive promotion strategy, action is taken on a number of negative issues when they are completely compelled to, and there is no communication policy. Consequently, organizations use appropriate communication strategies to respond quickly and effectively when or before they encounter reputational risks. It is estimated that approximately 20–30% of international companies prefer proactive reputation management (Hume, 2016).

Each organization has a unique cluster of attributes that enable organizations to respond to risks and problems, as well as proactively identify and address opportunities. This cluster can identify and classify the attributes that can affect the current value of each organization or create a new value (Foster, 2018). Various data and real-time analyses are needed to model reputation factors, compare, and foresee results. Figure 9.1 provides the reputation analysis framework, which presents the factors affecting reputation with a real-time and multi-indicator forecasting model. A reporting framework is obtained through this reputation analysis framework, which will strengthen the reputation over time and develop strategies by foreseeing how the situation can be addressed considering different scenarios, factors, and processes affecting reputation. Under the mentioned framework, first of all, internal and external data are collected on how and in which market a particular stakeholder will affect the reputation of an organization. Data-factor analysis is performed by integrating the collected data, and then a dynamic framework that affects corporate reputation is revealed by comparing and defining the impact of alternative

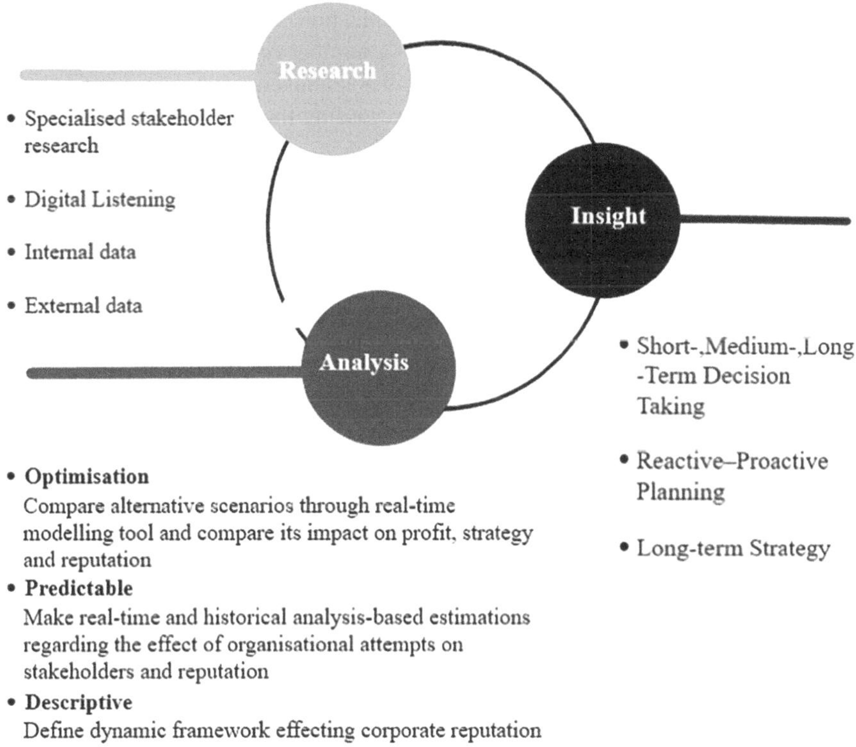

Fig. 9.1 Reputation analysis framework. Source: Foster (2018)

scenarios, profits, and strategies on reputation. At the last stage, concrete ideas about possible future events are determined and strategies are developed accordingly.

Management and maintenance of reputation requires two basic cognitive processes (Cañigueral & de Hamilton, 2019). Accordingly, first, it is necessary to understand what others think of us and to be aware that opinions can be manipulated or directed. Second, in order to manage reputation, it is necessary to care about how you appear in the eyes of others and to have the desire to be seen in a positive way. Therefore, reputation management also requires social motivation processes (Cañigueral & de Hamilton, 2019).

According to Soprano et al. (2009), who argue that there is no universally accepted definition of reputation risk in terms of financial industry and legal arrangements, reputational risks and operational risks are definitely interrelated. Because operational losses or damages have an impact on reputation, and managerial decisions that affect reputational risks cause reputation to be barely visible. Accordingly, reputation risk is the risk of damaging the reliability of the organization in the market where it is located, and the main element of reputation risk is defined as the effect of a certain event that may affect the perception of the organizations regarding its reliability, service quality, understanding of justice in management, or credibility (Soprano et al., 2009).

Gonzalez (2015) defines reputational risks as threats to the positive perception that others have or should have about the organization, its products or services, or managers and employees, which can lead to a number of negative consequences. These results are stated to be loss of current and potential customers, loss of employees, loss of talent, loss of income, bad faith regarding the public interest, separate review on behalf of government or regulatory agencies, shame, or loss of reputation. In addition, data loss, instant interruptions in the website, system errors, insufficient technical support, and other information technologies risks, which are mostly related to public relations activities and directly experienced by the target audience, can also pose threats to reputation (Gonzalez, 2015).

As the importance of corporate social responsibility and sustainability increases, it becomes more important to manage the reputation risk, which is deemed one of the most important and difficult risks to manage. A survey of senior executives by the Economist Intelligence Unit found that reputation risk ranks first by far, followed by regulatory risks and human capital risks. However, the main reasons for the difficulties in managing reputation risks are the inadequacy of existing tools and techniques; the inability to identify the responsible person; coordination inadequacy between management, risk management, and corporate communication; and the lack of communication with external stakeholders (Eccles & Krzus, 2010).

Reputation is built on trust with all stakeholders, thanks to past honest conduct, although it demonstrates belief that the organization is moving on a sustainable path. Despite the fact that reputation may seem more durable than initially thought, it can be dragged into failure or decline in case of annoying repeated abuses (Gaultier-Gaillard & Louisot, 2006). The Enron scandal is given as a suitable example for this (Larkin, 2003; Gaultier-Gaillard & Louisot, 2006; Aula & Heinonen, 2016). The damage to the organization's reputation in the Enron scandal resulted in bankruptcy. The same is true, in this scandal, for the trust placed in the audit firm. In fact, one of the basic components of trust and thus reputation is generally stated to be ethical behavior, and one of the important risks that organizations face is the risks related to ethical rules. The reputation damage that such risks cause for organizations that face them unprepared can be much greater.

According to Power (2004), reputational risk management can provide a potential knowledge transfer between organizations and social values systems. In some cases, organizations reveal that reputation risk will be forced to confront its social impact, causing the risk to be socially exaggerated. Risk management of everything, though a fad, states that the focus should be on individual, legal, and reputational risks rather than the primary risks embodied in the official mission. In fact, it should always be taken into account that even the gap between public expectations and actual performance creates a risk to reputation (Power, 2004).

According to Gaultier-Gaillard and Louisot (2006), it is sometimes possible to come out of a crisis situation where reputation is in danger, with a stronger image, as in the examples of Bank of America, Wachovia, and City Group. Likewise, in the crisis period, which is a very difficult process, organizations can seize the opportunity to "exist" in a way that will increase the public's trust by avoiding ethical misconduct violations, without paying any advertising fee in various media or television.

Organizations in today's society, defined as a multi-stakeholder and multichannel society, should not be left on their own to provide their stakeholders with all the information they need about the organization. Otherwise, organizations may be vulnerable to false information and hearsay information about themselves, thereby putting their reputations at risk (Eccles & Krzus, 2010).

The specificity of reputation risk, on the other hand, brings to light certain attributes that present certain challenges and dilemmas in terms of risk management. These attributes are stated as follows: (a) Reputation risks are relative (the fact that they will differ in degree, duration, and cost in other similar reputation crisis cases due to expectations and the diversity of factors that define effectiveness of meeting expectations); (b) reputational risk is a behavioral risk (stakeholder decisions and behavior are shaped by various unpredictable psychological and social factors such as, e.g., gossip, rapid mood swings, rumors, media news); (c) reputational risk is, due to the nature of causality, the risk of risks (caused by risks arising from other activities); and (d) it is difficult to measure and evaluate reputation risk due to its qualitative nature and complexity of cause and effect relationship (Szwajca, 2018).

Eccles et al. (2007) argue that there are three important determinants of reputational risks: accordingly, (a) the gap between reputation and reality, which is expressed as the situation where the organization's external reputation is greater than its ability to consistently meet expectations through actual performance; (b) actions considered acceptable become unacceptable as social norms and values change, or changing beliefs and expectations; and (c) inadequate internal coordination or the actions of one group creating expectations that another group cannot meet (Eccles & Krzus, 2010).

In field studies on reputation management, it is stated that organizations can manage reputation crises through strategic messages and communication channels including persuasion approach (Shanahan & Seele, 2015). The fundamental basis of risk communication is that perceived risk is just as important as actual risk, and risk perceptions are more emotional than rational. The Greek philosopher Epictetus said, "Perceptions are real because people believe them." If a person believes something, it is a fact for them, even if the facts or science shows it to be irrational. Risk communication, included in a comprehensive communication strategy, brings reality to negotiations that lead to discussion when it aims to eliminate concerns and respond to emotions (Griffin, 2014).

In this case, the most important role in reputation risks, which is considered behavioral risk, is apparently social media, which provides the opportunity to create a strong public opinion, and the predictability of reputation risk is very problematic due to its behavioral structure. Because it seems practically impossible to predict the occurrence probability of events determined by public opinion and behavior and to include it as a factor in risk schemes or models. It is stated that if the focus is on the expected lack of trust, arranging the communication in this direction will do more harm than good as it will put the communicator in a defensive position. In addition, complaints about the disappearing public trust and concerns that this will increase risks and weaken false dangers can be described as a model of trust deficiency (Bearth & Siegrist, 2021). As a result, the risks related to the new information environment arising from digitalization may also be among the risks that will harm trust, and thus reputation.

Gaultier-Gaillard and Louisot (2006) point out that attacks to reputation will involve not only threats but also opportunities, as is the case for many risky situations, because in times of crisis there will be partial reliance on how corporate behavior is perceived by key stakeholders. Larkin (2003) and Rayner (2003) state that there is a need for an ongoing process to assess and mitigate reputation risks, as well as to increase opportunities arising from trust in stakeholders.

9.4 Importance of Reputation Management

In studies on reputation and reputation management, it is stated that the organization should evaluate reputation and reality objectively in order to eliminate the gap between reputation and reality. Expectations and beliefs can appear suddenly or gradually develop over time, in which case, awareness of how social norms and values change will be raised by following the trends, social attitudes and behaviors, and the media, and thus awareness of the change in expectations comprehensively supported and followed at an earlier stage will be built (Eccles & Krzus, 2010).

As stated in the previous section, reputation risk includes qualitative risk rather than quantitative risk. Since reputation includes perception, perception must be measured. Three things determine the extent to which an organization is exposed to reputation risk. The first is whether the corporate reputation exceeds its real character, and the second is how much the beliefs and expectations of the stakeholders or the public toward the organization have changed, which can increase the gap or the difference or, on the contrary, reduce it. Third, is the quality of internal coordination and this is also a factor that can affect the mentioned difference or gap (Eccles et al., 2007). An important way to avoid inadequate internal coordination requires a well-defined process that encompasses public relations, investor relations, corporate communications, marketing, risk management, and all other groups. The input of this process is necessary for reputation management. In order to control and coordinate this process, an integrated reporting and a collaborative process is required (Eccles & Krzus, 2010).

According to Liehr-Gobbers and Storck (2011), who consider six basic ideas regarding reputation management, it is the reputation that drives corporate value first, followed by corporate value that depends on the behavior of various stakeholder groups or different target groups or the public. Reputation management, placed in the third stage, aims to create common interests with stakeholders or target groups. Stakeholder or target group perception is formed by each member of an organization, and building and maintaining the desired reputation is an essential part of leadership. In addition, reputational goals need to be linked to corporate strategy (Liehr-Gobbers & Storck, 2011). Accordingly, reputation cannot be determined by the views of a single stakeholder group, and in order for a strong and positive reputation to exist, all existing stakeholders are expected to have a positive perception of the organization. For this reason, the perception of reputation is apparently important in taking action to reveal the difference of opinion between internal and external stakeholders and to determine the factors behind such difference.

Stakeholders and related parties often associate reputation and risk, creating the perception that a good reputation can reduce the likelihood of risk or even not cover such risks. However, reputation includes beliefs, ideas, images, and some assumptions that reflect the position and dignity of certain people, social groups, products, organizations, and similar things (Ruso et al., 2012).

As stated above, the measure of reputation is the difference between level of the expected value and the actual performance, and such difference constitutes the reputation risk (Power, 2004; Çillioğlu Karademir & Şimşek, 2013). As Szwajca (2018) points out, reputation risks are relative, indeed, because there will be a gap or difference between the expectations of the stakeholders and the state of meeting the expectations. As a result, relationships with stakeholders will become a potential source of reputation risk. The level of this risk will depend on the size of the expectation on one hand and on the effectiveness of meeting those expectations on the other. Therefore, risk management needs to consider and compare expectations and the level of fulfillment of expectations. The main point here is the activities carried out to know, understand, and monitor expectations and to meet those expectations.

The purpose of reputation management is to persuade stakeholders or target groups to protect the positive image they have or to remedy the damaged perception and improve it in a positive way, and organizations achieve this by shaping the perception of public responsibility and influencing target audiences (Shanahan & Seele, 2015). In addition, according to Larkin (2003), the fact that an organization has multiple internal and external stakeholders causes the organization to have a wide variety of reputations, and reputation emerges as a result of a dynamic process.

Accordingly, the influences are built by the public perception of reputation, the activities of the organization and the experiences gained directly with its employees, the general perception of the public about the qualifications of the organization, and the information shared by other people through social media and social networks.

Reputation management theory suggests that our behavior in the presence of others changes to point to a good reputation (audience effect) (Cañigueral & de Hamilton, 2019). Exposure to reputation risk is not easy to measure; first of all, it will be extremely difficult to distinguish a purely reputation effect from other types of risk. Therefore, identifying a particular reputation component will require internal principles to be defined to avoid undue results or excessive capital charges. In fact, determining acceptable capital at risk is said to be the second challenge when the rules for what constitutes reputation impact are properly established (Soprano et al., 2009).

Freudenburg (1993) and Earle and Cvetkovich (1995, 1997) were the first researchers, in the field of risk, to realize the importance of trust in risk perception and management (Siegrist, 2021). In his study, the author expresses that Freudenburg (1993) states that one of the most important factors affecting risk perception is trust, and Earle and Cvetkovich (1995, 1997) states that trust not only is effective on risk perception but also affects the level of trust people have in important actors involved in danger management.

In addition, these researchers think that people tend to trust people with similar values, which constitutes the basis of social trust, and social trust often affects perception of dangers. This is expressed to be a consideration for people necessary to better understand risk perception (Siegrist, 2021). Public perception of risk regarding emerging risks and risk events often lags behind experts' risk decisions. The public must rely on influence and confidence in relevant social statuses (intuitive influence and trust) to decide whether a particular risk is relevant to them. It is important not to lose public trust in terms of the public's reaction to emerging risks and events (Bearth & Siegrist, 2021).

Overall, the risk of risks expressed to be the result of other risk types, especially operational risk, is indicated as reputation risk. For example, reputation of the organization will be affected when the expectations and interests of certain target groups or stakeholders are ignored, or since most risk types include a reputation risk element in the management process and risk types originating from the internet and social media affect the level of trust, the effects of which are more serious in the long term than the risks arising directly from the event itself.

9.5 Relationship Between Reputation Risk and Risk Management

Risk generally refers to the situation where the possible future consequences of an event cannot be exactly known. It is frequently stated that this is also due to the possibility of not obtaining the expected value or gain in financial terms and the existence of this possibility. However, reputation is an intangible economic asset, and as Eccles et al. (2007) stated, reputation includes perception and it is formed as a result of these general perceptions. When considered in this context, reputation risk apparently includes risks that lead to changes in attitudes and behaviors depending on the perception change and that eventually have material and nonmaterial effects. However, once the reputation is damaged, it is very difficult to regain it and clearly, it takes time.

In general, it is clear that there may be risks to reputation that can threaten reputation in many ways. In this context, we can consider reputation risk as a concept that points to a situation which will possibly have consequences that may adversely affect reputation and cannot be predicted or known with certainty because, in the event of a reputation risk, it is seen that in addition to its financial effects, it also has nonmaterial effects that can undermine the trust in and respect for the organization. Reputational risks include any event, situation, or action that may affect the reputation positively or negatively, regardless of their source, and sometimes the occurrence of the risk also reduces the trust in the organization (Rayner, 2003).

In the OECD Report (2020), the Canada Revenue Agency (CRA) defines reputation risk as any event that may damage not only the trust of stakeholders but also the respect they have for the organization. However, it is stated that it is important to manage such risks as reputation will have an impact on stakeholder behavior. When evaluated from this point of view, it is clear that if reputation risks are managed, they can provide both material and nonmaterial gain to the organization as well as competitive power.

Reputation risk is explained, in the literature, by the gap or difference between the expected value and the actual value. At the same time, it is pointed out that the gap or difference between these two values can be positively or negatively associated. Accordingly, it is stated that if there is a positive relationship between the expected and actual value, this may turn into an opportunity, and if a negative relationship develops, a reputation risk may arise. Figure 9.2 shows main factors that shape reputation risk and the relationship between them. Detailed information is given in the study titled "Global Survey on Reputation" by Deloitte (2014).

Describing reputation as the most important strategic corporate risk, Deloitte (2014) considers it as the performance against expectations. Because when the performance does not meet the expectations, reputation risk arises. As a result, how an organization manages expectations and performance in relation to its reputation determines whether it creates or loses value. In this case, it can be argued that the gap or difference between the expected value and the actual value can be controlled or reduced, thanks to an effective risk management in reputation management. As

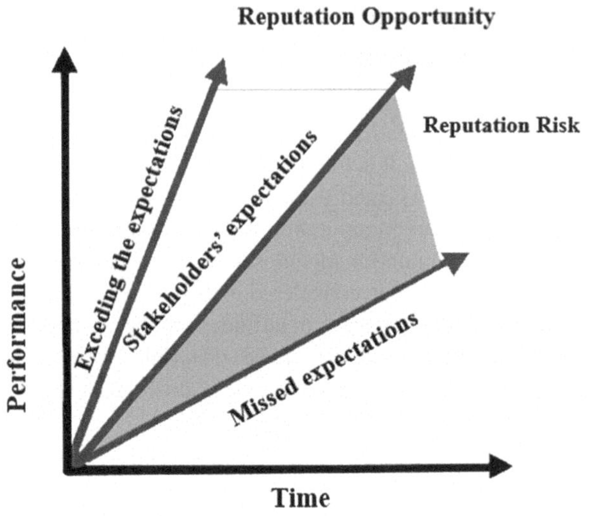

Fig. 9.2 Reputation risk or opportunity. Source: Deloitte (2014)

Szwajca (2018) states, risk management has to evaluate the expectations and the level of meeting expectations; otherwise, the severity of reputation risk will increase as the gap between expectations and meeting expectations (performance) grows. The main point here is that to know, define, and monitor the expectations and strategically planning the activities to be carried out in order to meet these expectations, through effective risk management, plays an important role.

The further the actual value deviates from the expected value, the more the reputation risk will increase, and accordingly, it can be predicted that the management effectiveness of risks to reputation will decrease. This will also risk the reputation of risk management as it may reduce the belief in the risk management practice used in the management of reputational risks. Does increased reputation risk actually require the management and taking under control of any type of reputational risk? In fact, the increase in reputation risk in such a case indicates that the perceived risk increases and therefore risk management reputation will be perceived in the same direction. For example, as stated by Power (2004), reputation appears to be at risk when there is a huge gap between the performance and public expectations of the service provided and perceptions of this performance. Likewise, as Szwajca (2018) states, reputation risk will arise when the expectations or needs of the stakeholders are not met since reputation is closely related to the expectations of the stakeholders. Therefore, the difference or gap between expectation and performance or reality will not only point to reputational risk but also reveal the effectiveness of reputation risk management.

At this point, by explaining the difference between the expected value and the actual value, the relationship between reputation risk and the reputation of risk management seems to be addressable. As a matter of fact, Kıral (2018) states that the effectiveness of risk management will be considered as reduced if the risks encountered are greater than the risks that can be prevented (risks that are intervened). He also states that one of the factors that reduces or even limits the effectiveness of risk management is the potential to be exposed to risks and our capacity to combat these risks. Accordingly, the more we face reputation risks, the more our life experience against reputation risks will increase and naturally, our perception of reputation risk will increase. As a result, our ability to prevent reputation risks, in other words our capacity to intervene in reputational risks, will increase, and this way, an effective risk management approach will be adopted in order to evaluate and manage events that may adversely affect reputation with a proactive approach, instead of the approach of risk management of everything. In short, our increasing efforts to combat reputation risks will begin to direct our risk management approach from a reactive approach to a proactive approach. After all, it is the fact that an understanding of risk management of everything will lead to management of nothing.

Indeed, the reputation of risk management requires the level of maturity needed to manage reputation risks. As the reputational risks are managed, the organization's reputational risk management maturity will increase, which will facilitate the prevention and mitigation of reputational risks. In addition, the organization's self-assessment will determine which aspects of the management of reputational risks should be strengthened. This way, the level of organizations' determination and evaluation of reputation risks will show their maturity level. It should be noted that if the risks to reputation are managed, the organization can be protected against the events that may damage the reputation with a proactive approach, and if they occur, the organization can effectively overcome it (OECD, 2020).

Many internal and external factors that can destroy reputation or cause loss of reputation are perceived as risks to reputation. Reputation risk, i.e., the expectation gap, also indicates the effectiveness of risk management. After all, an effective risk management requires knowing the expectations; identifying, defining, and monitoring the risks that will affect the fulfillment of the expectations; and controlling the said expectation gap through strategically planned activities. However, in terms of reputation management, everything that has an effect on corporate reputation is perceived as reputation risk. Risk management of everything points to secondary, i.e., reputation risk management.

Risk management reputation can be associated with the difference between the expected effectiveness (performance) of risk management in reputation management and the actual performance. It can be said that the methods, frameworks, and standards used in determining, defining, and controlling the reputational risks, or attitudes and behaviors toward reputational risks, and maybe the willingness to manage everything can be included among the factors that cause this difference between expected and actual performance to increase. Accordingly, as for reputation management, we intend to elaborate the factors that may have an impact on the reputation of risk management (the factors that cause the expectation gap to increase) as well as the approach of risk management of everything is management of nothing.

9.5.1 Factors That May Affect the Reputation of Risk Management

In general, the increase in risk management effectiveness in reputation management is important in terms of trying to understand and direct the attitudes and behaviors of stakeholders or public. But the most critical thing in this process is how to explain the factors that will affect the risk management reputation. According to Eccles et al. (2007), risk management plays an important role in defining, embodying, and managing risks to the reputation of the organization before they arise and turn into a problem. As a matter of fact, determining the value of reputation, evaluating the facts, identifying and closing the gaps, and monitoring the changing beliefs toward and expectations from the organization will not happen by itself (Eccles et al., 2007). Hence, it is apparently necessary to manage the risks related to reputation within the risk management. Indeed, the following question arises, "Could the common point of various crises emerged in the Enron scandal, which is known to be the most concrete example of the management of reputation risks, be the deficiencies or mistakes in risk management or human factors?"

It is stated that deficiencies or mistakes with regard to risk management are possibly among the reasons for the emergence of various crises; such that the reason why the methodology used in risk management and framework and standards are not effective in preventing the emergence of crises is still a hot topic (Kıral, 2018). In their study, Vinnari and Skærbæ (2014) found that risk management itself creates unexpected uncertainties that are otherwise unlikely to arise, instead of reducing uncertainty. In addition, according to Kıral (2018), it is clear that the framework and standards determined without considering the current conditions of the country or organizations will not as effective as desired in cases where a crisis situation may occur in general. Because when the current situation of the countries and organizations in question cannot be determined taking into account their facts, possible risks that the enterprise risk management approach are likely to face may arise (Kıral, 2018), and it can be argued that they may also include reputation risks.

It is important to take a more comprehensive perspective, given overall characteristics, nature, and interconnection of risks. In this context, it is deemed necessary to continuously develop a risk analysis framework that will enable multidimensional analysis of risk types and risk events and, above all, make the relationships between risks in organizations and reputation risks more visible (Kıral, 2018; Vinnari & Skærbæ, 2014).

Risk management often requires avoiding, mitigating, or controlling potential or actual hazards. Risk management includes assessing and mitigating the effects of financial volatility and evaluating operational risks specific to the field and sector in which an organization operates (Larkin, 2003). As stated by Szwajca (2018), one of the reasons for the difficulties in managing reputational risks is that reputational risks are risks of risks. This is said to be the result of other external risk types such as natural disasters, especially operational and financial risks. In particular, operational risks arise as a result of the attitudes and behaviors of people related to activity processes, and they point to the fact that they include human risks that arise as a result of the responsible persons not doing what should be done or doing what should not be done. While the reason for the emergence of these risks is considered a result of the inability to manage operational risks effectively, it is thought that man-made risks (human risks) may also be the cause (Power, 2004). Man-made risks can also be defined as human risks. Bombiak (2017) includes in the sources of man-made risk (human risk) the human flaws caused by the deliberate violation of corporate policy or laws by employees. Such man-made risks (human risks) are among the largest risk categories faced by organizations (Human Risk, 2020) and these risks seem to be among the risks to the reputation of organizations.

The OECD Report (2020) indicates that 83% of organizations experiencing a reputation crisis manage their reputation only at the strategic level, not at the operational level. In this context, it is shown that the primary categories of sources of risks to reputation are errors (human errors) and malevolent events. Human errors (man-made errors) are often a source of risk, which, in many cases, can be managed through high staff awareness, training, correction, continuous improvement, and good process design. Therefore, reputational risks in this category can be reduced at strategic level, mostly by establishing policies and corporate plans. These risk categories originate mainly from the employees of the organization who are in direct contact with the stakeholders at the operational level, when necessary, and it has an impact on the stakeholders.

Another issue that is deemed to affect the reputation of risk management is the reactions by the organization to the risks. Proactive or reactive strategies that organizations will determine in response to risks as a result of risk assessment will clearly play an important role in terms of the effectiveness of risk management. As a result, in some cases, it may be necessary to respond quickly to unexpected events that are of either internal or external origin. Reactive strategies are often expected to be used in such cases. However, proactive strategies always allow immediate response to expected events, while reactive strategy can provide significant advantages in dealing with unexpected events. On the other hand, while the proactive strategy minimizes the effort by the organization for crisis management, no effort is made until a crisis occurs in the case of reactive strategy. Proactive strategies are generally applicable to anticipated threats, challenges, and future conditions. Reactive strategies, on the other hand, tend to avoid more as they focus on existing problems and threats. In proactive strategies, expected events, threats, challenges, trends, and some cases where the predictions may be wrong may arise in which case there is no guarantee that proactive strategies will always be successful. From this point of view, the effectiveness of risk management can be increased by detecting faults that will reduce the management effectiveness of reputational risks, including proactive strategies. However, the OECD Report (2020) has determined that there is no universally accepted standard for reputational risk management in the public sector, and given the existing reputational risk management frameworks, it has been determined that organizations focus primarily on crisis management rather than proactive approach. It is stated that this aims to limit the damage it will cause only if an event occurs (OECD, 2020).

Such gaps between expectation and performance, also referred to as the expectation gap, are composed of the difference between performance and expectation. Such gaps can be managed by means of strategies that will change the performance dimension of the gap, and the changes in expectations can be managed by informing those concerned through risk communication and joint plans. At that point, the most important feature of risk management and risk communication is the management of reputation risk to the organization (Power, 2004). As a matter of fact, the OECD Report (2020) states that it is necessary to integrate three functions to determine the scope of reputational risk. Accordingly, when assessing existing reputational risk management frameworks and the identified gaps thereof, Canada Revenue Agency has identified a three-component theory underlying the reputational risk management framework (Fig. 9.3).

It is known that proactive risk management will enable organizations to anticipate and prevent or minimize threats that may damage reputation. Risk management capacity increase can be supported by ensuring active participation through communication. The function or duty of an effective communication is to attract the attention of stakeholders, to build trust, and to create an opportunity for the organization to "take precedence over the story" in all issues that shape the public perception of the organization. The effect of good communication made by influencing the public supported by explanations and sensitivity maintains trust and respect toward the organization. But the reputation of risk management requires the level of maturity necessary for managing reputation risks.

According to Power (2004), it is a kind of reputation management strategy for organizations to be open to the public about some risks that they cannot be unquestioningly held responsible for every possible failure. The aim of this strategy is stated to be the effort to change the zero-error expectation of the public, which increases due to zero tolerance rhetoric. Regardless of which risk-based communication strategies have previously been adopted for the purposes of reputation management, it may be difficult to take under control public reactions in a crisis situation as some people will be more affected than others. At this point, reputation

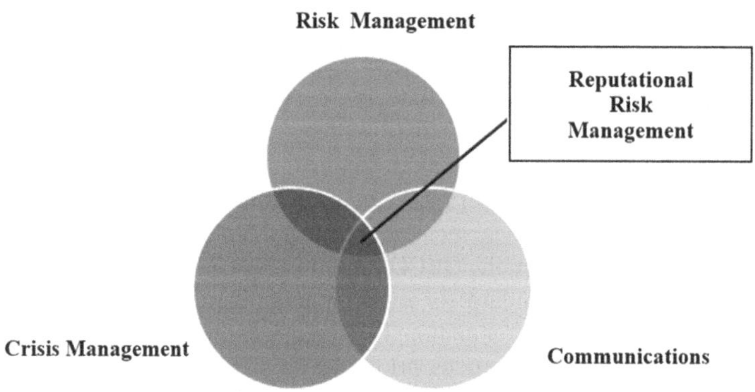

Fig. 9.3 Components of reputational risk management. Source: OECD (2020)

management has emerged to control such reactions of the public (Power, 2004). In this case, as the effectiveness of risk management increases, trust and credibility in risk management will increase, thus improving the reputation of risk management.

In fact, when reputation risk management is combined with communication and operational activities, it becomes possible to reduce the gap or difference between perception and reality. Thanks to such communication, it is apparent that the organization is both successful in managing its reputation risks and, on the other hand, that the impact of human-induced events with the potential to damage the reputation of the organization is reduced through public relations (OECD, 2020). Events, which are generally included in the daily news, reveal that the risks to the reputation of the organization will increase if they are not managed on time and in place.

While risk management is an integral part of strategy and value creation in the corporate sector in general, it introduced a new perspective to asset and income quality in financial organizations. According to Power (2004), misunderstanding or misinterpreting the cost/benefit ratio means that, even if it meets certain demands, it will be far from being economically efficient; in which case, it shows that risk management will also include economic risks. Indeed, some impacts of risk management are not only difficult to quantify but also require adequate conceptualization in the first place. The effectiveness of risk management in reputation management requires universal standards and frameworks established at the required level because risk management requires a process where risks can be identified, defined, and assessed and strategies developed. As Power (2004) states, it can be argued that the organization and even accounting firms systematically create fictitious legal risks in order to avoid liability, as well as fictitious risks related to reputation. The most fearful concern about reputation risk is that control categories will become less important as they become more nuanced. In this case, it will result in everything becoming unmanageable.

Larkin (2003) states that he sees reputational risks as an iceberg, and that most of the reputational risks are actually overlooked, potentially hindering the course of performance and reputation strategies, and most importantly, the scope and impact of reputation risk is often underestimated. Thus, it is seen that this leads to the fact that reputation risk perception may decrease or causes it to be ignored, and it becomes impossible to manage reputational risks, which shows that this will adversely affect the reputation of risk management.

According to Foster (2018), analytics involving real-time and big data can offer important skills necessary to model reputation factors, compare them and predict the outcomes. Reputation analysis framework given in Fig. 9.1 makes it possible to test how the situation can be handled in various scenarios and to monitor the factors and processes that affect global reputation. Thus, a reporting framework can be created in which strategies to strengthen reputation can be developed over time. In fact, it is clear that the methodology to be used in the management of reputational risks, as well as the framework and standards utilized, can play an important role in determining strategies to strengthen reputation and increasing the effectiveness of risk management for reputation. After all, it is seen that the methodology created and implemented can contribute to the determination of the strategies that will increase the reputation, as well as identification, definition, and analysis of the risks to the reputation, taking into account the organizations' environment and conditions.

Most organizations are often faced with many events or situations that involve risks to reputation. It is also clear that financial, operational, and legal (regulatory) risks will arise as a result of such events. However, the important thing is to determine, define, and quantify the reputation risks together with other risks before they turn into a problem, without damaging the reputation of the organization or losing its reputation. In fact, we can neither measure nor manage anything that we cannot identify or define. Determining the value of reputation, assessing the truth, detecting and closing the gaps, and following the changing beliefs and expectations will not happen by itself (Eccles et al., 2007). It should be noted that if a reputation risk occurs, the image and reputation of the organization may also be damaged.

From the perspective of reputation management, if the gap between expected value and performance indicates the risk to reputation, it seems that a relationship can be established between reputation risk and risk management effectiveness. The concept of reputation which cannot be evaluated, described, and distinguished at first glance can be affected by many sources. Foster (2018) states that insight should be developed in order to develop meaningful responses to shifts or changes in reputation. To that end, a large number of different data obtained from various sources must be collected, compiled, analyzed, and evaluated. As reputation consists of many sets of components, different approaches will be required for different organizations and different markets. In Fig. 9.4, Foster (2018) shows the relationship between the reputation strategy, which includes multiple action steps and processes based on environmental factors as well as the factors in the impact area of the organization, and stakeholder perceptions and expectations. Reputation strategies enable measurable, repeatable, reliable, and predictable actions.

In the literature, it is stated that the organization should objectively evaluate its reputation and reality in order to eliminate the gap between them. Expectations and beliefs can emerge suddenly or gradually over a long period of time. In such a case, first of all, trends, social attitudes, and behaviors should be followed, and awareness of how social values and adopted rules change should be built, and a process including an integrated reporting and cooperation is necessary in order to control and coordinate this process with the aim of determining the awareness of the change in expectations in detail at an early stage (Eccles & Krzus, 2010).

As Eccles et al. (2007) points out, reputation can be better or worse, different from the actual character or behavior of the organization. When an organization's reputation is more positive than the underlying reality, such gap or difference can seem like a significant risk. Therefore, when the effort of the organization to reach the expected value fails, the reputation of the organization is expected to decline until it becomes more compatible with reality. To bridge the gap or difference between reputation and reality, the organization must either improve its ability to meet expectations or reduce expectations by making fewer commitments. The only problem in this case is shown to be the fact the managers can resort to short-term manipulations. For instance, the difference or gap between reputation and reality in

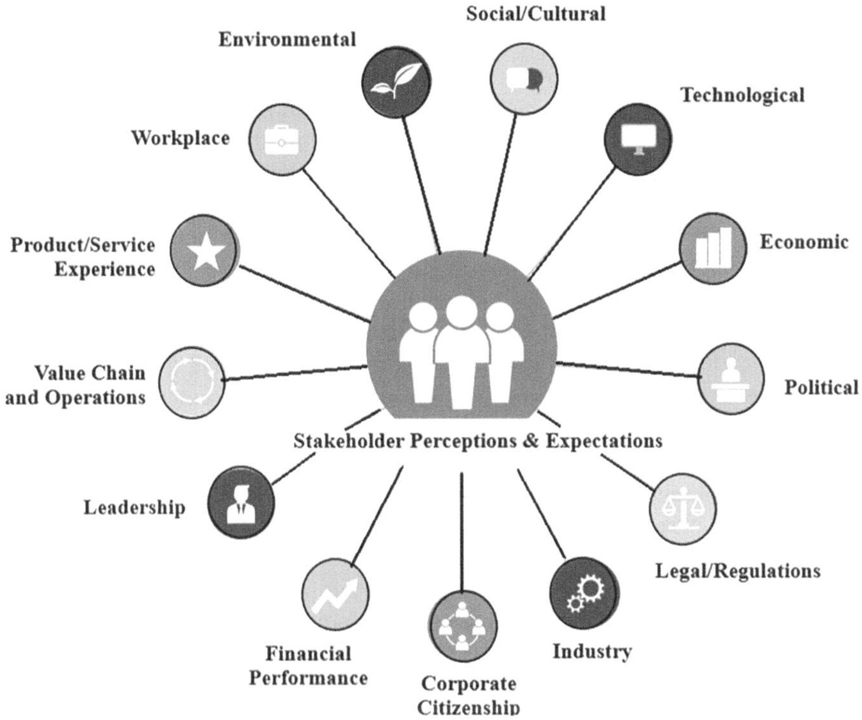

Fig. 9.4 Stakeholder perceptions and expectations. Source: Foster (2018)

financial performance can often lead to accounting fraud and ultimately re announcement of results.

Making an overall evaluation, it can be argued that an opposite relationship between reputation risk and risk management reputation is predicted for several reasons. As Maung et al. (2020) state, the first thing that comes to mind is the idea of reducing risk because it is known that there is a directly proportional relationship between reputation and brand value, and reputation includes tangible assets that create value such as quality management understanding, having ethical and talented employees and innovation capacity. If reputation risks are not strategically managed or properly addressed, they may have devastating consequences on key elements of reputation, such as financial performance, strategic plans, leadership, and sustainability. Having a strong and positive reputation will be the most important quality as it is a good reason for being preferred over others, and the relationship between reputation and attitudes and behaviors is generally expected to be positive. As a result, reputation is an important output that provides brand value and can add a strategic value to the individual, organization, society, or country (Chun and Davies, 2001). For this reason, according to Davies and Miles (1998), although being a complex phenomenon, reputation is a phenomenon worth managing. According to

Szwajca (2018), reputation risk management is apparently necessary in order to understand this complex structure of reputation and to identify any threats to it.

The resulting reputational risks and risk events increase the risk perception of both the organization and the stakeholder. If the perception of reputational risks often lags behind the risk judgments of experts, it will result in loss of or damage to trust of the public or stakeholders. It is stated in the OECD Report (2020) that the main issue to be considered is the trust in and respect for the organization and its components. For this reason, considering the material and nonmaterial consequences that may arise in case of damage to reputation, it is clear that the management of reputational risks is very important in order to prevent, with a proactive approach, any events that may damage reputation and to address them effectively. As Bearth and Siegrist (2021) states, disappearing or decreasing trust will lead to increased risks and result in a trust gap. Thanks to risk management in reputation management, the risks that may cause the aforementioned trust gap will be determined, evaluated, and made manageable.

Finally, combining reputation risk management with communication and operational activities makes it possible to reduce the gap or difference between perception and reality. This way, thanks to communication, the success of the organization in managing reputational risks becomes apparent while, on the other hand, the impact of human-induced events having the potential to damage the reputation of the organization can be reduced through public relations (OECD, 2020). After all, the events in the daily news can increase the risks to the reputation of the organization if they are not managed on time and in place.

In the light of the information given above, it is seen that the following conclusions have been reached regarding the risks to reputation in terms of individuals, organizations, or countries. Reputation risks are in the risk group with high economic and social effects, and are listed among the risk types that should be avoided, since the reasons for their emergence are difficult to identify and manage. If the risks to reputation cannot be identified, defined, and embodied, it means that it is not possible to take any strategic action and they cannot be taken under control.

9.5.2 The Approach of "Risk Management of Everything, Management of Nothing"

Another question that needs to be answered in terms of reputation management is, as Power puts it, does the understanding of risk management of everything lead to risk management of nothing? Risk management of everything is characterized by the emergence of secondary or reputational risk management (reputation risk management) because the "secondary effects" of a risk event that seems to be financially insignificant can lead to very important consequences for the reputation of the organization. The Shell incident revealed how external resources supported by the media resulted in jeopardizing the legitimacy and value of a large multinational company.

Therefore, according to Power (2004), given that the secondary effects of any risk event will affect reputation, if anything has an impact on corporate reputation, then reputational risk management requires risk management of everything. However, reputational risk management also reveals that in some cases, it will force organizations to confront its impact on society, resulting in a societal exaggeration of risk. Although risk management of everything is a whim, it is stated that, within the official mission, there should be more focus on human, legal, and reputation risks rather than primary risks. In fact, the difference between public expectations and actual performance indicates the risk to reputation (Power, 2004).

According to Davies and Miles (1998), although the organizations can do many things by themselves to reduce reputational risks, they are confined to the corporate environment in which they operate. In this context, it is seen as a kind of defense strategy for organizations to develop strategic partnerships, make efforts on external stakeholder and relationship management, and even carry out corporate social responsibility activities within the framework of reputation management. After all, anything that may threaten reputation should be managed, in which case reputation risk will require managing everything (Davies & Miles, 1998).

Overall, any subject has to be a part of risk management, thanks to internal control. Otherwise, it is clear that if reputation risks occur, it will cause serious material and nonmaterial losses to the organization. In such a situation, the credibility of risk management will reduce. After all, reputation is an intangible economic value created as a result of long-term strategic efforts. Reputation risks are also very difficult to manage as they are called qualitative risks. However, depending on the proactive or reactive approaches used in reputation risk management, risk management will decrease or increase reputation because, by and large, proactive approaches aim to increase public loyalty by creating trust and credibility among stakeholders, and they include more strategic approaches compared to reactive approaches.

Since risk management focuses more on financial and operational risks, it falls short in determining reputational risks. Hence, as the inadequacy of risk management in reputation risks increases, its effectiveness will decrease, which, in turn, suggests that reputation risks are likely to increase. Considering the understanding of "the risk management of everything is management of nothing," considering everything as a risk with a possible effect on reputation will lead to inability to manage risks and result in an environment where nothing can be managed. For instance, an environment where everything is evaluated as a risk with a possible effect on reputation will lead to the tendency to act overly cautiously, resulting in the understanding of controlling everything. In an overly cautious environment, burnout syndrome will appear over time, and as a result, the organization will gradually become insensitive to reputation risks. In this environment, necessary and sufficient measures will not be taken because of such insensitivity, and it is highly possible that an unmanageable situation will arise as a result of not being able to control reputation risks. Therefore, although the understanding of risk management of everything has led to the necessity of managing secondary risks, it is clear that an effective and systematic reputation risk management is necessary because the effects on society should not be exaggerated.

Organizations coming together to fulfill certain duties in the social structure act to serve the society. Therefore, they work to meet many needs of the people, particularly the basic needs (education, health, accommodation, etc.). Considering these needs, as Power (2004) states, the importance and even reputation of organizations for people is obvious. Trying to manage everything as a reputation risk, as is the case in internal control, which is a part of risk management approach of everything, inevitably brings the following question to mind: Will defining and evaluating everything regarding the reputation as a risk, as is the case for internal control, reduce the effectiveness of risk management? Or does it lead to the emergence of a controllability system, which is based on no reason, as is the case in the internal control system? And thereby creating new kinds of expectation gaps and thus reducing the reputation of risk management? Or will preparing reports on reputational risks and sharing them with the public increase public trust and credibility in organizations?

In fact, it is obvious that evaluations can be made as the risks to reputation are determined and defined. However, if the one moves away from the idea that everything is controllable without any justification, it will be possible to determine what the risks to reputation are and what they are not, and reputation risks can be managed with proactive and reactive approaches. Otherwise, the belief that risk management is inadequate will emerge, and it may reduce the confidence in risk management and thus may endanger the reputation of risk management. In addition, considering everything about reputation is a risk and the misconception that these risks can be controlled indicates that risk management will have a more defensive and uninformed form.

Besides, starting from Power (2004)'s study called "risk management of everything," we can reach the following important results: In terms of accounting, reputation risk has the power to overturn even the concept of materiality. Considered in terms of financial size, reputation means that even a seemingly small event or loss will cause undue public repercussions (such as the Shell incident, the Andersen incident). The critical point here is how most people believe that some events exaggerated, especially by the media and legal systems. Such exaggerated narrative processes are not normally under the control of organizations. This means reputation risk reflects a new understanding of vulnerability (exposure to attack or criticism) and new needs are emerging to keep reputation manageable. Organizations can actually do a lot themselves to mitigate these secondary or reputational risks, but it is clear that organizations are held hostage in their environment. This emerges as one of the most important risk situations to reputation for organizations.

Within this framework, it can be argued that many practices such as strategic partnerships, external stakeholder and relationship management, as well as corporate social responsibility are actually defense strategies for mitigating or reducing risks to reputation. Corporate social responsibility practices, in particular, reveal that it is a strategy carried out within the scope of reputation risk management. Therefore, Power (2004) states that if everything potentially threatens reputation, reputation risk requires management of everything and that risk management of everything is characterized by the emergence of secondary, i.e., reputational risk management. Because if everything has an impact on corporate reputation, then reputational risk management requires risk management of everything. Therefore, the rise of reputation risk management is not only a product of the emergence of the new economy but also a requirement of managing intangible assets. After all, all kinds of developments and changes in the twenty-first century cause our world to become more and more risky and dangerous, as Power (2004) states, and the most effective response can be through effective risk management. However, as Power (2004) specifically points out, "if a society and its organisations begin to spend increasing resources to defend themselves, then the consequences of the secondary risk management obsession will be severe."

9.6 Conclusion

Reputation is one of the most important values for both institutions and individuals. The significance of this value stems mainly from its damaging and destructive effects that can occur when it is lost. In such a case, loss of reputation can lead to economic and financial difficulties leading to bankruptcy and can also damage the moral values of the organization, such as prestige, image, or status. On the other hand, reputation is one of the valuable assets of an organization as it creates a strong public perception, at least as strong as material values; has the power to influence the target audience; provides a competitive advantage; and can be converted into an important economic value. For this reason, organizations would not want to lose this power, which they have built up through years of effort and strategic endeavors. On the contrary, they would seek to manage reputation risks effectively in order to protect and prevent loss of power and reputation that are important corporate assets.

Reputation is the social perception that emerges based on changing beliefs and views about the institution and affects and determines the position, competitive advantage, and value of organizations in the environment they operate. The ability to control and prevent events and situations that would affect reputation; to protect reputation against a number of risks that would negatively affect and naturally change the perspective of others, their attitudes, behaviors, perceptions, and trust; and to gain a competitive advantage is only possible by managing reputation risks. In determining the extent to which an organization is exposed to reputation risks and measuring reputation, it will be helpful to measure perceptions and monitor the change in expectations.

Formed on the basis of the experiences and comments about the organization, reputation is defined on the basis of which perception overrides—how the organization sees itself or how it is perceived. Therefore, when a reputation risk arises, perceived reputation of the organization can take on meaning beyond its actual qualifications, in which case it is important for organizations to adopt risk management that includes a proactive approach to protect their reputation and manage reputation risks. While this approach will enable the pursuit of policies that are in compliance with trust, honesty, and ethical values, it will also offer the benefits of a stronger reputation, maintaining this power and more strategic and value-based management. As a matter of fact, a strong reputation will ensure its durability and reliability and reduce the impact of reputation risks.

As a strategic risk, reputation risk is among the most difficult risks to manage and measure. Nevertheless, organizations increasing their capacity to intervene in reputation risks will begin to shift their risk management approach from a reactive approach to a proactive one. As is well known, proactive approaches mostly aim to increase public loyalty by building stakeholders' trust and confidence and have more strategic approaches compared to reactive ones. As a matter of fact, managing reputation risks with a proactive approach will help protect the brand value of the organization. Therefore, the most important requirement is to assess and measure reputation risks at the strategic goal-setting stage within enterprise risk management. This will lead to shifting to an effective risk management approach where the events or situations that will affect the reputation are evaluated with a proactive approach rather than risk management of everything approach.

Reputational risk is directly related to stakeholder expectations. The difference between stakeholder expectations and the performance of an organization is considered reputation risk. This gap can only be bridged through effective reputation risk management. Effective risk management requires understanding the expectations; identifying, defining, and monitoring the risks that will affect the realization of the expectations; and controlling the expectation gap in question. In this respect, there appears to be a significant relationship between reputation risk management and effectiveness of risk management. On the other hand, reputation risks are managed within the framework of risk management. Effective conduct of risk management is an indication that reputation risks are also addressed effectively.

This study seeks the answer to the question "Does the reputation of the risks decrease as the risks to reputation increase?" Organizations need to identify the risks they may face, assess them and take the necessary measures to achieve their goals in the areas they operate. It is clear that if reputation risks are underestimated and not managed, or if they cannot be managed or are ignored, the effectiveness of risk management will decrease, and the reputation of the organization will be further damaged, with potentially devastating consequences. Although reputation is a complex phenomenon, it is an economic asset worth managing. From this perspective, effective handling and management of reputation risks within the scope of risk management is important in turning reputation into an economic asset. However, it should be noted that, in risk management, uncertainties may increase due to the areas that seems different, unpredictable, or overshadowed or areas outside the framing, and this may increase the reputation of the risks and pose a threat to reputation. In this case, it should not be forgotten that associating every concrete risk with reputation risk will bring about the problem of "risk management of everything." Thus, it will create the risk of "managing no risks" and will negatively affect the reputation of risk management. Finally, it should not be forgotten that effective risk management is necessary in order to understand this complicated structure of reputation, to identify threats to reputation, and to uncover opportunities.

References

Aula, P., & Heinonen, J. (2016). *Risk of risks. The reputable firm. How digitalization of communication is revolutionizing reputation management* (pp. 133–162). https://doi.org/10.1007/978-3-319-22008-6_7. Retrieved from: Library Genesis^{2M}.

Banks, E. (2008). Overview of risk management and alternative risk transfer. In *Risk and return* (pp. 40–52).

Bearth, A., & Siegrist, M. (2021). The social amplification of risk framework: A normative perspective on trust?. *Risk Analysis, Early View*, 16 May 2021. https://doi.org/10.1111/risa.13757. Retrieved from: Wiley Online Library.

Bombiak, E. (2017). Human resources risk as an aspect of human resources management in turbulent environments. *Management and Leadership*. Retrieved from: ResearchGate.

Cañigueral, R., & de Hamilton, A. F. (2019). Effects of being watched on self-referential processing, self-awareness and prosocial behaviour. *Consciousness and Cognition, 76*, 1–15.

Chun, R., & Davies, G. (2001). E:Reputation: The role of mission and vision statements in positioning strategy. *Brand Management, 8*(4&5), 315–333. https://doi.org/10.1057/palgrave.bm.2540031

Çillioğlu Karademir, A., & Şimşek, A. (2013). Measuring corporate reputation: The case of a state University. In B. Baybars-Hawks & O. Samast (Eds.), *New challenges, new opportunities: interdisciplinary perspectives on reputation management* (Chapter 2, pp. 5–18).

Davies, G., & Miles, L. (1998). Reputation management: theory versus practice. *Corporate Reputation Review, 2*(1), 16–27.

Dell'Atti, S., Pacelli, V., Labini, S. S., & Trotta, A. (2016). Managing reputation: Reflections and operational suggestions. In S. Dell'Atti & A. Trotta (Eds.), *Managing reputation in the banking industry theory and practice* (Part III From Experience to Knowledge, pp. 162–187). Retrieved from: Library Genesis^{2M}.

Deloitte Touche Tohmatsu Limited. (2014). *Global survey on reputation risk: Reputation@risk*. Retrieved from https://www2.deloitte.com/content/dam/Deloitte/global/Documents/Governance-Risk-Compliance/gx_grc_Reputation@Risk%20survey%20report_FINAL.pdf

Deren van het Hoff. (2013). *Models in reputation measurement. New challenges, new opportunities: interdisciplinary perspectives on reputation management* (Chapter 4, 29–42). Retrieved from: Library Genesis^{2M}.

Earle, T. C., & Cvetkovich, G. T. (1995). *Social trust: Toward a cosmopolitan society*. PRAEGER.

Earlel, T. C., & Cvetkovichl, G. (1997). Culture, cosmopolitanism, and risk management. In *Risk analysis* (Vol. 17, Issue 1).

Eccles, R. G., & Krzus, M. P. (2010). It's time for one report. *One report integrated reporting for a sustainable strategy* içinde (Chapter 6, 153–156 ss.) Retrieved from: Library Genesis^{2M}.

Eccles, R. G., Newquşst, S. C., & Schatz, R. (2007). Reputation and its risks. *Harvard Business Review, 85*(2), 104–156.

Eckert, C. (2017). Corporate reputation and reputation risk definition and measurement from a (risk) management perspective. *Journal of Risk Finance, 18*(2), 145–158. https://doi.org/10.1108/JRF-06-2016-0075

Eisenegger, M. (2009). Trust and reputation in the age of globalisation. In J. Klewes & R. Wreschniok (Eds.), *Reputation capital building and maintaining trust in the 21st century* (Part 1 reputation in the 21st century – Good or evil?, s.: 15). Retrieved from: Library Genesis2M.

Finansal Ansiklopedi. (2021). *Spekülatif Risk Nedir?* Retrieved from https://tr.nesrakonk.ru/speculativerisk/

Fombrun, C. J. (1996). Reputation: Realizing Value from the Corporate Image. Harvard Business Review Press. p.72.

Foster, C. (2018). Hiper-Bağlı Bir Dünyada İtibar Stratejisi ve Analitiği (A. Parlar, Çev.). Koç Üniversitesi Yayınları. (2019).

Freudenburg, W. R. (1993). Risk and recreancy: weber, the division of labor, and the rationality of risk perceptions. *Social Forces, 71*(4), 909–932. https://doi.org/10.1093/sf/71.4.909

Gaultier-Gaillard, S., & Louisot, J. P. (2006). Risks to reputation: a global approach. *The Geneva Papers on Risk and Insurance-Issues and Practice, 31*(3), 425–445.
Gaultier-Gaillard, S., Louisot, J. P., & Rayner, J. (2009). Managing reputational risk-from theory to practice. In J. Klewes & R. Wreschniok (Eds.), *Reputation capital building and maintaining trust in the 21st century* (Part III: The 21st century of reputation crisis, 161–175 ss.). Retrieved from: Library Genesis2M
Glickman, G. L. (2014). Managing reputational risk. In T. H. Stanton & D. W. Webster (Eds.), *Managing risk and performance* (Chapter 11, 219–240 ss.). Retrieved from: Library Genesis^{2M}.
Gonzalez, D. (2015). Managing Online Risk Apps, Mobile, and Social Media Security. Retrieved from: Library Genesis^{2M}.
Griffin, A. (2014). Crisis, issues and reputation management. Kogan Page Limited.
Groza, M. D., Pronschinske, M. R., & Walker, M. (2011). Perceived organizational motives and consumer responses to proactive and reactive CSR. *Journal of Business Ethics, 102*(4), 639–652. https://doi.org/10.1007/s10551-011-0834-9
Heidinger, D., & Gatzert, N. (2018). Awareness, determinants and value of reputation risk management: Empirical evidence from the banking and insurance industry. *Journal of Banking and Finance, 91*(2018), 106–118. https://doi.org/10.1016/j.jbankfin.2018.04.004
Herkenhoff, F. (2009). Measuring risks to reputation. J. Klewes and R. Wreschniok (Eds.), *Reputation capital building and maintaining trust in the 21st century* (Part III The 21st century of reputation crisis) (pp. 197–210). https://doi.org/10.1007/978-3-642-01630-1. Retrieved from: Library Genesis^{2M}.
Honey, G. (2009). *A short guide to reputation risk.* https://doi.org/10.4324/9781315263618. Retrieved from: Library Genesis2M
Human Risk. (2020). *What is the human risk?* Retrieved from: What is Human Risk? | Human Risk (human-risk.com).
Hume, D. (2016). Evidence-based reputation management. In P. Aula & J. Heinonen (Eds.), *Risk of risks. The reputable firm. How digitalization of communication is revolutionizing reputation management* (pp. 163–199). Retrieved from: library Genesis2M.
Kıral, H. (2018). Kurumsal Risk Yönetiminin Riskleri. *Denetişim, 8*(18), 5–14.
Kıyat, B. D., & Sütçü, C. S. (2013). Research on measuring perceptions of reputation in the health sector through social media. In B. Baybars-Hawks & O. Samast (Eds.), *New challenges, new opportunities: Interdisciplinary perspectives on reputation management* (Chapter 3, 19–29).
Kwon, K., & Rupp, E. D. (2012). High-performer turnover and firm performance: The moderating role of human capital investment and firm reputation. *Journal of Organizational Behavior, 34*(2013), 129–150. https://doi.org/10.1002/job.1804
Larkin, J. (2003). *Strategic reputation risk management.* Palgrave Macmillan. Retrieved from: Library Genesis^{2M}
Liehr-Gobbers, K., & Storck, C. (2011). Reputation management. In S. Helm, K. Liehr-Gobbers, & C. Storck (Eds.). *Management for professionals reputation management* (pp. 17–21). https://doi.org/10.1007/978-3-642-19266-1_2. Retrieved from: Library Genesis^{2M}
Maung, M., Wilson, C., & Yu, W. (2020). Does reputation risk matter? Evidence from cross-border mergers and acquisitions. *Journal of International FinancialMarkets, Institutions & Money, 66*(2020), 1–16. https://doi.org/10.1016/j.intfin.2020.101204
OECD. (2020). *Communities of interest series enhancing reputational risk management.* https://www.oecd.org/tax/forum-on-tax-administration/publications-and-products/coi/enhancing-reputational-risk-management.htm
Outreville, J. F. (1998). The meaning of risk. *Theory and Practice of Insurance,* 3. https://doi.org/10.1007/978-1-4615-6187-3_1
Power, M. (2004). The risk management of everything rethinking the politics of uncertainty. *The Journal of Risk Finance, 5*(3), 58–65. https://doi.org/10.1108/eb023001
Rayner, J. (2003). *Managing reputational risk curbing threats, leveraging opportunities.* Retrieved from: Library Genesis2M.

Rim, H., & Ferguson, M. A. T. (2017). Proactive versus reactive CSR in a crisis: an impression management perspective. *International Journal of Business Communication, 57*(4), 1–24. https://doi.org/10.1177/2329488417719835

Ross, A. (2005). Reputation: Risk of risks. Gareth Lofthouse (Edit). The Economist Intelligence Unit. Retrieved from: Data Breach Insurance.

Ruso, J., Vujosevic, M., & Novakovic, M. (2012). Organization reputation and risk: Stakeholders perception. *Conference: International Conference SYMORG 2012: Innovative Management and Business. 5th to 9th June 2012 Zlatibor, Serbia.* Retrieved from: ResearchGate.

Scott, S. V., & Walsham, G. (2005). Reconceptualizing and managing reputation risk in the knowledge economy: toward reputable action. *Organization Science, 16*(3), 308–322. https://doi.org/10.1287/orsc.1050.0127

Shanahan, F., & Seele, P. (2015). Shorting *Ethos*: Exploring the relationship between Aristotle's *Ethos* and reputation management. *Corporate Reputation Review, 18*, 37–49. https://doi.org/10.1057/crr.2014.19

Siegrist, M. (2021). Trust and risk perception : a critical review of the literature. *Risk Analysis, 41*(3), 480–490. https://doi.org/10.1111/risa.13325

Soprano, A. Crielaard, B., Piacenza, F., & Ruspantini, D. (2009). *Measuring operational and reputational risk: A practitioner's approach*, p 164. Retrieved from GoogleBooks

Swanepoel, E., Esterhuyse, J., Van Vuuren, G., & Lotriet, R. (2017). Assessing reputational risk: a four point matrix. *Journal of Economic and Financial Sciences, 10*(2), 313–337. https://doi.org/10.4102/jef.v10i2.19

Szwajca, D. (2018). Dilemmas of reputation risk management: theoretical study. *Corporate Reputation Review, 21*, 165–178. https://doi.org/10.1057/s41299-018-0052-9

Tonello, M. (2007). *Reputation risk: A corporate governance perspective.* In Corporate/Investor Summit Series. https://ssrn.com/abstract=1077894

Tucker, L., & Melevar, T. C. (2005). Corporate reputation and crisis management: The threat and manageability of anti-corporatism. *Corporate Reputation Review, 7*(4), 377–387.

Vinnari, E., & Skærbæ, P. (2014). The uncertainties of risk management: A field study on risk management internal audit practices in a Finnish municipality. *Accounting, Auditing & Accountability Journal, 27*(3), 489–526.

Walter, I. (2016). Reputational risks and large international banks. *Financial Markets and Portfolio Management, 30*, 1–17. https://doi.org/10.1007/s11408-016-0264-x

Chapter 10
The Nexus Between Internal Control and Risk Management

Serpil Ceylan

Abstract After the 1990s, organizations faced new risks due to the facts that technology-intensive activities started to be carried out as a consequence of the changes in technology, the relations with the environment became more complex along with the acceleration of globalization, the organizations grew in scale, and new business models emerged. In addition to these developments, the importance of establishing an effective risk management and internal control system has gradually increased, with the effect of financial scandals, in order for organizations to achieve their goals and objectives. This study aims to examine the internal control (IC) and risk management (RM), becoming increasingly more important for organizations, to determine their scope and to reveal the relationship between them. In this context, the concepts of IC and RM are firstly discussed based on the literature and published frameworks, and then the relationship between IC and RM is examined. As a result, it has been determined that IC is an important tool used for effective RM, that they serve together to achieve the goals and objectives of the organization and therefore they are complementary elements that support each other, and that presenting a single guide through wholly consolidating the frameworks published to guide the practitioners will increase the efficiency in practice.

Keywords Internal control · Traditional risk management · Enterprise risk management · COSO confusion

S. Ceylan (✉)
Social Sciences University of Ankara, Ankara, Türkiye
e-mail: serpil.ceylan@asbu.edu.tr

H. Kıral (ed.), *Rethinking Enterprise Risk Management*, Accounting, Finance, Sustainability, Governance & Fraud: Theory and Application,
https://doi.org/10.1007/978-981-97-5983-5_10

10.1 Introduction

In management science, risk is considered as any situation or event that may prevent organizations from achieving their goals and objectives. These situations or events involve uncertainty, and organizations endeavor to identify risks and reduce their effects by making estimates using available data in order to achieve their goals. Particularly after the 1990s, uncertainty increased due to the rapid developments in science and technology and the fact that the relations became more complex due to the acceleration of globalization, which in turn led the organizations face new risks. Administrative structures of organizations have also taken their share from the change, and ownership and management have been separated from each other, upon establishment of a more anonymous structure and the adoption of the limited liability principle as a result. The fact that company owners and managers are different people has revealed the risk that managers will reduce the resources entrusted to them by taking more risks (Spira & Page, 2003). This is because it is the owners, not the managers, who are directly exposed to the consequences of risk. Therefore, the assurance requests of the company owners have also increased.

Mentioned rapid change has also led to changes in the business models of organizations, and these changes have created new risks that need to be managed. In the face of the increase in uncertainty and therefore the risks, organizations have started to develop control systems in response to the risk. With the effect of financial scandals experienced after the 1990s, the importance of establishing an effective RM and control system has gradually increased in order for organizations to achieve their goals. In the light of these developments, IC and RM have become the focal point of both academia and international organizations. This focus has resulted in the publication of guidelines on both RM and IC by various organizations, which brought up the question of what kind of relationship there is between IC and RM.

Apparently, two different approaches have emerged over time regarding the relationship between IC and RM. First, IC is a broader concept and encompasses RM; the second is the approach that IC is an effective tool in providing effective RM and therefore RM encompasses IC. Stating that control should include identifying and mitigating the risks, the Criteria of Control Framework[1] (CoCo) took the first approach (Page & Spira, 2004). Therefore, RM was considered as an element of IC. Similarly, risk assessment was defined as one of the five components of IC in the IC frameworks published by COSO[2] in 1992 and 2013, and it was stated that this component formed a basis for how the organization will manage its risks (Pang & Li, 2013; COSO, 2013).

On the other hand, stating that IC is a key element and an integral part of RM, the Turnbull Report published in 1999 clearly associated IC with RM. Referring to this explanation in the Turnbull Report, Page and Spira (2004) stated that the conceptualization of IC as an RM process allows managers to focus on a wide range of risks

[1] The CoCo Framework published by Canadian Institute of Chartered Accountants.

[2] Committee of Organizations Sponsoring the Treadway Commission.

faced by companies rather than more limited IC. Therefore, while COSO has considered risk assessment as one of the five components of IC in its IC Framework, the Turnbull Report has put RM at the center and defined IC as a key component in the management of risks. As is the case in the Turnbull Report, the Enterprise Risk Management-Integrated Framework published by COSO in 2004 considered RM in a broader context and emphasized that IC is an integral part of enterprise risk management (ERM) (COSO, 2004). The contradiction created by the fact that COSO considered IC as a part of ERM in the framework published in 2004, yet included risk assessment as a component of the IC framework in new IC framework updated in 2013, confused the practitioners.

Although different approaches have emerged over time regarding the relationship between IC and RM in the published frameworks and guides, studies in the literature examining the relationship between IC and RM are limited. However, it is observed that the relationship between them is included in the studies that examine the two concepts from different perspectives individually. These studies highlight the view that IC and RM should be integrated.

This study aims to reveal the relationship between IC and RM in a holistic manner. In this context, the concepts of IC and RM are described in the second part of the study while the relationship between IC and RM is examined in the third part. And determinations and evaluations are provided in the conclusion part.

10.2 Conceptual Framework

With a view to evaluating the relationship between IC and RM, this part of the study examines the concepts of IC and RM by considering the literature, widely used frameworks, and their development over time.

10.2.1 Internal Control

The earliest record of IC dates back to the early twentieth century. In that period, the essence of IC is the realization of the principle of segregation of duties in an economic activity or transaction, and its purpose is to reduce the risk of physical loss of goods (Pang & Shi, 2009). Therefore, IC helps to ensure the protection of assets and is limited to financial transactions.

The first official definition of IC was made by the AICPA[3] in 1949 (Spira & Page, 2003; Wilson et al., 2014). According to the definition by AICPA, IC includes all methods and measures adopted for planning the organization and protecting the assets of an enterprise, controlling the accuracy and reliability of accounting data,

[3] American Institute of Certified Public Accountants.

increasing operational productivity and promoting compliance with management policies foreseen (AICPA, 1949 cited by Pang & Shi, 2009). While this definition focuses on issues related to internal financial control, apparently, the scope has been expanded by taking into account management controls. There was no significant change in the abovementioned definition of Internal control (IC) until the 1990s. IC began to be reconsidered in the 1990s following the developments in information technology, changes in audit methods, and the financial scandals experienced (Spira & Page, 2003). In the Internal Control Framework published by COSO in 1992, IC is defined as "*a process, effected by an entity's board, management, and other personnel, designed to provide reasonable assurance regarding the achievement of objectives such as effectiveness and efficiency of operations, reliability of financial reporting, and compliance with regulation*" (COSO, 1992; cited by Chang et al., 2014). This framework transformed IC from being a checklist into a working machine. The framework has components that produce and exchange information (Leitch, 2008). Control environment, risk assessment, control activities, information and communication, and monitoring has been determined as components of IC. Therefore, RM has been addressed as a component of IC. The five components are not separate from each other; they have been considered as mechanisms that work together to achieve operational goals, financial reporting, and compliance goals (Woods, 2008).

However, after the framework was published, changes in business models such as the use of external service providers with expertise in a certain field, the increase in technology-intensive activities, the acceleration of globalization in the markets, and the increasing legal regulations have also increased the demand for an agile IC system that can catch up with this change. Hence, COSO published an updated framework in 2013. In the new framework, IC is defined as "*a process effected by the organization's board of directors, management and other personnel, designed to provide reasonable assurance regarding the achievement of objectives relating to operations, reporting and compliance*" (COSO, 2013). In both 1992 and 2013 frameworks, COSO described the relationship between the components of IC, objectives, and the organization's activities in the form of a cube. Such description highlights that IC is not an independent process conducted separately from the activities of the organization and is integrated into all its activities. The main difference between the two frameworks is while financial reporting was the target in the one published in 1992, it was expanded to include nonfinancial reporting in 2013. Although IC principles are included in the first framework, they are mostly hidden in the details. New framework clarified this by determining the principles for each component of IC (McNally, 2013). Principles regarding the risk assessment component are determined as follows (COSO, 2013):

- Defining corporate goals clearly
- Identifying the risks related to the mentioned objectives and analyzing them to determine how they should be managed
- Considering the possibilities of fraud when assessing the risks
- Determining and evaluating the changes to affect the IC system considerably

An effective IC system, on the other hand, helps reduce, to an acceptable level, the risks that may prevent the organization from achieving one, more or all of its operational goals, reporting goals, and compliance goals. An effective IC system includes establishing a control environment that includes setting out appropriate standards and procedures for the implementation of IC throughout the organization; identifying, analyzing and prioritizing risks, determining and implementing appropriate control activities for these risks, as well as providing relevant and necessary information flow related to both internal and external environment, and monitoring this process and its results. However, the framework has some limitations. IC may not be able to prevent the results of bad judgment or decisions and external events that may affect the achievement of the organization's goals, so an effective IC system may fail as well (COSO, 2013). Therefore, the IC system provides reasonable assurance to both internal and external stakeholders.

In addition to the IC definition of COSO, which is widely accepted around the world, and its frameworks guiding the practice, IC definitions are also included in the documents published by different organizations. New York State IC Framework defines IC as the whole of corporate policies, plans, activities carried out in order to realize them, and the efforts made by employees in this way, which together provide reasonable assurance for an organization to achieve its goals and objectives (Hevesi, 2005). CoCo defines control as "*comprising those elements of an organization (including its resources, systems, processes, culture and tasks) that, taken together, support people in the achievement of the organization's objectives*" (IFAC, 2006). CoCo emphasizes that, in order to achieve its goals and objectives, an organization must determine significant internal and external risks and create and implement policies to manage them, and in this context, control includes the identification and mitigation of risks (Pang & Shi, 2009). In ICAEW[4] (1999) Internal Control Guide, it has been stated that the IC system plays key role in RM because IC contributes to the appropriate management of risks in an organization. INTOSAI[5] (2004), on the other hand, expresses that IC is a process performed by an organization's management and personnel and designed to address the risks to achieve the organization's overall objectives and mission and to provide reasonable assurance.

The common point of these definitions is that IC helps organizations achieve their goals and objectives, the management of the organization and its employees at all levels are responsible for this, it should be integrated into all activities and processes of the organization, and it provides reasonable assurance for the organization to manage its risks effectively. Apparently, it is a process that started as internal financial control and spread to the nonfinancial activities and transactions of the organization because of the developments experienced over time, the increasing risks due to the more variable environment and more complex relations, and that is carried out systematically throughout the organization. An effective IC system helps

[4] The Institute of Chartered Accountants in England and Wales.

[5] The International Organization of Supreme Audit Institutions.

the organization reach its goals and objectives by contributing to mitigating the risks to an acceptable level.

After the financial scandals experienced, the importance of IC further increased upon the request from the management of the organization and those who audit these organizations to present their opinions on the efficiency of the IC system as provided for in various regulations published in different countries, such as the Sarbanes-Oxley Act in the United States and the Combined Code[6] in the United Kingdom. With the introduction of these regulations, the IC system has become an accountability tool. The reason why the IC system is gaining further importance for organizations is that, in addition to these regulations, it is a self-assurance mechanism, reporting and control activities are recorded, and it contributes to creating an institutionalized way of responding to failures and crises by providing a more formal structure (Power, 2004).

10.2.2 Risk Management

RM is a systematic process carried out to identify, assess, and mitigate the harmful effects of risks so that organizations can achieve their goals and objectives. This process also includes evaluating opportunities for organizations to achieve their goals. RM is a dynamic process and organizations have adopted different approaches over time to manage their risks. As for the historical development of RM, it is apparent that the risks were first managed individually with the traditional method, also called the "silo approach." The traditional understanding of RM includes setting out the responsibilities for the identification, management, and control of risks at the level of specific business functions (Krstić & Đorđević, 2012). In this method, only certain risks are taken into account, the correlations between the risks are ignored and risks are addressed as isolated from each other. Managers of business units are only responsible for the risks of their own units and their management (Krstić & Đorđević, 2012; Selimović et al., 2020). Therefore, each business unit develops tools and practices independently of the others to manage its own risks (Bromiley et al., 2015). A reactive approach is adopted in the management of risks and only the negative effects of risks on the organization are intended to be prevented (Eryılmaz, 2018). However, the inadequacy of the traditional RM approach due to the rapid developments in technology and the emergence of new ways of doing business, the legal and political environment, changes in interaction with the environment due to market conditions and globalization, and the financial scandals have led to new

[6] Combined Code is the arrangement combining the recommendations of the Cadbury, Greenbury, Hampel, and Turnbull Committees. According to this regulation, the board of directors in the United Kingdom is obliged to establish an effective RM and IC system and to review it at least once a year in order for the company to achieve its goals. Companies on the London Stock Exchange are required to comply with the code, to report how the provisions are applied, and to disclose any noncompliance.

searches. Since it is not possible to manage effectively the increasing risks in a rapidly changing and complex world by using the traditional method, the concept of ERM emerged in the 1990s.

In the ERM approach, risks are addressed with a more holistic perspective rather than dividing them. Dickinson (2001) defines ERM as managing all risks faced by the organization with a systematic and holistic approach. According to Sobel and Reding (2004), ERM supports organizational management in understanding and effectively managing uncertainties. It covers all business risks with a holistic approach. Brown et al. (2019) consider ERM as the activities carried out to effectively manage all risks throughout the organization rather than managing risks separately on the basis of business units. Meulbroek (2002) stated that ERM is the application of an enterprise-wide strategy to identify, assess, and manage all risks that affect the enterprise value. According to the author, the goal of ERM is not to minimize the overall risk faced by an organization but to choose the optimal risk level to maximize shareholder value. Farrell and Gallagher (2015) emphasized that the most important aspect that distinguishes ERM from traditional RM is that the main risks from all sources of the organization are gathered together in a risk portfolio and then managed. Bromiley et al. (2015) argues that the ERM approach also includes the management of strategic risks, unlike the traditional approach. In addition, this approach reveals that organizations should consider the potential of risks to provide a competitive advantage in RM.

This change in the understanding of RM has made RM a focal point for organizations to achieve their goals and objectives. Accordingly, RM guides have been prepared by international organizations to guide institutions. Among these, the framework prepared by COSO is the most common one around the world. In the Enterprise Risk Management-Integrated Framework published in 2004, COSO defines ERM as "*a process, effected by an entity's board of directors, management and other personnel, applied in strategy setting and across the enterprise, designed to identify potential events that may affect the entity, and manage risk to be within its risk appetite, to provide reasonable assurance regarding the achievement of entity objectives*" (COSO, 2004). The framework provides guidance on how to implement an effective ERM to help the organization achieve its objectives and consists of eight interrelated components. These components are internal environment, objective setting, event identification, risk assessment, risk response, control activities, information and communication, and monitoring. These components are associated with strategic goals, operational goals, reporting, and compliance goals (COSO, 2004). In addition, it is apparent that, upon inclusion of all units in the process, both the definition and the framework created reflect the approach in the academic literature that risks should be addressed and managed holistically. On the other hand, the COSO ERM framework is not intended to replace the COSO IC Framework. Rather, IC is included in the framework as an integral part of ERM (COSO, 2004).

However, considering the increasing uncertainty, complexity, and flexibility, it has become clear that risk should be taken into account in the determination of business strategy and corporate objectives in order to optimize the outputs of ERM. With this approach, COSO published a new framework in 2017 that combined ERM with strategy and performance. Mentioned new approach associated risk with the performance of the enterprise rather than being an individual study. In addition, the new framework highlighted the importance of ERM in strategic planning and ERM is integrated into the entire organization as risk affects strategy and performance in all units (COSO, 2017). This update integrates ERM with the decision-making process and lays out the main lines between IC and ERM (Dias, 2017). The framework consists of 5 components and 20 principles associated with these components.

The new framework shown in Fig. 10.1 is composed of five terms placed between the intersections of the colored stripes. Although the relationship between the mentioned terms and the stripes is not clear at first glance, the five terms below the figure (governance and culture, strategy and objective setting, performance, review and revision, information, communication and reporting) constitute the components of the model and are represented by a stripe in the color of each component icon. Thus, it is intended to indicate that each of the five components proceeds through the processes described in the stripes. In other words, the five components influence the mission, vision and core values, strategy development, setting out the business objectives, implementation, and performance, thus creating enhanced value through ERM (Prewett & Terry, 2018).

Apart from these frameworks published by COSO, 31000: 2018 Risk Management Guideline has been published by the ISO to guide enterprises in RM. ISO 73:2009 Guideline, published by ISO in 2009 to develop a common understanding of RM concepts and terms, defines RM as the activities organized to control and manage risks in an organization. ISO 31000:2018 states that the purpose of RM is to add value to the organization, it includes all activities related to an organization, it is a constantly repeated process rather than being a one-time process, and it helps organizations in determining strategy, achieving goals, and making strategic decisions. This definition shows that the ERM approaches of ISO and COSO are similar and stresses that ERM should also be taken into account when determining the strategy.

Considering these definitions and published frameworks, ERM is apparently a dynamic process. The main purpose of ERM is to help the organization achieve its goals and objectives. To this end, it is included in all processes, starting from the

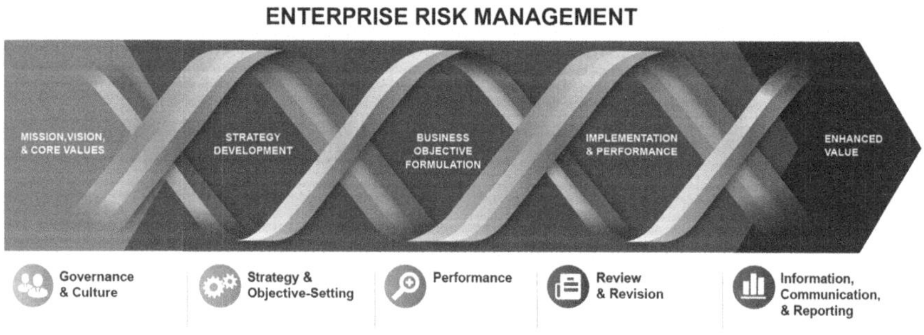

Fig. 10.1 Enterprise risk management framework integrated with strategy and performance (COSO, 2017)

determination of business strategies and goals to the implementation and monitoring of the results.

10.3 Relationship Between Internal Control and Risk Management

Considering the emergence and historical development of the concepts of IC and RM, it is evident that they have become increasingly important for enterprises since the 1990s. While the focus was initially on IC, RM has become the focus over time. Accordingly, opinions on the relationship between the two concepts also differ over time. While the opinions arguing that IC was a broad concept and included RM were prevailing, the view arguing that RM was more comprehensive and that IC was an important tool in carrying out an effective RM started to come to the fore over time.

Although the relationship between IC and RM has not been examined much in the literature, it is observed that the relationship between them is included in different studies that examine the two individually or in the published frameworks. However, the frameworks published to guide the organizations have also led to confusion and blurring of the relationship between the two.

10.3.1 COSO Confusion

Risk assessment is included as a component of IC in the IC frameworks published by COSO in 1992 and 2013. It is stated, in the frameworks, that the mentioned component is an ongoing process that includes the identification and assessment of risks and provides the basis for how risks should be managed for organizations (COSO, 2013; IFAC, 2006).

The ERM framework, published by COSO in 2004, considers RM as related to broader internal and external risks with regard to determining the strategy for achieving the organization's objectives. It also states that IC structures and procedures are included as a tool to achieve these objectives and are a part of the RM process (IFAC, 2006). Woods (2008) emphasized that considering IC a part of RM, and thus emphasizing the importance of RM, in the new framework led to a radical change in understanding. The author also stated that there are three main differences between the framework published in 1992 and the framework published in 2004. First, the framework published in 2004 considers ERM as a critical factor in achieving the goals and objectives of the organization, whereas IC is the critical factor according to the framework published in 1992. Second, the COSO, 2004 framework states that risks in an organization should be assessed and managed in the context of broader organizational objectives. From this point of view, the response to any risk may also be different. Third, COSO, 2004 deems RM as a strategic function. As such, the 2004 framework actually redefines IC in terms of RM.

Abovementioned change of understanding that emerged in the framework published in 2004 also led to confusion because risk assessment, control activities, information and communication, and monitoring are determined as components both within the framework of IC and within the framework of ERM. While the risk assessment component, which shows how risks should be managed and includes the identification, analysis, and prioritization of risks, is part of the IC framework, publication of an RM framework on how risks should be managed is the main reason for this confusion. Furthermore, it was stated, in the framework published in 2004, that the mentioned framework did not aim to replace the IC framework and that IC was also included in the ERM framework, which blurred the relationship between them. The existence of both an IC framework including risk assessment and an RM framework including IC makes it difficult to clarify the relationship. Moreover, the fact that both frames are depicted in the form of cubes is another factor that adds to the confusion. This confusion, which started upon the publication of framework in 2004, worsened with the publication of the updated IC framework in 2013 and the inclusion of risk assessment as one of the five components of IC in the new framework.

One cannot say that this confusion led by the COSO cubes is completely eliminated by the framework that combines the updated ERM, strategy, and performance published by COSO in 2017. The new framework reveals the importance of ERM in strategic planning and highlighted that risk is an element that should be taken into account in the process of determining business strategy and objectives of the organization because the strategies chosen by the organizations may not always be compatible with the mission, vision, and core values (COSO, 2017). Defining the strategy incorrectly can lead to deviation from the goals and objectives. Including ERM into the process also improves strategy selection. It was stated, in COSO, 2013, that an effective IC system may not prevent the consequences of erroneous forecasts or decisions. Incorporating ERM into key decision-making processes, with the new framework, the risk of erroneous forecasts and decisions is reduced. Thus, it is emphasized that RM also contributes to increasing the efficiency of IC. By clearly stating in COSO, 2017 that ERM is much more than IC, it became also clear that RM is the focus and that it is more comprehensive than IC. According to Prewett and Terry (2018), IC seems to be included in this new framework, as was the case for the framework published in 2004. The components of the framework are apparently restated versions of the COSO IC components. For instance, the principles of the performance component, namely, identifying risks, assessing the severity of risks, prioritizing the risks, and implementing risk responses (COSO, 2017), correspond to the elements of risk assessment and control activities components of IC.

In the new framework published by COSO in 2017, integrating IC with RM and determining it as the focal point of RM reveal that the two complement each other in achieving the goals and objectives of the organizations. Therefore, combining the frameworks and presenting a single guide that steer practitioners will contribute to increasing efficiency in practice by eliminating contradiction and confusion. It would be a more appropriate approach to integrate, both visually and as a process, these two elements, which are so intertwined and whose boundaries cannot be sharply separated, which support each other and create value when carried out together.

10.3.2 Integrating Internal Control with Risk Management

Despite the mentioned contradiction in the frameworks published by COSO, the relationship between IC and RM is clear in academic studies. The approach that emerged in these studies is that IC and RM should be integrated and both contribute to the achievement of the goals and objectives of the organizations. The difference is in how it should be integrated.

According to Krstić and Đorđević (2012), although RM has always been an integral part of IC, the scandals affecting the world's largest companies and the causes of these scandals have led the risk to be the focal point. Setting up a risk-based IC system has become an important tool for an effective RM. Pang and Shi (2009), on the other hand, suggest that the approaches in the literature arguing that both IC includes RM and vice versa are not comprehensive enough and that IC is actually integrated with RM from the very beginning. According to the authors, factors such as changes in technology, business models, and economic environment have affected the way of integration over time. The change experienced has been reflected in the development of both IC and RM, and their scope has gradually expanded. First, IC emerged, the control environment, which is a component of IC, developed the awareness of management risk, and controls such as authorization control and record control in the accounting system helped to ensure the protection of assets. Thus, the creation of an effective control system strengthened the RM idea. However, recurring financial scandals and the change in operation environment, which increased the uncertainty and risks, shifted the focus to RM. These two elements are integrated at a higher level, through designing the RM in a way to include IC as the main element, in the ERM framework published by COSO.

Wu (2013) stated that IC constituted the basis of RM and is an integral part of it. According to the author, the two are integrated and cannot be separated from each other. The author pointed out the difference between the two by stating that, in an organization, IC provides solutions to "*how to do things right*" and RM to "*how to do the right things*" and argued that both cannot be given up by comparing "*internal control to drive a car*" and "*risk management to look up the road conditions.*" In the context of this analogy, the author emphasizes that, in order to achieve their goals and objectives, the organizations must first closely follow the change in the environment, make the RM plans right, and determine their risks correctly, and then they can deal with these risks once they determine and implement appropriate control activities. He states that an organization must both check road conditions and drive to be successful; hence, IC and RM cannot be separated from each other.

The results of the study, in which Su and Zhao (2011) examined the relationship between IC and RM, revealed that the relationship between the two is mutually supportive and that raising the level of RM would have strong and positive effects on IC. According to Pang and Li (2013), IC and RM should be integrated. Both are dynamic processes and help organizations adapt to the changes in the environment in which they operate and survive by effectively managing their risks. The greatest benefit of IC and RM processes can only be achieved if they are integrated.

On the other hand, Leitch (2008) states that IC and RM should be combined and focuses on how to integrate them. The author argues that geometric abstractions of IC and RM within the COSO frameworks or elsewhere results in confusion and blurred the relationship between them. However, combining the two in practice is a matter of design, the essence of which is combining them conceptually. He used the concept of "*risk control*" to reflect this point of view. This concept implies that the control system includes controls that generates other controls, and many of them are intelligent controls that include risk-related thinking. Thanks to intelligent controls, IC and RM are integrated.

According to Leitch (2008), control activities are applied to cope with uncertainties in a world full of uncertainties. Some control activities implemented automatically create new control activities that are called "intelligent controls," and many of them involve risk-based thinking. Therefore, while designing controls against risks and uncertainties, the risks that may arise during the implementation of the designed control should also be taken into account. This way, it is ensured that new controls are automatically produced against unforeseen risks that may occur later. Intelligent controls produced this way contribute to RM for the next stages, and thus, IC and RM are integrated.

As a result of examining the studies mentioned above, IC has apparently come to the fore in the historical process regarding the relationship between IC and RM and it has been adopted as an effective process in order to mitigate the risks to an acceptable level. Accordingly, the first studies considered IC as a broader concept and the RM as a component of IC. However, the increase in uncertainty and complexity, the rapid change in technology and its reflection on business processes, growing corporate scales, and the change in managerial structures and business models have increased the risks faced by organizations. In such an environment, RM has become the focal point in order to achieve the goals and objectives with the effect of the experience gained in practice. IC was also included in this process and started to be deemed as a tool used for effective RM.

10.4 Conclusion

This study aims to reveal, with a holistic approach, the relationship between IC and RM, tools used by organizations to achieve their goals and objectives, in the face of increasing risks. In this context, first of all, the development of both tools is examined in the historical process.

The first IC practices started upon the implementation of the principle of separation of duties in economic activities against the risk of physical loss of assets at the beginning of the twentieth century. As the time went by, ex ante financial control practices came to the fore at first, and then, in the face of increasing risks, it expanded in a way to include administrative controls as well as financial controls. In the 1990s, IC turned into a systematic process that was applied throughout the organization and contributed to the achievement of goals and objectives through helping to mitigate risks to an acceptable level. Guidelines published by international organizations have also guided the organizations in establishing an effective IC system. Risk assessment was included as a component of IC in the IC frameworks published by COSO in 1992 and 2013, and that component constituted a basis for enterprises in identifying, assessing, and managing risks.

However, the increasing uncertainty and complexity over time required a more comprehensive perspective in addressing the risks in order for organizations to achieve their goals and objectives. Furthermore, financial scandals also highlighted RM studies. Thus, risks started to be managed holistically throughout the organization with the ERM approach. Over time, RM has been included in the key decision-making processes of the organizations, taken into account in determining the business strategy and corporate objectives, and IC has been integrated with the RM process.

However, the inclusion of IC in the ERM framework published by COSO in 2004 and the subsequent updating of the IC framework in 2013 and continuing to include risk assessment as a component of IC caused confusion among practitioners. In fact, the relationship between the two developed in the historical process. While IC was the focus in the 1990s, the approach that considers RM as a part of IC came to the fore. However, as a result of the necessity of addressing risks from a wider perspective over time, RM became the focal point in the 2000s and IC was also included in the RM process.

In this context, the confusion led by the COSO frameworks can be solved by incorporating the IC framework entirely into the ERM framework and publishing a single guide for practitioners. Studies in the literature also show that IC and RM together contribute to the achievement of the goals and objectives of the organizations, and that both, as dynamic processes, facilitate the adaptation of the organizations to environmental changes and support each other.

Consequently, IC system is a process designed to mitigate risks faced by the organizations to an acceptable level by the organization. Hence, the concept of risk is also the basis of IC. Effective management of risks helps organizations achieve their goals and objectives. IC also provides an appropriate control management system for organizations so that they can effectively manage their risks. Therefore, RM and IC are not interchangeable; on the contrary, they serve together to achieve the goals and objectives of the organization. Thus, they are complementary elements that support each other in an organization. The full integration of both conceptual and visual frameworks aimed at guiding practitioners contributes to increasing the effectiveness of the process by eliminating confusion.

References

Bromiley, P., McShane, M., Nair, A., & Rustambekov, E. (2015). Enterprise risk management: Review, critique, and research directions. *Long Range Planning, 48*(4), 265–276.

Brown, J., Duane, M., & Schuermann, T. (2019). What is enterprise risk management. *Journal of Risk Management in Financial Institutions, 12*(4), 311–319.

Chang, S. I., Yen, D. C., Chang, I. C., & Jan, D. (2014). Internal control framework for a compliant ERP system. *Information & Management, 51*(2), 187–205.

COSO. (2004). *Enterprise risk management-Integrated framework (Executive summary and framework)*. Committee of Organizations Sponsoring the Treadway Commission.

COSO. (2013). *Internal control – Integrated framework executive summary*. Retrieved on 18.06.2024, from https://www.coso.org/_files/ugd/3059fc_1df7d5dd38074006bce8fdf621a942cf.pdf

COSO. (2017). *Enterprise risk management integrating with strategy and performance*. Retrieved on 18.06.2024, from https://www.coso.org/_files/ugd/3059fc_61ea5985b03c4293960642fdce408eaa.pdf

Dias, A. P. (2017). A more effective audit after COSO ERM 2017 or after ISO 31000: 2009? *Revista Perspectiva Empresarial, 4*(2), 73–82.

Dickinson, G. (2001). Enterprise risk management: Its origins and conceptual foundation. *The Geneva Papers on Risk and Insurance Issues and Practice, 26*(3), 360–366.

Eryılmaz, M. (2018). Enterprise risk management: Past, today and future. In R. Efe et al. (Eds.), *Social sciences researches in the globalizing world* (pp. 244–254). St. Kliment Ohridski University Press.

Farrell, M., & Gallagher, R. (2015). The valuation implications of enterprise risk management maturity. *Journal of Risk and Insurance, 82*(3), 625–657.

Hevesi, G. A. (2005). *Standards for internal control in New York State Government*. Retrieved 12.05.2021, from https://ms.hmb.gov.tr/uploads/2019/01/intcontrol_stds.pdf

ICAEW. (1999). *Internal control: guidance for directors on the combined code*. Institute of Chartered Accountants in England & Wales.

IFAC. (2006). *Internal controls-a review of current developments*. IFAC.

INTOSAI. (2004). Guidelines for Internal Control Standards for the Public Sector. Retrieved 12.05.2021, from https://ms.hmb.gov.tr/uploads/sites/2/2019/09/INTOSAI.pdf

ISO. (2009). *ISO Guidance 73:2009*. Retrieved 09.05.2021, from https://www.iso.org/obp/ui/#iso:std:iso:guide:73:ed-1:v1:en

ISO. (2018). *ISO 31000:2018 risk management-guidelines*. Retrieved 09.05.2021, from https://www.iso.org/obp/ui# iso:std:iso:31000:ed-2:v1:en

Krstić, J., & Đorđević, M. (2012). Internal control and enterprise risk management–from traditional to revised COSO model. *Economic Themes, 50*(2), 151–166.

Leitch, M. (2008). *Intelligent internal control and risk management: Designing high-performance risk control systems*. Gower Publishing Limited.

McNally, J. S. (2013). The 2013 COSO framework & SOX compliance: One approach to an effective transition. *Strategic Finance, 6*(1), 1–8.

Meulbroek, L. K. (2002). *Integrated risk management for the firm: A senior manager's guide*. SSRN: https://ssrn.com/abstract=301331 or https://doi.org/10.2139/ssrn.301331

Page, M., & Spira, L. F. (2004). *The Turnbull report, internal control and risk management: The developing role of internal audit*. Institute of Chartered Accountants of Scotland.

Pang, Y., & Li, Q. (2013). Game analysis of internal control and risk management. *International Journal of Business and Management, 8*(17), 103–110.

Pang, Y., & Shi, D. (2009, July). Integration of internal control and risk management. In *2009 International Conference on Business Intelligence and Financial Engineering* (pp. 369–372). IEEE.

Power, M. (2004). The risk management of everything. *The Journal of Risk Finance, 5*(3), 58–65.

Prewett, K., & Terry, A. (2018). COSO's updated enterprise risk management framework—A quest for depth and clarity. *Journal of Corporate Accounting & Finance, 29*(3), 16–23.

Selimović, J., Grabovica, E., & Polić, T. M. (2020, June). Traditional and enterprise risk management: The case of Bosnia and Herzegovina. In *Proceedings of FEB Zagreb International odyssey conference on economics and business* (Vol. 2, No. 1, pp. 650–662). University of Zagreb, Faculty of Economics and Business.

Sobel, P. J., & Reding, K. F. (2004). Aligning corporate governance with enterprise risk management. *Management Accounting Quarterly, 5*(2), 29–37.

Spira, L. F., & Page, M. (2003). Risk management: The reinvention of internal control and the changing role of internal audit. *Accounting, Auditing & Accountability Journal, 6*(4), 640–661.

Su, X. H., & Zhao, X. (2011, September). Analysis on effects of risk management level on internal control. In *2011 IEEE 18th international conference on industrial engineering and engineering management* (pp. 1202–1205). IEEE

Wilson, T., Wells, S., Little, H., & Ross, M. (2014). A history of internal control: From then to now. *Academy of Business Journal, 1*, 73–79.

Woods, M. (2008). A commentary on the COSO internal control framework and its links with Sarbanes-Oxley. In M. Woods, P. Kajüter, & P. Linsley (Eds.), *International risk management* (pp. 33–48). Elsevier.

Wu, Y. (2013, June). Enterprise internal control from the perspective of risk management. In *2013 conference on education technology and management science (ICETMS 2013)* (pp. 1179–1182). Atlantis Press.

Serpil Ceylan graduated from the Department of Business Administration of the Faculty of Economics and Administrative Sciences at Gazi University in 2000. She worked as a State Revenue Expert in different units of the Revenue Administration between 2002 and 2012 and at the Prime Ministry between 2012 and 2013. She completed her master's degree at the TODAIE's Public Administration Department in 2011. In January 2014, she was appointed Internal Auditor at the Social Sciences University of Ankara (ASBU) and established the Internal Audit Unit. She is currently working as an Internal Auditor at ASBU. At the same time, she is continuing her doctoral education at the Department of Audit and Risk Management at ASBU. She has the CIA (Certified Internal Auditor) certificate. She wrote book chapters in the fields of audit and risk management.

Chapter 11
A Theoretical Examination of the Overlaps and Distinctions Between Risk Management and Crisis Management

Turgay Çağlayan

Abstract With the recently developing technology, the diversity and increase in demand, on the one hand, and the limited nature of resources used for supply, on the other hand, result in significant risks at the strategic level. Therefore, organizations have to carry on their activities in an environment where they are exposed to higher levels of risks compared to the past. This environment, full of uncertainty and risks, paves the way for unexpected and undesirable events, and in such an environment, suddenly arising crisis with negative consequences are also very likely to happen. In such cases, being aware of possible crises in advance, mitigating the negative effects of the crises, or managing them in a way that can offer opportunities may bring important advantages to the organizations. The most efficient factor in managing the crisis is to anticipate the crisis with a proactive approach and to take appropriate decisions in a timely manner. The aim of this study is to evaluate the similarities and differences between risk and crisis and risk management and crisis management and to evaluate whether organizations that cannot manage their risks will have to manage their crises. As a result of the examination conducted to that end, it has been seen that not every risk turns into a crisis or that not every crisis is caused by a risk. For this reason, in the event of a crisis, it is important to have a plan or system to manage the crisis, whether the risks are managed or not.

Keywords Risk · Crisis · Risk management · Crisis management

T. Çağlayan (✉)
Social Sciences University of Ankara, Ankara, Türkiye
e-mail: turgay.caglayan@student.asbu.edu.tr

H. Kıral (ed.), *Rethinking Enterprise Risk Management*, Accounting, Finance, Sustainability, Governance & Fraud: Theory and Application,
https://doi.org/10.1007/978-981-97-5983-5_11

11.1 Introduction

Until recently, most organizations of different sizes gave priority to the management of financial risks in line with the desire to maximize earnings, as well as to ensure efficiency and economy. Under normal circumstances, the management of financial risks can be considered as a necessary and prioritized factor compared to the other risks. However, according to the report on "Risk Management and Corporate Governance" published by the Organization for Economic Cooperation and Development (OECD) in 2014, *"It is not possible for organizations to protect themselves from risks and maintain corporate success by only managing financial risks."*

Organizations that need to holistically manage their financial risks as well as other risks commonly adopt a risk-oriented management approach. Acting with a risk-oriented approach, especially in the planning and control phases of processes and activities, positively affects the achievement of corporate goals. However, the risks encountered in an environment paving the way for unexpected and undesirable events may be affected by different events and risks, creating negative effects at a greater level than expected. Having more impact than expected, such situation is sometimes considered as a crisis for the organization. In such cases, a risk-oriented management style alone is not enough to manage the crisis, and it is important to run the crisis management process.

It was seen, during the literature review, that the relations and connections between risk and crisis and risk management and crisis management were evaluated in overall. However, these relationships and connections were evaluated only at concept level and it was concluded that, as a common view, organizations that cannot manage their risks will manage their crises. This study also evaluates, by examining previous studies, the similar and different aspects between risk and crisis as well as risk management and crisis management and brought a new perspective to the existing view in the literature.

The aim of this study is to examine the similarities and differences between risk and crisis as well as risk management and crisis management and to make an assessment about whether organizations that cannot manage their risks will have to manage their crises.

The study consists of five parts. In order to understand the subject more easily, explanatory information is given on the concept of risk and risk management in the next section which is followed by explanatory information on the concept of crisis and crisis management in the third section. The fourth part discusses the risk and crisis, whereas the fifth part addresses and assesses the similar and different aspects between risk management and crisis management. Conclusion part includes the detections and evaluations related to the subject.

11.2 The Concept of Risk and Risk Management

According to sociologist Niklas Luhmann, the origin of the word risk is derived from the word "*rhiza*" in Homer's Odyssey. Risk is a nautical term that emerged in England in the seventeenth century as the word "*rhizikon*," which means to describe the "*danger posed by the steep cliffs on the coast for sailors*" as a made-up language. In the eighteenth century, it started to be used in Germany in the meaning of "*to ensure success of businesses against the dangers they will face*" (Lupton, 1999).

According to another definition, the word risk used in the meaning of "*danger*" was evolved from French which is written as "*risque*", and it is also written as "*rischio*" in Italian, "*riesgo*" in Spanish, "*risko*" in German, and "*risk*" in English. It was first used as a *riziko* in our language and was later included in the literature as *risk*. It is defined as "danger of harm" in the Turkish Dictionary of the Turkish Language Association (TDK). Examining the definition, it can be inferred that risk is a source of danger and threat.

Unlike these definitions, it is also considered that the concept of risk derives from the word "*rızık*," which is written as "*rizq*" in Arabic culture. *Rızık* is everything material and nonmaterial that Allah offers to all living things for their benefit. Examining this definition, it can be thought that risk includes everything, both positive and negative, that is presented. When these definitions, coming from the past and explained above, are examined, it is seen that there is no agreed definition of the concept of risk, which has been recently used very frequently.

According to Regester and Larkin (2008), risk is the measure of the negative impact of an event. Risk is an effect or an adverse event that produces that effect. Risks are inherently uncertain and must be managed in order to avoid any negative situation they may cause. According to Conrow (2003), risk is the measurement of not reaching the desired level within the framework of predetermined costs, time, and some constraints for the defined objectives for an activity. According to this definition, risk consists of two components. These components are the possibility of not achieving the desired goal and the negative consequences in case of failure.

In most of the above definitions, it is clear that the outcome of risk mostly includes a negativity. However, in some definitions such as the definition derived from the word "*rizq*" in Arabic culture, it is seen that risk includes opportunities as well as negative consequences.

Traditional views on risk define risk as an adverse event, danger, and harm. The techniques and tools used against risk only deal with and focus on the negative side of the risk. However, recent definitions define risk by drawing attention to the opportunities it brings (Richard, 2003).

In the modern sense, risk can be defined as the probability of an event that will affect the process of achieving the goals, with a broader perspective than the purely negative consequences in the traditional view. Positive or negative deviations from the expected result in the objectives can also be called risks. Negativity can be defined as a threat while positive deviation can be defined as an opportunity. While every risk includes an opportunity, every opportunity naturally involves risk.

Opportunities and profits are the rewards of those who manage to carry out activities by taking risks.

Risks are red flags that can be encountered during any activity and they must be managed in order for the activities to result in the desired level. Risk management is the method applied in a logical and systematic way to identify, define, classify, analyze, and respond to risks related to any activity. Risk management is also used to maximize profits by making use of the opportunities while minimizing losses through helping organizations achieve their goals.

According to Chelst and Bodily (2000), risk management is the process of planning certain measures taken to reduce the probability of occurrence of undesirable events that are considered to prevent an activity or to mitigate its effects if the event occurs. Risk management is an important mechanism that aims to provide reasonable assurance on some issues such as continuation of the processes and activities of the organization uninterruptedly; compliance with legal regulations; reduction of errors, deficiencies, and losses; increasing profits; protection of image, reputation, and brand; safety and protection of employee health, etc.

The definition of risk management updated by the Committee of Organizations Sponsoring the Treadway Commission (COSO) in 2017 is "*the culture, capabilities and practices integrated into the formulation and execution of the strategy that the organization can rely on to manage risk in creating, protecting and realizing value*." It is clear from this definition that the main objectives of risk management are to create value for the organization, to raise awareness, and to protect the organization. Integrating the risk management mechanism into the processes of determining and executing the strategies of the organization will be beneficial in achieving the objectives set for these processes. The integration implemented here will not only enable reduction of the possibility or impact of risks but also evaluation of the opportunities that may arise.

According to Benton (2001), the risk management process generally consists of three steps. The first step is to identify, categorize, and classify risks that are measurable. The second step is the assessment, measurement, and prioritization (analysis) of risks using qualitative and/or quantitative methods. The last step is to manage risks (risk response) in order to prevent it from happening or reduce its impact to the desired level, if it happens.

11.3 Crisis Concept and Crisis Management

Crisis, which has its origins in the Greek word "*crisis*," is a word that has different meanings in various branches of science and is used in the meaning of "*suddenly appearing or emerging disease symptom*" or "*sudden progression of the disease to the fatal stage*," which is commonly used especially in medical science (TDK, 2021). In the field of social sciences, it is mostly used in the meaning of "*depression*," equivalent to its dictionary meanings.

It is seen, in the same reference, that the crisis has different meanings. Apart from the meanings described in medicine, crisis also has the meanings listed below:

- Someone's mental depression
- Situation where something is very scarce
- Sudden and excessive desire for something
- Collapse
- Hard times or depression in the life of a society or an organization, either in a country or between countries

Social sciences take into account especially the last two definitions. However, it is difficult, in this respect, to make a clear definition of the crisis concept because the phenomenon of crisis is evaluated considering the negativity of the situation, and it may change from person to person.

According to Barton (1993), a crisis is an event that has a huge impact, is difficult to predict, and has negative consequences in general. According to Caponigro (1998), a crisis is an action that negatively affects the results of an activity, damages the reputation and credibility of the organization, and can get out of control in a short time. Phillips (2004), on the other hand, defines crisis as a sudden situation that jeopardizes the existence of the organization and that occurs out of the planned or expected. In general terms, a crisis can be evaluated as the inability to intervene in a threatening event.

Not every problem that occurs in the ordinary process should be called a crisis. The common point of the definitions related to crises is the occurrence of certain unforeseen or impossible to know events which often have negative consequences that may have serious impact at any scale, from a large-scale structure such as the state to small organizations. In other words, it is correct to call the events that occur suddenly and unexpectedly and have negative consequences crises. Crises, which can spread like an epidemic and often have negative consequences, pose a great threat especially to organizations. Organizations need to manage the crisis in order to prevent these threats.

According to Fink (1986), crisis management is the process of deciding which strategies can be applied to achieve a positive outcome during a crisis, and planning and implementing these strategies. Wilson (1992), on the other hand, defines crisis management as a type of management that plans strategic actions which will prevent any crisis through defining the events and situations that may cause it or which will minimize the effects and damages after it has occurred. Crisis management is a management model developed to overcome unexpected situations emerging suddenly when normal functioning is disrupted; depression, stress, tension, and conflict increase; and time is limited to deal with these issues (Tekin, 2015).

Crisis management is divided into two depending on the crisis preparedness of the organization and the time and form of crisis management. Active crisis management is the process where the organization plans the necessary work in advance and develops a prevention-oriented strategy by considering this possibility before the crisis occurs. Reactive (passive) crisis management is the process of taking corrective measures as soon as a crisis occurs in the sense of eliminating the crisis that has become evident or minimizing its negative effects.

As is clear from the definitions above, there is a need to design and update separate procedures for each crisis type in crisis management that an organization will plan and implement. For this reason, crisis management includes different plans. Crisis management needs a management approach that can predict and evaluate the likelihood and impact of crises, and it is beneficial as long as it is implemented as planned. In this context, crisis management offers the organization and its stakeholders the ability to recognize and manage crises and creates an experienced crisis management team that can react to unexpected situations (Bhasin, 2020).

11.4 Similar and Different Aspects of Risk and Crisis

"Risk" and "crisis," which are often confused or considered as the same concepts, do not mean the same thing. While risk is an event whose probability and impact cannot be fully predicted and which do not result in a devastating impact as a crisis, a crisis is an unstable situation that, as a result of a sudden change in the environment of the organization, disrupts the routine functioning of the activities; poses a high threat to the basic structure, order, goals, and objectives of the system; and requires critical decisions to be taken under time pressure and uncertainty (Uras, 2017). Crises often occur as a result of the emergence of risks and the unpredictable increase in their impact. Therefore, risks often appear before crises occur, and such risks are generally perceived as a crisis signal. Although the risk management approach, which has been updated in the light of recent experiences, has developed a system to benefit the crisis management process, the risk management mechanism alone cannot always guarantee the prevention of the crisis or the efficient management of the crisis.

The uncertain and complex situation in the business environment constantly causes organizations to be exposed to risks, in other words to dangers or opportunities. The organization's ability to achieve its determined goals and objectives also depends on their protection from the dangers encountered as a result of risks or their ability to make use of the opportunities. As the risks faced by the organization, resulting in danger or opportunity, are sometimes impossible to predict in advance, they can lead organizations to some untimely changes and even drag them into crisis. Crises are often caused by changes that the organization never expected. Such changes cause the management of the organization to direct its existing resources to this change, and thus, routine activities, operations, and knowledge are of secondary importance. In fact, when the crises, natural disasters, and events that are not under the control of the organization are set aside, they usually follow strategic risks that occur untimely and/or create an unexpected impact (Dinçer, 1998).

Publishing Canadian musician Dave Carroll's song "*United Breaks Guitars*" on social media can be given as one of the most meaningful examples of how risk turns into a crisis for an organization. Dave Carroll will fly to the city where he will give a concert in 2008 by United Airlines. When he gets on the plane, watching out the window, he sees that his guitar which he will use in the concert was carelessly thrown into the cargo hold of the plane and fell to the ground. After the plane arrives at its destination, checking his luggage, he sees that his guitar is badly damaged. He has a concert as soon as the plane lands and he has no time. Without wasting any time, he takes his guitar to a mechanic to have it repaired and gives his concert that way. When the three-day concert program is over, he contacts the company to ask them to compensate the damage to his guitar by paying the repair fee amounting to $1200. However, the company's customer services refuse to pay the requested $1200 for the damage of the guitar, stating that the damage notifications must be made within 24 h from the completion of the flight where the damage is made, as per the company policy. After his request is denied, Dave tries to contact the company via various channels such as correspondence, phone, and e-mail for 9 months to claim his right and wants to talk to an official. However, all these attempts failed.

After failing to get anything from the communication process with the company, Dave shared it on social media by shooting a clip for his song "*United Breaks Guitars*" whose composition he completed in November 2008. Shares of United Airlines dropped about 11% within 4 weeks after the release of the video. Such decrease corresponds a loss of approximately $180 million. In the same period, United Airlines' cargo flights in the United States decreased by 13% and passenger traffic by 7%. It is observed, in the following period, that there are serious losses in the brand and reputation of the company (Soule, 2010). This event is a striking example of how a common and low-impact operational risk can turn into a major crisis when a company ignores it.

11.5 Similar and Different Aspects of Risk Management and Crisis Management

As can be understood from the definitions in the second and third sections, while risk management and crisis management are different mechanisms, it can be seen that the two mechanisms support each other when the purposes of use in the crisis process are examined. The main difference between risk management and crisis management can be summarized as follows: Risk management focuses on identifying, classifying, evaluating, and controlling any activity or event that is deemed to be harmful to the organization. Crisis management, on the other hand, focuses on intervening and managing an unforeseen event after it occurs and takes effort to ensure that the institution comes through this event with the least damage or with an opportunity.

Institutions need crisis management in two ways. In the first case, the event causing the crisis is not included under the scope of risk management. These types of crises usually occur through external factors, they can appear suddenly and create huge and devastating effects, and the organization can be caught completely unprepared. For instance, in case of a decrease in corporate sales as a result of the dissemination of unfounded news detrimental to the organization on social media by a competitor company, which is not addressed in the risk assessment process, it can be considered within the scope of crisis management to take urgent measures which have not been unplanned beforehand.

The second case in which crisis management will be necessary is when the event turns into a crisis and launches crisis management as a result of the realization of any of the risks evaluated in the risk management process. A technical failure affecting the information system center of the institution and the loss of some of the company's data can be given as an example. If the event described in the example is evaluated in the risk management process and a measure is planned, the impact of the adverse event can rapidly be reduced before the crisis begins by means of such measures.

As can be seen from the definitions made and the cyclic relationship between risk, crisis, risk management, and crisis management indicated in Fig. 11.1, being the subject of risk management risk sometimes has the potential to cause crises. A risk that is not managed efficiently under risk management can cause a crisis, and crisis management is needed upon the emergence of the crisis. The precrisis period is the phase where the most efficiency can be achieved during the crisis through risk management. Identifying, evaluating, monitoring the risks having the potential to cause a crisis, and taking measures to prevent them from turning into a crisis are the activities of the risk management mechanism affecting the crisis management process. The crisis management process begins to run once the possibility of the risks to turn into a crisis is realized, and the event is controlled within the scope of crisis management upon the emergence of the crisis. The crisis comes to an end once the crisis is taken under control and stability is ensured regarding the activities of the organization. Crisis management also ends upon the repair of the damage suffered by the organization after the crisis and resuming the previous routine order, in other

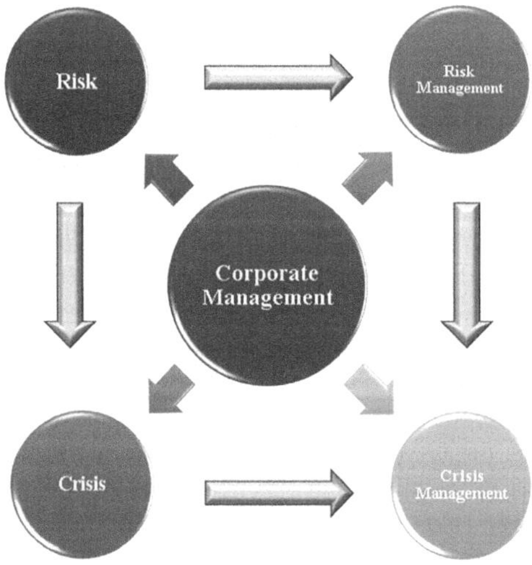

Fig. 11.1 Risk, crisis, risk management, and crisis management cyclic relationship. Source: Adapted from Turan and Çelikyay (2020)

words upon recovery and restructuring. Risk management, however, continues to run with a view to manage the risks that may arise during and after the crisis.

It is important to run risk management and crisis management in a cycle, especially in the process of emerging crises that cause great damage and last for a long time, which means that the risk management has a preventive effect before the crisis and an approach that will proactively manage the risks encountered during and after the crisis. As seen in Fig. 11.2, risk management helps develop the capability to prevent the risk in the precrisis period, mitigate the impact of the risk, and predict the crisis beforehand and early warning of the organization during the crisis. If all these risk management benefits cannot prevent the occurrence of a crisis, then crisis management should be implemented. Within the scope of crisis management, activities such as evaluating and reducing the impact of the crisis, responding to the crisis, postcrisis recovery, and restructuring of the institution are carried out (Wilhite & Knutson, 2008).

During the crisis, some activities should be carried out in order to prevent the crisis or to avoid the damage through detecting the crisis. As seen in Fig. 11.3, the stages of preventing the crisis, detection, management, recovery, and exit, define the activities to be carried out during the crisis. In the precrisis phase, it is aimed, at the stage of preventing the crisis, to mitigate and eliminate the effects of highly likely crisis with the help of risk management. In the period of exit with the least damage, efforts are made to detect the crisis and to increase the efficiency of the methods used to eliminate the crisis when the crisis begins. In the crisis period, the goal is to overcome the crisis by managing it through the activities and the measures taken against the factors causing the crisis, which have been determined by the crisis management planned before. In the postcrisis period, the damaged resources are recovered in order to eliminate the impact of the crisis and an exit from the crisis is provided with a sufficient recovery. Examining the crisis process, the benefit of risk

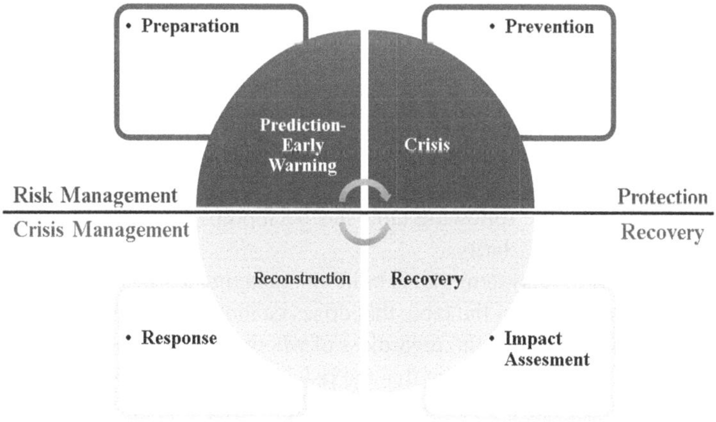

Fig. 11.2 Risk management and crisis management cycle. Source: Taken from Wilhite and Knutson (2008)

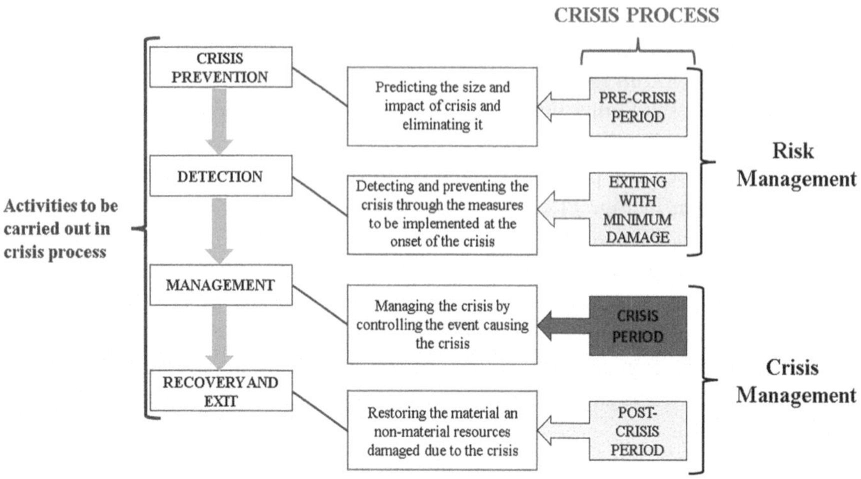

Fig. 11.3 Risk management and crisis management in crisis process. Source: Adapted from Tekin and Zerenler (2008)

Table 11.1 Relationship between risk management and crisis management

	Those who cannot manage crises	Those who can manage crises
Those who cannot manage risks	Cannot manage crises	Can manage crises (passive)
Those who can manage risks	Cannot manage crises	Can manage crises (active)

Source: Produced by the author

management is high, especially in the first two stages, and crisis management is activated when the crisis occurs (Tekin, 2020).

As mentioned at the beginning of the study, it is inferred from the studies on risk management and crisis management that there is a widespread opinion that those who cannot manage their risks will manage their crises. However, evaluating the similar and different aspects of risk management and crisis management together, four different conclusions were reached by examining the risk management and crisis management of the organization throughout the crisis process, i.e., in the pre-crisis period, crisis period, and postcrisis period. In the light of the information obtained in this scope, the following table has been prepared regarding the process and results for the sake of clarity.

Table 11.1 mentions a system that is built on managing a crisis that the organization will face. It is clear from the table that crises cannot be managed in the absence of an efficient crisis management, regardless of whether the risks are managed in the organization. Such that, in the event that the risks that are likely to cause a crisis are managed and their effects are mitigated before an efficient crisis management, the crisis can be managed actively and even the possibility of gaining benefits will increase by turning the crisis into an opportunity. However, all of the examinations and examples given in this study reach conclusions on assumption that a crisis occurs. If the risks that the institution is exposed to do not turn into a crisis, thanks to the efficient risk management, they will not be addressed in this study.

In order to have a more comprehensive understanding of the four different processes identified and results, the operation of risk management and crisis management in the crisis process and the results obtained are evaluated separately and enriched with examples.

11.5.1 Those Who Cannot Manage Risks May Not Manage Crises

The main reason for reaching such a conclusion is that the organization does not manage its risks and has not planned a crisis management process before the crisis arises or that it cannot manage the crisis efficiently despite the crisis management is planned in advance.

This can be defined by the crisis Dave Carroll caused to United Airlines by sharing the video titled "*United Breaks Guitars*" on social media, which describes the transformation of an operational risk into a crisis, included in the fourth section of the study. Even if there was no information about the risk management process of the company at that time, it could not be considered that such a large company did not run risk management. However, it can be thought that the risk has turned into a crisis since the risk management methodology is not implemented by the affiliated units/departments although the strategic risk management process is carried out by the senior management or since it is not carried out at the desired efficiency and appropriate controls are not planned or the planned controls are not implemented in the management of the emerging risk.

Apparently, the company does not have a planned crisis management process in place during the crisis. The company, which tried to solve this risk turning into a digital crisis due to a human error, by running a passive crisis management with a reactive approach, aggravated the crisis even more. The company suffered considerable financial loss as a result of the crisis and also made a loss due to remarkable decrease in number of passengers and cargo.

11.5.2 Those Who Cannot Manage Risks Can Manage Crises

An organization that has been able to manage the crises despite not being able to manage the risks has run passive crisis management process in a way to take appropriate measures from the moment the crisis arises and has planned crisis management and put this plan into action during the crisis even though it has never implemented the risk management process or has not operated it efficiently or there is no crisis management plan at all. "Tylenol Crisis" is an example in this regard.

On September 29, 1982, three people fell sick and died at the hospital in Chicago after taking Tylenol, an extra-strong painkiller manufactured by Johnson & Johnson (J&J) company. FBI officials, who suspected the assassination because those who lost their lives due to cyanide poisoning were also relatives, found evidence that the serial numbers written on the Tylenol boxes on the victims' residences were the same and they all smelled "*like almond*." At the time, Tylenol was the most used pain reliever with over 100 million users and 37% market share across the United States (Onat, 2020). The first deaths were followed by the statement of J&J company where they said that they were not related to the incident and "*there is no cyanide in their products*" (Benoit & Drew, 2009). However, a week later in California, four people died due to the same poisoning and an employee of the company told the press, during the investigation process, that "albeit at a lower amount, cyanide was used for testing in J&J laboratories," which started the process where the incident would be referred to as "Tylenol Crisis" on the headlines in the media which reported that the poisoning was due to the use of Tylenol.

Negative news in the media requires J&J executives to take urgent action against the crisis. The first action of the company officials would be to temporarily suspend Tylenol advertisements to reduce attention to the product. During the crisis, J&J president James Burke set up a seven-member strategy team (crisis team) in order to manage the process efficiently, firstly by giving an immediate response to negative news in the media and exhibiting an example of leadership (Rehak, 2002). The first strategy goal that the team received from Burke is "*How do we protect people?*" while the second one is "*How do we protect this product?*" (Berge, 1990). In addition, consumers nationwide are promptly warned through the media against consuming Tylenol products until the extent of the sabotage is determined, and all 31 million Tylenol capsules are recalled from store shelves in and around Chicago (Eaddy, 2012). Thanks to the coverage of this recall activity in the press, the negative impact on the company image is reduced and consumer support is provided (Benoit & Drew, 2009).

As a response to the strategy team's question "*How do we protect people?*," J&J sets up a free helpline for consumers in the first week of the crisis within the framework of public relations (Berge, 1990). However, a nationwide study is conducted to measure consumer reactions to Tylenol poisoning. Although 87% of the people participating in the research stated that the organization that produced Tylenol was not responsible for the deaths, 61% still stated that they would not buy Tylenol in the future (Time, 2021). The market share of the company drops to 7% in a short time due to the prevailing purchasing tendency although the company is not held responsible by the consumers in the survey.

In the framework of the strategic team's question "*How do we protect this product?*," packages with new triple protection, safer against fraud and sabotage, which are also $2.5 cheaper than previous drug packages are released to the market in order to prevent any similar crisis, and this is shared with all media organizations. These efforts are appreciated by the public, and its market share has risen again and reached 46% 100 days after the crisis (Onat, 2020). After a similar poisoning case in 1986, the production of Tylenol is stopped although the company is not considered guilty due to the positive effect of the well-managed process on the public.

The biggest proof that J&J company could not foresee the event that created such a crisis as a risk is the following statement made by James A. Murray, public relations deputy manager of J&J, after the incident: "*We had a written plan for other emergencies. Yet, we didn't have a crisis plan against such a huge incident. We reacted to what happened every day as information came in. It was like groping in the dark. First day, we weren't quite sure what was going on there*" (Snyder, 1983). The high impact of the emerging risk led to a crisis and, as included in the statement, J&J reacted to the negative situations encountered during the crisis once the crisis arises. In this scope, some activities that should have been carried out in the precrisis period of the crisis process, including risk management, were not carried out properly; the activities that should be done during the crisis were tried to be continued in an unplanned way and in line with the course of the crisis. After the efforts taken during the crisis period, the market share was brought to a higher level than the precrisis period and the company exited the crisis with minimum impact, and the crisis was managed efficiently by even turning it into an opportunity, with the contribution of restructuring.

11.5.3 Those Who Can Manage Risks May Not Manage Crises

This can be mostly observed in the process of a crisis stemming from a natural disaster or an event originating from external factors that are out of control of the organization. In a process that will ensure such a result, crisis occurs although the organization manages its risks efficiently, where the crisis management has not been planned or the crisis management that is planned or put into practice cannot efficiently manage the current crisis.

The most appropriate event setting an example in this regard is the chip crisis which continues today. Chips used in many fields from kitchen tools to defense industry, from electronics to automotive industry, are semiconductors. Although it is small, it is of great importance due to its use in technological tools. The chip industry is monopolized by the US and Far East companies.

Most of the companies producing vehicles in the automotive sector plan their activities periodically under normal conditions and take precautions in advance by managing the risks they will face. In addition, they prepare material requirement plans and procurement plans in accordance with their production capacities and carry out the procurement process as provided for by these plans. Semiconductor chips are the most important parts in the automotive industry for which the sector depends on foreign sources in the procurement process.

Since people had to stay at home and continued education, business, and entertainment activities from home due to the Covid-19 pandemic emerging at end of 2019, the use of computers, smart devices, tablets, and game consoles has increased.

Besides, many organizations started developing remote working systems or improving existing infrastructure for their staff to work from home. Use of technology in education has increased the demand for the sector called consumer electronics. Demand for chips, which is an input of the consumer electronics industry, has increased proportionally. In the same period, when the automotive sector, which stopped its production lines due to transition to flexible working system and falling demand for automobiles, resumed production upon the rapid recovery in Covid-19, it was hard to find the chips, whose production capacity continued at the same level, due to the supply-demand imbalance. As a result of the unforeseen events listed above caused by the pandemic, which is a global crisis, many automobile manufacturers have decided to stop their production for a short time due to the shortage in chip supply. Thus, the chip crisis, which caused a great loss in the automotive sector in the second half of 2020, caused a great decrease in the production volume of the sector.

Therefore, no matter how efficiently the companies which are dependent on chips for production have managed their risks, they will face a chip crisis as a result of external factors as well as supply-demand imbalance resulting from the global crisis. And not being able to supply the appropriate number of chips for their production plans, they will reduce their production volume, which will result in loss. There is still no example for efficient crisis management displayed by organizations during the ongoing chip crisis or for how they can get out of this crisis with the least damage.

11.5.4 Those Who Can Manage Risks Can Also Manage Crises

In this case, the organization manages its risks efficiently, and if the managed risks turn into a crisis, it also manages its crises efficiently by running the crisis management process it has planned and get benefits by taking advantage of the opportunities it encounters. It would be appropriate to give an example of a sports tournament held at the international level which is the only tournament that has survived the Covid-19 global crisis that has emerged recently and that we are still experiencing.

Due to the Covid-19 pandemic, giant sports tournaments such as the Tokyo Olympic Games, European Football Championship, NBA (American Basketball League), and UEFA (European Football Federations Association) Champions League and the majority of national leagues in different branches of sports have been cancelled or postponed since the beginning of 2020. Many organizers and clubs suffered great damage and financial losses due to these cancellations and postponements.

It was also the case for the tennis season. Evaluating this situation in advance, the French Open Tennis Tournament took immediate action and moved its calendar to September 2020 but still could not avoid losing 230 million pounds. The Wimbledon Tennis Tournament, the only tournament held on grass courts, was also cancelled after the French Open. However, despite the fact that the tournament was cancelled, the authorities of the All England Lawn Tennis & Croquet Club, which organizes the Wimbledon Tennis Tournament, did not announced any damage, which drew attention.

It was expressed, in the statement, that the authorities predicted, within the scope of the risk assessment made considering the SARS outbreak in 2003, that an epidemic may occur, which could adversely affect the tournament, and it was also expressed that this issue was included in the policy during the period when the tournament was insured for £1.61 million within the scope of transferring the risks. With this article, most of the ticket and broadcasting revenues of the Wimbledon Tennis Tournament, which was cancelled for the first time except for the world wars, were covered by approximately 142 million pounds paid by the insurance company during the global crisis when everyone was experiencing an economic depression.

Examining the policy with a view to evaluating the efficiency of the risk management process, it was seen that the company officials added many items to the policy, within the scope of transferring the risks, ranging from the death of the queen of the United Kingdom to the national mourning. As a result, the All England Lawn Tennis & Croquet Club, which organized the Wimbledon Tennis Tournament, was the winner of the year in the sports world, during the global crisis. Any kind of event that may cause a crisis were foreseen under efficient risk management and precautions were taken, and the risks encountered during the crisis were managed and it was ensured to exit the crisis with the least damage.

11.6 Conclusion

It is not quite possible not to be affected by risks and especially crises. The organizations have some difficulties due to the risks and crises they face. However, it is known that some organizations have come out of the crises, in particular, unscathed and even benefited by taking advantage of the opportunities emerging as a result of the crisis. All these experiences highlight the importance of the risk management and crisis management mechanisms run by the organizations in a timely and efficiently manner.

Organizations constantly encounter risks from the moment they are established. They also face the crises arising, time to time, due to not managing some of these risks efficiently. Techniques and strategies developed to detect and prevent a crisis before the crisis period can often create sufficient impact to prevent any crisis. However, in the event of a crisis, the effect of the crisis can be reduced to the level that will cause the least damage to the organization by running the crisis management.

This study evaluates similar and different aspects between risk and crisis as well as risk management and crisis management and aims at introducing a new perspective to the common view in the literature which argues that those who cannot manage their risks will manage their crises. In this context, four different results were reached after examining the risk management and crisis management operation status of the organization in the crisis process, i.e., in the precrisis period, crisis period, and postcrisis period, and these results are individually examined by giving examples.

Given the result of the examination, if those who cannot manage the risks cannot also manage the crises, they will suffer from the crisis, and if those who manage the risks cannot manage the crises, they will suffer from the crisis. However, those who cannot manage the risks but manage the crises will manage their crises by executing passive crisis management, and those who manage both the risks and the crises will manage their crises by executing active crisis management and even benefit from the opportunities arising as a result of the crisis.

As a result, it is important for organizations to manage their risks and crises in order to maintain their existence in a stable manner, to protect their reputation and value, and even to create value. However, evaluating the widespread view "*who cannot manage the risks manages his crises*," which is mentioned many times in the study, not every risk turns into a crisis or not every crisis is caused by a risk. For this reason, when faced a crisis, it is important to have a plan or system to manage it, whether the risks are managed or not; in which case, the crisis encountered can be managed efficiently, the damage can be minimized, and even benefits can be obtained by making use of the opportunities.

References

Barton, L. (1993). *Crisis in organizations*. South-Western.

Benoit, L., & Drew, S. (2009). Appropriateness and effectiveness of image repair strategies. *Communications Reports, 10*(2), 153–163.

Benton, A. B. (2001). *Step-by-step enterprise risk management*. Risk Management, *48*, 41–50.

Berge, D. T. (1990). *The first 24 hours; A comprehensive guide to successful crisis communications*. Basil Blackwell.

Bhasin, H. (2020). *Crisis management– Meaning, need, steps and examples*. Retrieved 09.05.2021, from https://www.marketing91.com/crisis-management/

Caponigro, J. (1998). *The crisis counselor*. Barker Business Books.

Chelst, K., & Bodily, S. (2000). *Structured risk management: Filling a gap in decision analysis education. The Journal of the Operational Research Society, 51*(12), 1420–1432.

Conrow, E. (2003). *Effective risk management: Some keys to success*. American Institute of Aeronautics and Astronautics Inc..

Dinçer, Ö. (1998). *Stratejik Yönetim ve İşletme Politikası*. Beta Yayınları.

Eaddy, L. L. (2012). *Johnson &Johnson's Recall Debacle*. Electronic Theses and Dissertations. Retrieved 15.05.2021, https://stars.library.ucf.edu/etd/2194. University of Central Florida.

Fink, S. (1986). *Crisis management: Planning for the inevitable*. American Management Association.

Lupton, D. (1999). *Risk* (2nd ed.). Routledge.

Onat, S. (2020). Retrieved 05.06.2021, from https://tr.sedatonat.com/post/tylenol-krizi

Phillips, D. (2004). *Handbook of corporate communication and public relations*. Routledge.

Regester, M., & Larkin, J. (2008). *Risk issues and crisis management in public relations* (4th ed.). Kogan Page.

Rehak, J. (2002). *Tylenol made a hero of Johnson & Johnson: the recall that started them all.* Retrieved 05.06.2021, from https://www.nytimes.com/2002/03/23/your-money/IHT-tylenol-made-a-hero-of-johnson-johnson-the-recall-that-started.html

Richard, L. (2003). *Management* (6th ed.). Thomson South-Western West.

Snyder, L. (1983). *An anniversary review and critique: the Tylenol crisis* (pp. 24–34). Retrieved 05.06.2021, from https://www.sciencedirect.com/science/article/pii/S0363811183801829

Soule, A. R. (2010). *Fighting the social media wildfire: How crisis communication must adapt to prevent from fanning the flames*. University of North Carolina.

TDK. (2021). *Türkçe Sözlük*. Türk Dil Kurumu Yayınları.

Tekin, Ö. F. (2015). *Crisis management and its importance for public administration*. Journal of Vocational School of Social Sciences, *18*(2), 119–135.

Tekin, M. (2020). *Krizi Yönetebilmenin Sırları*. Satınalma Dergisi, *90*, 21–26.

Tekin, M., & Zerenler, M. (2008). *İşletmelerde Kriz Yönetimi (6'ncı Baskı)*. Günay Ofset.

Time. (2021). *Tylenol crisis*. Retrieved 05.06.2021, from http://archive.timepr.com/c3.asp

Turan, A., & Çelikyay, H. H. (2020). *Türkiye'de Kovid-19 ile Mücadele: Politikalar ve Aktörler.* Uluslararası Yönetim Akademisi Dergisi, *3*(1), 1–25.

Uras, U. (2017). *Riskleri Yönetmede Başarısızlık, Krizleri Yönetmek Zorunda Bırakır.* Retrieved 04.05.2021, from https://www.kalderankara.org/bilgi-merkezi/makaleler/riskleri-yonetmede-basarszlk-krizleri-yonetmek-zorunda-brakr-14

Wilhite, D., & Knutson, C. (2008). *Drought management planning: Conditions for success.* Options Méditerranéennes, *80*, 144.

Wilson, B. G. (1992). *Crisis management: a case study of three American universities.* Pro Quest Dissertations Publishing, University of Pittsburg

Turgay Çağlayan graduated from the Military High School and the Military Academy between 1994 and 2002 and then graduated with the rank of Lieutenant in 2002. He served as a platoon and company commander in various units of the Turkish Armed Forces until 2012. During this period, he completed his master's in international relations at Konya Selçuk University. He worked as an internal auditor at the Ministry of National Defense in 2012 and continues to work in this position. He also continues his postgrad education at the Social Science University of Ankara.

Chapter 12
Risk Management in Digital Era: Opportunities and Challenges

Cem Dursun

Abstract This study aims to evaluate the risks faced by businesses embracing digitalization while assessing the opportunities, how to manage these risks in the mentioned new period, the supporting factors and opportunities, and the potential threats and challenges. In this context, we first address the historical development of the concept of digital transformation, its main benefit objectives, then the risks and adverse effects of digitalization, which is followed by a discussion, over the existing literature, of the change in risk management in the digitalized world and the conditions, opportunities, and challenges making this change necessary. As a result, digitalization can provide significant gains in operational processes and risk management approaches. On the other hand, it has been revealed that it is necessary to act with a new risk management approach in which this opportunity for gain can be made use of, taking into account the new risks arising after digitalization. Evaluating the opportunities and challenges regarding implementing the said approach, we have assessed the risk management approaches in businesses after digitalization under the titles of how businesses' reactions to risks change, the consequences of risks in changing businesses, and how the adverse effects of risk have changed.

Keywords Industrial revolution · Digitalization · Risk management · Data analytics · RPO · IoT

12.1 Introduction

We live in a world where borders have disappeared as a result of globalization, access to all kinds of products and services is possible, and initiatives in almost every field are facilitated with less resources and effort compared to the past. The

C. Dursun (✉)
Social Sciences University of Ankara, Ankara, Türkiye
e-mail: cem.dursun@student.asbu.edu.tr

H. Kıral (ed.), *Rethinking Enterprise Risk Management*, Accounting, Finance, Sustainability, Governance & Fraud: Theory and Application,
https://doi.org/10.1007/978-981-97-5983-5_12

reason behind the rapid spread of globalization lies in the fact that we live in a rapidly digitalizing world. This world makes it possible for a young university student to develop a simple application in a small room, on a single computer connected to the internet, and to compete with very large-scale companies in a short time. It is not surprising that the number of entrepreneurial actors is increasing with great momentum in such a dynamic world offering equal opportunities to every entrepreneur. In this new digital world, it is apparent that the products and services offered can be compared simultaneously with their counterparts in the world; intense competition prevails, and therefore the share of numerous organizations operating in various sectors from the cake is rapidly decreasing; and only those with high competitiveness survive. It is accepted that the changes in technology and competition reduce, along with digitalization, most of the disadvantages within the framework of the traditional role of the enterprise (Porter, 2000). On the other hand, the introduction of digital technologies increases the efficiency of existing business models and business processes as they reduce costs, increase product quality, and shorten delivery times (Brynjolfsson & Hitt, 2000). In short, digitalization leads to unprecedented economic size and sustainability advantages (Knudsen et al., 2021).

Instead of perceiving digitalization only as a technological development, it is a more valid approach to consider it as a structural transformation with many sociocultural, economic, and political reflections, including business models, culture, and processes. There are important gains that businesses have achieved in almost every field, thanks to digitalization. These gains also make it possible for digital transformation to be accepted within the businesses and spread rapidly. On the other hand, it is extremely important not to ignore the risks and negative effects of digital transformation. Depending on the effectiveness of the risk management approach they will follow, businesses may stay away from these negative effects. In such an environment, the key to success for businesses is in the hands of those who can manage digitalization and the threats and opportunities it brings.

Risk management is an approach that starts with traditional methods, renews itself with changing and developing conditions over time, and gives assurance that businesses can act in accordance with their strategies. The experiences have revealed that traditional risk management approaches will have to undergo a radical change after digital transformation. This change aims to proactively implement strategic decisions at the same time with the contribution of technical approaches such as data analytics, artificial intelligence, big data, and machine learning. On the other hand, this change is not as easy as expected for businesses in some cases due to compelling factors as well as some supportive factors. Completing the digital transformation, the applicability of the "digital risk management" approach will increase even more after the changing and developing processes, systems, and infrastructures as well as culture (Portilla et al., 2017).

In this context, this study aims to determine the new methods on how to manage the risks brought by this transformation in the most effective way, as well as the benefits to be provided by the businesses after digital transformation, and to evaluate the supporting factors and opportunities for the implementation of these methods, and potential threats and challenges.

The study is composed of five parts. In the following part of the study, the historical development of digital transformation is discussed. In the third chapter, the risks and side effects of digitalization are discussed. In the fourth part, risk management in the digitalized world is evaluated. In the fifth part, risk management approaches observed in businesses after digital transformation, supporting factors and opportunities for the implementation of these methods, and potential threats and challenges are examined. The conclusion part includes determinations and evaluations on the subject.

12.2 Historical Development of Digital Transformation

Three concepts that are associated with digital transformation and that have a very close relationship with each other are knowledge, technology, and economy. Considering their historical development, technologies have created economic systems and economic systems have created social structures. Three economic systems have emerged in history: agricultural economy, industrial economy, and knowledge economy. In this sense, being the first economy, the agricultural economy started along with the agricultural revolution in the 8000s BC when the human beings settled down and continued until the last quarter of the eighteenth century. The social structure formed by the agricultural economy was called the agricultural society, and after completing its mission in 1760, the industrial revolution took place upon the invention of the steam engine when the mechanical systems and machines working with steam power started to be used instead of human power (Xu et al., 2018). With the industrial revolution that started in England in the last quarter of the eighteenth century and spread in other European countries, Russia and Japan at the beginning of the nineteenth century, production reached an unprecedented volume, the capital grew, and the profitability of the enterprises increased to remarkable levels. This first step of the industrial revolution is called Industry 1.0. As can be seen in Fig. 12.1, which includes that period and the following periods, the invention of the telegraph in 1840 and the telephone in 1880 and the use of electrical energy in the last quarter of the nineteenth century were followed by the launch of mass production with the first moving production lines in 1870. It's called Industry 2.0. Although the industrial economy still continues, the information economy has emerged in the second half of the twentieth century with the design of the first microcomputer and the use of personal computers, in other words the integrated use of electronic and information technologies. In this process, mentioned technological developments have created the knowledge economy that later created the information society. To compare these two processes, capital and labor were accepted as basic inputs in the production function of industrial economy, and the production function was expressed as Y = f (K, L) with Y: production amount, K: capital, L: labor. In the knowledge economy, technology is also included in the production function, the production function is expressed as Y = f (K, L, T), with T: technology (Yıldırım, 2004).

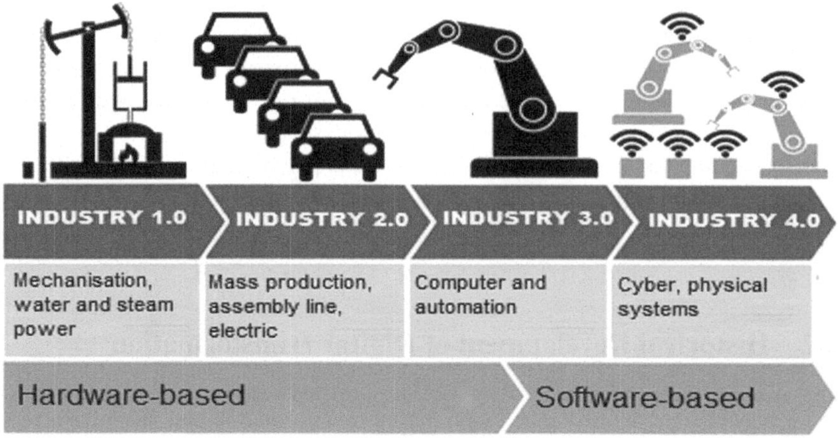

Fig. 12.1 Industrial revolutions. Source: Tarhan (2018)

Although they are not new technologies, digital technologies based on computer hardware, software, and networks have begun to become more advanced and interconnected, changing social structures and the economy in the beginning of the twenty-first century. Especially after the developments in information and communication technologies, digital systems and physical devices that can interact with each other on a worldwide network such as the internet have constituted smart systems. These smart systems have led to a structure that is directed by computers, can manage itself, and even make decisions, where automation is maximized and the effect of the human factor is reduced. This period was called Industry 4.0 (Schwab, 2017). Industry 4.0, which was first brought to the agenda at the 2011 Hannover Fair and later announced as the industrial modernization of Germany, is about digital transformations that will deeply affect all industries. An unprecedented progress has been achieved during this period considering the rapid changes in the design, production, operation, and service provision of production processes and products.

Within the framework of digital transformation, innovations are provided not only in technological development and change but also in employment, regulations, production, investment, and education. However, Industry 4.0 have some negative effects: employment problems of unqualified workers due to the spread of automation, the loss of mid-level competencies transferred to autonomous smart systems, and the increase in plant investments where robots work. On the other hand, it is predicted that the human factor will be more intensely included in critical decision mechanisms and a need for human resources with competencies in this regard will arise (Çakır, 2018). Currently, Industry 4.0 has not yet been completed in Turkey, and according to the studies, it is observed that, on one hand, many enterprises lag behind the required technological developments, and on the other hand, the number of enterprises that have made progress in this process within the scope of digital transformation has increased in number (Yıldırım, 2020).

Digitalization, which started upon the development of personal computers in the 1970s and their active use by end users, has reached a different level under the name of digital transformation where information and communication infrastructures have spread in recent years; effective usage areas have emerged, thanks to technologies such as 5G; and cloud computing has become mandatory in terms of continuity and accessibility despite regulatory limitations. The IoT, artificial intelligence new technologies such as machine learning, smart cities, smart factories, augmented reality, cyber physical systems, cybersecurity, autonomous robots, simulation, connected homes, driverless cars, robotic services, Bitcoin and Blockchain, 3D printers, big data, and data analytics have started to be used (Schwab, 2017; Bulut and Akçaci, 2017; Akben and Avşar, 2018; Soylu, 2018 Birkel et al., 2019; Eling and Lehmann 2018). With the use of 3D printers, which is the first development, production processes have been made considerably effective and efficient. The IoT, another development area, have provided benefits in many areas since it enables the physical systems used in homes and factories, and many facilities communicate with each other as a result of the integration of cyberspace, and it also enables rapid and effective detection and correction of possible malfunctions. Camera and sensor structures were used with augmented reality, especially in the field of operational technology; performance, problem, and efficiency monitoring were captured; and various analyses and measurements were started with the data collected from the aforementioned advanced ends. Finally, the use of autonomous robots provides benefits to humanity in many areas, both in business and private life (Bulut & Akçaci, 2017).

One of the areas where digitalization spread first and effectively is the banking sector. Considering as an indicator, there are said to be six main trends behind the digital transformation in this sector, either directly or indirectly:

- Customers and their ever increasing expectations
- More pressure for competitiveness
- In most cases, regulatory restrictions that place average return on equity below the cost of capital and cost pressures arising from low interest rates
- Types of emerging risks arising from new business models
- New arrangements
- Handling core functions such as fraud detection, compliance with the legislation, or audit reporting through different methods, namely, transferring to fintechs[1] (Portilla et al., 2017)

It is witnessed that digital transformation has started in the public sector as well as in the private sector and that it even provides serious benefits in some institutions. As a result of the encouragement by the government, the areas where digital transformation is handled as the highest priority are considered as public financial management, infrastructure and transportation, cybersecurity, and education (Akmeşe, 2020).

[1] The term "financial technology," or shortly "fintech," covers innovative financial solutions provided by IT and is also used for newly established companies that offer these solutions although it often includes established financial service providers such as banks and insurers (Puschmann, 2017).

With the effect of digital transformation, existing business models and processes are also digitalized and new models are emerging, and organizations are also subject to digital transformation in order to manage these models in the most effective way, and their basic goals such as production quality and operational performance increase. We have entered a period where businesses that cannot adapt to the new digital world and thus cannot reach this level are out of the game as they cannot compete (Schwab, 2017).

Digital transformation also includes significant revisions to a business's corporate strategy. It may affect policies and procedures, personnel, resources, operational practices, or the community. For this reason, how digital transformation is carried out is critical for the long-term structure of businesses (Henriette et al., 2016). At this point, digital transformation intersects with elements such as business strategies, governance and management approaches, internal control structures, and risk management. Among these elements, risk management stands out as it is the main starting point that guides the others. Understanding the risks coming along with many opportunities arising from the changing and developing process, system, and infrastructure, culture and business models after digital transformation, how to manage them, and what kind of opportunities and conveniences will appear in this sense are as important as digital transformation for businesses.

12.3 Risks of Digitalization

We have witnessed that digital technology has made our lives better than before for the last 70 years (Tian & Xu, 2015). With the developments experienced in this period, businesses increased their productivity and economies grew (Hitt & Brynjolfsson, 1996). As a result of these developments, the areas where digital technologies are beneficial have become new focal points of researchers. In parallel studies, besides the positive effects of digital transformation, it has also been determined that there are some negative effects due to the integrated and complex structure of information technologies, which are the foundations of digitalization.

Industry professionals and academics have assessed the advantages of digitalization as well as its costs and side effects to businesses, the threats and side effects associated with the increasing use of information technology-based applications, from the perspective of individuals, organizations, and communities to identify the net benefits of digitalization. The internet, which stands out the most among all technological developments, has sharply changed human history (Kim et al., 2011). This sharp change has brought very important benefits for individuals and institutions. On the other hand, it is observed that technology-related and unrelated crimes and negative actions such as spam, ransomware, cyber-aggression, violation of digital property rights, and cyberbullying are carried out over the internet for every individual and institution (Kim et al., 2011; Xu et al., 2018; Gimpel & Schmied, 2019). Later studies show that there are more negative effects with different aspects than those first observed. Especially with machine learning, put on the agenda upon digitalization, artificial intelligence enables the design of algorithms beyond human perception and ability, and due to the complex nature of digitalization, yet it can cause negative effects by making erroneous evaluations at points where there is no human initiative (Gimpel & Schmied, 2019). Furthermore, although it is stated that digitalization allows everyone to be an entrepreneur by enabling equality of opportunity, it helps the rise of very large companies or extremely powerful national and supranational organizations that can hinder competition, creativity, and control, and we witness some situations similar to the one where Facebooks takes actions that will affect political activities in the United States of America (Gimpel & Schmied, 2019). Therefore, it is extremely important to consider the risks that digitalization brings in addition to its benefits.

In short, it is apparently related to the negativities experienced in areas such as productivity, cost, efficiency, and security as a result of the effects of the risks that come to the agenda together with digital transformation for businesses. The effect is negative if it undesirably affects the benefits provided to the individuals in society above a certain level. These interests may be legal interests of natural persons such as the right to life, education, health, and freedom of movement or legal interests of legal persons such as physical or intellectual property (Gimpel & Schmied, 2019).

As stated above, due to the complex nature of digitalization, many of these impacts are uncertain and unknown, and it is difficult to identify and measure them which indicates that businesses have entered a period where they may have difficulties in the field of risk management beyond what they are accustomed to so far in an environment where digital transformation is becoming more and more widespread. Considering the risks related to digital transformation, it is understood that they are the result of actions, decisions, and digital technology tools related to digitalization rather than digital technology itself. Apart from the risks, it is also necessary to focus on the side effects of digital transformation. The risk and side effects of digitalization may stem from the dynamics of certain or uncertain, expected or unexpected, individual or collective actions. Side effects, either direct or indirect, often refer to negative effects (Decker, 2013). There is no objective criterion for fault or negativity that everyone agrees on across individuals, businesses, cultures, and periods. Therefore, an unbiased viewer perspective is required to qualify an effect as adequately negative, common, or as risk and adverse effect, and assess whether it is likely to happen or not (Raphael, 2007).

Maturity can be considered in multiple layers in terms of digitalization. It allows the digitalization of analogue signals and continuous storage of digital data if the digital technology tools are at a low technical level. Encryption at a higher but technical level enables operations such as big data processing. At a higher sociotechnical level, outputs such as lower transaction costs, automated decisions and actions, and rapid innovation and diffusion can be achieved. Increasing digital maturity with the realization of opportunities can have an impact at various levels, from the individual to the society scale. For example, when information systems do not work as intended at the individual level, it can cause technostress at the interpersonal level such as loss of motivation and socialization, and decreased work performance and error proneness at the organizational level (Gimpel & Schmied, 2019).

In environments where digital transformation takes place at certain levels, the risks are generally evaluated as follows:

- *Negative information exchange*: Digitalization enables some individuals or institutions to take actions that will allow socially inappropriate information sharing or exchange of goods.
- *Support for illegal actions*: Digitalization enables harmful actions such as individual attack, cybercrime, cyberwar, and cyberterrorism.
- *Negative economic changes*: Damage to traditional economic structures as a result of changes in digitalization, monopolization of effective national and supranational institutions, prevention of competition and increased dependence on these institutions, and loss of competitiveness of national states and institutions regarding their economic position in global competition due to regional concentrations.
- *Disturbing the political balances*: Digitalization can change political forces and dynamics in ways against the will of the majority, and the effects of marginal views increase as a result of the spread of such extremist views and the strengthening of the political controls of autocratic regimes that want to exert strict controls on the people.
- *Increasing vulnerabilities in IT operations*: Failures that may occur in critical digital technology devices, loss of performance and quality, disruptions in connected corporate processes due to dysfunctions, service interruptions affecting other connected systems and, thus, institutions experiencing reputational, regulatory, financial, and operational losses.
- *Negative health conditions*: Digitalization negatively affects the psychological health of individuals due to addiction and intensive use.
- *Environmental degradation*: Consumption of material resources due to the resource requirements necessary for the production of digital products, negative effects of digital wastes that can be recycled in a limited way, climate changes in parallel with meeting the demand for energy required for the functioning of digital technologies, and restriction of individual freedoms by digitalization.
- *Ethical violations*: Digitalization brings along dilemmas in the field of ethics, individuality intensifies instead of cooperation to provide social and economic support, and accountability is limited in digital environments.
- *Inappropriate decision environment*: Erroneous, incomplete, and misleading information is present in digitalized structures, and wrong decisions can be made due to this environment.
- *Loss of individual and institutional competencies*: Digitalization can lead to socially undesirable changes in traditional competencies and behaviors, loss of competency due to dependence on technology, production of manipulative information, and the dissemination of such information through digital technologies, thus directing social perception.

- *Lack of control over algorithms*: As a result of digitalization, the algorithms used in every structure work without human initiative, and social injustice and prejudices emerge as a result of the uncontrollability of such situations (Gimpel & Schmied, 2019).

12.4 Risk Management in Digitalized World

Digital transformation leads to remarkable changes in business models, technologies, business processes, and corporate cultures of enterprises. It offers expansions that will provide significant benefits to businesses in areas they have not had any contact until now. For this reason, although it is spreading rapidly all over the world, the rate of spread varies according to the risk perception of the enterprises. The reason for this is that besides the aforementioned benefits, the enterprises have different levels of awareness with regard to understanding the risks that come with digitalization and to determine how to manage them. It will not be appropriate to address emerging and future risks through known risk management approaches. Therefore, it becomes compulsory for businesses to expand their vision for digital risks in addition to digital transformation literacy.

This period brings along new opportunities and threats for the units responsible for risk management. In this context, the main developments that dramatically changed the risk ecosystem and how to respond to the related risks began to take place on the priority agenda of the said units and management units of the enterprises. The past assessments reveal the necessity of making changes not only to risks and responses to risks but also to the risk management discipline (Albinson et al., 2016). It provides an opportunity to examine the complex and rapidly evolving relationship between information systems, digital technologies, and risk. Within these possibilities, actions have been taken regarding both technical and administrative perspectives on risk management by making use of the competencies of information systems (Ciborra, 2006). In this context, businesses that have the opportunity to make more effective and productive decisions by utilizing the information obtained through data analytics and automation focus on solutions such as big data applications, pattern recognition and real-time preventive controls, and RPA.[2] It is aimed, especially through RPA, to increase productivity by 30–40%, to reduce the workload on personnel by 70% and to provide greater benefits by including competent personnel in the decision mechanisms of more critical processes (Thomas & Mitchell, 2017).

When businesses focus on creating their digital transformation strategies, risk management and cybersecurity issues are apparently at the forefront and center of these efforts. However, it is observed that the units responsible for risk management

[2] RPA: Robotic Process Automation is a new technology for automating the processes. It is an infrastructure using the graphical user interface and interacting with existing core systems just like a human worker would do (Kregel et al., 2021).

have hard time regarding the fact that risk management is a fundamental component of the digital transformation process. On the other hand, it has been understood that significant strategic benefits can be obtained with the risk management approach, which is planned to be carried out proactively rather than reactively by making use of the capabilities that digital transformation will bring (Xu et al., 2018). Barriers to the development and implementation of innovative risk management strategies are said to be lack of resources, absence of national policy, lack of data on risks, limitations in science and technology, barriers to local government and limited local community participation, restrictions on access to information and ineffective information management, gaps in decision-making processes, multiple command and control arrangements, and a broad and deep distrust against the public (Rao, 1995).

In order to create a successful digital risk program, there are seven components of digital risks for businesses, specifically for banks (Fig. 12.2). While the same level of maturity is not expected in each of these components, reasonable maturity is required in certain areas to operate the digital risk program in line with core business strategies. Being the business area where the digital transformation was experienced first and fastest, banking sets an example for other business areas. Hence, it is possible that the digital risk management processes that have already started to be operated in banking are also implemented in other businesses (Portilla et al., 2017).

If we are to explain the components of digital risk in detail:

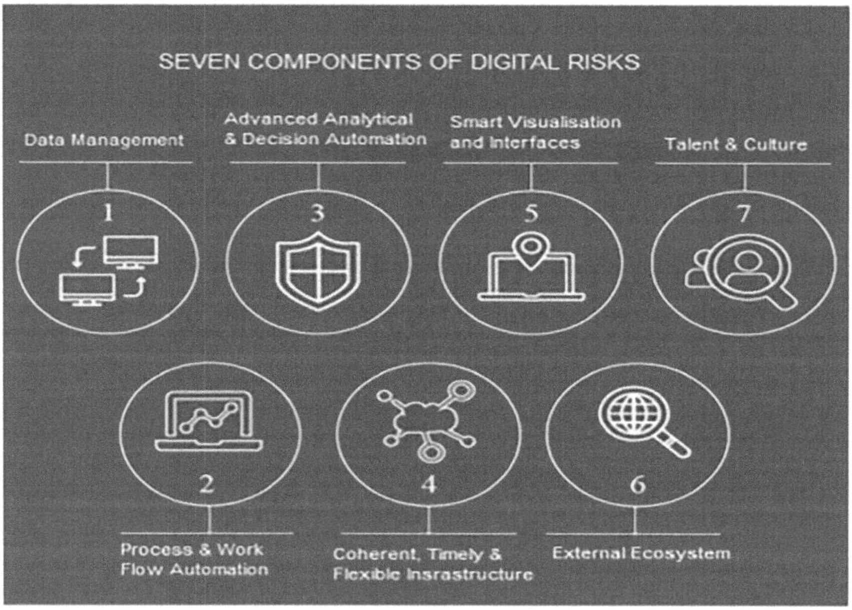

Fig. 12.2 Seven components of digital risks. Source: Portilla et al. (2017)

- *Data Management*: Data management and the development of operational models is an essential component in improving data quality, assuring consistency between risk and business preferences, and meeting risk-related data needs. It is at utmost importance that risk units can benefit from data in processes such as risk identification, analysis, assessment, and response to risks (Portilla et al., 2017; Khanboubi & Boulmakoul, 2018).
- *Automation of Processes and Workflows*: Routine processes are automated through RPA, and some repetitive activities, which are under the responsibility of the risk management unit, are carried out by these systems by integrating with smart workflows. This way, the risk management unit can take part in high value-added decision mechanisms (Portilla et al., 2017; Khanboubi & Boulmakoul, 2018).
- *Advanced Analytical and Automated Decision-Making*: Complex transactions performed through advanced risk models based on machine learning algorithms and transaction clusters detecting irregular transactions, used to be performed with difficulty, in long periods and in error-prone manner by the personnel working in the risk management units in the past. After digitalization, efficient results with low error rate can be obtained through these methods.
- *Combined, Reliable, and Adaptable Infrastructure*: The activity area of the risk management unit is expanding with a number of additional possibilities, including new data storage options, new interfaces, and convenient access to the supplier ecosystem.
- *Smart Visualization and User Interfaces*: Risk-related information can be followed in a more intuitive, understandable, and customized way through risk dashboards, augmented reality platforms for consumers, and other interfaces (Portilla et al., 2017).
- *External Ecosystem*: Cooperation can be made on the detection and monitoring of abuse and irregularity risks, with the participation of suppliers and external stakeholders through systemic integrations (Portilla et al., 2017; Khanboubi & Boulmakoul, 2018).
- *Talent and Culture*: The density of personnel such as data scientist, data analyst, and modelling specialists, who operate in an agile culture that values innovation and experience, and who have digital infrastructure and perspective in addition to having knowledge in both risk and business areas, is increased (Portilla et al., 2017; Khanboubi & Boulmakoul, 2018).

12.5 Risk Management Approaches Observed in Businesses in Post-digital Transformation

Digitalization is completed in three stages within businesses. First, the goals of the business are defined. Then, in order to achieve these goals, it is necessary to understand the benefits to be obtained from digitalization, to determine the level of competence required to achieve these benefits, and to evaluate which of these competencies exist in the enterprise. The last stage is developing a preparation model that includes three main levers: improving the competencies of the employee in terms of eliminating the gap between the current and the targets, the integration of databases, and the use of monitoring technologies (Khanboubi & Boulmakoul, 2018).

Businesses operating in various sectors are forced to reevaluate their business models and cope with new operational risks upon digitalization. The use of digital channels causes the evolution of existing risks and the emergence of new ones. In this case, risk managers make more effort to identify, assess, and reduce risks. In fact, many of these risks are not new but are increasing as a result of the structural changes brought about by the digitalization of business models and operations. However, critical risks such as cyber risk, model risk, and epidemic risk have increased in recent years and are considered to be the three main threats associated with digitalization (Gimblett, 2018). The businesses had to change their approaches toward risks in order to reduce the negative effects arising from these three main hazards and related issues.

12.5.1 Various Responses of Businesses to Risks

Risk management is related to the goals and objectives of businesses. In the digitalizing business world, goals and objectives apparently depend on new information and communication technologies. Dependence on technology is increasing day by day due to the fact that almost all business processes are started to be operated through information systems. As a result, business risks and information technology risks have become even more intertwined. In such a structure, it is obvious that risks such as systemic crashes, malfunctions, and cyberattacks will affect not only information systems but also business processes (Mazareanu, 2010). For this reason, a new approach has emerged in the digital age and risk management has evolved into information security risk management. The main purpose of information security risk management is to protect information technology assets such as data, hardware, software, personnel, and facilities from all threats that may arise from outside or inside the organization. The aim is to prevent or minimize losses by choosing and applying appropriate security measures (Khanboubi & Boulmakoul, 2018).

In this new approach, the main objective is to react to risks as quickly as possible and thus to minimize negative effects and ensure that the business overcomes this with as little loss as possible. It is important to be prepared in advance in order to react quickly and to monitor the risk more closely by making estimations based on the information to be obtained from data sources with regular dataflow. To that end, business intelligence systems are used. Thanks to the tools offered by these systems, the experiences of the enterprise throughout its life are evaluated under the title of "lessons learned" and risk scenarios for future situations can be obtained. The same tools can analyze the said scenarios by taking into account the new conditions of the internal and external environment and offer solutions that will respond to risk based on this analysis (Khanboubi & Boulmakoul, 2018).

There are various reasons behind the changes in risk management approaches of businesses after digital transformation. The most prominent among these are the integration of information technologies into the decision processes of enterprises day by day; making widespread and ensuring continuity of the controls established for the efficient, productive, and safe operation of the processes of the enterprises; requirements, in place, to maintain strong business immunity in order to be prepared for the adverse effects of new risks that are constantly changing and diversifying; and risk management being not only an assurance function against possible dangers but also an element that has an impact on the performance of the general processes of the enterprise, changing customer expectations and market dynamics.

12.5.1.1 Integration of Information Technologies into Decision Processes

After the developments in information technologies, artificial intelligence, big data, and data analytics, businesses that have easy access to large amounts of data can go beyond traditional risk management approaches in the steps of predicting, detecting, and preventing high-level risks by making use of this data. According to the estimates of IDC,[3] the volume of information in the world doubles every 2 years (Syuntyurenko, 2015). On the other hand, developments in this field continue and it is aimed to benefit from autonomous information systems in further steps. Autonomous information systems are structures that manage and potentially defend their selves and response to risks, which will assist and sometimes even replace human-controlled risk management in this area (Henderson et al., 2012). The emergence of new technologies such as process automation or RPA, cognitive information processing, and IoT is expected to play a key role in the digitalization of the financial sector which is the engine of digital transformation (Khanboubi & Boulmakoul, 2018).

12.5.1.2 Making Process Controls Widespread and Continuous

Intelligent devices equipped with various sensors, communication, and information processing capabilities, called IoT, have begun to be used in many areas. Businesses that benefit from these technologies are increasing day by day in the field of risk management, especially within the scope of monitoring risks. These structures offering a proactive risk management opportunity, as is the case in other areas of use, offer businesses the opportunity to identify risks, make important risk estimations, and even take measures against these risks. Thus, real-time widespread and dynamic risk management can be applied. In the digitalization period, where the

[3] International Data Corporation: US-based market research company.

dynamic risk management approach stands out, it is the main priority to simultaneously respond to the risks identified (Mazareanu, 2010).

12.5.1.3 The Necessity of Preparedness and Resilience Against Risks

There is an acceptable level of risk for businesses and this is determined by the risk appetite. It is essential to manage the risk in a way that does not exceed the mentioned level. Controls are the main instruments for managing risk in this dimension. However, controls sometimes fail to reduce the risk to the expected level, and the investments do not bring expected gains. Therefore, businesses have to be alert to risk by increasing their immunity and to be resilient in order to minimize the negative impact in case of risk. Being alert to risk is possible through structures that can detect or predict risk early. Resilience, on the other hand, is related to the ability to quickly control and eliminate the negative impact after the occurrence of the risk. Companies have recently adopted these two approaches and acted differently against the increasing and diversifying risks. Businesses attach importance to being prepared and resilient against risk through basic activities such as identifying and monitoring threats, identifying anomalies in business processes, and minimizing risks originating from third parties (Deloitte, 2016, 2017).

12.5.1.4 Risk Becoming a Performance Factor

With approaches such as artificial intelligence, machine learning, and data analytics, the possibilities of using data have begun to be used, and as a result of the risks being more measurable, approaches such as managing risks and even taking guidance in different areas based on risk values have begun to emerge. In the past, risk management was applied only as a process in which actions such as creating responses to risks at unacceptable levels or avoiding risks are carried out. In this approach, the top priority risk for businesses was compliance with regulations. In the new period, the fact that the risk values can be obtained concretely, thanks to the abovementioned opportunities, provide important guidance to the enterprises to use these values for performance and quality measurements. As management systems, enterprise risk management and enterprise performance management have similar objectives and positively influence each other (Klučka & Grünbichler, 2020). While the traditional risk management approach in enterprises is implemented in a way to control the risk periodically and take measures to avoid losses, other processes focus on performance and creating value. On the other hand, it has been generally observed that efforts to improve risk management processes have intensified recently. In this context, risk management can apparently have significant contributions in terms of performance and value enhancement for digitalized businesses (Thekdi & Aven, 2016).

12.5.1.5 Changing Customer Expectations and Market Dynamics

Within the framework of digital transformation, a faster-than-normal change has begun to be experienced, for businesses, in consumers, in sectors, and the ecosystem they are in. Effected by this, significant changes began to be experienced in their strategies, business models, products and services, customer experience processes, business processes, technological infrastructures, and organizational structures (Deloitte, 2016, 2017). Risk management has become even more important for businesses that understand consumer behavior and expectations, offer products and services in this direction, and act with the aim of gaining competitive power in the current market. Similarly, in such a dynamic ecosystem, it is important to closely monitor the risks that may cause deviation from the aforementioned targets and to give the necessary response as quickly as possible. In this context, the main instrument in the hands of enterprises will again be data analytics methods.

12.5.1.6 Supporting Factors and Opportunities as well as Potential Threats and Challenges

Risk management approaches may vary within the framework of the digital transformation level of the enterprises, their technological competencies, and different internal and external conditions specific to them. There are factors and opportunities that support changes in businesses' risk management approaches as well as potential threats and challenges that slow or hinder these changes.

Cases causing changes in risk management approach	Supporting factors and opportunities	Potential threats and challenges
Integration of Cognitive Technologies into Decision Processes	• Businesses have the opportunity to access large data sets that can benefit from big data technologies • The emergence of advanced artificial intelligence-based algorithms that can generate meaningful results from data • Increasing the competent human resources in the field of data science • Behavioral analytics applications being widespread in risk management	• Difficulty in applying cognitive technologies and related tools • Insufficient number of competent personnel in the current situation • Absence of assurance mechanisms on artificial intelligence • Insufficient data quality and inability to access complete and accurate data • Making inaccurate estimations based on data or system and encountering undesirable results

Cases causing changes in risk management approach	Supporting factors and opportunities	Potential threats and challenges
Making Process Controls Widespread and Continuous	• The widespread use of sensors measuring the activities of the processes for which risk data is obtained, in a way to support big data infrastructures • The increasing widespread presence of the IoT network among businesses • Automation of common risk assessment and control tests in areas such as internal audit, internal control, supply chain management, finance and cybersecurity, and improving risk-related decision-making processes • Automating compliance monitoring and reporting processes by placing risk controls in business technologies • Effective management of risks originating from customers as a result of simultaneous analysis of customer behavior with real-time dataflows	• Increased exposure to cyber risks in the relevant area due to IoT technology integrated into many points of business processes • Increasing privacy concerns among customers, staff, and business partners after monitoring became widespread in all areas • Management of the quality of the data constantly collected by widely installed sensors and similar structures being more difficult
The Necessity of Preparedness and Resilience against Risks	• Increasing opportunities to benefit from data science in the pre-detection and management of risks with increasing competencies in fields such as data analysis, machine learning, and artificial intelligence	• Limited access to data needed for risk monitoring and forecasting • Limited tools to be used in such analytical processes • General low level of expertise in this field • Work on resilience is very complex due to many interconnected processes and agility is limited
Risk Becoming a Performance Factor	• There are correlations between risk values obtained by using data analytics and performance. • Artificial intelligence becoming a usable approach in terms of risk detection and monitoring	• The absence of appropriate tools to correlate risk with performance or the absence of competent personnel to use these tools effectively

Cases causing changes in risk management approach	Supporting factors and opportunities	Potential threats and challenges
Changing Customer Expectations and Market Dynamics	• As for the entrepreneurs recently entering to the market, being able to compete with local businesses, thanks to the developments in technology • Innovations in business models encourage businesses to develop themselves • Customers expect more personalized products and services every day • Revising the corporate strategy development approach to bring greater agility and responsiveness to emerging threats • Using tools and techniques such as real-time monitoring, scenario planning, stress testing, war games, and simulations to manage risk • In today's competitive environment, the increase in the number of companies that innovate and bring innovation to the sector • Increasing the diversity of competitors as a result of the fact that everyone can easily access every product and service in the globalizing world and the spread of new free and subscription-based business models • Regulations taking control of innovations • Increasing innovations intentionally to steer regulations • Increasing consumption amount	• Brands becoming more vulnerable to geopolitical risks as a result of increasing dependency on stakeholders located in different locations • New enterprises lacking the ability to monitor and interpret strategic threats may be exposed to significant negative impacts in this area • The complexity and size of the data to be used in monitoring processes is hard to manage

Source: Abdikeev (2017), Mazareanu (2010), Khanboubi and Boulmakoul (2018), Henderson et al. (2012), Syuntyurenko (2015), Deloitte (2016, 2017) Ferguson (2012), Pfleeger and Caputo (2012), Hussain et al. (2012)

12.6 Conclusion

The concept of digital transformation starting in the 8000s BC upon the agricultural revolution has begun to be fully implemented upon the last industrial revolution which is today called Industry 4.0. In this process, the technological infrastructures, production processes, organizations, and, perhaps most importantly, the cultures of the enterprises undergo significant changes. Digital transformation, which offers opportunities such as the widespread use of RPA, the commissioning of autonomous smart systems, the analysis of large amounts of data collected with sensors and similar structures through artificial intelligence and machine learning and big data infrastructures, and providing important outputs not only for risk but also for associated strategic decisions, makes remarkable contributions to businesses. It is clear that productivity can be increased considerably, especially by means of RPA; the workload on personnel is reduced, and thus, human factor is started to be used in critical decision processes where it is more necessary compared to routine processes.

Although digital transformation provides significant benefits to businesses, it also brings along significant risks and adverse effects such as negative information exchange; support for illegal actions; negative economic changes; disruption of political balances; increase in vulnerabilities of IT operations; worsening of health conditions; environmental degradation; ethical violations; inappropriate decision environment; loss of competence, either individual or institutional; and lack of control over algorithms. It has been determined that the management of these risks will not be possible with traditional risk management approaches. In the digitalized world, it is necessary to act with a new risk management approach. The new approach should also consider the seven core components of digital risk: data management; automation of processes and workflows; advanced analytics and automated decision-making; unified, reliable, and adaptable infrastructure; smart visualization and user interfaces; external ecosystem; and talent and culture.

Consequently, it has become necessary to act by adopting a new risk management approach, where digitalization can provide important gains not only to the management and operational processes of enterprises but also to the risk management, yet make use of these gains by considering the new risks emerging after digitalization. As for implementing the mentioned approach, road maps have been prepared for effective risk management of businesses after digitalization, through evaluating the supporting factors and opportunities as well as potential risks and challenges in basic subjects such as integration of cognitive technologies into decision processes, making process controls widespread and continuous, risk preparedness and resilience, risk becoming a performance factor, changing customer expectations, and market dynamics. With its dynamic character, this road map will change in line with the new needs and risks that will arise over time and will also affect the new risk management approaches of the businesses.

References

Abdikeev, N. M. (2017, October). Cognitive technologies of business processes management in digital economy. In *2017 Tenth International Conference Management of Large-Scale System Development (MLSD)* (pp. 1–3). IEEE.

Akben, İ., & Avşar, İ. İ. (2018). ENDÜSTRİ 4.0 VE KARANLIK ÜRETİM: GENEL BİR BAKIŞ. *Türk Sosyal Bilimler Araştırmaları Dergisi, 3*(1), 26–37.

Akmeşe, S. (2020). Kamuda Dijital Dönüşümün Siber Güvenlik Ve Dijital Güvence Boyutları Ve İç Denetimin Rolü. *Denetişim*, (20), 108–119.

Albinson, N., Blau, A., & Chu, Y. (2016). *The future of risk: New game, new rules.*

Birkel, H. S., Veile, J. W., Müller, J. M., Hartmann, E., & Voigt, K. I. (2019). Development of a risk framework for Industry 4.0 in the context of sustainability for established manufacturers. *Sustainability, 11*(2), 384.

Brynjolfsson, E., & Hitt, L. M. (2000). Beyond computation: Information technology, organizational transformation and business performance. *Journal of Economic Perspectives, 14*(4), 23–48.

Bulut, E., & Akçaci, T. (2017). Endüstri 4.0 ve inovasyon göstergeleri kapsaminda Türkiye analizi. *ASSAM Uluslararası Hakemli Dergi, 4*(7), 55–77.

Çakır, N. N. (2018). Endüstri 4.0 Ve Çalışmanın Geleceği. *Ejovoc (Electronic Journal of Vocational Colleges), 8*(2), 97–105.

Ciborra, C. (2006). Imbrication of representations: Risk and digital technologies. *Journal of Management Studies, 43*(6), 1339–1356.

Decker, M. (2013). Technikfolgen. In A. Grunwald (Ed.), *Handbuch Technikethik* (pp. 33–38). Springer.

Deloitte, S. (2016). *Türkiye'deki Dijital Değişime CEO Bakışı.*

Deloitte. (2017). *The future of risk, New game, new rules.*

Eling, M., & Lehmann, M. (2018). The impact of digitalization on the insurance value chain and the insurability of risks. *The Geneva Papers on Risk and Insurance-Issues and Practice, 43*(3), 359–396.

Ferguson, R. B. (2012). Risky business: How data analytics and behavioral science can help. *MIT Sloan Management Review, 54*(1), 1.

Gimblett, R. (2018). *Operational risk management in the digital era in the Swiss banking industry* (Doctoral dissertation, Haute école de gestion de Genève).

Gimpel, H., & Schmied, F. (2019). *Risks and side effects of digitalization: A multi-level taxonomy of the adverse effects of using digital technologies and media.*

Henderson, G., Sawilla, R., Matwin, S., Bacic, E., Tremblay, L., Sayyad-Shirabad, J., & de Souza, E. N. (2012). Automated risk management system. *Decision making support for continuous improvement of IT mission assurance. Defence R&D Canada—Ottawa, technical report DRDC Ottawa TR, 60*, 2012.

Henriette, E., Feki, M., & Boughzala, I. (2016, September). Digital transformation challenges. In *MCIS* (p. 33).

Hitt, L. M., & Brynjolfsson, E. (1996). Productivity, business profitability, and consumer surplus: Three different measures of information technology value. *MIS Quarterly, 20*, 121–142.

Hussain, O. K., Dillon, T. S., Hussain, F. K., & Chang, E. J. (2012). *Risk assessment and management in the networked economy* (Vol. 412). Springer.

Khanboubi, F., & Boulmakoul, A. (2018). A roadmap to lead risk management in the digital era. In *Conference: Big data & Applications 12th edition of the Conference on Advances of Decisional Systems* (pp. 7–9).

Kim, W., Jeong, O. R., Kim, C., & So, J. (2011). The dark side of the internet: Attacks, costs and responses. *Information Systems, 36*(3), 675–705.

Klučka, J., & Grünbichler, R. (2020). Enterprise risk management–Approaches determining its application and relation to business performance. *Quality Innovation Prosperity, 24*(2), 51–58.
Knudsen, E. S., Lien, L. B., Timmermans, B., Belik, I., & Pandey, S. (2021). Stability in turbulent times? The effect of digitalization on the sustainability of competitive advantage. *Journal of Business Research, 128*, 360–369.
Kregel, I., Koch, J., & Plattfaut, R. (2021). Beyond the hype: Robotic process automation's public perception over time. *Journal of Organizational Computing and Electronic Commerce, 31*, 1–21.
Mazareanu, V. P. (2010, October). Advantages of using a dynamic risk management approach. In *Proceedings of the IVth International Conference Globalization and Higher Education in Economics and Business Administration,* GEBA.
Pfleeger, S. L., & Caputo, D. D. (2012). Leveraging behavioral science to mitigate cyber security risk. *Computers & Security, 31*(4), 597–611.
Porter, M. E. (2000). Location, competition, and economic development: Local clusters in a global economy. *Economic Development Quarterly, 14*(1), 15–34.
Portilla, A., Vazquez, J., Harreis, H., Pancaldi, L., Rowshankish, K., Samandari, H., & Staples, M. (2017). The future of risk management in the digital era. In M. Staples (Ed.), Institute of International Finance and McKinsey & Company (pp. 19–20).
Puschmann, T. (2017). Fintech. *Business & Information Systems Engineering, 59*(1), 69–76.
Rao, V. R. (1995). Risk management: Time for innovative approaches. *Environmental management, 19*(3), 313–320.
Raphael, D. D. (2007). *The impartial spectator: Adam Smith's moral philosophy*. Oxford University Press.
Schwab, K. (2017). *The fourth industrial revolution*. Currency.
Soylu, A. (2018). Endüstri 4.0 ve girişimcilikte yeni yaklaşımlar. *Pamukkale Üniversitesi Sosyal Bilimler Enstitüsü Dergisi, 32*, 43–57.
Syuntyurenko, O. V. (2015). The digital environment: The trends and risks of development. *Scientific and Technical Information Processing, 42*(1), 24–29.
Tarhan,U.(2018,May29).*Endüstri4.0makinelerinmi,insanlarınmıyükselişi?*RetrievedMay14,2021, from https://www.ufuktarhan.com/makale/endustri-40-makinelerin-mi-insanlarin-mi-yukselisi
Thekdi, S., & Aven, T. (2016). An enhanced data-analytic framework for integrating risk management and performance management. *Reliability Engineering & System Safety, 156*, 277–287.
Thomas, G., & Mitchell, J. (2017). *The future of risk management ten years after the crisis* [online]. Retrieved 12.05. 2019, from http://www.oliverwyman.com/content/dam/oliverwyman/v2/publications/2017/sep/OW-Future-of-Risk-2017.pdf
Tian, F., & Xu, S. X. (2015). How do enterprise resource planning systems affect firm risk? *Post-implementation Impact Mis Quarterly, 39*(1), 39–60.
Xu, M., David, J. M., & Kim, S. H. (2018). The fourth industrial revolution: Opportunities and challenges. *International journal of financial research, 9*(2), 90–95.
Yıldırım, S. (2004). Bilgi Ekonomisi Ve Bilgi Ekonomisinin Türkiye Açısından Değerlendirilmesi. *Balıkesir Üniversitesi Sosyal Bilimler Enstitüsü Dergisi, 7*(12), 105–124.
Yıldırım, B. (2020). İşletmelerde Dijital Dönüşüm Süreci: Nitel Bir Araştırma. *Ekonomi Maliye İşletme Dergisi, 3*(2), 204–223.

Cem Dursun has an MSc degree from Middle East Technical University—in Civil Engineering, an MBA degree from Bilkent University in business Administration, an MS degree from Middle East Technical University—in security, and he is currently studying for a Ph.D. degree in Social Sciences University of Ankara—Audit and Risk Management. He has worked in IT Audit, Risk Management, IT Governance, and Cyber Security areas in the Banking, Telecommunications, and Energy Industries for over 20 years. He is working as Chief Information Security Officer in "Enerjisa" of "Sabancı Group," the partner of E.ON Group, one of Europe's largest operators of energy networks and energy infrastructure. He is the past president and currently vice president of ISACA Ankara Chapter. He is certified as CISA, CISM, CDPSE, CRMA, ITIL v3, ISO 27001 Lead Auditor, COBIT 2019 Foundation, Accredited CISA Trainer and Accredited CISM Trainer. He has been participating as a trainer in ISACA certification exam preparation courses. He translated several ISACA materials into Turkish, including COBIT and Certified Information Systems Auditor (CISA) and Certified Information Systems Manager (CISM) certification exam manuals.

Part V
An Overview of ERM Literature

Chapter 13
Enterprise Risk Management: A Bibliometric Review

Deniz Erdem, Ertan Güvendi, Mecbure Aslan, Ramazan Acar, and Serkan Ülger

Abstract This study aims to perform a bibliometric analysis to map the development of the enterprise risk management (ERM) field. Post-1996 publications on enterprise risk management in the Web of Science database are analyzed in this scope. Bibliometric analysis of 597 publications provides a map of keywords, authors, countries, and institutions and a framework for following this literature over 25 years. According to the results of the research, in the field of ERM, an interdisciplinary field of study that attracts the attention of not only the academic world but also the business world, there has been a decrease in the number of publications in recent years. However, studies on new and different subjects have been conducted, and academic studies in ERM have shifted from developed to developing countries. It has been observed that proximity or language similarity does not affect the cluster formed by publishing countries.

Keywords Enterprise risk management · ERM · Bibliometric analysis

D. Erdem
Internal Audit Manager, Tanoto, Ankara, Türkiye
e-mail: deniz.erdem@tanoto.com.tr

E. Güvendi
Turkish Tax Audit Board, Ankara, Türkiye
e-mail: ertan.guvendi@vdk.gov.tr

M. Aslan · S. Ülger (✉)
Social Sciences University of Ankara, Ankara, Türkiye
e-mail: mecbure.aslan@student.asbu.edu.tr; serkan.ulger@student.asbu.edu.tr

R. Acar
The Turkish Court of Accounts, Ankara, Türkiye
e-mail: racar@sayistay.gov.tr

H. Kıral (ed.), *Rethinking Enterprise Risk Management*, Accounting, Finance, Sustainability, Governance & Fraud: Theory and Application,
https://doi.org/10.1007/978-981-97-5983-5_13

13.1 Introduction

Technological developments, digitalization, and the rapid increase in the amount of data have increased the importance attached to the concept of risk (Hopkin & Thompson, 2010). Increasing trade between countries, diplomatic relations, and technology-based transactions have not only increased the number of risks but also put on the agenda different risks such as supply chain risk. In a world where risks are mounting, managing these risks has become more important (Olson & Wu, 2010). The fact that it has become a growing and important field has also increased the interest of researchers in this field (Beasley et al., 2005; Choi et al., 2015; Gordon et al., 2009; Liu et al., 2011; Paape & Speklè, 2012). The desire of companies to manage their risks holistically has led to the development of enterprise risk management (ERM) (D'Arcy & Brogan, 2001).

In their study on the relationship between ERM practice and firm characteristics, Beasley et al. (2005) concluded that the presence of the chief risk officer, the apparent support of the chief executive officer and the chief financial officer, and firm size positively affect the implementation of ERM. Choi et al. (2015) emphasize that the ever-increasing risks in global markets may increase the importance attached to ERM. Gordon et al. (2009) emphasize that the relationship between ERM and firm performance depends on factors such as environmental uncertainties, competition, size, and complexity of the firm, and that an ERM should be implemented by considering these factors. While the work by Paape and Speklè (2012) is on the design of an ERM that could affect risk management efficiency, Liu et al. (2011) have conducted a study on the status of ERM implementation in the Chinese construction industry. Although there are publications on different subtopics related to ERM, in our research, we have found no bibliometric studies about ERM. Therefore, in order to contribute to the literature, we aim to analyze the studies in the field of ERM through bibliometric methods over the publications between 1997 and 2022.

Although the concept of ERM began to develop in the mid-1990s (Choi et al., 2015), risk assessment and risk management already existed before. Economic developments such as the termination of the Bretton Woods Agreement in 1972, the oil crisis in the 1970s, and the debt crisis in the 1980s brought to the agenda the financial risks such as volatility in exchange rates, prices, and interest rates. The effort to manage these risks has led to the emergence of enterprise risk management (ERM) (D'Arcy & Brogan, 2001).

ERM includes the holistic management of all risks faced by the organization (Bromiley et al., 2014). Categorizing risks, Banham (2004) defines ERM as identifying, analyzing, measuring, and comparing all risks arising from a company's operational, financial, and strategic activities. In another definition, ERM is a process by which organizations in all sectors assess, control, exploit, finance, and monitor risks from all sources in order to increase short- and long-term value (D'Arcy & Brogan, 2001). According to Verbrugge et al. (2003), ERM is organization wide as opposed to units and is an effort to manage all of the organization's risks in a way that helps it achieve its goal of maximizing the value of its assets. According to the

Risk Management Society (RIMS), ERM is a business discipline that supports an organization in achieving its goals by addressing all of its risks and managing the combined impact of these risks as an interrelated risk portfolio (RIMS, 2021). Similarly, the International Institute of Internal Auditors (IIA) defines ERM as a rigorous and coordinated approach to assessing and responding to all risks that affect an organization's achievement of its strategic and financial objectives (IIA, 2009).

According to Hopkin and Thompson (2010), ERM is neither a new nor different approach. It should be considered as a unifying approach that brings together the management of all kinds of risks. Given the definitions made until now, the common point of almost all of them is apparently the management of risks with a holistic approach. However, studies arguing that managing a small number of important risks instead of all risks will have positive effects on the efficiency and life of enterprise risk management (Kıral, 2018) also signal that the perspective on ERM may change over time.

The fact that no bibliometric studies have been found on ERM during the research process makes this study meaningful because, as stated by Baldemir and Ülger (2022), bibliometric studies are important since they allow researchers to be well informed of the literature in a short time. Therefore, this bibliometric study on ERM aims to enable researchers to focus, to see past and current trends, and to design new studies.

In the study, scientific studies with "enterprise risk management" in the keywords and titles of the publications were analyzed using bibliometric methods. It is aimed to be informed of the development of ERM by determining the most cited studies, the most active journals, institutions, authors, countries, and current keywords. To achieve this goal, the study is structured as follows. First, the development and definitions of enterprise risk management are briefly mentioned. The following part provides an explanation of the method used. In the third part, the results of bibliometric analysis and its evolution over time are presented. The analysis includes publications that allow the assessment of disciplinary trends. Finally, a discussion of the future of enterprise risk management literature is presented and possible future development of the field is addressed.

13.2 Material and Method

Web of Science (WoS) Core Collection database (by Clarivate Analytics, USA) was used for the literature review. Publication review was conducted using the "Title (TI)," "Author Keywords (AK)," or "Keyword Plus (KP)" fields. "Enterprise risk management" is used as a search keyword in WoS. Thanks to this search method, all publications related to enterprise risk management were obtained even if the expression of enterprise risk management is not included in the title. The study covers the 25 years between 1997 and 2022.

Bibliometric network visualizations and citation analyses were performed using the VOSviewer (Version 1.6.18, Leiden University's Centre for Science and Technology Studies) package program (van Eck & Waltman, 2010). A "thesaurus" file was created to arrange repetitive or similar words while using the VOSviewer application.

13.3 Findings

As a result of the literature review, a total of 629 publications on enterprise risk management published between 1997 and 2022 were found in the WoS database.[1] These publications are composed of Articles (458), Proceedings Papers (135), Book Chapters (45), Editorial Materials (13), Review Articles (12), Book Reviews (11), Early Access (11), Books (5), Corrections (1), Data Papers (1), and Meeting Abstracts (1).

Publications were differentiated by applying the following criteria:

- Document Type: Articles or Proceeding Papers or Book Chapters or Review Articles or Books
- Web of Science Index: Social Sciences Citation Index (SSCI) or Emerging Sources Citation Index (ESCI) or Science Citation Index Expanded (SCI-EXPANDED) or Conference Proceedings Citation Index—Social Science & Humanities (CPCI-SSH) or Conference Proceedings Citation Index—Science (CPCI-S) or Book Citation Index—Social Sciences and Humanities (BKCI-SSH) or Book Citation Index—Science (BKCI-S)
- Year: 1997–2021

With the criteria added due to the bibliometric analysis, the total number of publications decreased from 629 to 597. Figure 13.1 shows the distribution of publication types within the total number of publications.

It is clear from Fig. 13.1 that most of the studies published in the literature on ERM are articles.

Figure 13.2 shows the number of publications per year. Figure 13.2 clearly shows that the increasing trend in studies on ERM, which started in 2005, continued until 2018, and after then, there was a decrease in the number of studies made on this subject. We will see in the coming years whether this decrease is temporary or permanent.

[1] In the first review, the keyword "ERM" was also included in the research. Accordingly, the total number of articles was over 2000. However, it was noticed that the abbreviation ERM had other meanings such as ERM: Ezrin–Radixin–Moesin protein family or Enhanced Russell Measure model. For this reason, ERM was not used as a keyword.

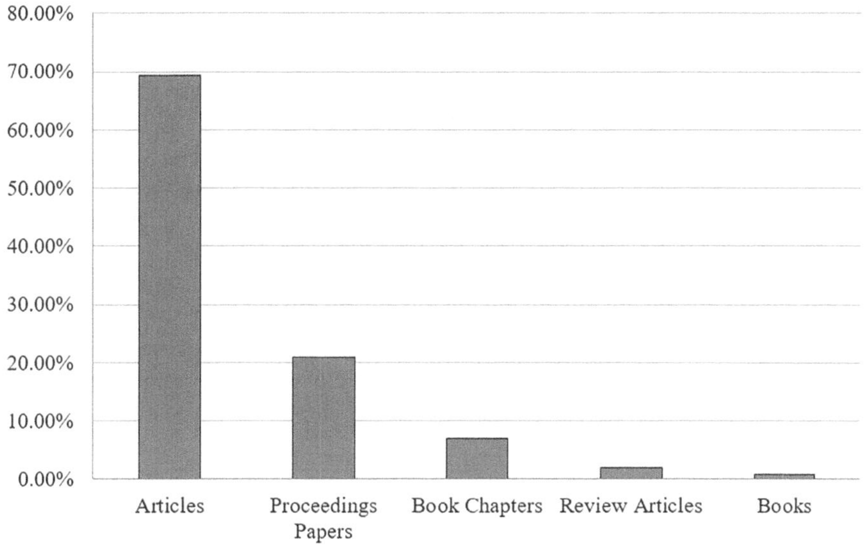

Fig. 13.1 Types of publications

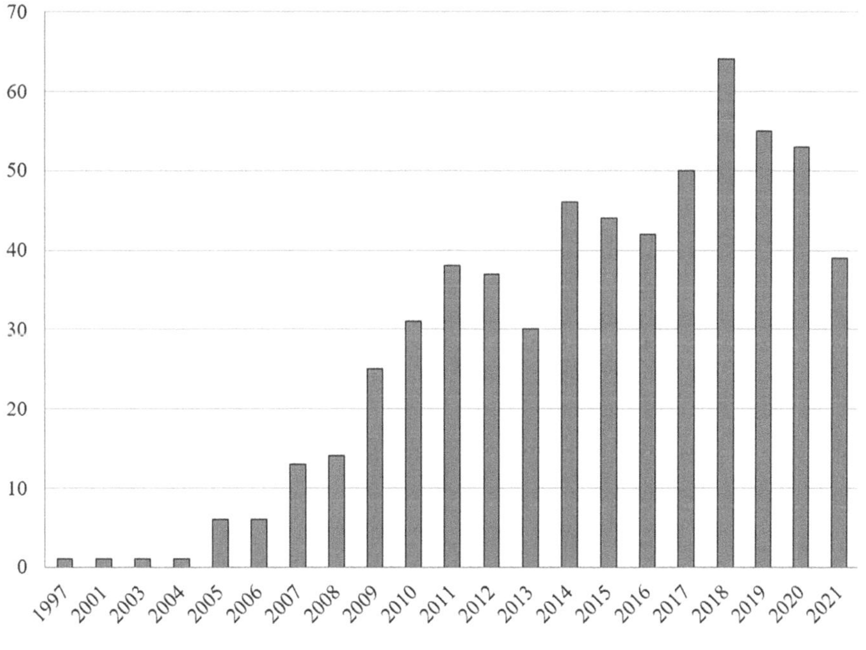

Fig. 13.2 Number of publications per years

13.3.1 Reference and Citation Review

As a result of the research conducted according to the WoS database reference analysis results, the H-index of 597 publications was observed as 45. The sum of times cited of the publications subject to the research is 7981 (without self-citations: 5809) and hence the average citations per article is 13.37. The citing articles are 4851 (without self-citations: 4496). Figure 13.3 indicates, by years, the total number of citations to the publications found as a result of the research.

Figure 13.3 indicates that the number of citations to the related articles has increased as the number of articles on ERM has increased since 2005. While the annual total number of citations increased at a rate varying between 50 and 100 between 2006 and 2017, it is seen that the annual total number of citations suddenly rose in 2018. Following that rapid increase continuing for 3 years, a slowdown is observed in the rate of increase as of 2021.

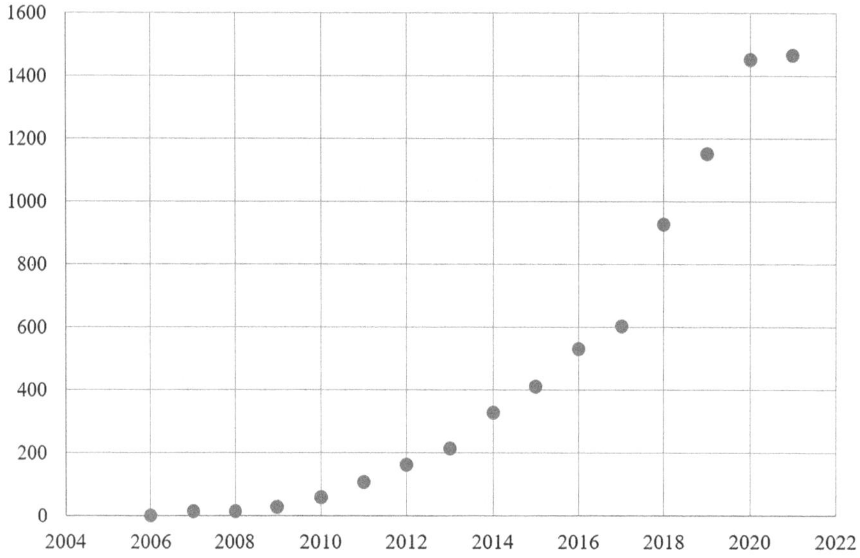

Fig. 13.3 Annual total number of citations per years

13.3.2 Keyword Frequency Analysis

A series of keyword queries were made using the "Author Keywords" and "KeyWords Plus[2]" filters in the "Web of Science" database in order to identify the study topics of interest in enterprise risk management.[3] In this context, the frequency of the 20 most frequently used keywords in studies in the field of enterprise risk management between 1997 and 2022 according to these two filter types is provided below.[4]

As it is clear in Fig. 13.4a, the most frequently used keywords by the authors in studies on ERM are corporate governance (23), internal control (17), firm (company) performance (17), performance (13), Chief Risk Officer (12), ISO 31000 (12), and COSO ERM (12). Figure 13.4b provides the most frequently encountered KeyWords Plus in studies on ERM. Accordingly, keywords such as determinants (45), performance (45), impact(s) (25), cost(s) (24), governance (23), and corporate governance (22) are the most common KeyWords Plus-type keywords. As a result of the 25-year literature review on ERM through both filters, it can be said that the concepts of firm performance and corporate governance come to the fore.

On the other hand, the inquiry was limited to last 5 years (between 2017 and 2022) in order to see the latest trends in the literature. Accordingly, Figs. 13.5a, b reveal the frequency status of the most frequently used keywords in studies in the field of ERM in the last 5 years through the mentioned two filter types.

As can be seen in Fig. 13.5a, the most frequently used keywords by the authors in studies published in the last 5 years on ERM are firm (company) performance (14), corporate governance (11), COSO ERM (9), COSO (7), firm value (7), performance (7), and SMEs (7). Among the keywords used by the authors in the last 5 years, keywords such as internal control, ISO 31000 (2009), and Chief Risk Officer fell behind in the ranking, while SMEs (7), firm value (7), value creation (5), risk culture (5), and emerging market (5) began to be used more frequently.

Figure 13.5b indicates the most frequently encountered KeyWords Pluses in studies published in the last 5 years on ERM. Accordingly, the most frequently encountered keywords such as determinants (33), performance (30), governance

[2] KeyWords Plus is based on a special algorithm specific to Clarivate databases, increasing the power of citation-reference search by searching across disciplines for all articles with common references. KeyWords Plus keywords include words or phrases that often appear in the titles of an article's references but do not appear in that article's title or among author keywords.

[3] The first sample of the study consists of 597 studies between the years 1997–2022. Only 494 of these studies have "Author Keywords" section. Six of these studies were excluded from the sample because they did not have the year information. Therefore, the final sample of the query made through the "Author Keywords" filter consists of the remaining 488 studies. A similar approach was used for the "KeyWords Plus" filter, and apparently, only 330 studies had the "KeyWords Plus" option. Five of these studies do not have year information. In this framework, the final sample of the query made through the "KeyWords Plus" filter consists of 325 studies.

[4] While identifying the most frequently used keywords, keywords that do not indicate a specific field of study, such as "enterprise risk management", "risk management", "risk(s)", "firm(s)", "enterprise(s)", "model(s)", "system(s)" were ignored.

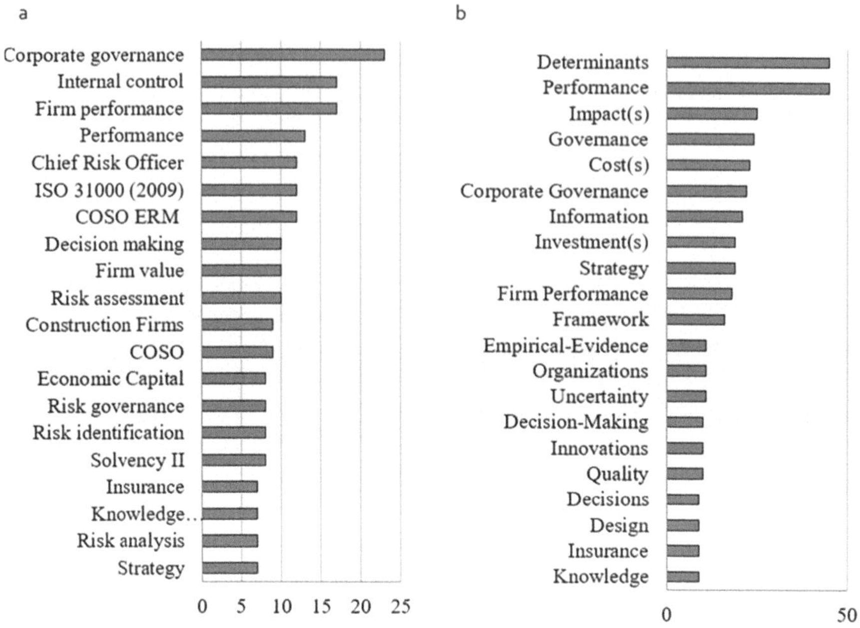

Fig. 13.4 Most frequently used keywords (Author Keywords and KeyWords Plus)

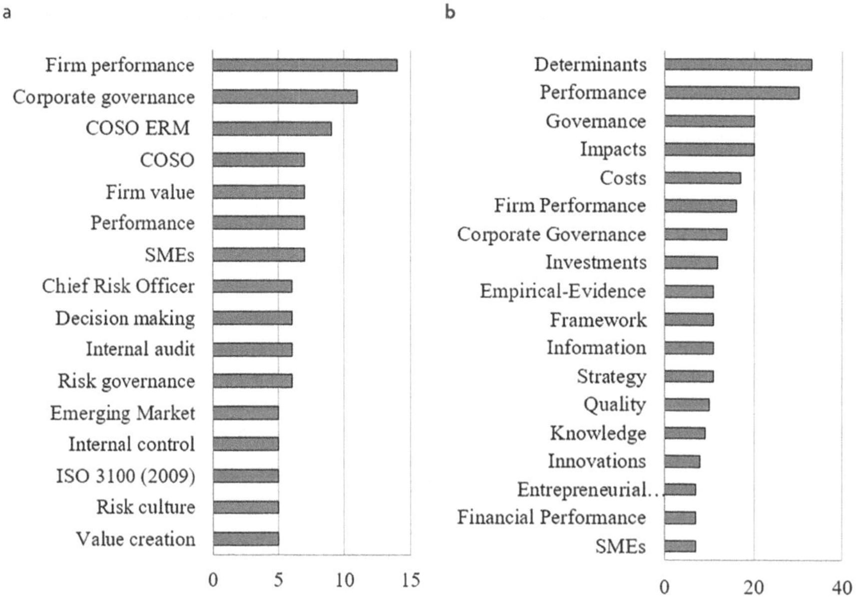

Fig. 13.5 Most frequently used keywords in the last 5 years (Author Keywords and KeyWords Plus)

(20), impact(s) (20), cost(s) (17), firm governance (16), and corporate governance (14)) are also the most common KeyWords Plus-type keywords between 1997 and 2022. However, keywords such as firm performance (16), empirical evidence (11), quality (10), innovations (8), entrepreneurial orientation (7), financial performance (7), and SMEs (7) are more common in the last 5 years, compared to the previous 20-year period.

Accordingly, in the last 5 years, while firm performance and corporate governance issues continue to maintain their importance, emerging markets and small- and medium-sized enterprises have apparently begun to come to the fore among research topics. This can be interpreted as a sign that ERM studies have matured and that the knowledge and experience accumulated in the field is now being applied to developing countries and smaller enterprises. On the other hand, more qualitative research topics such as firm value, value creation, quality, innovation, entrepreneurial orientation, and risk culture have begun to gain importance.

13.3.3 Reference Review

Among the analyzed publications, sources with at least 5 publications were evaluated. Accordingly, 13 institutions that published the most on this subject were identified. These institutions are shown in Fig. 13.6.

As can be seen in Fig. 13.6, the most publishing sources in the field of ERM are Journal of Risk and Financial Management, International Journal of Production Research, Journal of Risk Finance, Journal of Risk Research, Risk Management an International Journal, British Actuarial Journal, Annals of Operations Research,

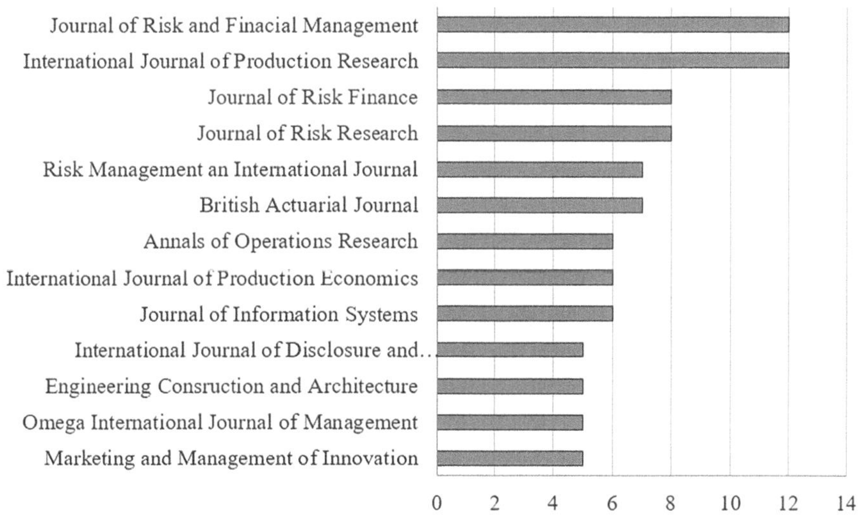

Fig. 13.6 The most publishing sources

International Journal of Production Economics, Journal of Information Systems, and International Journal of Disclosure and Governance. The existence of journals publishing in different fields is a natural consequence of ERM's being an interdisciplinary research area.

13.3.4 Author Review

Figure 13.7 shows the authors who have published the most in the field of ERM. According to the results of the analysis, 12 authors with 6 or more publications were determined.

As clear in Fig. 13.7, David Olson, Desheng Dash Wu, and Sui Peng Low have published more in this field. The point to be noted here is that some of the authors in this list conduct collaborative studies. However, the fact that an author has a large number of publications does not mean that he receives many citations. The most publishing authors in Fig. 13.7 are not the most cited ones.

The most cited authors and the number of publications of these authors are given in Fig. 13.8.

According to the results of the research, the publication by Cox (2008) titled "What's Wrong with Risk Matrices?" stands out. Although the author has one publication on ERM, he is the most cited author due to this publication. Cox (2008) points out in the said publication that although the risk matrix is a frequently used tool in risk management, it may give erroneous results in practice. This publication,

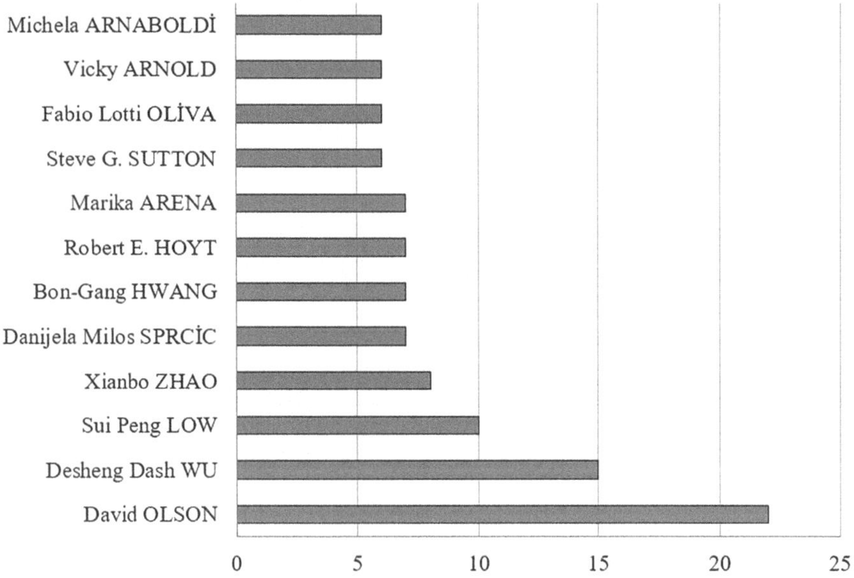

Fig. 13.7 The most publishing authors

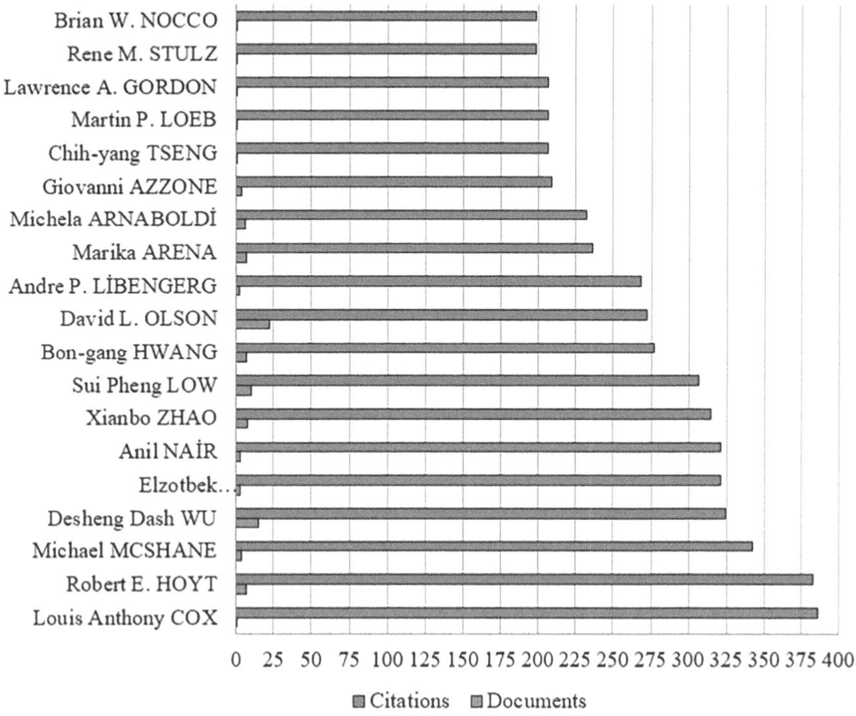

Fig. 13.8 The most cited authors and number of publications by authors

which was critical of the risk matrix, was found interesting by the researchers and was determined as the most cited publication. David Olson, who is ranked the first among the most published authors, is in the tenth place in the citation ranking, while Desheng Dash Wu, in the second place among the most published authors, is in the fourth place in the citation rankings.

13.3.5 Institution Review

Figure 13.9 shows the institutions that have at least three publications and at least three cited publications in the field of ERM, and the relationship between these institutions. The university with the highest number of publications in the field of ERM is the University of Nebraska with 26 publications, followed by the University of Toronto with 14 publications and the National University of Singapore with 12 publications, respectively.

Considering the citations, it is clear that these three institutions are at the top three in the same order. A total of 516 citations were made to 26 articles published by researchers at the University of Nebraska, 485 to 14 articles published by

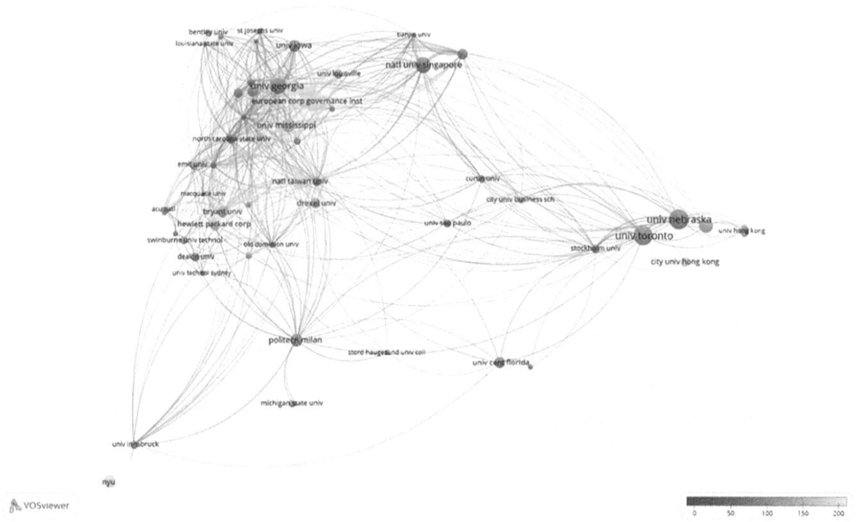

Fig. 13.9 Relationship among institutions with at least three publications and three cited publications

researchers at the University of Toronto, and a total of 345 citations to 12 articles published by researchers at the National University of Singapore. Considering the number of publications and the number of citations received by the publications, it is apparent that the number of citations received is directly proportional to the number of publications. However, when evaluated on the basis of the number of citations per publication, the University of Toronto is apparently in the first place with an average of 35 citations, followed by the National University of Singapore with an average of 29 citations and the University of Nebraska with 20 citations. The University of Nebraska, which has the most publications and total citations, has a lower average number of citations per publication than the other two universities.

Figure 13.9 also shows the clusters formed by these institutions. Examining the clusters of institutions, it is seen that the first three institutions that publish the most and receive the most citations are in the same cluster and all of them are universities. Considering the number of publications and citations, it is apparent that both universities and different research institutions such as European Corporation Governance Institute, National Taiwan University, and New York University are included in the second cluster.

Figure 13.10 shows the institutions with at least three publications in the field of ERM and at least three cited publications, as well as their publications and their citations. The left axis of the graph represents the total number of publications, and the right axis represents the total number of citations.

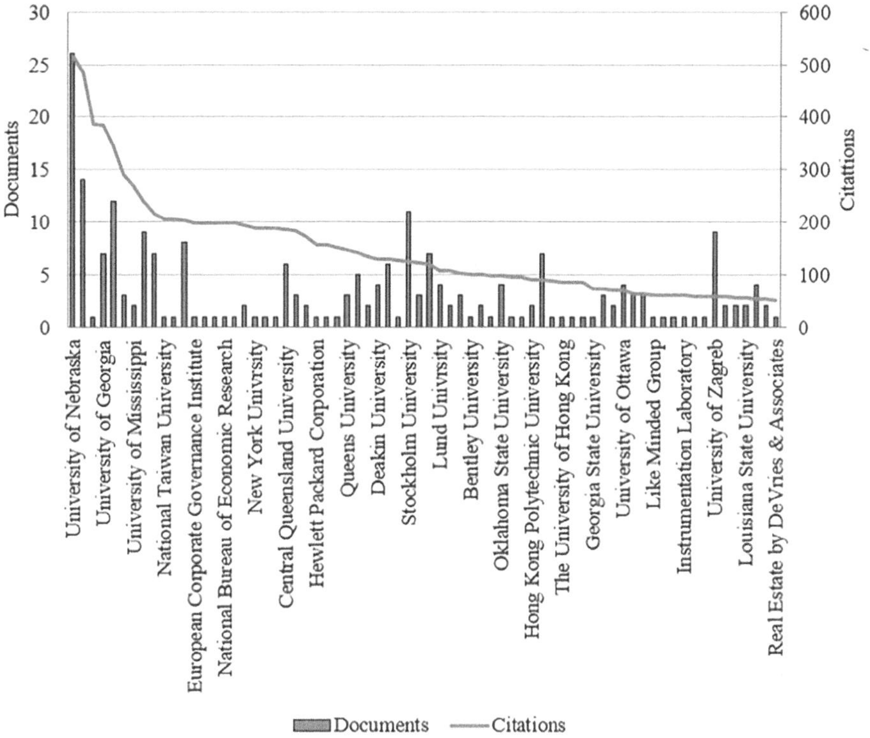

Fig. 13.10 Number of publications by institutions and number of citations they receive

13.3.6 *Country Review*

The breakdown of the articles as per countries are as follows: USA (158), People's Republic of China (78), Canada (41), Malaysia (38), England (37), Australia (33), Italy (21), Sweden (19), Germany (18), Brazil (17), Singapore (15), South Africa (15), Taiwan (13), Poland (12), Türkiye (12), Croatia (11), France (11), India (11), Nigeria (10), Pakistan (10), Scotland (10), Slovakia (10), Spain (10), Switzerland (10), Denmark (8), Indonesia (7), Netherlands (7), Romania (7), Austria (6), Norway (6), Colombia (6), Czech Republic (6), Greece (5), Slovenia (5), South Korea (5), United Arab Emirates (5), and Others (56).

Figure 13.11 shows the countries with the most publications in the field of ERM and the clusters formed by these countries. Examining Fig. 13.11, it is seen that most publications in this field are made in the USA, followed by China and Canada.

Considering the country clusters, the top three publishing countries are in the same cluster, and they mostly published in 2014 and 2015. Another cluster, including Malaysia, Brazil, and South Africa, consists of countries that mostly published in 2016 and 2017. The countries in the cluster, which includes Pakistan, Nigeria, and Indonesia, mostly published in 2020.

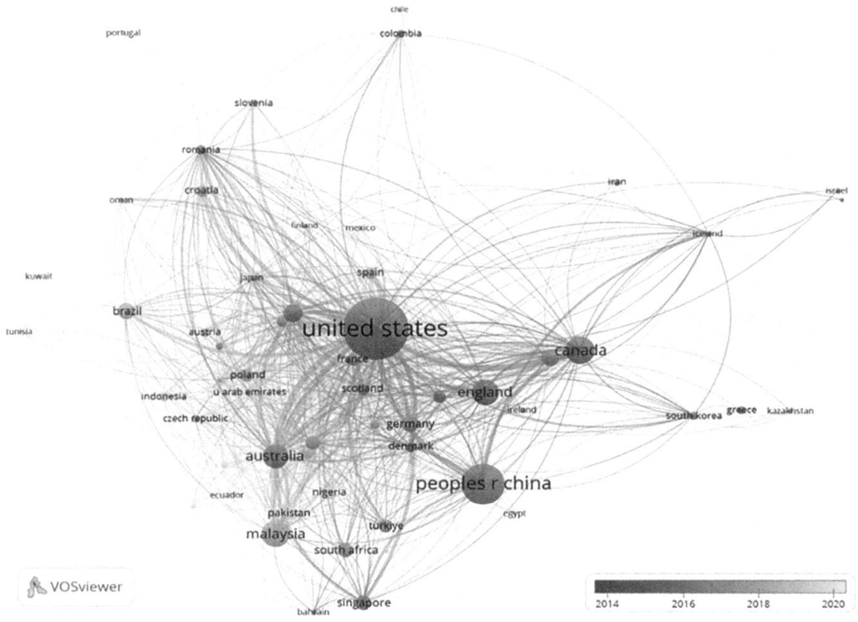

Fig. 13.11 Information on publishing countries

The above data reveal two important results. The first one is that countries cluster independently of their geographic proximity and linguistic similarity. The second one is that publications in the field of enterprise risk management have shifted from developed to developing countries.

13.4 Discussion

When the number of articles and citations is examined by years, it is observed that the years between 2006 and 2020 are the golden age for the studies on ERM. As of 2021, the number of publications decreased and the number of citations relatively slowed down. It is basically thought that the reason is that the expected benefit from ERM has not been achieved, and on the contrary, the concept "risk management of nothing" has emerged instead of an integrated risk management across the entire enterprise (Power, 2009; Kıral, 2018). We think that due to the fact that the benefit expected by the people, companies, and the academic world on ERM is not fully realized, research will shift to different subtitles. For this reason, it is predicted that the studies producing solutions to the deficiencies of the current approach and methodology and developing suggestions to increase the added value of ERM will increase rather than studies measuring the efficiency of ERM.

Frequency analysis on keywords revealed that in terms of both keyword filters, the most frequently encountered keywords in the last 5 years and the most frequently encountered keyword lists in all years largely overlap. However, it is apparent that new keywords began to be used in the studies in the last 5 years, such as SMEs (Small and Medium Entrepreneurships), Entrepreneurial Orientation, Financial Performance, Risk Culture, Firm Value, Value Creation, Balanced Scorecard, Tobin's Q Ratio, etc. Researchers who will carry out new studies on ERM should be expected to attach importance to these areas.

Reviewing the authors who publish on ERM, it is seen that the majority of the publications were made by more than one author. When the most published and the most cited authors are compared, it is seen that the most published authors are different from the most cited authors. The fact that the publications on ERM are sources that publish in different fields is a natural result of the fact that ERM is an interdisciplinary research area.

Examining the institutions that publish on ERM, it is seen that the first three institutions that publish the most and receive the most citations are in the same cluster and all of them are universities. On the other hand, when evaluated independently of clusters, it is seen that not only universities but also various institutes, information and technology companies, and professional organizations publish on ERM. This reveals that ERM is an area of interest not only to the academic world but also to the business world.

Examining the countries publishing in the field of ERM, the publishing density has shifted from developed countries to developing countries over the years. There may be two reasons for this situation. The first reason may be that pioneering studies and highly cited publications on ERM are mostly prepared by researchers in developed countries. Over time, the increasing interest of researchers in developing countries on this subject and putting it on their agenda has increased the number of publications in developing countries. The second reason can be explained by the presence of words such as SME in source word analysis. SMEs play an important role in economic activities in developing countries (The World Bank, 2022). The ERM in these organizations is important for the continuity of economic activities. Hence, the importance attached to the SMEs is reflected in the increasing number of publications in developing countries. Another important point about the publishing countries is that the geographical proximity and language similarity of these countries do not have an effect on the clusters they form.

13.5 Conclusion

As a result of the literature, the emergence of different risks together with the increasing uncertainty in the world has increased the interest in ERM. The number of academic studies on this subject has increased as of the 2000s. Changes and developments in the publishing world have been examined in order to predict future research on ERM. To that end, the evolution of studies on ERM over time was analyzed through keyword analysis. In the study, we intended to predict potential research areas on the subject, based on the development of the ERM subject over time. For this purpose, articles, papers, book chapters, review articles, and books published in the last 25 years in the selected indexes were analyzed. It was observed that the concepts of firm performance and corporate governance came to the fore as the subject of studies between 1997 and 2022. And in recent years, there have been developments in the field, such as the increase in studies on emerging markets and SMEs, indicating that ERM studies have matured.

The sources with the most publications in this field are the Journal of Risk and Financial Management and the International Journal of Production Research. It has been observed that collaborative studies are generally carried out in this area. Top published authors are David Olson, Desheng Dash Wu, and Sui Peng Low. Despite having the only publication in the field of ERM, Louis Anthony Cox is the most cited author.

Technological developments, digitalization, and the rapid increase in the amount of data have allowed risk to be addressed in different ways, which has been observed as a trend toward corporate management, performance, and governance, identified as a result of the analysis. We anticipate that future research questions will be more concerned with the integration of corporate management and governance as well as its impact on the performance of institutions.

References

Baldemir, R., & Ülger, G. (2022). A holistic investigation of the global outcomes of spontaneous pneumothorax during 1980–2021, including the COVID-19 pandemic A bibliometric approach. *Medicine, 101*(11), e29113.

Banham, R. (2004). Enterprising views of risk management: Businesses can use ERM to manage a wide variety of risks. *Journal of Accountancy, 197*, 65–71.

Beasley, M. S., Clune, R., & Hermanson, D. R. (2005). Enterprise risk management: An empirical analysis of factors associated with the extent of implementation. *Journal of Accounting and Public Policy, 24*(6), 521–531.

Bromiley, P., McShane, M., Nair, A., & Rustambekov, E. (2014). Kurumsal Risk Yönetimi: İnceleme, Eleştiri ve Araştırma Talimatlar. Accessed 26.04.2022, from http://www.elsevier.com/locate/lrp

Choi, Y., Ye, X., Zhao, L., & Luo, A. C. (2015). *Optimizing enterprise risk management: A literature review and critical analysis of the work of Wu And Olson*. Springer Science+Business Media. https://doi.org/10.1007/s10479-015-1789-5

Cox, L. A. (2008). What's wrong with risk matrices? *Risk Analysis, 28*(2), 497–512. https://doi.org/10.1111/j.1539-6924.2008.01030.x

D'Arcy, S. P., & Brogan, J. C. (2001). Enterprise risk management. *Journal of Risk Management of Korea, 12*(1), 207–228.

Gordon, L. A., Loeb, M. P., & Tseng, C. Y. (2009). Enterprise risk management and firm performance: A contingency perspective. *Journal of Accounting and Public Policy, 28*(4), 301–327.

Hopkin, P., & Thompson, C. (2010). *Risk management understanding, evaluating and implementing effective enterprise risk management*. First Published İn Great Britain And The United States In 2010 By Kogan Page Limited, Sixth Edition 2022.

IIA. (2009). *Role of internal audit in ERM*. Position Paper. Retrieved from na.theiia.org

Kıral, H. (2018). Kurumsal Risk Yönetiminin Riskleri. *Denetişim, 8*(18).

Liu, J. Y., Low, S. P., & He, X. (2011). Current practices and challenges of implementing enterprise risk management (ERM) in Chinese construction enterprises. *International Journal of Construction Management, 11*(4), 49–63.
Olson, D. L., & Wu, D. (2010). *Enterprise risk management models*. Springer. https://doi.org/10.1007/978-3-642-11474-8_2
Paape, L., & Speklè, R. F. (2012). The adoption and design of enterprise risk management practices: An empirical study. *European Accounting Review, 21*(3), 533–564.
Power, M. (2009). The risk management of nothing. *Accounting, Organizations and Society, 34*(6), 849–855.
RIMS. (2021). *The risk management society: About strategic and enterprise risk management*. Retrieved from www.rims.org/resources/strategic-enterprise-risk-center/about-serm (archived at https://perma.cc/5WJ4-TQGN).
The World Bank. (2022). *Small and Medium Enterprises (SMEs) Finance*. Retrieved June 26, 2022, from https://www.worldbank.org/en/topic/smefinance
Van Eck, N. J., & Waltman, L. (2010). Software survey: VOSviewer, a computer program for bibliometric mapping. *Scientometrics, 84*(2), 523–538. https://doi.org/10.1007/s11192-009-0146-3
Verbrugge, J., Smith, C., Niehaus, G., et al. (2003). University of Georgia roundtable on enterprise-wide risk management. *Journal of Applied Corporate Finance, 15*(4), 8–26.

Deniz Erdem works as an Internal Audit Manager at Tanoto, which operates in the automotive industry. She graduated from Bilkent University, Department of Business Administration. Then, she started her career at KPMG, one of the Big 4 companies in independent auditing and consultancy. During her studies at KPMG, she completed the non-thesis master's program in accounting and auditing from Okan University, the Institute of Social Sciences. After KPMG, she moved to PWC, another Big 4 company. At PWC, she was a senior risk and assurance services department consultant. She also has CPA, POAASA Independent Auditor, and CMB certificates. She has completed ISO 9001-2008 Internal Auditor and ISO 27001 training.

Ertan Güvendi is a chief tax inspector at the Turkish Tax Audit Board. He holds a bachelor's degree in public finance from the Dokuz Eylul University in Izmir/Türkiye and a master's in international development policy from Duke University in North Carolina/United States. He wrote several articles and book chapters on taxation, tax policy, and systems.

Mecbure Aslan is an internal auditor at the Internal Audit Department of the Ministry of Agriculture and Forestry in Turkey. She holds a Certified Internal Auditor, International Government Auditor Certificate, and ISO 27001 LA certificates. She worked as a culture and tourism expert at the Ministry of Culture and Tourism and as a youth and sports expert at the Ministry of Youth and Sports. She graduated from Hacettepe University, Faculty of Economics and Administrative Sciences, Department of Economics, and Anadolu University, Vocational School of Justice. She holds a master's degree in economics from Hacettepe University Department of Economics and a master's degree in public administration from Ankara Hacı Bayram Veli University (formerly Turkey and Middle East Institute of Public Administration). She is currently pursuing her PhD at the Social Sciences University of Ankara.

Ramazan Acar is a principal auditor at the Turkish Court of Accounts. He holds a bachelor's degree in economics from the Middle East Technical University and a master's degree in applied economics from Washington State University in Pullman/Washington.

Serkan Ülger is a Finance and Treasury expert at the Ministry of Treasury and Finance. He earned his bachelor's degree in computer engineering from Bilkent University in Ankara/Türkiye and his master's in international development policy from Duke University in North Carolina/United States. He is currently pursuing his PhD at the Social Sciences University of Ankara. He is interested in project management, project risk management, strategic risk management, machine learning, and public administration.

Index

H. Kıral (ed.), *Rethinking Enterprise Risk Management*, Accounting, Finance, Sustainability, Governance & Fraud: Theory and Application,
https://doi.org/10.1007/978-981-97-5983-5

The manufacturer's authorised representative in the EU is Springer Nature Customer Service Centre GmbH, Europaplatz 3, 69115 Heidelberg, Germany. If you have any concerns regarding our products, please contact ProductSafety@springernature.com

Printed and bound by CPI Group (UK) Ltd, Croydon, CR0 4YY
01/10/2026
02225909-0006